Zhisheng (Edward) Wen, Richard L. Sparks, Adriana Biedroń, Mark Feng Teng
Cognitive Individual Differences in Second Language Acquisition

Trends in Applied Linguistics

Edited by
Ulrike Jessner

Volume 19

Zhisheng (Edward) Wen, Richard L. Sparks,
Adriana Biedroń, Mark Feng Teng

Cognitive Individual Differences in Second Language Acquisition

Theories, Assessment and Pedagogy

ISBN 978-1-5015-2366-3
e-ISBN (PDF) 978-1-61451-474-9
e-ISBN (EPUB) 978-1-5015-0045-9
ISSN 1868-6362

Library of Congress Control Number: 2022950035

Bibliographic information published by the Deutsche Nationalbibliothek
The Deutsche Nationalbibliothek lists this publication in the Deutsche Nationalbibliografie;
detailed bibliographic data are available on the internet at http://dnb.dnb.de.

© 2024 Walter de Gruyter Inc., Boston/Berlin
This volume is text- and page-identical with the hardback published in 2023.
Cover image: Martin Zech, Bremen, using a photo by Roswitha Schacht/morguefile.com
Typesetting: Integra Software Services Pvt. Ltd.

www.degruyter.com

Acknowledgments

The publication of this book has been a long journey in the making. We wish to thank all those who have helped in this long process in one way or another. First of all, we sincerely thank the Series Editor of "Trends in Applied Linguistics" (Prof. Ulrike Jessner) and the commissioning editors and the editorial staff at the Mouton de Gruyter for their complete trust, enormous encouragement and support in the production of this volume. Then, we wish to acknowledge our sincere thanks to Professor Peter Skehan for writing the Foreword to the volume at such short notice, his long-term mentorship and endorsement of our academic endeavors over the years are highly appreciated. Last but not least, we are indebted to our respective families for their endurable love and care over the years while we were preoccupied with writing this book. Without their excessive patience and extreme tolerance, the present book would definitely take much longer to go into print.

Edward, Richard, Adriana & Mark
November, 2022

Contents

Acknowledgments —— V

Foreword —— IX
Peter Skehan

1   SLA and Individual Differences: An Overview —— 1
Zhisheng (Edward) Wen & Richard L. Sparks

Part I: Age, Intelligence, Aptitude and Affect

2   The Age Factor and the Critical Period Hypothesis —— 19
Adriana Biedroń

3   Intelligence —— 35
Adriana Biedroń

4   Foreign Language Aptitude —— 53
Adriana Biedroń

5   Language Aptitude, Psychological and Affective Factors —— 73
Adriana Biedroń

Part II: Memory, Attention and Noticing

6   Phonological and Executive Working Memory —— 97
Zhisheng (Edward) Wen

7   Consciousness, Attention and Noticing —— 125
Zhisheng (Edward) Wen

Part III: Learning Strategies, Metacognition and Self-Regulation

8 Language Learning Strategies —— 147
Mark Feng Teng

9 Metacognition —— 175
Mark Feng Teng

10 Self-Regulation —— 201
Mark Feng Teng

Part IV: L2 Skills, Learning Difficulties, and Anxiety

11 L2 Reading and Writing Skills —— 225
Richard L. Sparks

12 L2 Learning Difficulties and Disabilities —— 257
Richard L. Sparks

13 L2 Anxiety: An Affective Factor or a Linguistic Variable? —— 287
Richard L. Sparks

Epilogue

14 Individual Differences in SLA–Looking Back and Looking Forward —— 321
Richard Sparks & Zhisheng (Edward) Wen

Author Profiles —— 335

Index —— 337

Foreword

Peter Skehan

Many, possibly most, approaches within applied linguistics take what might be termed a universalist perspective. In other words, they focus on structures and processes which are assumed to be operative across all individuals. Not necessarily in exactly the same way, but the presumption is that such processes are pervasive and vital, and are central to understanding how language learning occurs. Studying feedback and interaction, or developmental sequences, or how tasks operate are examples of this. The challenge in this approach is to explore how different types of feedback or different tasks produce better acquisitional results or influences on performance. Developmental sequences, for example, are studied to explore how comprehensively they operate, and how they can be accounted for through linguistic or cognitive theory. They might also be studied to explore the best timing for instruction, and the limits of instructional interventions.

Obviously, these approaches have made huge, even dominant contributions to applied linguistics and second language acquisition, and probably account for an extremely high percentage of research that is carried out, and of publications which have appeared. But there is an alternative, albeit more recent approach, and this is to explore how learners differ from one another, and how these differences can have an impact on the nature and rate of second language learning. In earlier days, the approach was characterised by a focus on specific individual difference variables, such as foreign language aptitude, particularly through John Carroll's work (1962), or motivation, with Robert Gardner (1985) a pioneer in this area. Typically, researchers conducted studies on the particular variable that interested them, and that was that. But as time went on, these particular studies built into an *individual differences approach*, with a wider range of possible IDs, (including intelligence, style, affective and conative factors), and a clear perception of some sort of commonality amongst them. The central feature has been to think that, if learners are different from one another in some major ways, we need to understand these differences, have some sense of their malleability, and how instruction may need to be modified to take account of them. Indeed, this approach connects with what might be termed 'mixed ability' teaching within pedagogy, where teachers are concerned with the techniques which enable them to support development in classes where students may differ markedly from one another.

In fact, we can broaden this discussion to go well beyond the specific areas of language and language learning. The contrast, which has been termed the differential and the universal, reflects a long-standing debate in general psychology (Cronbach & Meehl, 1955). This debate, as the date of the Cronbach-Meehl reference makes clear, has been influential for many years, and provoked a certain amount of tension. The intention of this particular reference was to try to reconcile the two approaches and reduce the tension by suggesting that each approach has a lot to offer the other! Universalist approaches, e.g. of learning, might be suggestive of areas where individual differences might exist and be worth measuring and applying. Equally, an approach based on the structure of human abilities might suggest areas under-represented in universalist approaches (Carroll, 1993). Interestingly, an excellent example of such cross-fertilisation is relevant to one of the chapters in the present volume – the case of foreign language aptitude. The most influential recent work in this area, as described in Chapters 4 and 5, is the development of the Hi-LAB. This relatively new aptitude test demonstrates the effects of basic psychological research, of a generalist nature, into processes of memory and learning, which was then applied to the (differential) area of foreign language aptitude, as specific aptitude tests have been developed based on this general psychological theorising (also see Hughes et al., 2023). The aptitude sub-tests concerned are quite innovative compared to most existing aptitude tests, and show how one area can contribute insights to the other.

Cognitive Individual Differences in Second Language Acquisition makes a major contribution to this tradition of exploring differential factors in second and foreign language learning. Over the last few decades, there has been a steady output of textbooks, monographs and edited volumes, as well as general review articles in this area. These have tried to explicate the common interests of those who research in the area, the findings, and the research techniques. Most of these have attempted to cover the entire field of ID work, and so have covered cognitive, and affective, and conative work. This raises one of the distinctive qualities of the present volume. It focusses on *cognitive* individual differences, and this reflects the way the field has grown, and that coverage of all individual differences in one book may run the risk of lacking depth. Consequently, in this book we have a focus only on the major areas from the cognitive domain, of talents for language learning, of basic psychological processes, of the learner being self-aware about their own learning, and of difficulties in language learning as well as reactions to success (and failure). In addition, all sections of the book show strong influences of 'feeder' disciplines such as contemporary psychology and education in the way they approach these different cognitively-oriented areas, an important point of connection with neighbouring disciplines.

Another major contribution comes from the way the volume has been written. It is multi-authored, and this, in turn, leads to two advantages. First, as the field has grown, so it has become more difficult for individuals to maintain a level of expertise over all the diverse sub-domains. In the present volume, four authors have collaborated effectively to do justice to developments in individual differences. Adriana Biedroń specialises in aptitude, intelligence, and age and critical period issues. Zhisheng (Edward) Wen covers the areas of working memory and processing. Mark Feng Teng handles learning strategies, metacognition, and self-regulation. Richard Sparks covers reading and writing, language disabilities, and anxiety. All draw on their own areas of scholarship and current research, and so the coverage is authoritative and up-to-date. Authors are able to draw upon their particular areas of expertise to make sure that coverage is comprehensive and informed 'from the inside' as it were. They are also well placed to convey the excitement of the latest research – often their own. The reader gets the best of both worlds – comprehensive, co-ordinated coverage but also depth that flows from personal expertise.

The second advantage of having sections written by specialists is that chapters can, more easily, have multiple goals. They do provide even-handed coverage of each area concerned, as issues are raised and discussed. But there is also scope for personal voices to emerge, so that, in addition to the general discussion of theories, findings, and issues, one can have a greater sense that there are personal viewpoints which motivate the authors. Each author has a point of view, and can then combine general, authoritative coverage of their area with a freshness that comes from being an active researcher, with a viewpoint on the area concerned. Sparks exemplifies this with his coverage of anxiety. A first reaction here might be that the discussion of anxiety research is misplaced in a book on *cognitive* individual differences. Sparks, though, argues cogently that anxiety is the *result* of cognitive individual differences and relates this claim to a considerable research base. Similarly Wen, after general coverage of the key area of working memory, outlines his own approach to resolving some of the more difficult issues within this domain, using his Phonological/Executive model to discuss phonological memory and language processing within the second language area. Biedroń and Teng offer similar personal interpretations of aptitude and learning strategies and self-regulation. As a result, 'voice' has a distinctive role in this book, showing that personal interests (and motivations) have an important role in our field.

The volume also makes another contribution, and with this, we return to a point made at the beginning of this Foreword – the distinction between differential and universalist approaches, and how these two approaches have often happily walked separately along their own merry paths! We have seen one brief example of how this separation can be overcome in Chapter 4, discussing the development of the Hi-LAB. But there is a more general nature to the way this volume tries to be outward-looking and to bridge the differential-universalist divide, and this concerns the important place, in an IDs book, for the general field of second language acquisition. SLA has grown exponentially over the last fifty years, but a lot of that development has not had much of a 'differences' component. But things are changing and we now see many points of contact, with SLA studies integrating some ID measures (Li, 2015; Skehan, 2015), and vice versa. What has been termed the 'micro' approach to language aptitude relates to second language processes such as restructuring, and to processes such as exploiting feedback, or engaging in implicit or explicit learning. Similarly, memory and attention, central to SLA, now figure naturally in a book such as this, as Section Two indicates. Noticing, and attention to feedback, and its integration into an interlanguage system presuppose effective memory function, for example, and so the two approaches need to work more tightly together. The book aptly reflects the way these two, previously disparate areas, are coming together in fascinating ways.

A final point is that these different features, comprehensive up-to-date reviews, personal voice, and integration of ID work with an area like SLA, come together to make this book an unusual combination of textbook, suitable to underpin ID courses, and research publication, making distinctive contributions to the field. The former quality comes from the authoritative, even-handed coverage in each of the areas. The latter connects with the research linkages of the different sections, coupled with the personal voice that drives each of them. As a result, the volume has a considerable range of appeal, across undergraduate and postgraduate levels. It is to be hoped that it will have a considerable impact on the field of individual differences, specifically, and second language acquisition, more generally.

References

Carroll, John B. 1962. The prediction of success in intensive foreign language training. In Robert Glaser (Ed.). *Training, Research, and Education*, 87–136. Pittsburgh, PA.: University of Pittsburgh Press.

Carroll, John B. 1993. *Human Cognitive Abilities: A survey of factor analytic studies*. Cambridge: Cambridge University Press.

Cronbach, Lee J. & Paul E. Meehl. 1955. Construct validity of psychological tests. *Psychological Bulletin, 52,4*, 281–302.

Gardner, Robert. 1985. *Social Psychology and Second Language Learning: The role of attitudes and motivation*. London: Edward Arnold.

Hughes, Meredith, Ewa Golonka, Alison Tseng & Susan Campbell. 2023. The High-Level Language Aptitude Test Battery (Hi-LAB): Development, validation, and use. In Zhisheng (Edward) Wen, Peter Skehan & Richard Sparks (eds.), *Language aptitude theory and practice*. Cambridge: Cambridge University Press.

Li, Shaofeng. 2015. The associations between language aptitude and second language grammar acquisition: A meta-analytic review of five decades of research. *Applied Linguistics, 36 (3)*, 385–408.

Skehan, Peter. 2015. Foreign language aptitude and its relationship with grammar: A critical overview. *Applied Linguistics, 36 (3)*, 367–384.

1 SLA and Individual Differences: An Overview

Zhisheng (Edward) Wen & Richard L. Sparks

Abstract: The introductory chapter summarizes the background and rationale for this volume. It illustrates how the current volume expands on previous publications with new and distinctive features. In particular, important individual differences (IDs) of age, intelligence, aptitude, working memory, attention, strategies, meta-cognition, self-regulation, anxiety, reading, and writing as well as L2 learning difficulties are featured as they have not been discussed so systematically. In essence, this volume provides systematically organized (as its subtitle indicates, theories, assessment, research, and pedagogy), comprehensive and in-depth reviews on each of the key IDs believed to play an important role in SLA.

Keywords: Individual differences, second language acquisition, Universal Grammar (UG), Usage-based accounts, complex dynamic systems theory (CDST), L2 learning

1.1 Conceptualizing SLA: From UG to UB Approaches

Research into second language acquisition (SLA) has witnessed rapid growth in both 'quantity and quality' in the past few decades, resulting in substantial progress in areas of theory construction, research methodology, empirical investigations, and accumulative evidence as well as pedagogical implications and applications (Long 2016). In terms of theoretical paradigms, for example, a multitude of epistemological approaches to SLA is gradually taking shape and becoming well-established. These approaches range from the more conventional mainstream paradigms such as the universal grammar (UG) based generative accounts (e.g., Rothman and Slabakova 2018; Slabakova et al. 2020), to an increasing interest in the emergentist, connectionist, construction-oriented, usage-based (UB) accounts (Dornyei 2009; Li et al. 2022; Mitchell, Myles and Marsden 2019; MacWhinney et al. 2022; VanPatten and Williams 2014), broadly grouped as alternative accounts (Atkinson 2011).

Most of the time, these approaches have co-existed peacefully and blossomed independently, proceeding within their research camps or teams of advocates and followers, pursuing their own research agendas with specific research methodologies, organizing their own conferences, and publishing in journals focusing on their respective domains. However, there are occasional skirmishes when contrasting approaches exchange views face to face. The recent interchanges between the generative SLA approaches (represented by Slabakova et al. 2014, 2015) and the complex, dynamic, systems theory (CDST) approach (represented by de Bot 2015) amply demonstrated the differences and arguments in their epistemological stances regarding three fundamental factors pertaining to language design and acquisition (Chomsky 2005, 2011; Hauser et al. 2002; Slabakova et al. 2020): (1) Genetic endowment (UG), which determines the general course of the development of the language faculty; (2) Experience (comprehensive input), which leads to (narrow) variation; and (3) Principles of data-analysis & computation efficiency.

In this respect, the mainstream generative camp tends to treat UG as the primary factor, and thus puts input (experience) and computation as something on the periphery of SLA, while the UB-based accounts (including the CDST approach) embrace the other end of the spectrum, i.e., language experience or input as a priority. There is also a third perspective on epistemological stances, which emphasizes computation efficiency (e.g., Gibson et al. 2019) or the constraints of the ubiquitous memory limitations (Gomez-Rodriguez et al. 2019) as the primary factor that constrains and shapes language evolution, acquisition, and processing (cf. Lu and Wen 2022). These perspectives have included the emergentist accounts (MacWhinney and O'Grady 2015; O'Grady 2012, 2015; MacWhinney et al. 2022) and the processing accounts (Christiansen and Chater 2015, 2016, 2017).

Despite these seemingly disparate perspectives, the research paradigms provide complementary insights into the most intriguing 'mysteries' of high-level and distributed human cognition, i.e., language (Ellis 2019). Though the jury is still out as to which paradigm will find the "holy grail", i.e., by solving the logical problem of language acquisition, these multidisciplinary insights are injecting much dynamism into the exciting and thriving field of language sciences in general and SLA in particular. As such, the current volume adopts an open-minded approach towards these diverse epistemological stances in SLA with a view to achieving some balance among them. To put it in Lantolf's (1996) words, "let all the flowers blossom."

In another line of development, the past two decades in SLA have also witnessed steady growth in both the breadth and depth of research on instructed SLA (ISLA; Loewen and Sato 2017). In his 2016 plenary address to the annual SLRF conference, Michael Long offered two types of reasons for this exponential growth in ISLA, both external and internal (see also Long 2017). Externally, most major geopolitical forces have linguistic consequences, which have helped to raise wider recognition of the importance of designing effective language instruction for specific populations. Internally, advances in instruction have been facilitated by several developments: (1) renewed attention to *instruction, language,* and *acquisition,* the 'I', 'L' and 'A' of ISLA; (2) publication of detailed state-of-the-science surveys, including both narrative accounts and particularly the growing body of meta-analyses (e.g., Norris and Ortega 2000; Li 2010); (3) deployment of new technology, e.g., eye-tracking (Godfroid 2019), ERP, and fMRI, etc.; (4) creation and validation of new aptitude measures, e.g., the Hi-LAB (Linck et al. 2014; Doughty 2019; see also Wen et al. 2019; Wen, Skehan and Sparks 2023); (5) establishment of the field's first collaborative research network (CRN) and a free, publicly accessible digital repository of data-collection instruments, materials and stimuli (IRIS; Paquot et al. 2019); (6) a growing number of process-product studies, including aptitude-treatment-interaction (ATI) studies, that employ both linguistically focused and communicative assessment of outcomes; (7) improvements in the ways studies are conducted, replicated and reported; and (8) increased journal and conference space for the dissemination of findings. These developments demonstrate that ISLA has blossomed in the past two decades (Long 2017; Loewen and Sato 2017).

Conceptualizing SLA and IDs: Towards a CDST Approach

The frameworks adopted in some chapters of this book incorporate emerging trends and approaches of SLA in which L2 acquisition or development is no longer reduced to a monolithic and static concept, but rather is increasingly recognized as a *multi-dimensional, emergent, complex, dynamic,* and *adaptive* process (e.g., de Bot 2015; Larsen-Freeman 1997, 2019; Larsen-Freeman and Cameron 2008). SLA is conceived as a process consisting of multiple (sub-level) components and dimensions, comprising of an array of sub-domains and sub-skills that transcend across acquisition/learning, processing/performance, evolution, and development. More specifically, these L2 sub-domains encompass three aspects or facets of L2 acquisition (e.g. VanPatten 2010; Wen 2016).

First, there are *linguistic knowledge and representation aspects* of L2 domains such as phonemes (speech) sounds, vocabulary (lexis), formulaic sequences/chunks, and morpho-syntactic constructions or grammatical structures as conceived in the connectionist account advocated by Ellis (1996a) and Krishnan et al. (2016). Second, there are *processing and performance aspects* that straddle L2 sub-skills such as listening, speaking, reading, writing, and (bilingual) translation/interpreting. Finally, there is the sub-domain of L2 proficiency *development* which implicates aspects of evolution, emergence, and changes. These developmental stages represent conceptualizations of L2 proficiency at the beginning (*ab initio* or novice), intermediate, and post-intermediate/advanced levels and native-like stages (e.g., Hulstijn 2015).

These categories of SLA knowledge, processes, and skills are derived mainly from those of VanPatten's (2010, 2013) recent argument for a two-facet view of SLA (i.e., representation vs. skills), augmented by a third time-based longitudinal dimension of L2 development (Wen 2016; Christiansen and Chater 2016). In this sense, the first two categories of SLA sub-domains proposed here can be interpreted as equivalent to VanPatten's conceptions of the 'mental representation' and the concept of 'sub-skills' (subsuming listening, reading, speaking, and writing), though we have also included the additional (fifth) skill of 'translation/interpreting' as combining language comprehension and production (Dong et al. 2018). Then, the third aspect of L2 developmental domains is added to represent the *complex, dynamic, and adaptive* nature of L2 proficiency, which has gained increasing credence in the current SLA arena (Douglas Fir Group 2016, 2019; Hiver, Al-Horrie, and Evans 2021).

It should be acknowledged that the working definition of SLA adopted by this volume does not just embrace the mainstream generative grammar (MGG) approach to first language acquisition (e.g., from Chomsky 1965), which prioritizes grammar or grammatical rules as the core of language learning, and puts everything else (such as memory) in the periphery (Hauser et al. 2002). More importantly, the SLA domains are interpreted through the lens of the increasingly prevalent approaches of dynamic systems theory and complexity theory (Larsen-Freeman, 1997, 2015a, 2015b) in which vocabulary (lexis) and grammar (syntax) are no longer regarded as separate entities (cf. Marchman and Bates 1994; also see Römer 2009; Vulchanova et al. 2014), but rather as intermingled linguistic sequences, formulaic chunks or morpho-syntactic constructions that co-adapt (Ellis 1996, 2012, 2013). Given the sometimes elusive nature and problematic concept of the generative term 'grammar' (Cook and Singleton 2014; also see de Bot 2015), the current volume follows the emerging usage-based trends in SLA and thus opts for the terms 'lexis', 'formulae' and 'morpho-syntactic constructions' (or 'morpho-syntax') to represent the variegated units of linguistic sequences/constructions in the SLA representational and developmental sub-domains.

Overall, we hope it is clear from the above discussion that SLA categories of *representational, processing,* and *developmental* domains are being aligned in a *new* order by incorporating these latest accounts of the emergentist, connectionist, and construction-oriented views of language acquisition, language use and language development (Ellis 2013). We also hope that such definitions not only echo but also expand the ideas initiated by Nick Ellis regarding the complex relationships between the individual difference (ID) factors such as language aptitude, working memory, etc., on the one hand, and their corresponding roles in the representation, acquisition, and development of these SLA sub-domains on the other (Ellis 1996b, 2012, 2013).

1.2 Rationale and Motivation for the book

Individual differences (IDs) in second language (L2) learning have been researched for many years (Li et al. 2022). A host of both well-established and emerging ID variables such as intelligence, personality, gender, language aptitude, motivation, willingness to communicate, working memory, field dependence-independence, learning strategies, attitudes, identity, anxiety, and their respective impact on L2 outcomes have been studied as far back as the 1950s. A casual search (conducted on 24 July 2022) in the *Pubmed* database with the three keywords of "individual differences", "second language" or "L2" and 'language learning' generated over 9,000 entries between 1985 to 2022, not to mention other databases (such as Scopus). Just in 2021 alone, there are over 168 entries. The research of IDs has always occupied a central role not just in SLA and applied linguistics, but also in other broader fields of education, cognitive development, psychology and neuroscience, to name but a few.

In the early days when the field of SLA had just started, Fillmore (1979) discussed IDs in cognitive and social strategies for learning a second language. Ten years later, Skehan (1989) moved on to propose that in addition to studying how learners are similar, the study of IDs between learners in, e.g., aptitude, motivation, learning strategies, would be beneficial to research in L2 learning. Another ten years later, Skehan (1998) further elaborated his 'psycholinguistics' or 'cognitive approach' to second language learning and teaching as complementary to mainstream linguistic-oriented SLA research. Then, Robinson (2002) presented research on the "fit between person (second language learner) and situation/context (learning conditions) in the second language (L2) classroom" (p. 1). After the turn of the new millennium, prolific publications by Dörnyei and colleagues significantly boosted the IDs enterprise towards developments in L2 learning motivation. Dörnyei (2005, 2009) significantly broadened the terrains of the study of IDs into the 'cognitive neuroscience' perspective and the complex dynamic systems theory (CDST) approach that Larsen-freeman had first advocated in 1997 but not received much attention until recent years. Most well-established IDs of language learning are being re-conceptualized in these new lenses, including language aptitude and motivation, as well as additional variables such as mood and personality, learning styles and cognitive styles, and learner beliefs, including self-esteem (the recent special issue of *Studies in Second Language Learning and Teaching* (SSLLT), 2020).

In more recent years, Wen (2016), Wen et al. (2015) and Granena et al. (2016) provided theoretical and empirical studies on key cognitive IDs such as working memory and language aptitude. Then, Reiterer (2018) and Wen et al. (2019) focused on language aptitude particularly and presented perspectives on IDs in L2 learning from multidisciplinary fields including applied linguistics, educational and cognitive psychology, and cognitive neuroscience. The chapters in those two volumes described research on IDs in language aptitude from aptitude tests, age and ultimate attainment, working memory, aptitudes for explicit and implicit learning, and neurophysiological indicators of the linguistic components of language aptitude. Most recently, the themed special issue of the *Annual Review of Applied Linguistics* (ARAL), and the volume on language aptitude by Wen, Skehan and Sparks (2023) continued this interdisciplinary tradition to further push the boundaries in both language aptitude theoretical conception and aptitude testing practice.

Despite these cognitive-oriented works, IDs in affect such as motivation, willingness to communicate, and anxiety have continued to thrive with new and emerging topics such as L2 self, L2 engagement, and (classroom) boredom being added to the 'affective' family (Dewaele 2009). Overall, the past four decades of intense ID research in SLA have witnessed some twists and turns as well as competition between the 'cognitive' and the 'affective' ID variables. Each tradition is adhering to its preferred research paradigms and methodologies to pursue research interests and agendas (see Li et al. 2022 for recent overviews).

To be fair, research into affective variables, particularly L2 motivation, has dominated the field of IDs in SLA in the past two decades or so. Another quick search with the keywords of "second language motivation" or "L2 motivation" in the Scopus database generated over 1400 entries (with Dörnyei alone producing over 30 entries). This partly explains why we have not included lengthy discussions on motivation in this volume. As such, the current volume includes major chapters on more 'cognitive' and linguistic-oriented ID variables that, in most cases, have not been systematically covered by previous and extant monographs and textbooks/handbooks of SLA.

In essence, we intend this volume as providing recent updates and extension of the seminal volumes by Skehan (1989, 1998) and Dornyei (2009), focusing on cognitive approaches to IDs, particularly on age, intelligence, language aptitude, working memory and attention, learning strategies, metacognition as well as linguistic oriented constructs such as anxiety (which is different from previous conceptualizations). These past decades have witnessed significant progress being made in ID research in both SLA and the neighboring fields of educational psychology, cognitive psychology, and cognitive neuroscience.

The current volume expands on these previous volumes but distinguishes itself with several new and distinctive features. First, rather than including all conceivable cognitive and affective ID variables, this volume provides systematically organized (as its subtitle indicates, theories, assessment, research, and pedagogy), comprehensive and in-depth reviews on each of the key IDs believed to play an important role in SLA. In this case, we highlight the important IDs of age, intelligence, aptitude, working memory, attention, strategies, meta-cognition, self-regulation, anxiety, reading, and writing as well as L2 learning difficulties. All of these IDs, despite their significant influence on SLA, have not been discussed in previous volumes so systematically. We are hoping to provide a comprehensive and updated view of these previously marginalized topics.

Second, the volume includes relevant, updated evidence and insights from the latest developments in SLA and cognitive sciences (Miller 2003), multidisciplinary perspectives from anthropology (evolutionary perspectives), educational and cognitive psychology, developmental psychology, and neuroscience. To some extent, Dornyei's 2009 volume initiated and underscored the trend of '*a cognitive neuroscience approach*' in terms of theoretical account, but did not address the emerging issues of assessment techniques and meta-analytical studies that have thrived in the subsequent decade. In the current volume, perspectives from these multiple disciplines (in particular, psychology, education, and neuroscience) offer an in-depth, interdisciplinary understanding of these IDs and their potential effects on L2 sub-domains and processes.

As the subtitle of the book denotes, the surveys for each of the cognitive IDs in SLA are mostly organized into four levels by subsuming theoretical conceptualizations, elaborating on methodological issues regarding measurement and assessment procedures, reviewing empirical studies and meta-analytical results, and examining pedagogical implications for L2 instruction and classroom practice. Hopefully, each chapter will prove to be an invaluable source for readers (i.e., SLA researchers, language teachers, TESOL practitioners, and postgraduate students) to have a comprehensive, thorough, and updated review of each key cognitive ID and overview of theories, research and practice.

1.3 Organization and Contents

As such, the volume is organized in the presentation of each ID in focus first, culminating with a constellation of their effects towards the end. Following the introductory chapter, **Part I** of the book consists of four major chapters contributed by **Adriana Biedroń**. **Chapter 2 considers** the **age factor** as situated in the controversies and debates surrounding the **critical period hypothesis (CPH) and age of onset**. The chapter also reviews the emerging literature investigating the neurobiological brain mechanisms of the critical period, as well as the combined effects of age and genetic variations on second language learning (Vaughn and Hernandez 2018).

Chapter 3 examines the role of **intelligence** in SLA. It begins by reviewing the history of intelligence research and then summarizes the major theoretical models and perspectives and key assessment procedures for intelligence from the traditional IQ tests to the modern and the latest development of the implicit theory of **mindset** (Dweck 2006). The chapter concludes by considering some possible venues for future research on this intriguing topic for SLA.

Chapter 4 traces the developments of **foreign language aptitude** theoretical models and language aptitude test batteries, including those informed by educational psychology, e.g., the Modern Language Aptitude Test (MLAT), the Linguistic Coding Differences Hypothesis (LCDH), the Cognitive Analysis of Novelty in the Acquisition of Language – Foreign (CANAL-F), and those informed by cognitive psychology and SLA, including LLAMA, the Staged model, the aptitude complexes model, and the latest Hi-LAB model/test. In the end, the role of working memory is also mentioned, though it receives full-length discussion in Chapter 6.

Chapter 5 provides a commentary on the connections between **foreign language aptitude and the psychological factors** that include a cognitive component. It begins with a discussion of the theoretical foundations of psychological factors in SLA, which is followed by detailed analyses of the relationship between language aptitude and psychological factors in terms of theory, research, and practice. Then, the chapter turns to discuss the development of linguistic giftedness and multilingual talents or polyglots. The chapter concludes with an outline of pedagogical implications and proposals for further research.

Part II consists of Chapters 6 and 7 by Edward (Zhisheng) Wen. **Chapter 6** conducts a thorough review of the complex relationship between the limited capacity of **working memory** and its implications for various SLA sub-domains and skills. The chapter begins by summarizing the three major theoretical models of working memory in cognitive psychology that have provided the methodological inspiration for SLA research (see also Schwieter and Wen 2022). These reviews culminate in an integrative model of working memory as an overarching framework for implementing the working memory construct in SLA (Wen 2016; Wen and Schwieter 2022). Within the framework, two key components, phonological working memory (PWM) and executive working memory (EWM), take center stage (i.e., the Phonological/Executive model; Wen 2015, 2016, 2019; Wen and Skehan 2021) and their componential mechanisms and finer-grained effects on SLA are highlighted (see also Wen and Schwieter 2022). Then, a comprehensive review of related literature, including major strands of independent empirical studies and recent meta-analytical studies, explains the intricate relationships between the general premise and component mechanisms of working memory and SLA domains and skills. The chapter concludes by calling for a paradigm shift from WM components to finer-grained WM functions (**updating**, task **switching**, and **inhibitory control**; cf. Miyake and Friedman 2012) in future WM-SLA explorations (see also Bunting and Wen 2023).

Chapter 7 builds on chapter 6 by examining the three closely related but sometimes confusing constructs of **consciousness, attention, and noticing**, focusing on a historical evaluation of the noticing hypothesis, to be augmented by two more recent attentional models in current SLA and within task-based language teaching (TBLT). Specifically, the chapter highlights Richard Schmidt's *noticing hypothesis* in terms of its theoretical frameworks, key tenets, and measurement and assessment procedures, as well as evaluating the empirical support it has received from Schmidt himself and other SLA researchers, including emerging evidence from corrective feedback. Then, within TBLT, Skehan's Limited Attention Capacity (LAC) Hypothesis (2015) and Robinson's 'Cognition Hypothesis' (CH 2022) are elaborated as viable and complementary frameworks for explaining L2 task-based performance. In the pedagogy section, some instructional techniques such as focus-on-form (e.g., consciousness-raising activity, textual enhancement exercises, Focus-on-form strategies) are introduced with their implications for classroom practice.

Part III consists of three chapters by Mark Feng Teng. **Chapter 8** introduces the historical development of **L2 learning strategies** and then presents the assessment of language learning strategies by reviewing the survey instruments that have been implemented by SLA researchers and educational practitioners over the years. The research findings shed light on IDs in **strategy use** and the inherent factors that result in IDs in **strategy choice** and L2 learning performance. Research findings highlight the effectiveness of **strategy-based instruction** on L2 learning. The chapter concludes by presenting the remaining challenges for instruction and pedagogy related to language learning strategies.

Chapter 9 and **Chapter 10** turn to **metacognition and self-regulation** that are currently gaining increasing prominence in current SLA research. The chapter first provides a theoretical basis for understanding metacognition and self-regulation. Through synthesizing theories, this chapter highlights the importance of **metacognition** as a tool for language learning and teaching. This chapter introduces **key instruments** for assessing metacognition in language learning as well as **intervention studies based on metacognitive instruction** for listening, reading, and writing outcomes. The author emphasizes that students should be aware of how they can activate their existing knowledge to enhance the language learning process, build awareness of knowledge gaps, and set goals for bridging the gaps. The author argues that language **teachers play a key role in supporting their students to develop metacognitive awareness** through modeling key metacognitive strategies. Most importantly, language teachers should be metacognitively aware of their own teaching in order to help students' language learning.

Previous research on IDs in SLA has been overly dependent on a monolithic view in which each ID factor is discussed as if it is independent and unrelated to other IDs (Dornyei 2009). As one approach to addressing and resolving this issue, Dornyei has proposed the CDST framework as a meta-theory for viewing IDs in SLA, which calls for ID amalgamates instead of single ID variables. To bring other views on IDs in L2 learning, we include three innovative perspectives in the current volume.

Taken together, the three chapters in **Part IV** by Richard L. Sparks invite SLA researchers to consider seriously the role of IDs for more and less successful L2 learning respectively. Specifically, **Chapter 11** focuses on the assessment of cognitive skills found to be important for the mastery of English reading and writing skills. Sparks proposes the Simple View of Reading (SVR) and Simple View of Writing (SVW) models as viable frameworks for explaining and assessing L2 reading and writing for English language learners (ELLs). In reading research, word decoding and oral language comprehension skills have been found to explain the bulk of variance for reading comprehension. For writing, transcription and ideation are the cognitive components largely responsible for writing ability. The author describes both models, examines the relationships between reading comprehension and listening comprehension and oral language and writing, and explains how to assess English reading and writing with readily available standardized tests. He concludes by discussing pedagogical strategies for teaching English reading and writing to ELLs based on assessment using the models' frameworks.

Chapter 12 scrutinizes the subject of IDs in L2 learning and learning disabilities (LD). The author has studied this topic in the U.S. for over 30 years and found that there is not a specific "disability" for L2 learning. The term LD has different meanings in the U.S., where LD implies specific academic deficits, and in Europe, where the term is used broadly to include many different types of disabilities. In this chapter, the author explains how the differences in the definitions and diagnosis for LDs cause problems in the identification of students with L2 learning problems. Sparks explains the construct of LD, reviews research showing that both L1 and L2 difficulties are cognitive problems in the domain of language, examines the relationship between LDs and L2 learning problems, and explores teaching methods for students with L2 problems. He also examines several beliefs about LDs and L2 learning and explains how the beliefs have been falsified by empirical evidence.

Chapter 13 argues that L2 anxiety is more likely to be a consequence of language problems rather than an affective construct. Since the 1990s, the author has questioned the claims of L2 educators about the role of anxiety in L2 learning and presented evidence showing that L2 anxiety is strongly related to learners' L1 skills, L2 aptitude, and L2 achievement, and that L2 anxiety measured in high school predicts growth in L1 skills many years prior to engaging in L2 coursework. In this chapter, he examines theories about the role of anxiety in L2 learning, the measurement of anxiety, and evidence that challenges the L2 anxiety hypothesis. Next, he presents the results of a new longitudinal study using hierarchical regression analyses to determine whether IDs in L2 anxiety would explain unique variance in the growth of L2 reading comprehension skills over time. The findings from this study and others suggest that L2 anxiety surveys serve as a proxy for students' language learning skills, their self-perceptions of their language skills, or both. The chapter concludes by exploring how confusion about the role of anxiety in L2 learning may affect L2 pedagogy.

Chapter 14 by Richard Sparks and Edward (Zhisheng) Wen concludes the book by looking back and looking forward to the topic of ID research and SLA. The authors propose some blueprints for future research in cognitive IDs, general IDs research, and beyond. Though the focus of the current volume has been placed on the 'cognitive' end, they propose that isolated treatment of cognitive (and other) variables (i.e., the 'siloing' practice), will likely be unproductive in generating a "Grand Theory" for L2 acquisition. In the chapter, the authors examine Richard Snow's framework for language aptitude and propose their own framework for aptitude theory construction by examining domain-specific and domain-general variables for L2 aptitude. They also raise the question of whether the results of language aptitude tests can generate practical applications for language instruction. The chapter concludes by encouraging collaboration among researchers with multiple perspectives on L2 aptitude and offering some examples of important, albeit outstanding, questions guiding future research on IDs in SLA.

1.4 Concluding Remarks

Overall, the chapters are structured in a similar format and focus on a distinctive ID construct. Within each chapter, four aspects of relevant research are discussed and synthesized in an integrated manner: a) theoretical models and conceptions, b) assessment tools, techniques, and procedures, c) empirical research and evidence, and d) pedagogical implications. Furthermore, surveys of ID factors draw on not only the latest developments in applied linguistics and SLA research, but also incorporate insights from neighboring multidisciplinary fields such as educational psychology and cognitive psychology, biology and genetics, and neuroscience. Taken as a whole, we aim to provide readers with an interdisciplinary understanding of key cognitive and related affective factors underlying second language learning and performance.

References

Atkinson, Dwight (ed.). 2011. *Alternative approaches to second language acquisition*. New York: Routledge.
Bunting, Michael F. & Zhisheng (Edward) Wen. 2023. Working memory in language and bilingual development. In Robert H. Logie, Zhisheng (Edward) Wen, Susan E. Gathercole, Nelson Cowan & Randall W. Engle (eds.), *Memory in science for society*, 301–327. Oxford, UK: Oxford University Press.
Chomsky, Noam. 1965. *Aspects of the theory of syntax*. Cambridge, Mass: MIT Press.
Chomsky, Noam. 2005. Three factors in language design. *Linguistic Inquiry* 36(1). 1–22.
Chomsky, Noam. 2011. Language and other cognitive systems. What is special about language? *Language Learning and Development* 7(4). 263–278.
Christiansen, Morten H. & Nick Chater. 2015. The language faculty that wasn't: A usage-based account of natural language recursion. *Frontiers in Psychology* 6. 10.3389/fpsyg.2015.01182
Christiansen, Morten H. & Nick Chater. 2016. *Creating language: Integrating evolution, acquisition, and processing*. Cambridge, MA: MIT Press.
Christiansen, Morten H. & Nick Chater. 2017. Towards an integrated science of language. *Nature Human Behaviour* 1(8). 1–3.
Cook, Vivian & David Singleton. 2014. *Key issues in second language acquisition*. Multilingual Matters.
Cowan, Nelson. 2005. *Working memory capacity*. New York and Hove: Psychology Press.
De Bot, Kees. 2015. Moving where? A reaction to Slabakova et al. *Applied Linguistics* 36(2). 261–264.
Dewaele, Jean-Marc. 2009. Individual differences in second language acquisition. In Tej K. Bhatia & William C. Ritchie (eds.), *The new handbook of second language acquisition*, 623–646. Bingley, United Kingdom: Emerald.
Dong Yanping, Yuhua Liu & Rendong Cai. 2018. How Does Consecutive Interpreting Training Influence Working Memory: A Longitudinal Study of Potential Links Between the Two. *Frontiers in Psychology* 9: 875. 10.3389/fpsyg.2018.0087
Dörnyei, Zoltán. 2005. *The psychology of the language learner: Individual differences in second language acquisition*. Mahwah, New Jersey: Lawrence Erlbaum.
Dörnyei, Zoltán. 2009. *The psychology of second language acquisition*. Oxford: Oxford University Press.
Dörnyei, Zoltán. & Stephen Ryan. 2015. The psychology of the language learner revisited. Mahwah, NJ: Erlbaum.
Doughty, Catherine J. 2019. Cognitive language aptitude. *Language Learning* 69. 101–126. https://doi.org/10.1111/lang.12322
Doughty, Catherine, & Allison Mackey. 2021. Language aptitude: Multiple perspectives. *Annual Review of Applied Linguistics. 41*. 1–5. https://doi.org/10.1017/S0267190521000076
Douglas Fir Group. 2016. A transdisciplinary framework for SLA in a multilingual world. *Modern Language Journal* 100 (S1). 19–47.
Dweck, Carol S. 2006. *Mindset: The new psychology of success*. New York, NY: Random House.
Ellis, Nick C. 1996a. Sequencing in SLA: Phonological memory, chunking and points of order. *Studies in Second Language Acquisition* 18(1). 91–126.
Ellis, Nick C. 1996b. Working memory in the acquisition of vocabulary and syntax: Putting language in good order. *The Quarterly Journal of Experimental Psychology Section A* 49(1). 234–250.
Ellis, Nick C. 2012. Formulaic language and second language acquisition: Zipf and the phrasal Teddy Bear. *Annual Review of Applied Linguistics* 32. 17–44. https://doi:10.1017/S0267190512000025
Ellis, Nick C. 2013. Second language acquisition. In Graeme Trousdale & Thomas Hoffmann (eds.), *Oxford handbook of construction grammar*, 365–378. Oxford: Oxford University Press.

Ellis, Nick C. 2019. Essentials of a theory of language cognition. *Modern Language Journal* 103. 39–60.
Fillmore, Lily Wong. 1979. Individual differences in second language acquisition. In Charles Fillmore, Daniel Kempler, & William S-Y Wang (eds.), *Individual differences in language ability and language behavior*, 203–228. Academic Press.
Gibson, Edward, Richard Futrell, Steven P. Piantadosi, Isabelle Dautriche, Kyle Mahowald, Leon Bergen & Roger Levy. 2019. How efficiency shapes human language. *Trends in Cognitive Science* 23(5). 389–407. http://dx.doi.org/10.31234/osf.io/w5m38
Godfroid, Aline. 2019. *Eye tracking in second language acquisition and bilingualism: A research synthesis and methodological guide*. New York: Routledge.
Gómez-Rodríguez, Carlos, Morten H. Christiansen & Ramon Ferrer-i-Cancho. 2019. Memory limitations are hidden in grammar. https://doi.org/10.7910/DVN/XHRIYX
Granena, Gisela, Daniel O. Jackson & Yucel Yilmaz (eds.). 2016. *Cognitive individual differences in L2 processing and acquisition*. Amsterdam: John Benjamins.
Hauser, Marc D., Noam Chomsky & W. Tecumseh Fitch. 2002. The faculty of language: What is it, who has it, and how did it evolve? *Science* 298. 1569–1579.
Hiver, Phil, Ali H. Al-Hoorie, & Reid Evans. 2021. Complex dynamic systems theory in language learning. Studies in Second Language Acquisition 44(4). 913–941. https://doi.org: 10.1017/S0272263121000553
Hiver, Phil, Ali H. Al-Hoorie & Diane Larsen-Freeman. 2022. Toward a transdisciplinary integration of research purposes and methods for complex dynamic systems theory: Beyond the quantitative-qualitative divide. *International Review of Applied Linguistics in Language Teaching* 60(1).
Hulstijn, Jan H. 2015. *Language proficiency in native and non-native speakers: Theory and research*. Amsterdam/Philadelphia: John Benjamins. https://doi.org/10.1075/lllt.41
Kidd, Evan, Seamus Donnelly & Morten H. Christiansen. 2018. Individual differences in language acquisition and processing. *Trends in Cognitive Sciences* 22(2). 154–169. https://doi:10.1016/j.tics.2017.11.006
Krishnan, Saloni, Kate E. Watkins & Dorothy V. M. Bishop. 2016. Neurobiological basis of language learning difficulties. *Trends in Cognitive Sciences* 20. 701–714. http://dx.doi.org/10.1016/j.tics.2016.06.012.
Lantolf, James P. 1996. Second language theory building: Letting all the flowers bloom! *Language Learning* 46(4). 713–749.
Larsen-Freeman, Diane. 1997. Chaos/complexity science and second language acquisition. *Applied Linguistics* 18(2). 141–165.
Larsen-Freeman, Diane. 2015a. Saying what we mean: Making a case for 'language acquisition' to become 'language development'. *Language Teaching* 48(4). 491–505.
Larsen-Freeman, Diane. 2015b. Ten 'lessons' from complex dynamic systems theory: What is on offer. *Motivational dynamics in language learning*. 11–19.
Larsen-Freeman, Diane. 2019. On language learner agency: A complex dynamic systems theory perspective. *Modern Language Journal* 103. 61–79.
Larsen-Freeman, Diane & Lynne Cameron. 2008. *Complex systems and applied linguistics*. Oxford: Oxford University Press.
Li, Shaofeng. 2010. The effectiveness of corrective feedback in SLA: A meta-analysis. *Language Learning* 60(2). 309–365.
Li, Shaofeng, Phil Hiver & Mostafa Papi. 2022. Individual differences in second language acquisition: Theory, research, and practice. In Shaofeng Li, Phil Hiver & Mostafa Papi (eds.), *The Routledge Handbook of SLA and individual differences*, 3–34. Routledge.

Linck, Jared A, Meredith M. Hughes, Susan G. Campbell, Noah H. Silbert, Medha Tare, Scott R. Jackson, Benjamin K. Smith, Michael F. Bunting & Catherine J. Doughty. 2014. Hi-LAB: A new measure of aptitude for high-level language proficiency. *Language Learning* 63(3). 530–566.

Loewen, Shawn & Masatoshi Sato. 2017. *The Routledge handbook of instructed second language acquisition*. Routledge.

Long, Michael. 2016. ISLA: Methodological Issues and Some Major Research Questions. Plenary speech at the *35th Second Language Research Forum (SLRF 2016)*, Columbia University.

Long, Michael M. 2017. Instructed second language acquisition (ISLA): Geopolitics, methodological issues, and some major research questions. *Instructed Second Language Acquisition* 1(1). 7–44.

Lu, Bingfu & Zhisheng Edward Wen. 2022. Working memory and the language device. In John W. Schwieter & Zhisheng (Edward) Wen (eds.), *The Cambridge handbook of working memory and language*. Cambridge: Cambridge University Press.

MacWhinney, Brian. 2018. A unified model of first and second language learning. In Maya Hickmann, Edy Veneziano & Harriet Jisa (eds.), *Sources of Variation in First Language Acquisition: Languages, contexts and learners*, 287–312. New York, NY: John Benjamins.

MacWhinney Brian & William. O'Grady. 2015. *The Handbook of Language Emergence*. Boston: Wiley-Blackwell.

MacWhinney Brian, Kempe Vera, Brooks Patricia, and Li Ping. 2022. Editorial: Emergentist approaches to language. *Frontiers in Psychology. 12*: 833160. doi: 10.3389/fpsyg.2021.833160

Marchman, Virginia A & Elizabeth Bates. 1994. Continuity in lexical and morphological development: A test of the critical mass hypothesis. *Journal of Child Language* 21(2). 339–366.

Miller, George A. 2003. The cognitive revolution: A historical perspective. *Trends in Cognitive Science* 7 (3). 141–144.

Mitchell, Rosamond, Florence Myles & Emma Marsden. 2019. *Second language learning theories* (5th ed.). London: Routledge.

Miyake, Akira & Naomi P. Friedman. 2012. The nature and organization of individual differences in executive functions: Four general conclusions. *Current Directions in Psychological Science* 21(1). 8–14.

Miyake, Akira, Naomi P. Friedman, Michael J. Emerson, Alexander H. Witzki, Amy Howerter & Tor D.Wager. 2000. The unity and diversity of executive functions and their contributions to complex "frontal lobe" tasks: A latent variable analysis. *Cognitive Psychology* 41(1). 49–100.

Norris, John M & Lourdes Ortega. 2000. Effectiveness of L2 instruction: A research synthesis and quantitative meta-analysis. *Language Learning* 50(3). 417–528.

O'Grady, William. 2012. Three factors in the design and acquisition of language. Wiley Interdisciplinary Reviews: Cognitive Science 3(5). 493–99.

O'Grady, William. 2015. Processing determinism. *Language Learning* 65(1). 6–32.

O'Grady, William. 2017. Working memory and language: From phonology to grammar. *Applied Psycholinguistics* 38(6). 1340–1343.

Paquot, Magali, Emma Marsden, Luke Plonsky, & Sophie Thompson. 2019. Open science in language learning research. IRIS and OASIS: EUROCALL 2019 (Louvain-la-Neuve, du 28/08/2019 au 31/08/2019).

Reiterer, Susanne M. (ed.). 2018. *Exploring Language Aptitude: Views from Psychology, the Language Sciences, and Cognitive Neuroscience*. Springer.

Robinson, Peter (ed.). 2002. *Individual differences and instructed language learning*. Amsterdam: Benjamins.

Robinson, Peter. 2022. The Cognition Hypothesis, the Triadic Componential Framework and the SSARC Model: An Instructional Design Theory of Pedagogic Task Sequencing. In Mohammad

Ahmadian & Michael H. Long (eds.), *The Cambridge Handbook of Task-Based Language Teaching*, 205–225. New York: Cambridge University Press.
Römer, Ute. 2009. The inseparability of lexis and grammar: Corpus linguistic perspectives. *Annual Review of Cognitive Linguistics* 7(1). 140–162.
Rothman, Jason & Roumyana Slabakova. 2018. The generative approach to SLA and its place in modern second language studies. *Studies in Second Language Acquisition* 40(2). 417–422.
Schwieter, John W & Zhisheng (Edward) Wen (eds.). 2022. *The Cambridge handbook of working memory and language* (Cambridge Handbooks in Language and Linguistics). Cambridge: Cambridge University Press.
Skehan, Peter. 1989. *Individual differences in second-language learning*. London: Edward Arnold.
Skehan, Peter. 1998. *A cognitive approach to language learning*. London: Oxford University Press.
Skehan, Peter. 2015. Limited attention capacity and cognition: Two hypotheses regarding second language performance on tasks. In Martin Bygate (ed.), *Domains and directions in the development of TBLT: A decade of plenaries from the international conference*, 123–156. Amsterdam: John Benjamins.
Slabakova, Roumyana, Tania L. Leal & Judith Liskin-Gasparro. 2014. We have moved on: Current concepts and positions in generative SLA. *Applied Linguistics* 35(5). 601–606.
Slabakova, Roumyana, Tania L. Leal & Judith Liskin-Gasparro. 2015. Rumors of UG's demise have been greatly exaggerated. *Applied Linguistics* 36(2). 265–269.
Slabakova, Roumyana, Tania L. Leal, Amber Dudley & Micah Stack. 2020. *Generative second language acquisition*. Cambridge: Cambridge University Press.
Ullman, Michael T. 2005. A Cognitive Neuroscience Perspective on Second Language Acquisition: The Declarative/Procedural Model. In Cristina Sanz (ed.), *Mind and Context in Adult Second Language Acquisition: Methods, Theory, and Practice*, 141–178. Washington, DC: Georgetown University Press.
Ullman, Michael T. 2012. The declarative/procedural model. In Peter Robinson (ed.), *Routledge Encyclopedia of Second Language Acquisition*, 160–164. Routledge.
Van Patten, Bill. 2010. The two faces of SLA: Mental representation and skills. *International Journal of English Language Studies* 10(1). 1–18.
Van Patten, Bill. 2013. Mental representation and skill in instructed SLA. In John W. Schwieter (ed.), *Innovations in SLA, bilingualism, and cognition: Research and practice*, 3–22. Amsterdam: John Benjamins.
Van Patten, Bill & Jessica Williams. 2014. *Theories in second language acquisition: An introduction*. New York and London, UK: Routledge.
Vaughn, Kelly A & Arturo E. Hernandez. 2018. Becoming a balanced, proficient bilingual: Predictions from age of acquisition & genetic background. Journal of Neurolinguistics 46. 69–77.
Vulchanova, Mila, Camilla H. Foyn, Randi A. Nilsen & Hermundur Sigmundsson. 2014. Links between phonological memory, first language competence and second language competence in 10-year-old children. *Learning and Individual Differences* 35. 87–95.
Wen, Zhisheng (Edward). 2015. Working memory in second language acquisition and processing: The Phonological/Executive model. In Zhisheng (Edward) Wen, Mailce Borges Mota & Arthur McNeill (eds.), *Working memory in second language acquisition and processing*, 41–62. Bristol: Multilingual Matters.
Wen, Zhisheng (Edward). 2016. *Working memory and second language learning: Towards an integrated approach*. Bristol. UK: Multilingual Matters.

Wen, Zhisheng (Edward). 2019. Working memory as language aptitude: The Phonological/Executive Model. In Zhisheng (Edward) Wen, Peter Skehan, Adriana Biedroń, Shaofeng Li & Richard L. Sparks (eds.), *Language aptitude: Advancing theory, testing, research and practice*, 187–214. New York: Routledge.

Wen, Zhisheng (Edward) & John W. Schwieter. 2022. Towards an integrated account of working memory and language. In John W. Schwieter & Zhisheng (Edward) Wen (eds.), *The Cambridge handbook of working memory and language*, 909–927. Cambridge University Press.

Wen, Zhisheng (Edward) & Peter Skehan. 2021. Stages of acquisition and the P/E Model of working memory: Complementary or contrasting approaches to foreign language aptitude? *Annual Review of Applied Linguistics* 41. 6–24. https://doi:10.1017/S0267190521000015.

Wen, Zhisheng (Edward), Peter Skehan, Adriana Biedroń, Shaofeng Li & Richard L. Sparks. 2019. *Language aptitude: Advancing theory, testing, research and practice*. New York: Routledge.

Wen, Zhisheng (Edward), Peter Skehan & Richard L. Sparks. 2023. *Language aptitude theory and practice*. Cambridge: Cambridge University Press.

White, Lydia. 2018. Formal linguistics and second language acquisition. In David Miller, Fatih Bayram, Jason Rothman & Ludovica Serratrice (eds.), *Bilingual cognition and language: The state of the science across its subfields*, 57–78. Philadelphia/Amsterdam: John Benjamins.

Part I: **Age, Intelligence, Aptitude and Affect**

2 The Age Factor and the Critical Period Hypothesis

Adriana Biedroń

Abstract: Critical Period Hypothesis concerns the phase of heightened sensitivity when it is possible to gain a native-like level of proficiency in a language. Despite controversies surrounding this concept, there is ample evidence for a negative correlation between the age of onset of acquisition and ultimate attainment in a foreign language. The purpose of this chapter is to review the relevant research on the concept of critical/sensitive periods for language learning with an emphasis on the inverse correlation between the age of onset and ultimate attainment in foreign language learning of both children and adults. We will also shed light on the cases of linguistically gifted people, polyglots and savants who seem not to be subject to the universal constraints of the critical period.

Keywords: age, age of onset, critical period hypothesis, ultimate attainment, native-like proficiency, linguistic talent, polyglots

2.1 Introduction

For many people, professionals and layman alike, it is taken for granted that second/foreign language learners whose L2 acquisition starts in early childhood and is followed by years of immersion tend to outperform late starters, in particular those post-pubescent learners in the language classroom. More importantly, in contrast to adult foreign language learners whose ultimate attainment varies substantially, children seem to stand a better chance of attaining a native-like level of proficiency. This observation of the age effects is usually interpreted as evidence for a 'critical/sensitive period' for second language acquisition (SLA), which refers to a period after which the acquisition of a foreign language becomes more arduous and less successful. The concept of the critical, or sensitive, period is one of the most hotly debated issues in current SLA, in particular in the domain of foreign language aptitude, and it is connected with the relationship between age of onset, rate of acquisition, and ultimate attainment (Long 2013). This term 'critical period' was introduced into the field of language acquisition by Penfield and Roberts (1959) and developed by Lenneberg in 1967, who claimed that language acquisition usually takes place between age two and puberty, which is the period he assumed to correspond to the lateralization process of the plastic brain.

However, Lenneberg's theory of the critical period was based on findings related to first language development in deaf children, feral children, and children with serious cognitive impairments and it was much later when the concept was used in second or foreign language acquisition (Vanhove 2013). Although the discussion of this concept and its effects on ultimate attainment has figured prominently in SLA research for the last 50 years, the causes of the so-called "critical period" are unclear: "There is now broad agreement that age of onset is the most reliable predictor of success in second language learning, but disagreement persists as to why" (Long 2013, p. 3). The problem of changes in brain lateralization over age is very complex. As Olulade et. al. (2020, p. 23477) elucidate: "Studies of the anatomy, physiology, and fMRI activation of the two hemispheres show that language is lateralized to the left hemisphere from birth". However, fMRI studies (Olulade et. al. 2020) conducted on children aged 4–13 and adults show strong activation in right-hemisphere homologs of the left-hemisphere language areas in the youngest children, which declines over age, and is completely absent in most adults. For this reason, it is difficult to state unequivocally the relationship between the process of lateralization and the critical period for language learning.

Problems such as when the critical period begins and ends, how long it lasts, and whether learning ability continues to decline, or reaches a floor are yet to be resolved. Hartshorne, Tenenbaum and Pinker (2018) contend that "there is little consensus as to whether children's advantage comes from superior neural plasticity, an earlier start that gives them additional years of learning, limitations in cognitive processing that prevent them from being distracted by irrelevant information, a lack of interference from a well-learned first language, a greater willingness to experiment and make errors, a greater desire to conform to their peers, or a greater likelihood of learning through immersion in a community of native speakers" (p. 264). Regardless of the theoretical underpinnings, post-pubescent foreign language learners predictably fail to attain native-like proficiency in a foreign language. Among all linguistic skills, phonological abilities are believed to be the most susceptible to a critical period effect. Even speakers whose proficiency level is generally assessed as native-like usually do not achieve native-like pronunciation of a language (cf. Abrahamsson and Hyltenstam 2009; Long 1990, 2013; Moyer 1999).

The purpose of this chapter is to review the relevant research into the concept of critical/sensitive periods for language learning with an emphasis on the inverse correlation between the age of onset and ultimate attainment in a foreign language. First, the theory of the critical/sensitive period will be presented, followed by a discussion of the relevant research findings in this area, in particular the concept of "native-likeness" of post-pubescent foreign language learners as moderated by language aptitude. Next, neurological evidence supporting the existence of a critical/

sensitive period will be reviewed. Finally, pedagogical implications for the language classroom will be considered.

2.2 Critical period for language development – theoretical foundations

Critical Period Hypothesis (CPH; Lenneberg 1967) concerns the deterioration of abilities to acquire a foreign language after a certain age (Abrahamsson and Hyltenstam 2008, 2009; Birdsong 2007; DeKeyser 2000; Harley and Hart 1997; Long 2013; Moyer 2014; Muñoz and Singleton 2011). Age of onset, which is the age of initial exposure to a foreign language, has been identified as the independent variable that accounts for the largest proportion of variance (approximately 30%) in ultimate attainment. The correlation between the age of onset and ultimate attainment is well-documented and accepted among SLA researchers (Granena and Long 2013). Importantly, a critical or sensitive period refers to the phase of heightened sensitivity when it is possible to gain a native-like level of proficiency in a language. This possibility is unavoidably linked to the constraints imposed by critical/sensitive periods (Birdsong 2018; Hartshorne et al. 2018; Long 1990, 2013). Many researchers contend that there are multiple sensitive periods for different aspects of a language and the decline of abilities is not abrupt, but instead is gradual (Long 2013). Critical/sensitive periods are attributed to neurobiological changes in the brain occurring over age, which result in plasticity deficits (Birdsong 2018).

The contention that the age of onset of acquisition is a crucial factor in ultimate attainment is rather uncontroversial. However, the claim that starting to learn a foreign language after the closure of sensitive periods typically results in non-native attainment has been a subject of discussion and a source of controversy for many years (see Long 2013, for a discussion). There is ample evidence for a negative correlation between the age of onset of acquisition and ultimate attainment in a foreign language (Abrahamsson and Hyltenstam 2008, 2009; Granena and Long 2013). Moreover, native-like proficiency is limited to certain phonetic, lexical, and morphosyntactic aspects and depends on many learner variables, such as language aptitude (DeKeyser 2000). Nevertheless, the opinions of researchers on this matter are not uniform. For example, researchers generally agree that the inability to learn a language is not abrupt, but rather continuous and refers mainly to grammar and pronunciation learning, as well as some more complex lexical aspects (cf. Bongaerts 2005; Bongaerts, van Summeren, Planken, and Schils 1997; Long 2013; Spadaro 2013; Van Boxtel, Bongaerts, and Coppen 2003), but there is no consensus regarding the beginning of the decline. According to Long (2013), the decline of language learning ability represents a stretched "z" shape, where the period of gradual deterioration goes after years of peak sensitivity following birth. After the offset when the decline is most pronounced, there are years of a slower decline, when achievement in the language depends on other factors, such as the length of residence, amount of exposure, language aptitude, and/or motivation.

As it has been said, there are different critical/sensitive periods for different linguistic aspects. Phonology is the most susceptible to the effects of the critical period. Ruben (1997) suggested the end of the critical period for phonology at the age of 12 months. According to Long (1990; 2013), native-like pronunciation is most possible for learners from 0–6 years, feasible but less likely for those who were first exposed between 6 and 12 years, and impossible in the case of onset over 12 years of age. After this age, success in a native-like accent will depend on factors such as the proportion between first and second language exposure and use, training, aptitude, and motivation. For various aspects of syntax and morphology the pattern is quite similar, however, the offset is more extended and continues until approximately 15 years of age (plus/minus two years). Comparable to pronunciation, the ultimate level of proficiency will depend on proportions between first and second language exposure and use, training, aptitude, and motivation, as well as metalinguistic knowledge. Spadaro (2013) investigated the sensitive period for the acquisition of lexical and collocational aspects of a foreign language and found that this sensitive period closes around the age of six years. Importantly, however, there were no significant differences between the scores of participants with the age of onset of 7–12 vs. 13+ years. These results suggest that non-native speakers may differ significantly from native speakers in their use of both core vocabulary and multi-word units. In addition, the knowledge of the latter category was significantly lower than that of native speakers and strongly dependent on the current age and the age of onset of the participants. Also, the findings suggest that non-native speakers, especially older participants, may have a much smaller scope of memorized chunks in their lexicon.

In a more recent study, Hartshorne et al. (2018) tested 669,498 native and non-native English speakers with the purpose of relating language aptitude, age of onset, years of exposition, and current age of the participants to ultimate attainment. They applied an Internet grammar quiz to attract a large number of participants. The test included a comprehensive measure of syntactic knowledge without an artificial ceiling as well as demographic data about age and linguistic background. The analysis focused on three groups: monolinguals, immersion learners and non-immersion learners. Their proposed model of Exponential Learning with Sigmoidal Decay (ELSD) offers support for the existence of a critical period for language acquisition. In particular, grammar learning ability for both easy and difficult structures preserves until the age of 17.4 years, which is much later than what is usually suggested for the offset of the critical period for native-like ultimate attainment of syntax, and then declines steadily. The researchers suggest that the relationship between the critical period and the ultimate attainment is complex and depends on different factors, for example, the learning duration. Moreover, they found that learners with an age of onset as late as 10–12 years old (both immersion and non-immersion) reach comparable levels of ultimate attainment to native bilinguals. After that age, a continuous decline as a function of the age of onset was observed. The researchers interpreted these results as evidence for the sharply defined critical period for grammar, which takes place in late adolescence, not childhood, and therefore can be attributed to factors such as social changes in adolescence, non-linear interference from the first language, or late-emerging neural maturation.

2.3 Research in native-like competence

The discussion of native-like L2 learners has always been related to the CPH. There is ample evidence that starting to learn a foreign language after this period typically results in non-native attainment. According to Gregg, "truly native-like competence in an L2 is never attained" (1996, p. 52). Nonetheless, there are studies of highly proficient foreign language learners, who seem, at least in part, to escape the critical period limitations. These unusual cases of adult native or near-native-like attainment in an L2 have been attributed to exceptional language aptitude (Abrahamsson and Hyltenstam 2008, 2009; Biedroń 2012; 2019; DeKeyser 2000; Erard 2012; 2019; Harley and Hart 1997; Hyltenstam 2016; Ioup, Boustagui, El Tigi and Moselle 1994; Novoa, Fein and Obler 1988; Sawyer and Ranta 2001; Schneiderman and Desmarais 1988). Individuals who attain high levels of proficiency in foreign languages – termed high achievers, gifted, talented, or exceptional foreign language learners, polyglots and hyperpolyglots–have attracted the attention of researchers and language teachers as examples of extraordinary abilities of the human mind (see Biedroń and Pawlak 2016; Biedroń and Birdsong 2019; Erard 2012, 2019 for recent reviews). These talented individuals are capable of learning several languages (up to 11, according to Erard) at high proficiency levels. There is also anecdotal evidence of more impressive numbers of languages mastered by professional linguists such as Rasmus Christian Rask (fluent in 25 languages and literate in 35 languages), André Martinet (12 languages), Donald Kenrick (communicative in 30 languages and able to translate from 60 languages), Stephen Wurm (working knowledge of 50 languages), as well as Kenneth Hale, Emil Krebs and Kató Lomb. Many researchers believe that the brains of these talented individuals are different from the brains of "normal" foreign language learners. Their exceptional abilities have been explained in terms of specific neurological characteristics conceptualized as *the Extreme Male Brain Theory of Autism* (Baron-Cohen 2002), distinct cytoarchitecture in Broca's region (Amunts, Schleicher, and Zilles 2004), the specific anatomy of the Heschl's gyrus (Turker, Reiterer, Schneider, and Seither-Preisler 2018), and the small but efficient brain-based language network (Jouravlev, Mineroff, Blank, and Fedorenko 2021).

The most important hypothesis that contributed to the discussion on child-adult differences in learning a language is Bley-Vroman's *Fundamental Difference Hypothesis* (1988), which hypothesizes that children are equipped with a language acquisition device that allows for the attainment of mastery in an L1. In line with this reasoning, the process of first language acquisition in children was generally believed to be uniform, effortless, and unconscious. This ability is domain-specific, that is restricted to the linguistic domain. In contrast, adult L2 learners no longer have access to the innate mechanisms for implicit language acquisition and have to rely on general cognitive mechanisms for explicit learning. Therefore, adult L2 learners must draw on domain-general analytic abilities. This gave rise to the stereotype that all children, irrespective of their cognitive abilities, acquire their L1 effortlessly and perfectly. This common belief has been challenged by Kidd and Donnelly (2020) (see also Biedroń and Véliz-Campos 2021, for a discussion) who convincingly argue that there is a systematic and meaningful variation in L1 development.

In contrast to L1 acquisition, a large body of research indicates that it is very difficult, if not virtually impossible, for adults to attain a native-like proficiency level (cf. Abrahamsson and Hyltenstam 2008, 2009; Hyltenstam and Abrahamsson 2003; Long 2005). Kasper and Kellerman have argued that "learners' interlanguage is deficient by definition" (1997, p. 5). Therefore, research examining the interface between language aptitude and age has focused mainly on two hypotheses: (1) language aptitude is related to adults, but not to children's language learning; (2) children attaining high levels of proficiency vary in their language aptitude, whereas adults who achieve very high proficiency are all exceptionally gifted (Li, 2019).

A significant contribution to the CPH effects came from DeKeyser (2000) who found that "only adults with a high level of verbal ability are expected to succeed fully at second language acquisition" (p. 500). Because adults have no access to implicit learning mechanisms, they have to draw on verbal-analytic problem-solving skills, which are characterised by significant individual differences. His second goal was to verify Johnson and Newport's (1989) claim that ultimate attainment in an L2 is strongly correlated with the age of acquisition before 17 years of age, but there are weak correlations once learners pass this age. DeKeyser based his hypotheses on the findings on ultimate attainment from Birdsong (1992), Coppieters (1987), Johnson and Newport (1989), Patkowski (1980), and others. In all of these studies, the participants were university language students and faculty members as well as other language professionals, which implied that they possessed high verbal aptitude that "may allow L2 speakers to perform morphosyntactically like native speakers"

(DeKeyser 2000, p. 507). The research hypotheses formulated by DeKeyser (2000) were confirmed, that is, all of the child language learners achieved a native or near-native level, whereas only adults with above-average aptitude overlapped with native speakers. Evidently, in the case of the early age of onset, aptitude is irrelevant, and only adult learners with high verbal ability can bypass the constraints of the critical period. This study confirmed Bley-Vroman's (1988) Fundamental Difference Hypothesis but also provided evidence in support of the CPH. As DeKeyser explained: "there really is a critical, and just not a sensitive or optimal, period for language acquisition" (2000, p. 518). Even so, DeKeyser related the CPH only to the implicit learning of abstract grammatical structures. DeKeyser placed the critical period between the ages of 6–7 years and 16–17 years. An important conclusion was that explicit learning is the only possibility for post-pubescent L2 learners to achieve a high level of proficiency, as they no longer have access to implicit learning mechanisms.

DeKeyser's claim that child acquirers inevitably succeed in L2 learning, irrespective of their aptitude, was challenged by Swedish researchers Abrahamsson and Hyltenstam (2008, 2009), who discovered small but vital effects of language aptitude on child SLA. They conducted a seminal study, which aimed at a) testing DeKeyser's hypothesis that only late learners with a high level of language aptitude will reach native-like levels of L2 proficiency; and b) testing a hypothesis that both early and late L2 learners who pass for native speakers in ordinary conversation will consistently overlap with native speakers in ten criteria of a comprehensive linguistic examination. The target sample consisted of 31 adult speakers with the age of onset of Swedish between one and eleven years, and 11 late adult speakers between the age of onset 12–23 years, selected from candidates who passed for a native speaker of Swedish with recommendations from at least six of ten native judges. The subjects were permanent residents of Sweden, with a mean length of residence of 25 years. The researchers used 20 different instruments for language testing and speech elicitation such as measures of pronunciation, speech perception, grammatical intuition, grammatical and semantic inferencing, formulaic language, and language aptitude. They focused on demanding linguistic aspects to determine the participants' strengths and weaknesses in Swedish. The study confirmed the researchers' hypotheses, that is, most of the learners who passed for native speakers in everyday conversation appeared to be less than native-like when thoroughly scrutinised in all linguistic aspects, but none of the late learners performed within the native-speaker span. Even for child L2 learners, an early age of onset was not a guarantee of native-like attainment. The researchers formulated a challenging conclusion: "when faced with a rather demanding linguistic task, nearly half of those who began to acquire the L2 between ages 1–11 exhibited less than native-like grammatical intuition" (2008, p. 496). The researchers also found that high L2 attainment was connected with high language aptitude. In line with DeKeyser (2000), the participants with late age of onset (over 12 years) who attained a level of proficiency indistinguishable from that of native speakers, displayed a high degree of language aptitude. This finding led Abrahamsson and Hyltenstam to conclude that adult native-like L2 learners do not exist, and instead should be classified as near-native because scrupulous linguistic examination for broad-based proficiency showed that they failed to achieve a level that overlapped with that of native speakers. Hyltenstam and Abrahamsson (2003) introduced the term *non-perceivable nonnativeness* to describe apparent native-likeness, which is a level of proficiency that cannot be distinguished from a native in everyday conversation, but can only be discovered through methodical linguistic investigation.

Hyltenstam and Abrahamsson's study has provoked much discussion and controversy about the criteria for the selection and evaluation of near-native participants as well as the interpretation of results. For example, Birdsong (2018; Biedroń and Birdsong 2019) attributes the alleged lack of native-like speakers to the effects of bilingualism. The proponents of the CPH claim that across-the-board native-like competence is impossible. This claim could be falsified only if at least one late foreign language learner indistinguishable from a native speaker in all possible linguistic aspects is identified (Long 1990). Birdsong considers this position implausible because of the reciprocal influence of both languages in an active bilingual. This suggests that a bilingual is not equal to two monolinguals. The effects of both languages are bidirectional, so a theoretical perfect monolingual native-likeness cannot be a criterion for rejection of the CPH. What is more, not only late but also bilinguals-from-birth and early bilinguals reveal differentiated levels of proficiency in both languages. Birdsong suggests that maturation within a critical period cannot explain all of the variety in ultimate L2 attainment and that other factors, such as the level of language activation, attrition, or L1/ L2 dominance, may affect the ultimate attainment.

A number of researchers (Andriga and Dąbrowska 2019; Birdsong and Vanhove 2016; Pfenninger and Singleton 2019) question the existence of the CP and claim that the language ability decline can be explained by a number of other factors, for example, the quality and quantity of input, motivational dynamics and contextual factors. Especially, the role of the native speaker as a point of reference in studies on ultimate attainment is questioned: "There is growing evidence that native speaker convergence is a myth: There are, in fact, considerable individual differences in adult L1 speakers' linguistic competence" (Andriga and Dąbrowska 2019, p. 6). The differences in L1 competence are ascribed to external factors, such as education and print exposure as well as to internal factors, for example, statistical learning abilities, intelligence and metalinguistic awareness. Moreover, the majority of ultimate attainment studies involve highly educated participants, which evidently falsifies the observed differences. If a native control sample includes lower-socioeconomic-status users, many L2 learners perform within the native range (Dąbrowska 2019).

Age of onset as a factor determining second language attainment was challenged by Pfenninger and Singleton (2019) who tested the effectiveness of early (age 8) versus late (age 12) starters in foreign language learning in Swiss elementary schools. The participants were tested at 12 and 18 years old. The researchers reported that by 18 the effects of an early start largely disappeared, except in the group of simultaneous biliterates. Apparently, the context of learning, that is parents' attitude and support and the number of books at home, compensated for the late start. A similar conclusion was drawn by Muñoz (2019), who analysed research on early L2 learning in different educational systems and found the rate advantage of older starters, but no evidence of an ultimate attainment advantage. This means that not only do the older starters learn faster than the younger ones, but the latter do not necessarily catch up in the long run. Among the factors explaining these results were internal, such as metalinguistic knowledge and literacy level, as well as external, for example, the amount and quality of input.

In 2013, Bylund, Hyltenstam, and Abrahamsson (see also Bylund, Abrahamsson and Hyltenstam 2012) decided to test the hypothesis that bilingualism, not the age of acquisition, affects ultimate attainment. As a starting point, they theorized that age effects on ultimate attainment are due to L1 entrenchment, which means that higher proficiency in an L1 could lead to the entrenchment of L1 forms, and, consequently, to more interference with an L2. The idea that the mother tongue interferes with the attainment of native-like proficiency in an L2 has been supported by many researchers (Birdsong 2006, 2009; Herschensohn 2007; Muñoz and Singleton 2011; Van Patten and Benati 2010). This team of Swedish researchers presented viable evidence that contradicted the above-mentioned arguments by showing results from studies testing three different populations: simultaneous bilinguals, bilingual L2 speakers, and international adoptees who lost their functional knowledge of an L1. They argued that the effects of bilingualism on the ultimate attainment of a foreign language are a complex phenomenon due to the intricacy of the bilingual experience. For example, different linguistic domains are more or less susceptible to bilingualism, and contexts in which language proficiency develops affect linguistic behavior, besides, age of onset effects and bilingualism effects do not have to be mutually exclusive.

Norrman and Bylund (2016) decided to investigate whether the maintenance of an L1 in bilingual speakers constrains the development of an L2. To this end, they examined phonetic discriminatory abilities in early second-language speakers of Swedish, who had maintained their L1 (immigrants), and those who had lost it (adoptees) using native speaker controls. The results showed no significant differences between the L2 groups, both of which scored significantly lower than native controls. Thus, the researchers concluded that L1 loss is not a necessary condition for acquiring an L2. However, the available evidence did not allow any conclusions concerning the effects of bilingualism on ultimate attainment. The authors suggested that more research into factors mediating the effects of the critical period on ultimate attainment is needed.

Another issue in CPH is the cognitive differences between children and adults. Li (2019) hypothesizes that both children and adults draw on domain-specific abilities but that the abilities are different in nature. For children, the domain-specific ability is the language acquisition device or universal grammar. For adults, the domain-specific ability is language aptitude. Therefore, the difference is in cognitive aptitudes for *explicit* versus *implicit* learning. Most aptitude tests are thought to measure explicit knowledge (DeKeyser 2019). The traditional belief based on Bley-Vroman's theory (1988) and DeKeyser's (2000) study that children hinge on implicit and adults on explicit learning mechanisms has been verified by subsequent studies. Recently, researchers have stated that aptitude for implicit learning predicts learning for both children and adults (DeKeyser 2019; Granena 2015) and the same applies to explicit learning. Tellier and Roehr-Brackin (2013) found that children can benefit from an explicit explanation in the case of a typical limited-input foreign language classroom. What is more, language analytic ability is a strong predictor of their achievement.

Neurological studies have confirmed the existence of sensitive periods for language acquisition (Dehaene et al. 1997; Indefrey and Gullberg 2006; Reiterer et al. 2011a; Reiterer, Pereda, and Bhattacharya 2011b). For example, completely native-like patterns even in very proficient foreign language learners, especially in syntactic processing, are rarely found. However, semantics seems to be less affected by the age of onset. Reiterer, Hu, Sumathi and Singh (2013) presented counterevidence claiming that exceptionally gifted foreign language learners might have avoided the critical period constraints. They contend that in contrast to average learners, gifted foreign language learners seem to experience no interference in phonological learning from the L1 as a result of their higher neuro-cognitive language flexibility. Hübener and Bonhoeffer (2014) have argued that a long-lasting belief, namely that neuronal plasticity in the brain is significantly enhanced during critical periods early in life and rather limited after their closure, should be revised because studies in primary sensory areas of the neocortex have uncovered a substantial degree of plasticity in the adult brain. Although plasticity in the adult neocortex stays dormant, it can be reactivated by modifications of sensory input or sensory-motor interactions, which modify the level and pattern of activity in cortical circuits. Summing up, the research into near-native achievement in an L2 yields intriguing and controversial results. Undoubtedly, neurological studies in the future will cast more light on critical/sensitive period effects on foreign language learning.

2.4 Conclusions and pedagogical implications

The literature surveyed in this chapter supports the existence of a critical/sensitive period for learning languages. Age effects belong to the most widely accepted and attested phenomena in SLA research (Long 2013). The controversies and doubts about age effects that have arisen are connected to the difficulty in establishing definite time thresholds for various linguistic aspects in L2 learning. New hypotheses and discoveries in SLA connected with such issues as multilingualism, language attrition, acquisition of L3s, effects of an L2 on an L1, and aging of the brain have contributed to the complexity of this issue. The problem of the critical period for foreign language learning seems to be of vital importance from a teaching perspective. There is not only variation in the ultimate attainment of post-pubescent foreign language learners but also unsuccessful learners who fail to achieve a satisfactory level of competence. Knowledge of limitations imposed by sensitive periods and differences between pre- and post-pubescent foreign language learners can raise awareness about the expected effects of learning and the methods of instruction appropriate for an age group. For example, an aptitude-treatment-interaction (ATI) approach could offer tailored instruction for post-pubescent foreign language learners, who have limited access to implicit learning mechanisms and are exposed to insufficient linguistic input.

Most researchers agree that human learning is subject to some limitations connected with a continuous decline in working memory, reasoning ability, and attention span starting around puberty and gradually decreasing our learning ability, making the process of learning more difficult, more effortful, and less successful in terms of ultimate language attainment (cf. Birdsong 2006; Long 2013). Adult L2 learners probably have more limited access to innate mechanisms for implicit language acquisition and have to rely on general cognitive mechanisms for explicit learning, which means that it is very difficult, if not virtually impossible, to attain a native-like proficiency level (cf. Bley-Vroman 1988). For the exceptional cases of near-native L2 learners, it appears that the most plausible explanation is the one offered by DeKeyser (2000), Abrahamsson and Hyltenstam (2008), and Long (2013), which states that such cases should be attributed to high FL aptitude.

Recommended readings

Granena, Gisela & Michael Long. 2013. *Sensitive periods, language aptitude, and ultimate L2 attainment.* Amsterdam/Philodelphia: John Benjamins.

This volume presents theoretical and empirical studies reflecting on age effects, bilingualism effects, maturational constraints, and sensitive periods in SLA. In addition, the volume reviews subcomponents of language aptitude, the development of new aptitude measures, and evidence on aptitude-treatment interactions.

Hyltenstam, Kenneth (ed.). 2016. *Advanced proficiency and exceptional ability in second language.* Boston/Berlin: Mouton de Gruyter.

The book focuses on highly successful and spectacular accomplishments in SLA. It covers a wide range of topics related to very high levels of proficiency such as morphosyntax, lexicon, formulaic language, reading proficiency, and pragmatics in advanced L2 users as well as amazing examples of second language users, that is, polyglots.

Hyltenstam, Kenneth, Bartning Inge & Lars Fant (eds.). 2018. *High-level language proficiency in second language and multilingual contexts.* Cambridge: Cambridge University Press.

This volume presents the issue of high-level language proficiency approached from different perspectives including linguistic/structural, psycholinguistic/cognitive, and sociolinguistic. Specifically, the volume attempts to answer two important research questions: Which conditions allow learners to attain an outstanding level of proficiency in a second language, and which factors prevent them from attaining a native-like proficiency level?

References

Abrahamsson, Niclas & Kenneth Hyltenstam. 2008. The robustness of aptitude effects in near-native second language acquisition. *Studies in Second Language Acquisition, 30(1),* 481–509.

Abrahamsson, Niclas & Kenneth Hyltenstam. 2009. Age of onset and native-likeness in a second language: Listener perception versus linguistic scrutiny. *Language Learning, 59(2),* 249–306.

Amunts, Katrin, Axel Schleicher & Karl Zilles. 2004. Outstanding language competence and cytoarchitecture in Broca's speech region. *Brain and Language, 89(2),* 346–353.

Andriga, Sible & Ewa Dąbrowska. 2019. Individual differences in first and second language ultimate attainment and their causes. *Language Learning, 69 (S1),* 5–12.

Baron-Cohen, Simon. 2002. The extreme male brain theory of autism. *Trends in Cognitive Sciences, 6(6),* 248–254.

Biedroń, Adriana. 2012. *Cognitive-affective profile of gifted adult foreign language learners.* Słupsk: Wydawnictwo Akademii Pomorskiej w Słupsku.

Biedroń, Adriana. 2019. Language aptitude: Insights from L2 exceptional learners. In Zhisheng Wen, Peter Skehan, Adriana Biedroń, Shaofeng Li & Richard Sparks (eds.), *Language aptitude: Advancing theory, testing, research and practice,* 168–184. New York/ London: Routledge.

Biedroń, Adriana & David Birdsong. 2019. Highly proficient and gifted bilinguals. In Annick De Houwer & Lourdes Ortega (eds.), *The Cambridge handbook of bilingualism (Cambridge handbooks in language and linguistics,* 307–323. Cambridge: Cambridge University Press.

Biedroń, Adriana & Mirosław Pawlak. 2016. New conceptualizations of linguistic giftedness. *Language Teaching, 49(2)*, 151–185.

Biedroń, Adriana & Mauricio Véliz-Campos. 2021. Trainability of foreign language aptitudes in children. In Joanna Rokita-Jaśkow & Agata Wolanin (eds.), *Facing diversity in child foreign language education*, 39–53. Springer.

Birdsong, David. 1992. Ultimate attainment in second language acquisition. *Language, 68*, 706–705.

Birdsong, David. 2006. Age and second language acquisition and processing: A selective overview. *Language Learning, 56*, 9–49.

Birdsong, David. 2007. Native-like pronunciation among late learners of French as a second language. In Bohn Ocke-Schwen & Murray J. Munro (eds.), *Language experience in second language speech learning*, 99–116. Amsterdam: John Benjamins.

Birdsong, David. 2009. Age and the end state of second language acquisition. In William Ritchie & Tej K. Bhatia (eds.), *The new handbook of second language acquisition*, 401–424. Amsterdam: Elsevier.

Birdsong, David. 2018. Plasticity, variability and age in second language acquisition and bilingualism. *Frontiers in Psychology, 9*.

Birdsong, David & Jan Vanhove. 2016. Age of second language acquisition: Critical periods and social concerns. In Elena Nicoladis & Simona Montanari (eds.), *Language and the human lifespan series. Bilingualism across the lifespan: Factors moderating language proficiency*, 163–181. American Psychological Association.

Bley-Vroman, Robert. 1988. The fundamental character of foreign language learning. In William Rutherford & Michael Sharwood Smith (eds.), *Grammar and second language teaching: A book of readings*, 19–30. Rowley, MA: Newbury House.

Bongaerts, Theo. 2005. Introduction: Ultimate attainment and the critical period hypothesis for second language acquisition. *IRAL, 43*, 259–267.

Bongaerts, Theo, Chantal van Summeren, Brigitte Planken & Erik Schils. 1997. Age and ultimate attainment in the pronunciation of a foreign language. *Studies in Second Language Acquisition, 19*, 447–465.

Bylund, Emanuel, Niclas Abrahamsson & Kenneth Hyltenstam. 2012. Does first language maintenance hamper nativelikeness in a second language? A study of ultimate attainment in early bilinguals. *Studies in Second Language Acquisition, 34(2)*, 215–241.

Bylund, Emanuel, Kenneth Hyltenstam & Niclas Abrahamsson. 2013. Age of acquisition effects or effects of bilingualism in second language ultimate attainment. In Gisela Granena & Michael Long (eds.), *Sensitive periods, language aptitude, and ultimate L2 attainment*, 69–101. Amsterdam: John Benjamins.

Coppieters, René. 1987. Competence differences between native and near-native speakers. *Language, 63*, 544–73.

Dąbrowska, Ewa. 2019. Experience, aptitude, and individual differences in linguistic attainment: A comparison of native and nonnative speakers. *Language Learning, 69 (S1)*, 72–100.

Dehaene, Stanislas, Emmanuel Dupoux, Jacques Mehler, Laurent Cohen, Eraldo Paulesu, Daniela Perani, Pierre Francois Van De Moortele, Stéphane Lehéricy & Denis Le Bihan. 1997. Anatomical variability in the cortical representation of first and second language. *NeuroReport, 8*, 3809–3815.

DeKeyser, Robert. 2000. The robustness of critical period effects in second language acquisition. *Studies in Second Language Acquisition, 22*, 499–533.

DeKeyser, Robert. 2019. The future of language aptitude research. In Zhisheng Wen, Peter Skehan, Adriana Biedroń, Shaofeng Li & Richard Sparks (eds.), *Language aptitude: Advancing theory, testing, research and practice*, 317–330. New York/ London: Routledge.

Erard, Michael. 2012. *Babel no more. In search for the world's most extraordinary language learners*. New York, NY: Free Press.

Erard, Michael. 2019. Language aptitude: Insights from hyperpolyglots. In Zhisheng Wen, Peter Skehan, Adriana Biedroń, Shaofeng Li & Richard Sparks (eds.), *Language aptitude: Advancing theory, testing, research and practice*, 153–168. New York/ London: Routledge.

Granena, Gisela. 2015. Cognitive aptitudes for implicit and explicit learning and information-processing styles: An individual differences study. *Applied Psycholinguistics*, *37*, 577–600

Granena, Gisela & Michael Long. 2013. Age of onset, length of residence, language aptitude, and ultimate attainment in three linguistic domains. *Second Language Research*, *29(1)*, 311–343.

Gregg, Kevin R. 1996. The logical and developmental problems of second language acquisition. In William Ritchie & Tej K. Bhatia (eds.), *Handbook of second language acquisition*. 49–81. San Diego, CA: Academic Press.

Harley, Birgit & Douglas Hart. 1997. Language aptitude and second language proficiency in classroom learners of different starting ages. *Studies in Second Language Acquisition*, *19(3)*, 379–400.

Hartshorne, Joshua K., Joshua B. Tenenbaum & Steven Pinker. 2018. A critical period for second language acquisition: Evidence from 2/3 million English speakers. *Cognition*, *177*, 263–277.

Herschensohn, Julia. 2007. *Language development and age*. Cambridge: Cambridge University Press.

Hübener, Mark & Tobias Bonhoeffer. 2014. Neuronal plasticity: Beyond the critical period. *Cell*, *159*, 727–737.

Hyltenstam, Kenneth. 2016. The exceptional ability of polyglots to achieve high-level proficiency in numerous languages. In Kenneth Hyltenstam (ed.). *Advanced proficiency and exceptional ability in second language*, 241–272. Boston/Berlin: Mouton de Gruyter.

Hyltenstam, Kenneth & Niclas Abrahamsson. 2003. Maturational constraints in SLA. In Cathrine J. Doughty & Michael H. Long (eds.), *Handbook of second language acquisition*, 539–589. Malden, MA: Blackwell Publishing.

Indefrey, Peter & Marianne Gullberg. 2006. Introduction. In Peter Indefrey & Marianne Gullberg (eds.), *The cognitive neuroscience of second language acquisition*, 1–8. Oxford: Blackwell Publishing.

Ioup, Georgette, Elisabeth Boustagui, Manal El Tigi & Martha Moselle. 1994. Re-examining the CPH. A case study of successful adult SLA in a naturalistic environment. *Studies in Second Language Acquisition*, *16*, 73–98.

Johnson, Jacqueline S. & Elissa Newport. 1989. Critical period effects in second language learning: The influence of maturational state on the acquisition of English as a second language. *Cognitive Psychology*, *21*, 60–99.

Jouravlev, Olessia, Zachary Mineroff, Idan A Blank & Evelina Fedorenko. 2021. The small and efficient language network of polyglots and hyper-polyglots, *Cerebral Cortex*, *31(1)*, 62–76.

Kasper, Gabriele & Eric Kellerman (eds.). 1997. *Communication strategies. Psycholinguistic and sociolinguistic perspectives*. London: Longman.

Kidd, Evan & Seamus Donnelly. 2020. Individual differences in first language acquisition. *Annual Review of Linguistics*, *6(1)*, 319–340.

Li, Shaofeng. 2019. Six decades of language aptitude research: A comprehensive and critical review. In Zhisheng Wen, Peter Skehan, Adriana Biedroń, Shaofeng Li & Richard Sparks (eds.), *Language aptitude: Advancing theory, testing, research and practice*, 78–97. New York/London: Routledge.

Long, Michael H. 1990. Maturational constraints on language development. *Studies in Second Language Acquisition*, *12*, 251–86.

Long, Michael H. 2005. Problems with supposed counter-evidence to the Critical Period Hypothesis. *IRAL, 43*, 287–317.
Long, Michael H. 2013. Maturational constraints on child and adult SLA. In Gisela Granena & Michael H. Long (eds.), *Sensitive periods, language aptitude, and ultimate L2 attainment*, 3–41. Amsterdam: John Benjamins.
Lenneberg, Eric H. 1967. *Biological foundations of language*. New York, NY: Wiley.
Moyer, Alene. 1999. Ultimate attainment in L2 phonology. *Studies in Second Language Acquisition, 21*, 81–108.
Moyer, Alene. 2014. What's age got to do with it? Accounting for individual factors in second language accent. *Studies in Second Language Learning and Teaching. Special issue: Age and more, 4(3)*, 443–464.
Muñoz, Carmen. 2019. A new look at "age": Young and old L2 learners. In John Schwieter & Alessandro Benati (eds.), *The Cambridge handbook of language learning (Cambridge handbooks in language and linguistics*, 430–450. Cambridge: Cambridge University Press.
Muñoz, Carmen & David Singleton. 2011. A critical review of age-related research on L2 ultimate attainment. *Language Teaching 44 (1)*, 1–35.
Norrman, Gunnar & Emanuel Bylund. 2016. The irreversibility of sensitive period effects in language development: evidence from second language acquisition in international adoptees. *Developmental Science, 19(3)*, 513–20.
Novoa, Loriana, Deborah Fein & Loraine K Obler. 1988. Talent in foreign languages: A case study. In Loraine K Obler & Deborah Fein (eds.), *The exceptional brain: Neuropsychology of talent and special abilities*, 294–302. New York, NY: Guilford Press.
Patkowski, Mark. 1980. The sensitive period for the acquisition of syntax in a second language. *Language Learning, 30*, 449–472.
Olulade, Olumide, Anna Seydell-Greenwald, Cathrine E. Chambers, Peter E. Turkeltaub, Alexander W. Dromerick, Madison M. Berl, William D. Gaillard & Elissa L. Newport. 2020. The neural basis of language development: Changes in lateralization over age. *Proceedings of the National Academy of Sciences of the United States of America, 117(38)*, 23477–23483.
Penfield, Wilder & Lamar Roberts. 1959. *Speech and brain mechanisms*. Princeton University Press.
Pfenninger, Simone E. & David Singleton. 2019. Starting age overshadowed: The primacy of differential environmental and family support effects on L2 attainment in an instructional context. *Language Learning, 69(S1)*, 207–234.
Reiterer, Susanne M., Xiaochen Hu, Michael Erb, Giuseppina Rota, Davide Nardo, Wolfgang Grodd, Susanne Winkler & Hermann Ackermann. 2011a. Individual differences in audio-vocal speech imitation aptitude in late bilinguals: Functional neuro-imaging and brain morphology. *Frontiers in Psychology, 2(271)*, 1–12.
Reiterer, Susanne M., Xiaochen Hu, T. A. Sumathi & Nandini C. Singh. 2013. Are you a good mimic? Neuro-acoustic signatures for speech imitation ability. *Frontiers in Psychology (Cognitive Science), 4(782)*, 1–13.
Reiterer, Susanne M., Ernesto Pereda & Joydeep Bhattacharya. 2011b. On a possible relationship between linguistic expertise and EEG gamma band phase synchrony. *Frontiers in Psychology, 2(334)*, 1–11.
Ruben, Robert J. 1997. A time frame of critical/sensitive periods of language development. *Acta Otolaryngologica, 117*, 202–205.
Sawyer, Mark & Leila Ranta. 2001. Aptitude, individual differences, and instructional design. In Peter Robinson (ed.). *Cognition and second language instruction*, 319–354. Cambridge: Cambridge University Press.

Schneiderman, Eta I. & Chantal Desmarais. 1988. A neuropsychological substrate for talent in second-language acquisition. In Loraine K. Obler & Deborah Fein (eds.), *The exceptional brain. Neuropsychology of talent and special abilities*, 103–126. New York, London: The Guilford Press.

Spadaro, Katherine. 2013. Maturational constraints on lexical acquisition in a second language. In Gisela Granena & Michael H. Long (eds.), *Sensitive periods, language aptitude, and ultimate L2 attainment*, 43–68. Amsterdam: John Benjamins.

Tellier, Angela & Karen Roehr-Brackin. 2013. The development of language learning aptitude and metalinguistic awareness in primary-school children: A classroom study. *Essex Research Reports in Linguistics 62(1)*. 1–28.

Turker, Sabrina, Susanne M. Reiterer, Peter Schneider & Annemarie Seither-Preisler. 2018. The neuroanatomical correlates of foreign language aptitude. In Susanne M. Reiterer (ed.). *Exploring language aptitude: Views from psychology, the language sciences, and cognitive neuroscience*, 119–149. Springer.

Van Boxtel, Sonya, Theo Bongaerts & Peter-Arno Coppen, P-A. 2003. Native-Like attainment in L2 syntax. In Susan H. Foster-Cohen & Simona Pekarek-Doehler (eds.), *Eurosla Yearbook 3*, 157–181. University of Canterbury/University of Basel: John Benjamins.

Van Patten, Bill & Alessandro G. Benati. 2010. *Key terms in second language acquisition*. London: Continuum.

Vanhove, Jan. 2013. The critical period hypothesis in second language acquisition: a statistical critique and a reanalysis. *PLoS ONE 8 (7)*, e69172.

3 Intelligence

Adriana Biedroń

Abstract: Among cognitive factors, intelligence was least studied, and even forgotten, in SLA research in the last three decades. For many years it was believed that it is only correlated with analytical abilities and important in formal teaching. This perspective has changed a bit lately. Recent research has revealed that intelligence plays a significant role in learning a language and that foreign language aptitude and general intelligence largely overlap. In this chapter, we will discuss definitions and models of intelligence, intelligence genetics and training, measurement methods, but first and foremost we will look at intelligence as a factor influencing the learning of a foreign language.

Keywords: intelligence, models of intelligence, intelligence testing, intelligence and SLA

3.1 Introduction

Intelligence is defined by Plomin and Stumm (2018, p. 148) as the ability to learn, reason, and solve problems, which predicts educational, occupational, and health outcomes better than any other individual difference factors. It is often called general cognitive ability and is considered the most stable psychological trait. Moreover, it is in large part heritable. There is massive evidence from family studies, twin studies, and adoption studies that inherited differences in the DNA sequence are responsible for about half of the variance in measures of intelligence.

In this chapter, we will present a discussion of the theory of intelligence, defined as the general cognitive ability, as well as the most significant hierarchical models of intelligence, proposed by Spearman (1927), Cattell (1971), and Carroll (1993), and multi-primary-factor models, in particular those developed by Thurstone (1938), Guilford (1967), Gardner (1983) and Sternberg (2002). This will be followed by presenting alternative views of cognitive abilities, specifically the theory of mindset (Dweck 2007). Next, we will refer to the genetic basis of human cognitive abilities as well as the environmentalists' perspective on intelligence development. Then, we will briefly present the methods of intelligence measurement. In the following part, the focus will shift to the research on the role of intelligence in second language learning (SLA). Finally, some conclusions and pedagogical implications will be offered.

3.2 Theories and models of intelligence

Although our knowledge of the general cognitive factor has evolved considerably over the last 30 years, its definition has not changed fundamentally. Gottfredson (1997) defined intelligence as a general cognitive ability, which includes the abilities of reasoning, planning, solving problems, abstract thinking, understanding complex problems, fast learning, and learning from experience. Generally, intelligence is described as the ability to deal with cognitive complexity (Gottfredson, 1997, p. 25). More complex tasks such as detecting similarities and inconsistencies, drawing inferences, and understanding new concepts require more mental manipulation, in other words, more intelligence. This academic definition is consistent with the layman's perspective, which associates intelligence with behaviors that require "smarts." Sternberg and Detterman (1986) presented three broad groups of intelligence definitions including (1) the ability to learn based on previous experience; (2) the ability to adapt to a new environment; and (3) metacognitive ability, which is the awareness of one's mental processes and the ability to control them.

The most significant information included in a contemporary definition of intelligence is that this construct covers a range of cognitive abilities. According to Plomin and Deary (2015, p. 99):

> Although there are many types of cognitive ability tests of individual differences, they almost all correlate substantially and positively; people with a higher ability on one cognitive task tend to have a higher ability on all of the others. Intelligence (more precisely, general cognitive ability or g, as discovered and defined by Spearman in 1904) indexes this covariance, which accounts for about 40 percent of the total variance when a battery of diverse cognitive tests is administered to a sample with a good range of cognitive ability [. . .]. Intelligence is at the pinnacle of the hierarchical model of cognitive abilities that includes a middle level of group factors, such as the cognitive domains of verbal and spatial abilities and memory, and the third level of specific tests and their associated narrow cognitive skills.

In most contemporary theories, general intelligence is recognized as a higher-order factor of human abilities (Carroll 1993). Such models conceptualize cognitive abilities as a pyramid made of different cognitive factors surmounted by the general cognitive factor. Alternative models, far less popular in cognitive psychology, present cognitive abilities as a set of different abilities or 'intelligences' functioning at the same level. Basically, all intelligence theories can be divided into two groups: *hierarchical models* and *multi-primary-factor models*.

3.2.1 Hierarchical models

An observation that all tests of mental ability produce results that rank people similarly gave rise to a claim that there must be one factor underlying both global and specific cognitive abilities. The first influential theory of human intelligence was the *two-factor* theory proposed by Charles Spearman in 1904. Using factor analysis, he tested intercorrelations between ability test scores to identify the factors underlying the observed patterns of correlations among them. The factor analysis revealed the existence of two factors: the general *"g"* factor, which explains most differences among individuals in performance on intelligence tests, and several specific *"s"* factors influencing abilities on specific tasks. The "g" factor was hypothesized to be a reflection of the general mental ability. Spearman's two-factor theory of intelligence (1904, 1927) was extended into different hierarchical models of intelligence, of which the most often referred to include Cattell's (1971) *Hierarchical Model of Cognitive Abilities* and Carroll's (1993) *Cognitive Abilities Model.*

A model of intelligence universally accepted in contemporary psychology was proposed by Cattell (1971). Cattell supported Spearman's view of intelligence but argued that there are two "g" factors: *fluid* (*Gf*) and *crystallized* (*Gc*). He defined fluid intelligence as the ability to analyze, remember, understand, and think inductively and deductively, to perceive complex relations among symbols, and to manipulate them irrespective of their meaning. Fluid intelligence is genetically inherited and independent of the previous experience of a person, and therefore cannot be modified. It is the potential with which a person is born. The best measures of *Gf* are abstract tasks that cannot be trained, such as number series, matrix problems, and abstract analogies. On the other hand, crystallized intelligence, which originates from fluid intelligence, is the result of experience reflected in the accumulation of knowledge and skills important in a certain socio-cultural context. It is the ability of a person in a given context and, logically, can be increased by practice. Good measures of *Gc* are tests based on previously-acquired knowledge such as comprehension, ability to define words, and general information. Both fluid and crystallized intelligence are interrelated. *Gf* is a genetically inherited factor, which as a result of appropriate 'investments' such as education and training, crystallizes to form particular abilities. *Gf* deteriorates with cognitive aging of the brain, whereas *Gc* can be developed by gaining knowledge and experience (Hunt, 1998). Cattell's *Investment Theory* (1971) states that fluid abilities are invested in learning, the results of which are evident in crystallized abilities.

The nature of the *g* factor aroused a debate among researchers. In the original version of the two-factor theory, the *g* factor is superior to *Gf* and *Gc*. Employing factor analysis, Gustaffson (1984), questioned the separation between general g and fluid Gf and provided evidence that Gf is identical to general g. Jensen (1998) postulated that the g factor can be depicted as a distillate permeating all individual differences in intelligence tests. This statement is based on the observation of the stability of g across tests. Moreover, it affects different life situations and correlates with a variety of behavioural factors such as decision time, as well as non-cognitive factors such as the speed of neural and synaptic transmission. Although there is still much discussion about the specificity of the g factor, a hierarchical model with the g factor at the top and several other factors subordinate to it is the mainstream model in the theory of intelligence.

Another hierarchical model of human abilities was introduced by Carroll (1993). His contribution to the discussion on general cognitive ability was based on data obtained between 1927 and 1987 from over 130,000 people. The three-stratum model derived from factor analysis has the g factor at the top and specific abilities placed at successively lower levels. Stratum II includes group-factor abilities, for example, verbal ability, spatial reasoning, and memory. Stratum I includes specific abilities more dependent on skills and experience, for example, spelling ability and speed of reasoning. Carroll's detailed analyses led to the recognition of 2,272 first-order factors, 542 second-order factors, and 36 third-order factors. All of these factors were grouped into twenty broad domains, e.g., *general abilities, reasoning abilities, abilities in the domain of language behaviour, memory abilities, attention and concentration abilities, auditory perception abilities,* and *visual perception abilities,* among others. What makes this model different is that it includes cognitive and non-cognitive factors. According to Carroll, "The first nine of these groups are regarded as representing true cognitive abilities in the sense of being relatively fixed, long-term attributes of individuals respecting the kinds of cognitive tasks they can and cannot perform with varying degrees of success, at a particular stage of development" (1993, p. 137). Other groups encompass personality characteristics, for example, *interest and motivation factors,* and *personality and affective factors,* and social factors referred to as *educational & social status background factors.* What is more, knowledge and school achievement are also present in the model. To sum up, we may say that Carroll's model constitutes probably the most multileveled and multifactor paradigm of human abilities.

Carroll is widely recognized as the originator of the most influential theory of foreign language aptitude (FL aptitude) and also the famous test – the *Modern Language Aptitude Test (MLAT)* (Carroll & Sapon 1959/2002). His model of human abilities is not only a link between psychology and SLA but also provides evidence for the interdependence between FL aptitude and intelligence. In the area of language, 367 minor factors are recognized and subsumed under five higher-order factors, essential in the linguistic domain: *verbal comprehension, language development, spelling ability*, *phonetic coding*, and *vocabulary*. Carroll's model of FL aptitude is only partly based on the language domain and partly on more general factors, reasoning ability, and memory. As he explained, "The line between this domain and many others, such as that of reasoning, is difficult to draw. Many factors appear to depend on both language abilities and other abilities, such as reasoning and memory" (1993, p. 145). His famous model of FL aptitude (1959) includes four factors: *grammatical sensitivity, phonetic coding, inductive reasoning,* and *associative memory*, of which only the first two are language-specific.

As stated above, Carroll's model situates FL aptitude within the structure of human intelligence. Carroll also observed the correlation between native and FL abilities. The *language development* factor, which reflects general development in spoken native language skills, contains different components and is dominated by the third-order *g* factor. It is measured by native-language vocabulary tests and knowledge tests, such as, for example, specific subtests from the Wechsler Intelligence Scales (Wechsler 1997). On the other hand, the *verbal comprehension* factor is dominated by the *g* factor or the crystallised intelligence factor, *Gc*. Therefore, the verbal factor is a good indicator of general intelligence. In line with Spearman's theory, Carroll states that all language abilities, including also *reading speed, cloze ability, spelling ability, phonetic coding, grammatical sensitivity, communication ability, listening ability,* and *oral production* are highly correlated and that their correlation is attributed to the influence of the *g* factor. Carroll described the relationship between language abilities and the *g* factor, i.e., "measures of vocabulary are among the best predictors of general intelligence" (1993, p. 193), and also stated, "It is probable that the level of general cognitive development that is or can be attained by an individual at a given age tends to set limits on the level of language development that can be attained at that age" (ibid. p. 194). Summing up, Carroll's model describes language abilities as distinct from the general intelligence factor, but also highly correlated with it. Evidence for this relationship was also provided by Biedroń (2012), who tested 44 accomplished multilinguals with the Wechsler scale and found that they had consistently very high verbal comprehension scores–over 130–accompanied by high general IQ scores.

3.2.2 Multi-primary-factor models

Apart from hierarchical models that describe intelligence as two or three levels of factors hierarchically subsumed under a general factor, alternative multi-primary-factor models have also been proposed. The four most important are Thurstone's (1938) *Theory of Primary Mental Abilities*, Guilford's (1967) *Structure-of-Intellect*

Model, Sternberg's (2004) *Triarchic Theory of Human Intelligence*, and Gardner's (1983) *Theory of Multiple Intelligences*. The joint feature in all the theories is regarding intelligence as several factors of equal importance.

Thurstone (1938) distinguished seven primary mental abilities given equivalent status: *verbal comprehension, verbal fluency, number, perceptual speed, inductive reasoning, spatial visualization,* and *memory*. In a similar vein, Guilford (1967) proposed a model of intelligence that organized cognitive abilities along three dimensions: content, product, and process. Moreover, he emphasized the role of creativity in human cognitive development. Although not popular today, both theories formed the foundation for cognitive ability theories particularly influential in SLA research proposed by Gardner (1983) and Sternberg (1985).

Gardner (1983) created a model of multiple intelligences assuming that there is no single intelligence factor, but rather a set of independent intelligences: *linguistic, logical-mathematical, spatial, musical, bodily-kinesthetic, interpersonal, intrapersonal, naturalist, spiritual* and *existential*. This theory aims to identify a person's profile of natural abilities to develop strengths and improve weak points. Due to its egalitarian character and simplicity, it became quite popular, especially among educators and foreign language pedagogues. Nevertheless, it has met with strong criticism from professional researchers and, consequently, is rarely treated as a truly scientific theory of intelligence. One of the main complaints concerned the weakness of the theoretical basis of the multiple intelligences theory, not related to research into intelligence (Sternberg 2004).

Another alternative theory was offered by Sternberg, an opponent of the traditional, psychometric notion of intelligence (1985, 2002, 2004). A *Triarchic Theory of Human Intelligence* is to some extent similar to Gardner's theory of Multiple Intelligences (1983) because it assumes identifying individual profiles and matching abilities, instruction, and assessment. The theory proposes that there are three groups of abilities: *analytic abilities* used in analysing, judging, comparing, and contrasting; *creative abilities* used in creating, inventing, and discovering; and *practical abilities* used to implement the acquired knowledge. In line with this view, abilities are modifiable rather than fixed and, as such, can be trained. This approach not only proposes the dynamic, continuous process of ability development but also minimizes hereditary influences on human intelligence. Therefore, intelligence is defined as a conglomerate of knowledge, cognitive strategies, and experience (see also Ceci 1996). Consequently, Sternberg criticizes traditional intelligence tests as unfair and unsatisfactory measures of human intellectual potential.

In a similar vein, Dweck (2007) and Mercer (2012), emphasize the social and cultural context over congenital cognitive factors. Dweck's theory of mindset shifts the focus of attention to the power of the mind as a stimulator of intellectual growth and success. In her book: *Mindset: The new psychology of success*, she argues that success in every area of human endeavor depends on the way we think about our abilities. Those who believe that abilities are fixed – people with a fixed mindset – are less likely to succeed than those with a growth mindset, which is those who assume that their abilities can be developed. Mercer (2012) extended this theory to the field of foreign language learning and postulated that the way people think about their aptitude to learn foreign languages affects their success or failure. Those who believe that their abilities are fixed are not likely to succeed, unlike those who are convinced that abilities, as well as other traits, can be trained and increased. This theory fits into the ideology of positive psychology, which emphasizes the role of positive emotions in the process of learning.

3.2.3 Nature or nurture

Intelligence is a factor that has been hotly debated for over 100 years, and one that arouses the most emotions and controversies. This may occur because intelligence affects all aspects of life including education, work, income, health, and life expectancy. Intelligence is in large part genetically determined and fixed and, consequently, undemocratically distributed. It is no wonder that many people reject the theory of inheritance of intelligence as socially dangerous, which is reflected in the sharp criticism of the recent book, *Blueprint. How DNA makes us who we are*, written by a behavioral geneticist, Robert Plomin (2018). Paradoxically, despite widespread criticism of intelligence theory, the popularity of various commercial methods of increasing IQ levels is not diminishing.

Evidently, genetics contributes significantly to differences between people and this contribution is not just statistically significant, but massive. Plomin writes that "Psychological traits are all substantially heritable, about 50% on average" (p. 11). Basically, most individual differences, including cognitive traits, may be determined by genes. It is the DNA that makes us who we are. Scientists have studied twins and adoptees and discovered a phenomenon that changed our thinking about human nature. To quote Plomin, "for the first time, nature and nurture can be disentangled" (2018, p. viii). This statement means that nurture, for the most part, cannot exist without nature. For example, most measures of a person's functioning within the environment, like social support, are affected by genes. This phenomenon can be explained by the fact that the environment does not act independently, but is selected and modified by us following our genetic endowment. According to Plomin, the influence of family has been long overestimated. For instance, the environment makes siblings raised in the same family different from siblings raised in different families. In fact, random experiences are more powerful in changing genetic trajectories than systematic family influence, but even these changes do not last. Another important discovery is that it is not one single gene or a set of genes that makes us different, but rather thousands of small factors, whose accumulative effect makes a substantial difference in our traits. This type of knowledge can help, for instance, in the early prevention of some highly heritable mental diseases. As Plomin explains, a common misunderstanding concerning heritability refers to the difference between what is and what could be. Another misunderstanding comes from looking at genes in terms of an individual rather than a population. A heritability estimation refers to a given population at a given time and may work otherwise in another population.

Quite often, there are significant differences in abilities observed between one family member and the others. Exceptional talent cannot be explained by the additive effects of genes, differences in upbringing, or hard work alone. Jensen (1997) presents examples of geniuses such as Beethoven, Ramanujan (a mathematical genius), and the great conductor Toscanini, whose parents, siblings, and children did not reveal any talents. Such a genius seems to 'come out of the blue' and emerges as a result of an unusual and rare combination of many genes (polygenes), which simultaneously influence several different abilities and traits. Such a combination is called *emergenesis* (Jensen 1997, pp. 43–44). As both parents provide only half of their genes each to their child, it is very unlikely that such a random half will include the rare combination of genes to create a genius. General IQ is not an emergenic trait, whereas exceptional abilities and talents are. However, an above-average level of intelligence is considered to be a critical condition for the development of an emergenic talent. Some psychologists claim that there is a threshold in IQ level, above which it does not influence achievements.

Evidence for the heritability of intelligence is undeniable (Jensen 1997; Plomin & Deary 2015; Plomin 2018). In line with Plomin (2018), all the aspects of personality and intellect are shaped by inherited differences in DNA. In other words, we are driven by genes far more than we realize. Moreover, a large body of evidence from twin, adoption, and genome studies indicates that genetic effects increase with age rather than decrease. According to Plomin and Deary (2015), the heritability of intelligence rises from about 20% in infancy to approximately 80% in adulthood. Family environment effects decrease with age, to finally become of minor importance in adulthood. These conclusions come mainly from large-scale twin studies and have been corroborated by a new quantitative genetic technique – Genome-wide Complex Trait Analysis (GCTA) – a method that assesses genetic influence using genome-wide genotypes in large samples of unrelated individuals (Plomin & Deary, 2015).

A recurrent question concerns the possibility of IQ improvement. Unfortunately, despite the efforts of researchers to develop a method to raise the level of intelligence, increasing intelligence seems to be a myth (Haier 2014). There have been a few attempts to increase IQ levels through training or various kinds of intervention. Eysenck and Schoenthaler (1997) suggested that the supplementation of diet with vitamins and minerals affects children's cognitive development. However, any positive effect concerns only fluid intelligence and it is more noticeable for younger than for older children. In fact, the benefits of supplementation are detectable only when there are deficiencies in the level of vitamins and minerals, whereas, in the case of proper nutrition, no increase in intelligence was observed. It is also questionable whether this intervention has long-term effects.

The most often quoted study by Jaeggi, Buschkuehl, Jonides, and Perrig (2008) was an attempt to increase fluid intelligence by training. The researchers claimed an observable transfer from training on a demanding working memory task to measures of *Gf*. This transfer was observed even if the trained task was completely different from the intelligence test itself. In light of the hypothesis that some executive functions are clearly related to general intelligence (Ardila 2018), one cannot reject the possibility of intelligence training, but this would require further research.

Nevertheless, given the shortage of research studies on the trainability of intelligence, especially fluid intelligence, it is not unexpected that behaviour-genetic theorists recommend caution about interpreting their findings and offering generalizations on their basis (Haier 2014; Scarr 1997).

3.3 Intelligence testing

The main goal of testing intelligence is to achieve a diagnosis of an individual's potential for military, educational, occupational, clinical, and academic purposes. The first test of intelligence was proposed by Binet and Simon in 1905. Their model of intelligence was based on an assumption that measures of intelligence should focus on individual differences in higher processes, namely memory, imagination, judgment, and comprehension. The Binet-Simon test was acknowledged as a major contribution to the assessment of intelligence in Europe and the United States and its adapted versions became popular among cognitive ability researchers.

One of the most popular models of intelligence is the *Wechsler Intelligence Scale* (1939, 1997, 2008). This model is based on three assumptions, namely: (1) intelligence is a complex factor consisting of different abilities; (2) the measure is based on deviation intelligence quotient; and (3) it includes verbal and performance scales.

Most measures of intelligence such as the Wechsler Scale are based on deviation IQ. Every person in a population represents a certain intensity of a feature, in this case, intelligence. The scoring is based on a projection of the subject's measured rank on the Gaussian bell curve with a center value (average IQ) of 100 and a standard deviation of 15. In a normal distribution, the IQ rank of one standard deviation above and below the mean (i.e., between 85 and 115) is where approximately 68% of all adults would fall. To know the deviation IQ of an individual, we have to determine his/her standard deviation above/below the mean. This method enables us to conclude that a person whose IQ result is, for example, 130 is placed two standard deviations above the mean. That means that his/her result is better than the results of 97.7% of the population. A person with an IQ result of 145, which is three standard deviations above the mean, is better than 99.9% of the population with respect to their intelligence quotient. The results below the mean are calculated analogically. In addition, the results are always interpreted according to age norms. Intelligence tests are standardized and normalized to suit the conditions of the target country.

The recent (fourth) edition of the Wechsler Scale, WAIS-IV, was released in 2008. It is composed of ten subtests and five supplemental subtests. The scale is divided into four index scores representing major components of intelligence: *Verbal Comprehension, Perceptual Reasoning, Working Memory*, and *Processing Speed*. Consequently, four intelligence indices are obtained as well as a *Full-Scale IQ* score. Moreover, two of the four indices, namely Verbal Comprehension and Perceptual Reasoning yield *a General Ability Index* score. The Verbal Comprehension Index comprises the following subtests: *Similarities, Vocabulary*, and *Information*. The Perceptual Reasoning Index includes *Block Design, Matrix Reasoning*, and *Visual Puzzles*. The Working Memory Index involves *Digit Span* and *Arithmetic*, and the Processing Speed Index contains *Symbol Search* and *Coding*. In the interpretation of the results, much importance is attached to disproportions between particular test results in particular scales, which enables a researcher to conduct a deep, clinical diagnosis of intellect (Wechsler, 1997). The scales are designed for adults, aged 16–90 years. For people under 16 years and children, there are different Wechsler scales.

3.4 Research into the relationship between intelligence and SLA

It is generally believed that intelligence is weakly related to FL aptitude. Undoubtedly, everyone who has high motivation can learn a a foreign language in favorable conditions. For many years it was taken for granted that among FL aptitudes only analytic abilities are related to intelligence. Now, this perspective has changed. Research into this relationship, after a period of stagnation, is now becoming more popular.

In the last three decades of the 20th century, FL aptitude and intelligence were treated as unrelated variables (Gardner 1985; Gardner & Lambert 1972; Skehan 1982). Nonetheless, the role of general intelligence in SLA was acknowledged by some researchers (Bachman 1990; Carroll 1993; Flahive 1980; Oller 1983; Wesche, Edwards & Wells 1982). Bachman (1990), suggested that information-processing ability is correlated with general cognitive abilities. Oller (1983) studied the relationship between general intelligence and first language learning ability and found that language proficiency is correlated with intelligence and all other abilities related to language in a higher-order structure. Flahive (1980) reported high positive correlations (in the range of .59 and .84) between proficiency in a second language and non-verbal intelligence, which indicates that not only verbal intelligence but also abstract reasoning ability may be relevant to foreign language learning outcomes. Wesche et al. (1982), found a positive correlation between aptitude test, the MLAT scores, and intelligence test scores, with the highest correlation between the MLAT total score and reasoning ability (.65). Factor analysis revealed the existence of one second-order general factor, identified as general intelligence, and three first-order specific factors characterized as first language verbal knowledge, number/reasoning/spatial intelligence, and aptitude. A correlation was found in a higher-order structure. It should be emphasized that the traditional Carroll's (1993) Cognitive Abilities Model presents language abilities as primary cognitive abilities subsumed under a general cognitive ability factor g. Moreover, as Dörnyei (2005) points out, both the MLAT (Carroll & Sapon 2002) and the PLAB (Pimsleur 1966) include an L1 test of vocabulary, which is a fundamental component of the measurement of intelligence.

In line with the above-described results, Sasaki (1996) conducted a study in which she assumed that aptitude and intelligence share a more abstract level of general cognitive ability. She attempted to examine to what extent and in what aspects FL aptitude is dependent on the general factor and in what aspects it is independent of it, which is language-specific. She investigated the relationship among three measures: second language proficiency, FL aptitude, and two types of intelligence, verbal and reasoning. Along the lines of the hierarchical view of cognitive abilities, Sasaki assumed the existence of a second-order latent factor of general cognitive ability and several first-order cognitive abilities. The assumed general factor represents an abstract level of cognitive ability that includes FL aptitude, verbal intelligence, reasoning, and other cognitive abilities relevant to SLA. Although first-order factor analysis of the aptitude and intelligence scores showed separation between these factors, second-order factor analysis confirmed the existence of one specific factor, which is the analytic ability, explaining the variance in some of the aptitude variables as well as in the intelligence quotients. Other aptitude factors, namely phonetic coding ability and memory, did not correlate with intelligence. The effect of this study was confirmation of a longstanding belief that intelligence and analytic ability are interrelated, whereas phonetic coding ability and memory factors are separate components of FL aptitude, independent of intelligence (cf. Skehan, 1998).

Another finding was reported by Grigorenko, Sternberg, and Ehrman (2000), who correlated the results of their FL aptitude test – the Cognitive Ability for Novelty in Acquisition of Language (CANAL-FT) – with fluid and crystallized IQ scores. There was a positive correlation between the scores, which supported the conclusion that there is a first-order correlation between FL aptitude and IQ to the extent that the concepts overlap.

Sparks, Humbach, Patton and Ganschow (2011) found that MLAT 5 (Rote Learning) clustered with intelligence measured with the Test of Cognitive Skills. Granena (2013), in turn, discovered that the scores on the general intelligence test GAMA loaded on the same factor as the scores on three LLAMA aptitude battery subtests (B, E, F). Consequently, she termed intelligence and the three LLAMA subtests "explicit aptitude."

Another study that verified the myth of the irrelevance of intelligence in SLA was conducted by Biedroń (2012). Forty-four gifted language learners whose L1 was Polish were tested employing the Polish version of Wechsler Intelligence Scale (Brzeziński, Gaul, Hornowska, Machowski, Zakrzewska 1996), which includes eleven subtests, six verbal and five performance. The results consist of the full-scale, verbal and performance IQ scores, as well as the scores for the three indices of Verbal Comprehension, Perceptual Organization, and Memory and Resistance to Distraction. Findings showed that the general IQ of the participants was high (125), with the verbal intelligence (130) being higher than the performance (119) and with high Memory and Resistance to Distraction index (128). These results confirmed that the IQ of the gifted L2 learners was higher than that in a normal Polish population. Contrary to Skehan's (1998) claim that gifted L2 learners are not characterized by a very high IQ level, the study reported that high and very high intelligence accompanies high FL aptitude. Moreover, gifted L2 learners obtained high scores on Vocabulary, Similarities, Information, and Comprehension, which are subscales of the verbal IQ. The scales measuring verbal intelligence include abilities similar to those measured by FL aptitude tests, especially the measure of Vocabulary which represents verbal comprehension, native language proficiency, a range of vocabulary knowledge, and intellectual readiness to define words, and is highly saturated with the g factor. Analogically, the MLAT includes a measure of vocabulary, although this skill is measured differently from that on the Wechsler scale. The high score on verbal IQ indicates that verbal abilities in the gifted L2 learners are very well developed. They have a wide range of vocabulary in both Polish and English, are good at defining words, can classify and create concepts, perceive relations between them, and differentiate between important and unimportant information. They are also good at logical and abstract thinking, analogical reasoning, drawing conclusions, efficient retrieval and reproduction of memorized verbal material (long-term memory).

Moreover, gifted L2 learners obtained high scores on the following Wechsler Intelligence subscales: Arithmetic, Digit-Span, and Digit Symbol Coding (the Memory and Resistance to Distraction index). These subtests measure short-term and working memory, focusing of attention, and resistance to distraction. This finding indicates a balanced level of verbal and memory abilities in gifted L2 learners. The memory abilities as measured by the Wechsler Scale were high, and in some talented L2 learners, very strong. Half of the participants scored over 130 on the Memory and Resistance to Distraction index, which is over two standard deviations above the mean. Four participants whose scores were close to the maximum (between 144 and 150 points) were very advanced polyglots, the highest-scoring participants on the MLAT. The Wechsler scales correlated with the MLAT scales in the range of .32–.48. The MLAT general score correlated with the full-scale IQ at .40, with the Memory and Resistance to Distraction at .44, the Verbal Comprehension at .33, and the Perceptual Organization at .32. The strongest correlations were reported between the Memory and Resistance to Distraction Index and MLAT 1 (.48), MLAT 4 (.40), and MLAT 5 (.37).

In his meta-analysis, Li (2016) found significant correlations between FL aptitude measures and intelligence: .64 for the MLAT and .50 for hybrid aptitude measures. Factor analysis did not yield a clear separation between these two variables, which suggests a large overlap. Still, in the author's interpretation, they do not seem to be the same constructs, mainly because tests of FL aptitude are better predictors of foreign language learning achievement.

In a recent small-scale study, Ameringer (2018) hypothesized that a greater capacity of declarative memory, operationalized as a component of intelligence, results in a higher language aptitude and that a higher education level increases both aptitude and declarative memory capacity. As instruments, she used the *Mehrfachwahl-Wortschatz-Intelligenztest* designed to measure the mental lexicon (an element of verbal intelligence) and Part 5 of the MLAT, which measures rote-learning ability. Her research samples included two groups differing in the length of education, namely university students and physical workers. As expected, a positive correlation was found between verbal IQ and MLAT 5 scores, and significant differences between the results of the tested groups, with the results of the students being higher. The researcher suggests that sufficient training in declarative memory, by being exposed to complex material in lectures or seminars, can increase memory abilities and, consequently, result in the development of language aptitude. Ameringer's results resonate with Biedroń's (2012) study in which the tested accomplished multilinguals – university students or professional linguists– achieved very high results on verbal IQ Wechsler scales. Interesting as they seem, the results should be treated with caution due to the limited number of participants.

Different results were obtained by Dąbrowska (2019), who compared the performance of native speakers and adult L2 learners on tasks measuring proficiency in grammar, vocabulary and collocations. Other variables included nonverbal intelligence and analytic ability. As expected, the native speakers outperformed the L2 learners on all three tasks, with the highest differences for collocations. Nonverbal intelligence and analytic ability were the best predictors of performance on the grammar test for adult native speakers, but not for L2 learners. Analytic ability but not nonverbal IQ accounted for variance in the test of vocabulary in L2 learners. Unlike in previously cited studies, the L2 sample was not a homogenous population of highly educated learners, but a heterogeneous group of people with different language backgrounds. This difference coupled with differences in the amount and quality of instruction might have masked the effects of IQ in L2 speakers.

Finally, Brooks and Kempe (2019), using evidence from both L1 and L2 studies argued that the majority of relevant research on intelligence confirms a more-is-more view of linguistic development. This means that higher intelligence and more capacious working memory lead to higher achievement in both L1 and L2.

3.5 Conclusions and pedagogical implications

Although much evidence suggests that there are strong positive correlations between intelligence and FL aptitude, there is a marked lack of research on the relationship between specific FL aptitude components and both higher-order and primary cognitive abilities. The analysis of correlations between tests of different abilities from the Wechsler Intelligence Scale and FL aptitude components can provide interesting insights into the domain of FL aptitude. An inspection of the Wechsler subscales indicates that many of the abilities tested are reflected in FL aptitude models. For example, besides the above-described *Vocabulary*, the verbal subscale *Similarities* tests inductive reasoning (discovering common features and classifying), the ability to perceive relations between concepts, abstract logical thinking, analogical reasoning, associative thinking, and differentiation between important and unimportant details, that is abilities facilitative in SLA.

Another underinvestigated and controversial problem is IQ increase and development. Much evidence indicates that this factor is relatively immutable and that training does not increase intelligence test results. However, this seems in contrast with the so-called *Flynn effect* (Flynn 2007), which accounts for the observed rise in the average IQ scores over the last 50 years. The average rate of progress has been three points per decade. This is too short a time for genetic modification to take place. Probably, this phenomenon can be explained by several interrelated factors such as civilization achievements reflected in improved nutrition, the smaller number of children in families, better education, a more complex environment, and technological development.

Intelligence is a cognitive factor that is least amenable to pedagogic intervention. Nevertheless, many socialization theorists (Ceci 1996; Mercer 2012; Sternberg 2002) emphasize the dynamic nature of intelligence as well as the role of the social and cultural context in the process of education. They highlight the role of efficient pedagogic interventions directed at compensating for weaknesses in intellectual functioning. Clearly, the attainment of a communicative level of proficiency is available to every learner if his/her motivation is sufficiently high and if he/she has access to high-quality language input. Moreover, the efficient use of language learning strategies, high self-esteem, low anxiety level, and positive attitudes toward learning could increase the probability of success (Gregersen & MacIntyre 2014).

The concepts of cognitive abilities, intelligence, and language aptitude have evolved considerably over the last 15 years. Including new cognitive abilities such as working memory, procedural and declarative memory, and implicit abilities in the set of FL aptitudes is a potential source of new discoveries in the field of SLA. In light of the new research, it is clear that the separation of intelligence and FL aptitude may not be as clear as it has been assumed. This is a potential research area for many years.

Recommended Readings

Reiterer, Susanne M. 2018. *Exploring language aptitude: Views from psychology, the language sciences, and cognitive neuroscience.* Springer- Nature.

The chapters in this volume were based primarily on the research work by Susanne Reiterer and her colleagues in their investigation of individual difference factors such as working memory, intelligence, personality, self-concept, bilingualism and multilingualism, education, musicality, and gender. As its subtitle indicates, a distinctive feature of the volume is its multidisciplinary perspectives.

Biedroń, Adriana & Mirosław Pawlak. 2016. New conceptualizations of linguistic giftedness. *Language Teaching 49/2*, 151–185.

This state-of-the-art paper focuses on the issue of linguistic giftedness, a somewhat neglected topic in the SLA literature, and attempts to reconceptualize, expand, and update this concept in response to the latest developments in the fields of psychology, linguistics, and neurology.

References

Ameringer, Victoria. 2018. Cognitive abilities: Different memory functions and language aptitude. In Susanne M. Reiterer (ed.), *Exploring language aptitude: Views from psychology, the language sciences, and cognitive neuroscience*, 19–43. Springer.

Ardila, Alfredo. 2018. Is intelligence equivalent to executive functions? *Psicothema, 30(2)*, 159–164.

Bachman, Lyle F. 1990. *Fundamental considerations in language testing*. Oxford: Oxford University Press.

Biedroń, Adriana. 2012. *Cognitive-affective profile of gifted adult foreign language learners*. Słupsk: Wydawnictwo Akademii Pomorskiej w Słupsku.

Binet, Alfred & Théodore Simon. 1905. *The development of intelligence in children*. Baltimore, MD: Williams and Wilkins.

Brooks, Patricia J. & Vera Kempe. 2019. More is more in language learning: reconsidering the less-is-more hypothesis. *Language Learning, 69*, 13–41.

Brzeziński Jerzy, Marek Gaul, Elżbieta Hornowska, Aleksandra Jaworowska, Andrzej Machowski & Marzenna Zakrzewska. 1996. *Skala inteligencji D. Wechslera dla dorosłych. Wersja zrewidowana. WAIS-R (PL). Podręcznik* [*Wechsler adult intelligence scale. A revised version. WAIS-R (PL). Manual*]. Warszawa: Pracownia Testów Psychologicznych PTP.

Carroll, John B. 1993. *Human cognitive abilities: A survey of factor-analytic studies*. Cambridge: Cambridge University Press.

Carroll, John B. & Stanley M. Sapon. 1959. *Modern Language Aptitude Test (MLAT)*. New York, NY: The Psychological Corporation. (Reprinted in 2002).

Cattell, Raymond B. 1971. *Abilities: Their structure, growth, and action*. Boston: Houghton Mifflin.

Ceci, Stephen J. 1996. *On Intelligence. A bio-ecological treatise on intellectual development* (2nd ed.). Cambridge, MA: Harvard University Press.

Dąbrowska, Ewa. 2019. Experience, aptitude, and individual differences in linguistic attainment: A comparison of native and nonnative speakers. *Language Learning, 69*, 72–100.

Dörnyei, Zoltán. 2005. *The psychology of the language learner: Individual differences in second language acquisition*. Mahwah, NJ: Lawrence Erlbaum.

Dweck, Carol S. 2007. *Mindset: The new psychology of success*. New York, NY: Random House.

Eysenck, Hans J. & Stephen J. Schoenthaler. 1997. Raising IQ level by vitamins and mineral supplementation. In Robert J. Sternberg & Elena Grigorenko (eds.), *Intelligence, heredity, and environment*, 363–392. Cambridge: Cambridge University Press.

Flahive, Douglas E. 1980. Separating the *g* factor from reading comprehension. In John W. Oller & Kyle Perkins (eds.), *Research in language testing*, 34–46. Rowley, MA: Newbury House.

Flynn, James R. 2007. *What is intelligence? Beyond the Flynn effect*. Cambridge: Cambridge University Press.

Gardner, Howard. 1983. *Frames of mind: The theory of multiple intelligences*. New York, NY: Basic Books.

Gardner, Robert C. 1985. *Social psychology and second language learning: The role of attitudes and motivation*. London: Edward Arnold.

Gardner, Robert C. & Wally E. Lambert. 1972. *Attitudes and motivation in second language learning*. Rowley, Mass.: Newbury House.

Gottfredson, Linda S. 1997. Mainstream science on intelligence: an editorial with 52 signatories, history, and bibliography. *Intelligence, 24*, 13–23.

Granena, Gisela. 2013. Cognitive aptitudes for second language learning and the LLAMA Language Aptitude Test. In Gisela Granena & Michael Long (eds.), *Sensitive periods, language aptitude, and ultimate L2 attainment*, 105-129. Amsterdam: John Benjamins Publishing.

Gregersen, Tammy & Peter D. MacIntyre. 2014. *Capitalizing on language learners' individuality. From premise to practice*. Bristol: Multilingual Matters.

Grigorenko, Elena L., Sternberg, Robert J. & Madeline E. Ehrman. 2000. A theory based approach to the measurement of foreign language learning ability: The CANAL-F theory and test. *Modern Language Journal, 84*, 390-405.

Guilford, Joy P. 1967. *The nature of human intelligence*. New York, NY: McGraw-Hill.

Gustafsson, Jan-Eric. 1984. A unifying model for the structure of intellectual abilities. *Intelligence, 8*, 179-203.

Haier, Richard J. 2014. Increased intelligence is a myth (so far). *Frontiers in Systems Neuroscience, 8, 34*.

Hunt, Earl B. 1998. Intelligence and human resources: Past, present, and future. In Philip L. Ackerman, Patrick C. Kyllonen & Richard D. Roberts (eds.), *Learning and individual differences: Process, trait, and content determinants*, 3-30. Washington, DC: American Psychological Association.

Jaeggi, Susanne M., Martin Buschkuehl, John Jonides & Walter J. Perrig. 2008. Improving fluid intelligence with training on working memory. *Proceedings of the National Academy of Sciences, 105(19)*, 6829-6833

Jensen, Arthur R. 1997. The puzzle of nongenetic variance. In Robert J. Sternberg & Elena L. Grigorenko (eds.), *Intelligence, heredity, and environment*, 42-88. Cambridge: Cambridge University Press.

Jensen, Arthur R. 1998. *The g factor: The science of mental ability*. Westport, CT: Praeger/Greenwood.

Li, Shaofeng. 2016. The construct validity of language aptitude. *Studies in Second Language Acquisition, 38*, 801-842.

Mercer, Sarah. 2012. Dispelling the myth of the natural-born linguist. *ELT Journal, 66(1)*, 22-29.

Oller, John W. 1983. Evidence for a general language proficiency factor: An expectancy grammar. In John W. Oller (ed.), *Issues in language testing research*, 3-10. Rowley, Mass.: Newbury House.

Pimsleur, Paul. 1966. *Pimsleur Language Aptitude Battery*. New York, NY: Harcourt Brace Jovanovich.

Plomin. Robert. 2018. *Blueprint. How DNA makes us who we are*. UK: Penguin Random House.

Plomin, Robert & Ian Deary. 2015. Genetics and intelligence differences: Five special findings. *Molecular Psychiatry, 20*, 98-108.

Plomin, Robert & Sophie von Stumm. 2018. The new genetics of intelligence. *Nature Reviews Genetics, 19*, 148-159.

Sasaki, Miyuki. 1996. *Second language proficiency, foreign language aptitude, and intelligence. quantitative and qualitative analyses*. New York: Peter Lang Publishing.

Scarr, Sandra. 1997. Behavior-Genetic and socialization theories of intelligence: Truce and reconciliation. In Robert J. Sternberg & Elena L. Grigorenko (eds.), *Intelligence, heredity, and environment*, 3-41. Cambridge: Cambridge University Press.

Skehan, Peter. 1982. *Memory and motivation in language aptitude testing*. PhD thesis, University of London.

Skehan, Peter. 1998. *A cognitive approach to language learning*. Oxford: Oxford University Press.

Sparks, Richard L., Nancy Humbach, Jon Patton & Leonore Ganschow. 2011. Subcomponents of second-language aptitude and second-language proficiency, *Modern Language Journal, 95*, 253-273.

Spearman, Charles. 1904. General intelligence, "objectively determined and measured". *The American Journal of Psychology, 15(2)*, 201-292.

Spearman, Charles. 1927. *The abilities of man: Their nature and measurement*. New York, NY: Macmillan.
Sternberg, Robert J. 1985. Implicit theories of intelligence, creativity, and wisdom. *Journal of Personality and Social Psychology, 49*, 607–627.
Sternberg, Robert J. 2002. The theory of Successful Intelligence and its implications for language aptitude testing. In Peter Robinson (ed.), *Individual differences and instructed language learning*, 13–43. Philadelphia: John Benjamins Publishing Company.
Sternberg, Robert J. 2004. *International handbook of intelligence*. Cambridge, UK: Cambridge University Press.
Sternberg, Robert J. & Douglas K. Detterman (eds.). 1986. What is intelligence? Norwood, NJ: Ablex.
Thurstone, Louis L. 1938. *Primary mental abilities*. Chicago, IL: University of Chicago Press.
Wechsler, David. 1939. *The measurement of adult intelligence*. Baltimore, MD: Williams & Wilkins.
Wechsler, David. 1997. *Manual for the Wechsler Adult Intelligence Scale – Third edition (WAIS III)*. San Antonio, TX: The Psychological Corporation.
Wechsler, David. 2008. *Wechsler Adult Intelligence Scale. Fourth edition (WAIS–IV)*. Pearson.
Wesche, Marjorie, Henry Edwards & Winston Wells. 1982. Foreign language aptitude and intelligence. *Applied Psycholinguistics, 3*, 127–140.

4 Foreign Language Aptitude

Adriana Biedroń

Abstract: Foreign language aptitude is the most studied factor among cognitive differences. The topics gaining increasing popularity are the relationship between aptitude and different kinds of memory, psychological and socio-environmental factors as moderating variables, musical ability, gender and bilingualism. Testing different aptitudes, aptitude dynamics and aptitude differences among children are topics also often taken up by researchers. There are more and more neurological studies shedding new light on this fascinating problem. As a result, the construct has been gradually updated and reconceptualized. This chapter covers the development of the concept of foreign language aptitude and aptitude testing, as well as the latest research and its pedagogical implications. In particular, we will focus on the dynamics and modification of foreign language aptitude and various types of pedagogical interventions.

Keywords: foreign language aptitude, aptitude testing, MLAT, Hi-LAB, LLAMA, LCDH, CANAL-F, PLAB, aptitude dynamics, aptitude-treatment-interaction, working memory

4.1 Introduction

Foreign language (FL) aptitude is a powerful factor accounting for the largest proportion of variances in the outcomes of learning a FL and its study has been high on the agenda of second language acquisition (SLA) researchers over the last two decades. FL aptitude is related to the domain of human cognitive abilities and resembles the psychological construct of intelligence, in that it covers a wide variety of cognitive learner differences and is an effective predictor of success in SLA (Dörnyei 2005, p. 34), however, these constructs are clearly different. Similar to the research on general cognitive ability, early research on FL aptitude focused on tests designed to predict the learner's *rate* of progress in learning a FL. The most popular model of FL aptitude by Carroll (Carroll & Sapon 1959/2002) and his famous instrument, the *Modern Language Aptitude Test* (*MLAT*), became a milestone in FL aptitude measurement and the most often cited paradigm in the literature. The MLAT, now 60 years old, is still considered to be one of the best tools for measuring FL aptitude and a point of reference for both advanced and beginning researchers.

Recently, there has been a remarkable growth of research in the fields of SLA, cognitive psychology, genetics, and neurology, which affected the definition and measurement of FL aptitude. As a result, the construct has been gradually updated and reconceptualized. In recent times, this factor has witnessed renewed enthusiasm across diverse disciplines of educational psychology, SLA, and neuroscience (Reiterer 2018; Wen, Biedroń & Skehan 2017; Wen, Skehan, Biedroń, Li & Sparks 2019).

Originally described as a set of three groups of abilities–analytical, memory, and phonetic–FL aptitude is now defined as an amalgamation of cognitive and perceptual abilities (i.e., aptitudes) (Granena & Yilmaz 2019; Robinson 2007; Skehan 1998). However, the classic tripartite division is still popular in theoretical reviews as well as research studies. FL aptitude is still used for prognostics, but the scope of research is expanding (Wen et al. 2019). Among the topics gaining increasing popularity are the relationship between aptitude and different kinds of memory, psychological and socio-environmental factors as moderating variables, musical ability, neurological factors, gender, and bilingualism (Reiterer 2018). A problem that appears in many research studies concerns FL aptitude dynamics (Biedroń & Véliz-Campos 2021; Thompson 2013). Another interesting topic is linguistic giftedness and high-level language proficiency (Biedroń 2019; Erard 2019, Hyltenstam, Bartning & Fant 2018). Finally, the problem of measurement of the construct to predict high levels of proficiency as well as cater to different kinds of aptitude (Doughty 2019; Granena 2020) is a potential breakthrough in this area of study. Unfortunately, due to the limited space, some of these fascinating problems are beyond the scope of this review.

In this chapter, we present the theory of FL aptitude with emphasis on constructs and models, namely the classic Carroll's (1959/2002) aptitude model, Skehan's *Stages Model* (1998), Robinson's *Aptitude Complex Model* (2002), Sparks and Ganschow's *'LCDH'* model (1991), and Sternberg and Grigorenko's *'CANAL-F'* theory (2002). In the following sections we focus on FL aptitude tests, starting with the MLAT (Carroll & Sapon 1959), Pimsleur Language Aptitude Battery (PLAB) (1966), the Cognitive Ability for Novelty in Acquisition of Language (CANAL-FT) (Grigorenko, Sternberg & Ehrman 2000), the LLAMA Language Aptitude Test (Meara, 2005), and the High-Level Language Aptitude Battery (HiLab) (Doughty et al. 2010). We also discuss various aspects concerning the construct of FL aptitude, including prospects for further test development. A short section is devoted to research into FL aptitude, in particular correlations with other variables. The final section is intended as an overview of selected empirical research aiming to investigate different pedagogical aspects of FL aptitude.

4.2 Theory: Definition and models of FL aptitude

FL aptitude is defined as a combination of cognitive and perceptual abilities (i.e., aptitudes) (Doughty 2019; Granena & Yilmaz 2019; Robinson 2007; Skehan 1998).

The contemporary definition of FL aptitude is based on the construct originated by Professor John B. Carroll. As he claimed: "[. . .] there exists such a thing as an aptitude for learning foreign or second languages, [. . .] aptitude can be measured, [. . .] measurements of aptitude can be useful in a variety of ways in connection with the teaching and learning of FLs" (1981, p. 83). Carroll emphasized the variety of the degree of aptitude among learners "[. . .] the individual's initial state of readiness and capacity for learning a FL, and probable degree of facility in doing so [. . .]" (ibid. p. 85) and "It may be that all people, or practically all of them, can and do achieve a satisfactory degree of mastery of a second language when the situation demands it, but it could also be true that they differ in the ease or rate of achieving that mastery" (Carroll 1981, p. 86). Carroll defined aptitude as a fixed and stable trait, but also accepted the possibility of its development by admitting that aptitude measures partly test some kind of achievement and depend to some extent on past learning (1981, 1990, 1993). Similar to other classic FL aptitude tests, Carroll's construct of FL aptitude was restricted to the rate and ease of learning a FL, not to its ultimate attainment.

With regard to the structure of the construct, Carroll (1981) divided aptitude into four, rather independent subcomponents, which can be described as follows:
1. *Phonetic coding ability* (PCA)- the ability to make sound discriminations and to analyze and code unfamiliar sounds in a way that makes retention and successful retrieval after a time interval possible. PCA involves coding, assimilation, and memory for phonetic material. It is associated with mimicry ability, which requires a subject to mimic a novel sound accurately. PCA was considered untrainable.
2. *Grammatical sensitivity* – the ability to identify and understand grammatical functions performed by words in sentences. This ability is considered passive as it is concerned with the recognition of the function of a given material, rather than an explicit representation. It is connected with an awareness of grammatical relationships.
3. *Inductive language learning ability* – an aspect of general reasoning capacity enabling learners to make generalizations and extrapolate from input to produce new sentences. This ability is perceived as active because it refers to the ability to examine a corpus of language material, notice, and identify patterns.
4. *Associative memory* – the ability to form associations in memory between stimuli and responses, for instance, native language lexical items and target language equivalents and to strengthen such connections. This ability is of special importance in vocabulary development, which is an essential part of FL learning (Carroll, 1981, p. 105).

The following research elaborated and extended Carroll's construct of FL aptitude. The two most important are Skehan's (1998, 2002) and Robinson's (1996, 2002, 2005, 2007, 2012) concepts of FL aptitude. Sparks and Ganschow's 'LCDH' model and Sternberg and Grigorenko's 'CANAL-F' theory are also considered significant contributions to the discussion.

Contrary to Carroll's model, which considered FL aptitude an autonomous area, Skehan's (1998) concept of aptitude, the *Processing Stage Model*, consists of components related to the stages of information processing in SLA. Therefore, Carroll's phonetic coding ability corresponds to input processing; language analytic ability, including Carroll's (1959/2002) grammatical sensitivity and inductive language learning, could be related to central processing; and memory-as-retrieval corresponds to output and fluency. Skehan identifies four broad stages of SLA processing: *Noticing, Patterning, Controlling*, and *Lexicalising*. The first stage, noticing, includes such aptitude components as working memory and phonetic coding ability; patterning involves grammatical sensitivity and inductive ability; and controlling and lexicalizing embrace different memory processes such as automatization and proceduralization.

Skehan emphasizes the role of pedagogical interventions, such as modifications of input and types of feedback, in interlanguage development. Different manipulations like input flooding, input enhancement, and negotiation for meaning or *recast* may be more or less efficient depending on the learner's aptitude profile. For example, recast as a very popular focus on form technique, depends on noticing ability, and, therefore, has its limitations in the case of learners with low working memory capacity. Skehan ascribes a special role to memory as a source of individual differences affecting language learning outcomes, with special emphasis being placed on the operations carried out within working memory. Summing up, this model introduces innovative aptitude components, such as working memory or noticing ability, which are considered vital in SLA development. Moreover, it informs second language teaching by emphasizing the relevance of the stages of information processing on the one hand, and the role of appropriate pedagogical intervention, on the other.

Robinson's (2007) Aptitude Complex Model went one step further and focused mainly on matching individual profiles of aptitude to types of instruction, termed as 'aptitude-treatment interaction' (ATI). Adopting Snow's (1987) cognitive-affective-conative triad of factors contributing to aptitude, Robinson (1996) defined FL aptitude as the ability to work at a specific task and in a specific situation. The model is based on the pedagogical assumption that by profiling individual differences and matching the individual profiles to specific types of instruction, differences in aptitudes can be minimized. Two hypotheses resulting from Robinson's (2007) 'aptitude-treatment interaction' research summarize his research findings, namely the *Aptitude Complex Hypothesis* and the *Ability Differentiation Hypothesis*. The first one refers to variation in FL learning outcomes as a function of different FL aptitudes operating under different learning conditions. According to Robinson, FL aptitude is not a homogeneous construct but constitutes sets of abilities or aptitude complexes, which are differentially related to learning under different psycholinguistic processing conditions corresponding to different levels of awareness. Robinson's model (2002) encompasses such primary abilities as *working memory capacity, pattern recognition, grammatical sensitivity*, and the *speed of processing*. Second-order abilities are combinations of primary abilities to establish cognitive constructs such as *noticing the gap, memory for contingent speech, memory for contingent text*, and *metalinguistic rule rehearsal* and their combinations make four aptitude complexes. The second, the *Ability Differentiation Hypothesis*, explains child-adult and high-low aptitude differences in FL learning outcomes. Similar to Skehan's model, Robinson emphasizes the role of working memory and the ability to learn from recasts as FL aptitudes. The value of Robinson's model lies in its pedagogical implications. Some learners might possess strengths in abilities facilitative under specific learning conditions, but less effective in other instructional exposure or teaching technique. The ultimate aim of his approach is to "make predictions about how to optimally match learners to instructional options" (Robinson 2007, p. 274), that is, to create an optimal environment for individual learner needs.

Sternberg (1997) proposed an alternative view on human cognitive abilities stating that abilities are forms of developing *expertise*, which means that they are not stable, but can be taught and developed. He transformed his *Theory of Successful Intelligence* (2002) into FL aptitude theory. Just as Robinson, he suggested that individual differences in FL aptitude should be matched to appropriate teaching methods. This principle is reflected in a method of testing proposed by Sternberg (2002)–dynamic testing–in which learners are given feedback to improve their scores. This idea provided the basis for a FL aptitude test – the *Cognitive Ability for Novelty in Acquisition of Language* (*CANAL-FT*) (Grigorenko et al. 2000), which reflects Sternberg's theory of FL aptitude.

Sparks' and Ganschow's (1991; see also Sparks, Patton, Ganschow, Humbach & Javorsky 2006; Sparks, Humbach, Patton & Ganschow 2011) *Linguistic Coding Difference Hypothesis* is based on research findings that at-risk FL learners have linguistic coding difficulties, which affect both L1 and L2 acquisition. As they postulate, "Inefficiency of the language processing codes may produce interference resulting in individual differences in FL acquisition. [. . .] We suggest, then, that native language factors are likely to be implicated as the main variable in FL learning" (Sparks & Ganschow 1991, p. 10). They propose that native-language (L1) skills in phonology/orthography, grammar, and semantics operate as the basis for L2 learning. Consequently, any problems with these language aspects will have a negative impact on both L1 and L2 learning.

Summing up, a few common characteristics emerge from the five models of FL aptitude, which are a hierarchical structure of cognitive abilities, differentiation of ability profiles, the importance of learning experience, and the role of pedagogical interventions. Two of the models, that is Carroll's and Sternberg's models, offer FL aptitude tests developed from a theoretical base. The remaining three have not developed aptitude instruments but instead, focus on causal explanations and pedagogical implications for FL aptitude theory.

4.3 FL aptitude testing

The most famous test of FL aptitude is the Modern Language Aptitude Test (MLAT) designed in 1959 by John Carroll and Stanley Sapon. The MLAT is a battery valid for literate native and near-native speakers of English and predicts the rate and ease of learning both modern and ancient languages.

The battery consists of five subscales, which can be described as follows:
- Part One: *Number Learning*. This part measures one aspect of the memory component of FL aptitude, but additionally reflects a special auditory alertness factor, which plays a role in auditory comprehension of a FL. Moreover, it partly measures inductive learning ability, a component of FL aptitude that is weakly represented in the MLAT.
- Part Two: *Phonetic Script*. This part measures sound-symbol association ability, which is the ability to learn correspondences between speech sounds and orthographic symbols. It also measures memory for speech sounds.
- Part Three: *Spelling Clues*. This part measures both the examinee's native vocabulary knowledge and sound-symbol association ability.
- Part Four: *Words in Sentences*. This part measures grammatical sensitivity and has particular relevance to the ability to learn the grammatical aspects of a FL. No grammatical terminology is present, so no metalinguistic knowledge is required from the examinee; however, the result may reflect the formal training in grammar.
- Part Five: *Paired Associates*. This part measures the rote memory aspect of FL aptitude.

The four-component model of FL aptitude proposed by Carroll as well as his famous measurement device, the MLAT (Carroll & Sapon 1959), have become a base for all subsequent FL aptitude research, resulting in the development of other FL aptitude tests, such as those devised by Pimsleur (1966), Horne (1971), Child (1973), Petersen and Al-Haik (1976), Grigorenko et al. (2000), Meara, Milton and Lorenzo-Dus (2002), and Doughty et al. (2010), among others.

Pimsleur's test of FL aptitude, the PLAB (1966) proposed a model of aptitude comprised of three factors, which are verbal intelligence, auditory ability, and motivation – a new factor, which constitutes a major distinction between the PLAB and other aptitude tests. Besides the inclusion of motivation in the battery, there are some other differences between the MLAT and the PLAB, such as a greater emphasis on the auditory factor and the inclusion of the item *grade point average* in the PLAB, which represents data about a student's past academic achievement. The test also contains a language analytic ability factor measured by a test in an artificial language but does not contain a measure of memory. The MLAT and the PLAB are still believed to be the most reliable tools for predicting FL learning outcomes and remain points of reference for contemporary researchers (Doughty 2019; Ehrman 1998).

The Cognitive Ability for Novelty in Acquisition of Language FL aptitude test (CANAL-FT) (Grigorenko, et al. 2000), reflects Sternberg's (1997) Theory of Successful Intelligence, which emphasizes aptitude training. The main assumption guiding the test's development was the significance of the ability to cope with novelty and ambiguity in SLA. The authors of the test claim that the CANAL-FT measures creative and practical abilities in addition to analytic and memory abilities. Moreover, the authors suggest that the results will point to appropriate forms of instruction and also reflect the dynamic nature of FL aptitude, which means that testing and instruction occur simultaneously. The test is based on an artificial language, *Ursulu*, which is presented gradually during the test, so that the participants have a chance to master it through cognitive processes of encoding, comparison, transfer of rules, and information synthesis. The processes of encoding, storage, and retrieval of information are evaluated through immediate and delayed recall tasks. The CANAL-FT score allows for identifying preferred modes of learning (visual *versus* auditory), levels of processing (lexical, morphological, semantic, and syntactic), and memory processes (immediate and delayed).

The LLAMA Language Aptitude Test (Meara et al. 2002; Meara 2005) is roughly based on the MLAT. It is a computer-administered battery and consists of four subtests designed to measure different aspects of FL aptitude: *a vocabulary learning task, a test of phonetic memory, a test of sound-symbol correspondence, and a test of grammatical inferencing*. This user-friendly test is available online free of charge, which makes it probably the most popular aptitude test worldwide. However, the validation process has not been completed, so the results of studies based on this battery must be treated with caution (Bokander & Bylund 2020).

Finally, the High-Level Language Aptitude Battery (HI-LAB) (Doughty et al. 2010; Doughty 2019) is a ground-breaking, computer-delivered tool designed to identify individuals with high FL aptitude who can reach advanced levels of FL proficiency. In other words, this battery is an attempt to answer the question which of cognitive aptitudes can predict a ceiling on the level of ultimate attainment that can be achieved by post-critical period adult learners (Doughty 2019). The authors of the test hypothesize that certain cognitive and perceptual abilities compensate for the post-critical period decline in language learning abilities. They assume a componential structure of FL aptitude. Consequently, the test contains the constructs hypothesized to underlie high-level FL aptitudes such as working memory capacity, rote memory, auditory perceptual acuity, processing speed, primability, implicit and explicit induction, inhibition, and attention control. In the most recent study, Doughty (2019), provides evidence that HI-LAB scores predict high attainment beyond other variables, such as language learning background. Moreover, aptitude profiles comprising components of both the MLAT and the HI-LAB could be used to target instruction to specific learners' aptitudes. The test is still under construction and its predictive validity has yet to be established. However, the HI-LAB appears to be the most groundbreaking instrument to measure FL aptitude constructed in the last decade.

Recently, the recognition of the difference between explicit and implicit cognitive aptitudes has been repeatedly proposed in the literature (Granena 2020; Granena & Yilmaz 2019). Explicit aptitudes, such as analytic ability, emphasize attention to linguistic features of the input. They are dominant in studies of FL aptitude and FL aptitude tests. In contrast, implicit aptitudes facilitate unaware and unintentional learning. Granena (2020, p.7) defines implicit aptitude as cognitive abilities which facilitate implicit learning and processing in an L2. Selective attention, but not executive attention, is required for implicit learning. In line with Bley-Vroman's (1989) *Fundamental Difference Hypothesis*, adults can no longer rely on innate implicit mechanisms for language learning and have to use alternative, problem-solving cognitive mechanisms associated with explicit aptitude (see also DeKeyser 2000). Contrary to this hypothesis, in the opinion of Granena and Yilmaz, the capacity for implicit learning "does not disappear in adulthood; it just deteriorates in efficiency" (2019, p. 240). Adults also learn an L2 implicitly, especially in naturalistic or study-abroad contexts. Apart from implicit learning ability, implicit language aptitude involves implicit memory ability. The measurement of implicit cognitive abilities is a challenge due to task categorization problems (implicit vs explicit) and the lower reliability index of implicit tasks (see Granena 2020, for a review of testing methodology).

In response to the development of tests such as Canal FT, the LLAMA, and the HI-LAB, Skehan (2016) proposes to relate aptitude testing to the contrasts between domain-generality and domain-specificity, on the one hand, and explicit and implicit processes, on the other. Domain-specific tests are based on linguistic material, whereas domain-general measures are not. Skehan argues that an imbalance can be observed between explicit tests emphasizing knowledge acquisition such as the

MLAT, and tests based on implicit learning such as the HI-LAB, which focuses on control over the system which has been developed. The latter group is in the minority; however, the development of such tests may be necessary in order to predict advanced-level language achievement. Evaluating FL aptitude tests from this angle, the MLAT and most subtests of the LLAMA and CANAL FT are domain-specific, explicit, and knowledge-based, designed for a conventional 'macro' approach to researching aptitude. In the macro approach, the main purpose of testing is to find correlations between subcomponents of FL aptitude and language learning outcomes. Due to growing interest in the acquisition process, this approach is losing its popularity and is gradually being replaced with a 'micro' approach, characterized by more focused investigations and manipulations of instruction (Skehan 2016).

According to Skehan, apart from the HI-LAB, which has made important progress in developing implicit aptitude components, only LLAMA D and part of CANAL-FT meet these expectations. LLAMA D, a phonetic memory measure (Meara 2005), concerns the ability to recognize sounds in a spoken language. Granena (2015) found that LLAMA D is a measure of implicit learning since it contains no explicit presentation. CANAT FT is more mixed in nature, with *Meaning of passages, Sentential inference*, and *Delayed tests* being implicit measures. A notable exception is the above-mentioned HI-LAB which involves mainly domain-general and implicit tests such as *Long-term memory retrieval, Implicit learning*, and *Processing speed*. There is a need to develop such tests as they appear to predict high levels of accomplishment in a FL, where improvement does not depend on learning new things so much as the capacity to sustain real-time processing and to use language more idiomatically (Wen et al. 2017).

In a similar vein, DeKeyser (2019) suggests focusing on FL aptitude tests measuring implicit aptitudes as well as established measures of fine-grained constructs, such as attention inhibition, switching, or updating, instead of more general ones such as working memory. Accordingly, more narrowly focused and strictly controlled learning experiments would contribute to a better understanding of the construct.

A totally different perspective on FL aptitude testing has been offered by Sedaghatgoftar, Karimi, Babaii, and Reiterer (2019) and Sedaghatgoftar and Reiterer (2022), who designed a test for measuring pragmatic aptitude. In the authors' opinion, current aptitude tests fail to measure the ability to learn pragmatics, which is the language at an appropriate level of formality required in different social situations. Because aptitude tests such as the MLAT do not test the full range of abilities necessary in various language learning situations, especially those pertaining to more naturalistic settings, the authors decided to construct a new tool to measure pragmatic aptitude. The test comprises three sections including *memory for pragmatic rule learning, mind-reading from films*, and *mind-reading from voices*. The first section, memory for pragmatic rule rehearsal, is thought to measure the ability to remember pragmatic rules from other languages that are culturally different from English. The second section, mind-reading from films, requires watching muted clips to determine what the actors mean only through their body language, facial expressions, and gestures. In the last section, mind-reading from voices, the participants are required to listen to ten recorded utterances in Persian (an unfamiliar language) and then determine the emotional or mental state of the speaker. Factor analysis revealed that the three subtests measure the same construct. Given the reliability and validity results, the authors claim that the test can likely be regarded as a reliable and valid measure of the cognitive ability to learn the pragmatics of a second language. So far, this is the first attempt to create a tool for measuring pragmatic aptitude in FL learners.

4.4 Research into FL aptitude

Over the last six decades, knowledge about FL aptitude has accumulated. Li (2015a, 2019) conducted a meta-analysis and synthesis of research investigating relationships between FL aptitude and FL learning outcomes, between aptitude and other individual differences, and the impact of different types of corrective feedback and reported several generalizations emerging from these studies. Learning outcomes were operationalized as overall proficiency, the learning of language skills (speaking, listening, reading, and writing), and linguistic knowledge (grammar and vocabulary). Individual differences included anxiety, motivation, intelligence, and working memory. As regards the correlations between FL aptitude and individual differences, the findings confirmed that the correlation with motivation is low (.16); with anxiety it is negative (- .35); with intelligence, it is high (.64); and with working memory, it is relatively low (.37, for executive working memory and .16, for phonological short-term memory). The low correlation between motivation and aptitude provides evidence that these two strongest predictors of FL learning success may be distinct. The negative correlation between aptitude and anxiety may not be surprising, i.e., low aptitude may trigger high anxiety and high anxiety may reduce cognitive potential and lower online performance, especially under a time constraint. The strong correlation between aptitude and intelligence may also be predictable as many studies provided evidence for the overlap of these constructs (see Chapter 3). The low correlation between aptitude and working memory suggests that these two constructs may be separate, with working memory being more domain-general and FL aptitude more domain-specific.

Regarding language learning outcomes, FL aptitude correlated significantly (.50) with general L2 proficiency, a relationship that is much stronger than any other factors. As Li posits: "These findings constitute evidence for the strong predictive power of language aptitude compared with other variables in the affective and cognitive domains" (2019, p. 86). As far as language skills and subsystems are concerned, significant correlations with FL aptitude were found for listening, speaking, reading, and grammar (in the range of .30 and .39) and a weak correlation was found for vocabulary learning (.15). It is worth emphasizing that these correlations were stronger for less advanced learners, which suggests that FL aptitude may be more predictive at the initial stages of FL learning. Finally, FL aptitude showed a stronger correlation with the effectiveness of explicit than implicit feedback (.59 and .32, respectively). This effect was even stronger for analytic ability, which very weakly correlated with implicit feedback. For comparison, working memory correlations with both types of feedback were smaller, which suggests that working memory is less crucial than FL aptitude in SLA. It has to be borne in mind that most of the tests of FL aptitude were based on the MLAT. Taking a different perspective, that is using an instrument such as the HI-LAB, which operationalizes FL aptitude differently, may yield different results.

4.5 Pedagogy and instruction

With regard to pedagogical implications of the theory of FL aptitude, we can identify two general approaches, namely: (1) FL aptitude training/L2 learning experience to accelerate development and (2) aptitude-treatment-interaction (ATI). Traditionally, FL aptitude was considered a stable factor (Carroll, 1981). Recently, this postulate has been criticized (Rogers et al. 2016; Rogers, Meara, Barnett-Legh, Curry & Davie 2017; Sáfar & Kormos 2008; Singleton 2014, 2017), although studies have produced mixed and contradictory results (Ameringer 2018; Turker, Reiterer, Schneider & Seither-Preisler 2018). In line with Sternberg's theory of cognitive abilities, FL aptitude is considered dynamic and potentially modifiable rather than genetically determined and stable. Accordingly, it is thought that aptitude may be increased in the process of education (cf. Sternberg 2002). The most important factor capable of increasing the score of FL aptitude is the L2 learning experience, an idea that is reflected in the CANAL-FT. Research shows that learners with previous language learning experiences outperform inexperienced learners (Grigorenko et al. 2000; Planchón & Ellis 2014; Rogers et al. 2017; Thompson 2013). In addition, learners' scores on the MLAT and other FL aptitude tests may significantly increase as a result of instruction (Ganschow & Sparks 1995; Sáfár & Kormos 2008; Sparks et al. 1997). A recurring question is whether bi/multilingualism contributes to an increase in FL aptitude (see Biedroń & Birdsong 2019, for a review). The bi/multilingual experience likely increases language learning abilities. Studies of various populations of high achievers, including polyglots and hyperpolyglots (Biedroń 2019; Erard 2019; Hyltenstam et al. 2018; see also Biedroń & Pawlak 2016, for a review), indicate that they are above-average linguistically talented. An interesting result was obtained by Bylund, Abrahamsson, and Hyltenstam (2012) who tested whether bilinguals' performance in both languages can be predicted by factors associated with native-like attainments, such as FL aptitude, age of onset, and frequency of language use. Only FL aptitude appeared to be a good predictor of bilingual performance, in that a high degree of aptitude correlated with nativelikeness in both languages and vice versa.

Neurological research conducted by Susan Reiterer and her colleagues also provides interesting and controversial evidence for the role of FL aptitude training. The possibility of the dynamic nature of FL aptitude is confirmed in studies that explain variation in FL aptitude as a result of complementary influences of inborn predispositions and experience-dependent brain flexibility (Reiterer et al. 2011a; Reiterer, Pereda & Bhattacharya 2011b; see also Biedroń 2015, for a review). However, more recent studies conducted by Reiterer and her team produced mixed results, not just calling into question but weakening the arguments for FL aptitude dynamics. For example, Turker et al. (2018) tested morphological scans of 30 German monolingual native speakers intending to compare the auditory cortex anatomy between extremely high- and low-aptitude participants. The variables tested included speech imitation aptitude, English pronunciation skills, MLAT scores, and the factor of musicality. The study confirmed that the high-aptitude L2 learners outperformed the less gifted ones on all the tests, played more musical instruments, and had more complete posterior duplications of the Heschl's gyrus, the region responsible for auditory processing in the right hemisphere and, consequently, differently developed primary auditory cortex. Heschl's gyrus, which is characterized by great anatomical variation among individuals, is responsible for both linguistic and music processing. Because the auditory cortex is rather stable over time and has a strong genetic component, the authors suggested that FL aptitude be defined as a rather innate capacity that develops over time but remains quite stable. Another result of the study also seemed to cast doubt on FL aptitude pliability, that is, the lack of a correlation between the number of languages spoken and any of the scores. Consequently, FL aptitude may not be such a highly dynamic construct as supposed.

The second perspective, ATI, presumes that various FL aptitude profiles should correspond to appropriate teaching methods. The idea to recognize learners' cognitive profiles to find the best teaching method to match their weaknesses and strengths is represented by Robinson's (2002) model. The concept guiding ATI is to match learners with different types of instruction and assess whether or not a given teaching method or technique is effective for them and whether students with different profiles perform differently under varied learning conditions (for a review of ATI research see Vatz, Tare, Jackson & Doughty 2013).

A practical application of FL aptitude is offered by Gregersen and MacIntyre (2014) who draw on Skehan's (1998) theory of FL aptitude to suggest activities that may improve the learner's skills required for the four stages of SLA, i.e., noticing, patterning, controlling and lexicalizing. They recognize two principles included in ATI, namely *matching* versus *compensatory*. The matching principle follows Robinson's ATI approach since it suggests teaching according to the strengths of the learner to increase his/her chances for success. The compensatory principle, compatible with Skehan's (2002) model, recommends teaching that is directed at compensating for learners' weaknesses. For example, the compensatory approach includes explicit teaching of grammar as a suitable instruction for learners with weaker analytic skills (Ranta 2008; White & Ranta 2002). It is the teacher's decision which means of remediation he/she decides to employ.

In line with ATI principles, contemporary literature abounds in research on the effectiveness of different types of instruction. In particular, grammar instruction as moderated by individual differences has captured researchers' attention. Li (2015a) reports 16 interactional studies that examined the relationship between aptitude and the effectiveness of instructional treatments. Most of the studies produced contradictory results as to the effectiveness of implicit versus explicit type of feedback (Sheen 2007a, 2007b; Trofimovich Ammar & Gatbonton 2007) and the role of the learner's proficiency level to benefit from different types of feedback (Li 2009). Li (2015b) suggests that explicit instruction coupled with metalinguistic explanation is more appropriate for beginners, especially those with poor analytic ability, whereas for more advanced learners, who draw more on working memory capacity, memory strategies may be helpful to process and retrieve new information and reconceptualize old information.

A handful of suggestions have also been offered by Doughty and her team developing the HI-LAB aptitude test. Tare et al. (2013) and Doughty (2019) emphasized both the necessity to recognize learners' cognitive profiles and their needs to create optimal instruction conditions. The authors offer pedagogical recommendations related to the constructs measured by the HI-LAB. For example, learners who have the aptitude for explicit learning may benefit from direct, explicit grammar instruction, learning by induction, and metalinguistic explanation. For those less explicitly oriented who are not good at extrapolating rules, a more traditional, deductive approach is suggested, where structures are first explained and then applied. Learners with high implicit learning ability prefer to cope with complex or unfamiliar language in a full context rather than be taught explicitly. For this group, the best technique is to avoid the explicit presentation of rules and to provide a variety of language examples in a context instead. Implicitly-oriented learners can benefit from exposure to input, such as extensive listening and reading, meaning-based tasks, and feedback in the form of recasts.

4.6 Conclusions and directions for further research

FL aptitude has attracted researchers' attention for over 60 years. Since the 1950s, the theory and research related to abilities have been subject to evolution, although the idea of the construct of language aptitude itself has remained generally unchanged. Now, we have witnessed a renewed interest in this topic, which gives hope for its future. However, the interest in aptitude topics is uneven, with some subjects being readily undertaken, while others suffer from a lack of systematic investigation. Among the best-researched topics are neurological aspects of FL aptitude, especially phonological aptitude, investigated by Susan Reiterer and her colleagues (Reiterer 2018; 2019), working memory as a potential FL aptitude (Wen 2019, Wen et al. 2017), high achievement in SLA (Biedroń 2019; Hyltenstam et al. 2018), FL aptitude testing (Doughty 2019; Linck et al. 2013) and the role of musicality in FL phonological aptitude (Reiterer 2019; Turker et al. 2018). Moreover, the number of studies that heed Skehan's call to a 'micro' approach and ATI principles is increasing. Many of these studies focus on implicit versus explicit kinds of feedback (Li, Ellis & Zhu 2019) or implicit versus explicit types of knowledge (Pawlak & Biedroń 2019), however, the latter are in the minority. It is worth emphasizing that many of the aforementioned studies have investigated working memory as a mediating variable, rather than other aptitudes. Another line of inquiry is connected with explicit and implicit aptitudes for language learning, with the emphasis being placed on the latter, as poorly studied and underestimated (Granena 2020; Granena & Yilmaz 2019). Studies into gender (Wücherer & Reiterer, 2018), motivation, and personality (Biedroń 2012; see also Reiterer 2018, 2019) as factors affecting FL aptitude have largely remained on the sidelines of mainstream research. A poorly researched area is FL aptitude dynamics and its connections with bilingualism (Biedroń & Birdsong 2019). The lack of research may occur because of the complexity of this relationship as well as methodological difficulties in the process of investigation. Longitudinal studies on large populations are needed in this field.

Another appealing line of investigation is the relationship between FL aptitude and other cognitive variables that may augment SLA (Skehan 2019). Given new research results in the field of intelligence and different memory abilities, this call is reasonable and timely. The idea of investigating interconnections between FL aptitude and other factors was introduced by Dörnyei (2009), who proposed to study this factor within the complex dynamic systems theory (CDST) paradigm. The main assumption guiding CDST is that all factors and processes that come into play in SLA are dynamic, open to change, and mutually affect each other. Dörnyei proposes to replace statistical analyses with qualitative studies, which take into account individual trajectories of development. Taking into consideration potentially irrelevant factors, "background noise", might produce a more complete description of a subject's profile.

Finally, an investigation of procedural and declarative memory systems as significant cognitive variables may be a potential source of information about FL aptitude (Buffington & Morgan-Short 2019; Ruiz, Tagarelli & Rebuschat 2018). Observing the growth of research in FL aptitude, it is hoped that these topics will be investigated by researchers in the future.

Recommended Readings

Wen, Zhisheng, Adriana Biedroń, Peter Skehan, Shaofeng Li & Richard Sparks (eds.). 2019. *Language aptitude: Advancing theory, testing, research and practice*. Routledge.

This recent volume covers broad issues in language aptitude theory and test developments in global contexts and includes studies investigating the role of language aptitude in L2 learners with different proficiency levels ranging from intermediate learners to exceptionally gifted learners, or polyglots. It revisits previous aptitude models and tests but also presents innovative perspectives and empirical evidence, as well as clear pointers for future research.

Biedroń, Adriana & David Birdsong, D. 2019. Highly proficient and gifted bilinguals. In Annick De Houwer & Lourdes Ortega (eds.), *The Cambridge Handbook of Bilingualism* (Cambridge Handbooks in Language and Linguistics, 307–323). Cambridge: Cambridge University Press.

This chapter examines the relationship between linguistic giftedness and bi/multilingualism, in particular, studies of gifted foreign language learners achieving very high levels of proficiency. It includes the description of different populations of multilingual gifted foreign language learners, including polyglots and savants, along with their cognitive, affective, and neurological characteristics.

DeKeyser, Robert (ed.). 2019. *Aptitude-treatment interaction in second language learning*, John Benjamins.

This edited volume brings together empirical studies about aptitude-treatment interactions, that is, the interactions between different aptitude profiles and different educational contexts as well as different aptitude profiles and different testing conditions.

Wen, Zhisheng, Peter Skehan & Richard Sparks (eds.). 2023. *Language aptitude theory and practice*. Cambridge, UK: Cambridge University Press.

This edited volume provides updated reviews and the latest developments in language aptitude test batteries, theoretical models, and aptitude-treatment interaction studies. Commentary chapters written by the editors call for a re-analysis and a paradigm shift of language aptitude research from its previous focus on aptitude testing to theory construction and practical applications. The volume consolidates the achievements made in language aptitude testing and pushes for further developments in aptitude theory and practice.

References

Ameringer, Victoria. 2018. Cognitive abilities: Different memory functions and language aptitude. In Susanne M. Reiterer, (ed.), *Exploring language aptitude: Views from psychology, the language sciences, and cognitive neuroscience*, 19–43. Springer.

Biedroń, Adriana. 2012. *Cognitive-affective profile of gifted adult foreign language learners*. Słupsk: Wydawnictwo Akademii Pomorskiej w Słupsku.

Biedroń, Adriana. 2015. Neurology of FL aptitude. *Studies in Second Language Learning and Teaching*, 5(1), 13–40.

Biedroń, Adriana. 2019. Language aptitude: Insights from L2 exceptional learners. In Zhisheng Wen, Peter Skehan, Adriana Biedroń, Shaofeng Li & Richard Sparks (eds.), *Language aptitude: Advancing theory, testing, research and practice*, 168–184. New York/ London: Routledge.

Biedroń, Adriana & David Birdsong. 2019. Highly proficient and gifted bilinguals. In Annick De Houwer & Lourdes Ortega (eds.), *The Cambridge handbook of bilingualism (Cambridge handbooks in language and linguistics*, 307–323. Cambridge: Cambridge University Press.

Biedroń, Adriana & Mirosław Pawlak. 2016. New conceptualizations of linguistic giftedness. *Language Teaching*, 49(2), 151–185.

Biedroń, Adriana & Mauricio Véliz-Campos. 2021. Trainability of foreign language aptitudes in children. In Joanna Rokita-Jaśkow & Agata Wolanin (eds.), *Facing diversity in child foreign language education*. Springer.

Bley-Vroman, Robert. 1989. What is the logical problem of FL learning? In Susan Gass & Jacquelyn Schachter (eds.), *Linguistic perspectives on second language acquisition*, 41–68. New York, NY: Cambridge University Press.

Bokander, Lars & Emanuel Bylund. 2020. Probing the internal validity of the LLAMA language aptitude tests. *Language learning*, 70(2).11–47.

Buffington, Joshua & Kara Morgan-Short. 2019. Declarative and procedural memory as individual differences in second language acquisition. In Zhisheng Wen, Peter Skehan, Adriana Biedroń, Shaofeng Li & Richard Sparks (eds.), *Language aptitude: Advancing theory, testing, research and practice*, 215–238. New York/ London: Routledge.

Bylund, Emanuel, Niclas Abrahamsson & Kenneth Hyltenstam. 2012. Does first language maintenance hamper nativelikeness in a second language? A study of ultimate attainment in early bilinguals. *Studies in Second Language Acquisition*, 34(2), 215–241.

Carroll, John B. 1981. Twenty-five years of research on FL aptitude. In Karl C. Diller (ed.), *Individual differences and universals in language learning aptitude*, 83–118. Rowley, MA: Newbury House.

Carroll, John B. 1990. Cognitive abilities in FL aptitude: Then and now. In Thomas Parry & Charles W. Stansfield (eds.), *Language aptitude reconsidered*, 11–29. Englewood Cliffs, NJ: Prentice-Hall.

Carroll, John B. 1993. *Human cognitive abilities: A survey of factor-analytic studies*. Cambridge: Cambridge University Press.

Carroll, John B. & Stanley M. Sapon. 1959. *Modern Language Aptitude Test (MLAT)*. New York, NY: The Psychological Corporation. (Reprinted in 2002).

Child, James R. 1973. *VORD*. Washington DC. U.S. Department of Defense.

DeKeyser, Robert M. 2000. The robustness of critical period effects in second language acquisition. *Studies in Second Language Acquisition*, 22, 499–533.

DeKeyser, Robert M. 2019. The future of language aptitude research. In Zhisheng Wen, Peter Skehan, Adriana Biedroń, Shaofeng Li & Richard Sparks (eds.), *Language aptitude: Advancing theory, testing, research and practice*, 317–330. New York/ London: Routledge.

Doughty, Catherine J. 2019. Cognitive language aptitude. *Language Learning, 69*, 101–126.
Doughty, Catherine J., Susan G. Campbell, Meredith A. Mislevy, Michael M. Bunting, Anita R. Bowles & Joel T. Koeth. 2010. Predicting near-native ability: The factor structure and reliability of HiLab. In Matthew T.Prior, Yukiko Watanabe & Sang-Ki Lee (eds.), *Selected proceedings of the 2008 Second Language Research Forum*, 10–31. Somerville, MA: Cascadilla Proceedings Project. Retrieved from www.lingref.com, document #2382.
Dörnyei, Zoltan. 2005. *The psychology of the language learner: Individual differences in second language acquisition*. Mahwah, NJ: Lawrence Erlbaum.
Dörnyei, Zoltan. 2009. *The psychology of second language acquisition*. Oxford: Oxford University Press.
Ehrman, Madline E. 1998. The Modern Language Aptitude Test for predicting learning success and advising students. *Applied Language Learning, 9(1–2)*, 31–70.
Erard, Michael. 2019. Language aptitude: Insights from hyperpolyglots. In Zhisheng Wen, Peter Skehan, Adriana Biedroń, Shaofeng Li & Richard Sparks (eds.), *Language aptitude: Advancing theory, testing, research and practice*, 153–168. New York/ London: Routledge.
Ganschow, Leonore & Richard Sparks. 1995. Effects of direct instruction in Spanish phonology on the native-language skills and foreign-language aptitude of at-risk foreign-language learners. *Journal of Learning Disabilities, 28(2)*, 107–120.
Granena, Gisela. 2015. Cognitive aptitudes for implicit and explicit learning and information-processing styles: An individual differences study. *Applied Psycholinguistics, 37*, 577–600.
Granena, Gisela. 2020. *Implicit language aptitude. Elements in second language acquisition*. Cambridge: Cambridge University Press.
Granena, Gisela & Yucel Yilmaz. 2019. Cognitive aptitudes for explicit and implicit learning. In Zhisheng Wen, Peter Skehan, Adriana Biedroń, Shaofeng Li & Richard Sparks (eds.), *Language aptitude: Advancing theory, testing, research and practice*, 238–257. New York/ London: Routledge.
Gregersen, Tammy & Peter D. MacIntyre. 2014. *Capitalizing on language learners' individuality. From premise to practice*. Bristol: Multilingual Matters.
Grigorenko, Elena L., Robert J. Sternberg & Madeline E. Ehrman. 2000. A theory based approach to the measurement of FL learning ability: The CANAL-F theory and test. *Modern Language Journal, 84*, 390–405.
Horne, Kibbey M. 1971. *Differential prediction of FL testing*. Paper presented before the Bureau of International Language Coordination. London.
Hyltenstam, Kenneth, Inge Bartning & Lars Fant (eds.), 2018. *High-level language proficiency in second language and multilingual contexts*. Cambridge: Cambridge University Press.
Li, Shaofeng. 2009. The differential effects of implicit and explicit feedback on L2 learners of different proficiency levels. *Applied Language Learning, 19*, 53–79.
Li, Shaofeng. 2015a. The associations between language aptitude and second language grammar acquisition: A meta-analytic review of five decades of research. *Applied Linguistics, 36(3)*, 385–408.
Li, Shaofeng. 2015b. Working memory, language analytical ability and L2 recasts. In Zhisheng Wen, Mailce B. Mota & Arthur McNeill (eds.), *Working memory in second language acquisition and processing*, 139–160. Bristol: Multilingual Matters.
Li, Shaofeng. 2019. Six decades of language aptitude research: A comprehensive and critical review. In Zhisheng Wen, Peter Skehan, Adriana Biedroń, Shaofeng Li & Richard Sparks (eds.), *Language aptitude: Advancing theory, testing, research and practice*, 78–97. New York/London: Routledge.
Li, Shaofeng, Rod Ellis & Yan Zhu. 2019. The associations between cognitive ability and L2 development under five different instructional conditions. *Applied Psycholinguistics, 40(3)*, 693–722.

Linck, Jared A., Meredith M. Hughes, Susan G. Campbell, Noah H. Silbert, Medha Tare, Scott R. Jackson, Benjamin K. Smith, Michael F. Bunting & Catherine J. Doughty. 2013. HiLab: A new measure of aptitude for high-level language proficiency. *Language Learning, 63(3)*, 530–566.

Meara, Paul M. 2005. *LLAMA language aptitude tests*. Swansea, UK: Lognostics.

Meara, Paul M., James L. Milton & Nuria Lorenzo-Dus. 2002. *Language aptitude tests*. Newbury: Express.

Pawlak, Mirosław & Adriana Biedroń. 2019. Verbal working memory as a predictor of explicit and implicit knowledge of English passive voice. *Journal of Second Language Studies. Special issue. Aptitude- Treatment Interaction in Second Language Learning, 2(2)*, 283–305.

Peterson, Calvin R. & Antoine R. Al-Haik. 1976. The development of the defense language aptitude battery (DLAB). *Educational and Psychological Measurement, 36*, 369–380.

Pimsleur, Paul. 1966. *Pimsleur Language Aptitude Battery*. New York, NY: Harcourt Brace Jovanovich.

Planchon, Anita & Elizabeth Ellis. 2014. A diplomatic advantage? The effects of bilingualism and formal language training on language aptitude amongst Australian diplomatic officers. *Language Awareness, 23(3)*, 203–219.

Ranta, Leila. 2008. Aptitude and good language learners. In Carol Griffiths (ed.), *Lessons from good language learners*, 142–155. Cambridge: Cambridge University Press.

Reiterer, Susanne M. (ed.). 2018. *Exploring language aptitude: Views from psychology, the language sciences, and cognitive neuroscience*. Springer.

Reiterer, Susanne M. 2019. Neuro-psycho-cognitive markers for pronunciation/ speech imitation as language aptitude. In Zhisheng Wen, Peter Skehan, Adriana Biedroń, Shaofeng Li & Richard Sparks (eds.), *Language aptitude: Advancing theory, testing, research and practice*, 277–279. New York/ London: Routledge.

Reiterer, Susanne, M., Xiaochen Hu, Michael Erb, Giuseppina Rota, Davide Nardo, Wolfgang Grodd, Susanne Winkler & Hermann Ackermann. 2011a. Individual differences in audio-vocal speech imitation aptitude in late bilinguals: Functional neuro-imaging and brain morphology. *Frontiers in Psychology, 2(271)*, 1–12.

Reiterer, Susanne M., Ernesto Pereda & Joydeep Bhattacharya. 2011b. On a possible relationship between linguistic expertise and EEG gamma band phase synchrony. *Frontiers in Psychology, 2(334)*, 1–11.

Robinson, Peter. 1996. Learning simple and complex second language rules under implicit, incidental, rule-search and instructed condition. *Studies in Second Language Acquisition, 18*, 27–67.

Robinson, Peter. 2002. Learning conditions, aptitude complexes and SLA: A framework for research and pedagogy. In Peter Robinson (ed.), *Individual differences and instructed language learning*, 113–133. Philadelphia, PA: John Benjamins.

Robinson, Peter. 2005. Aptitude and second language acquisition. *Annual Review of Applied Linguistics, 25*, 46–73.

Robinson, Peter. 2007. Aptitudes, abilities, contexts, and practice. In Robert M. DeKeyser (ed.), *Practice in second language*, 256–286. Cambridge: Cambridge University Press.

Robinson, Peter. 2012. Individual differences, aptitude complexes, SLA processes, and aptitude test development. In Mirosław Pawlak (ed.), *New perspectives on individual differences in language learning and teaching*, 57–75. Berlin Heidelberg: Springer-Verlag.

Rogers Vivienne E., Paul Meara, Rachel Aspinall, Louise Fallon, Thomas Goss, Emily Keey & Rosa Thomas. 2016. Testing aptitude. *EUROSLA Yearbook, 16(1)*, 179–210.

Rogers Vivienne E., Paul Meara, Thomas Barnett-Legh, Clare Curry & Emma Davie. 2017. Examining the LLAMA aptitude tests. *Journal of the European Second Language Association, 1(1)*, 49–60.

Ruiz Simón, Kaitlyn M. Tagarelli & Patrick Rebuschat. 2018. Simultaneous acquisition of words and syntax: effects of exposure condition and declarative memory. *Frontiers in Psychology, 9*, 1–11.
Sáfár, Anna & Judit Kormos. 2008. Revisiting problems with FL aptitude. *International Review of Applied Linguistics in Language Teaching, 46(2)*, 113–136.
Sedaghatgoftar, Nasrin, Mohammad N. Karimi, Esmat Babaii & Susanne M Reiterer. 2019. Developing and validating a second language pragmatics aptitude test. *Cogent Education, 6 (1)*.
Sedaghatgoftar, Nasrin & Susanne M. Reiterer. 2022. Second language pragmatics aptitude. *Cogent Arts & Humanities, 9(1)*. 2129473.
Sheen, Younghee. 2007a. The effect of focused written corrective feedback and language aptitude on ESL learners' acquisition of articles. *TESOL Quarterly, 41(2)*, 255–283.
Sheen, Younghee. 2007b. The effects of corrective feedback, language aptitude, and learner attitudes on the acquisition of English articles. In Alison Mackey (ed.), *Conversational interaction in second language acquisition*, 301–322. New York: Oxford University Press.
Singleton, David. 2014. Apt to change: The problematic of language awareness and language aptitude in age-related research. *Studies in Second Language Learning and Teaching, 4*, 557–571.
Singleton, David. 2017. Language aptitude: Desirable trait or acquirable attribute? *Studies in Second Language Learning and Teaching, 7(1)*, 89–103.
Skehan, Peter. 1998. *A cognitive approach to language learning*. Oxford: Oxford University Press.
Skehan, Peter. 2002. Theorising and updating aptitude. In Peter Robinson (ed.), *Individual differences and instructed language learning*, 69–95. Philadelphia, PA: John Benjamins.
Skehan, Peter. 2016. FL aptitude, acquisitional sequences, and psycholinguistic processes. In Gisela Granena, Daniel O. Jackson & Yucel Yilmaz (eds.), *Cognitive individual differences in L2 processing and acquisition*, 17–40. Amsterdam: John Benjamins.
Skehan, Peter. 2019. Language aptitude implicates language and cognition skills. In Zhisheng Wen, Peter Skehan, Adriana Biedroń, Shaofeng Li & Richard Sparks (eds.), *Language aptitude: Advancing theory, testing, research and practice*, 56–78. New York/ London: Routledge.
Snow, Richard E. 1987. Aptitude complexes. In Richard E. Snow & Marshall Farr (eds.), *Aptitude, learning and instruction, cognitive process analyses of aptitude* (2 vols.), 11–34. Hillsdale, NJ: Erlbaum Associates.
Sparks, Richard L. & Leonore Ganschow. 1991. FL learning difficulties: Affective or native language aptitude differences? *Modern Language Journal*, 7, 3–16.
Sparks, Richard L., Leonore Ganschow, Jon Patton, Marjorie Artzer, David Siebenhar & Mark Plageman. 1997. Prediction of FL proficiency. *Journal of Educational Psychology, 89(3)*, 549–561.
Sparks, Richard L., Jon Patton, Leonore Ganschow, Nancy Humbach, N. & James Javorsky. 2006. Native language predictors of FL proficiency and FL aptitude. *Annals of Dyslexia, 56*, 129–160.
Sparks, Richard L., Nancy Humbach, Jon Patton & Leonore Ganschow. 2011. Subcomponents of second-language aptitude and second-language proficiency, *Modern Language Journal, 95*, 253–273.
Sternberg, Robert J. 1997. *Successful intelligence*. New York, NY: Plume.
Sternberg, Robert J. 2002. The theory of Successful Intelligence and its implications for language aptitude testing. In Peter Robinson (ed.), *Individual differences and instructed language learning*, 13–43. Philadelphia, PA: John Benjamins.
Sternberg, Robert J. & Elena L. Grigorenko. 2002. The theory of successful intelligence as a basis for gifted education. *Gifted Child Quarterly, 46*, 265–277.
Tare, Medha, Carrie L. Bonilla, Karen Vatz, Martyn Clark, Jared Linck & Catherine J. Doughty. 2013. *Building a language learner's profile: Characteristics which inform training and pedagogy*. CASL technical report. College Park, MD: Center for Advanced Study of Language.

Thompson, Amys S. 2013. The interface of language aptitude and multilingualism: Reconsidering the bilingual/multilingual dichotomy. *Modern Language Journal, 97*, 685–701.

Trofimovich, Pavel, Ahlem Ammar & Elizabeth Gatbonton. 2007. How effective are recasts? The role of attention, memory, and analytical ability. In Alison Mackey (ed.), *Conversational interaction in second language acquisition*, 171–195. New York: Oxford University Press.

Turker, Sabrina, Susanne M. Reiterer, Peter Schneider & Annemarie Seither-Preisler. 2018. The neuroanatomical correlates of foreign language aptitude. In Susanne M. Reiterer (ed.), *Exploring language aptitude: Views from psychology, the language sciences, and cognitive neuroscience*, 119–149. Springer.

Vatz, Karen, Medha Tare, Scott R. Jackson & Catherine J. Doughty. 2013. Aptitude-treatment interaction in second language acquisition: Findings and methodology. In Gisela Granena, & Michael H. Long (eds.), *Sensitive periods, language aptitude, and ultimate L2 attainment*, 273–292. Amsterdam: John Benjamins.

Wen, Zhisheng. 2019. Working memory as language aptitude: The Phonological/Executive Model. In Zhisheng Wen, Peter Skehan, Adriana Biedroń, Shaofeng Li & Richard Sparks (eds.), *Language aptitude: Advancing theory, testing, research and practice*, 187–214. New York: Routledge.

Wen, Zhisheng, Peter Skehan, Adriana Biedroń, Shaofeng Li & Richard Sparks (eds.). 2019. *Language aptitude: Advancing theory, testing, research and practice*. London/ New York: Routledge.

Wen, Zhisheng, Adriana Biedroń & Peter Skehan. 2017. Foreign language aptitude theory: Yesterday, today and tomorrow. *Language Teaching, 50(1)*, 1–31.

White, Joanna & Leila Ranta. 2002. Examining the interface between metalinguistic task performance and oral production in a second language. *Language Awareness, 11*, 259–290.

Wücherer, Barbara & Susanne M. Reiterer. 2018. Language is a girlie thing, isn't it? A psycholinguistic exploration of the L2 gender gap. *International Journal of Bilingual Education and Bilingualism, 19*, 1–17.

5 Language Aptitude, Psychological and Affective Factors

Adriana Biedroń

Abstract: Despite contemporary psychological theories treating cognitive and affective/ psychological factors as complementary, they are rarely analysed together in SLA studies. Nevertheless, individual differences such as motivation, language anxiety and openness to experience have a clear cognitive component. Although their impact on ultimate attainment in foreign language learning is definitely less significant than that of foreign language aptitude, it is also observable, which is clearly illustrated by the cases of linguistically gifted people. This chapter aims to present the connections between foreign language aptitude and the psychological factors that include a cognitive component. To this end, the theoretical foundations of psychological factors are described as well as the relationship between FL aptitude and psychological factors in theory, research and practice. We will also focus on the contribution of psychological factors to the development of linguistic giftedness.

Keywords: foreign language aptitude, psychological factors, affect, personality, linguistic talent

5.1 Introduction

The purpose of this chapter is to present controversial factors thought to affect foreign language (FL) aptitude, which are psychological variables. First of all, it should be clarified that the terms "affective/ psychological factors" or "personality factors" are not quite correct to refer to the number of individual differences affecting FL aptitude. This is because apart from personality factors such as openness to experience or empathy, there are a number of individual differences including both a personality and cognitive aspect, for example, motivation or language learning styles. Even empathy could be classified as emotional or cognitive, and openness to experience has a strong cognitive component. Moreover, unlike personality factors, which are in large part heritable and stable, some individual differences such as language learning strategies are teachable and often consciously chosen by the learner, whereas others, like motivation or willingness to communicate, are subject to fluctuations. Although increasingly popular in SLA studies, non-cognitive factors generally remain on the margins of research into FL aptitude. One reason is that correlations between FL aptitude and personality factors have often been disappointing (Robinson & Ellis 2008). Personality factors and learning styles and strategies are not included in the concept of FL aptitude on equal terms with such factors as working memory or implicit aptitude; however, they may affect ultimate FL attainment in a non-linear way. The need for investigating these relationships within the framework of dynamic systems theory (DST) is regularly voiced in the literature (Lowie, van Dijk, Chan & Verspoor 2017).

This chapter aims to shed light on the connections between FL aptitude and the psychological factors that include a cognitive component. To begin with, the theoretical foundations of psychological factors in SLA are briefly explained. Next, we examine the relationship between FL aptitude and psychological factors, in theory, research, and practice. A section is devoted to the contribution of psychological factors in the development of linguistic giftedness. Finally, some pedagogical implications and suggestions for further research are offered.

5.2 Psychological factors in SLA-theoretical foundations

Individual factors in SLA are traditionally divided into cognitive and affective/personality characteristics, but there is controversy about their classification. It is a fairly arbitrary division, partly adapted from the psychology of individual differences and partly developed within SLA theory. Individual differences constitute a continuum with strictly cognitive factors, such as working memory located on one extreme, and strictly affective factors such as basic emotions (e.g., anger, fear, joy) on the other. Other factors cover a wide spectrum of individual differences to a greater or lesser extent containing cognitive and affective elements. According to the conventional classification adopted in linguistics (Arnold & Brown 1999; Gregersen & MacIntyre 2014), cognitive factors include intelligence, various types of memory, FL aptitude, and learning strategies and styles (e.g. cognitive and metacognitive learning strategies). Affective factors include personality traits, emotions, language anxiety, and a few learning styles and strategies (e.g. socio-affective learning strategies). Most individual differences are placed on a continuum, e.g., motivation, willingness to communicate, learner beliefs, and ego permeability. The latter group is nowadays described as "psychological factors" (e.g., Reiterer 2018) or simply individual differences (de Bot & Bátyi 2017) as opposed to cognitive factors whose affiliation is most often defined (e.g., Biedroń 2012; Doughty 2019; Gregersen & MacIntyre 2014). While borderline factors constitute a broad and diverse category, cognitive factors (intelligence, abilities) are treated as a closed homogeneous group (Doughty 2019; Doughty et al. 2010; Gregersen & MacIntyre 2014; Long 2013). This division is also visible in research methodology where borderline and affective factors are examined with the use of both quantitative (Biedroń 2011a; Dewaele & Alfawzan 2018) and qualitative methods (Biedroń 2011b; Lowie et al. 2017; Pavelescu & Petrić 2018), while cognitive factors are analyzed almost exclusively quantitatively (Doughty 2019; Pawlak & Biedroń 2019; Zychowicz, Biedroń & Pawlak, 2017).

Some researchers have speculated that affective experiences are intertwined with cognition (Clore, Schiller & Schacked 2018; Damasio 1994, LeDoux 1996) and perform a central role in human experience (Shackman & Wagner 2019). The controversy regarding the primacy of these two aspects is slowly disappearing and it seems reasonable to treat both concepts as complementary. Recently, there has been significant progress in brain imaging techniques and a remarkable acceleration of research focused on the interplay of emotion and cognition (Okon-Singer, Hendler, Pessoa & Shackman 2015). Generally, this research suggests that negative emotions like stress and anxiety seriously affect key elements of cognition. Neural circuits responsible for cognitive functioning in turn may affect the regulation of emotions. Okon-Singer et al. (2015, p. 1) challenge the separation between 'cognitive' and 'emotional' brains:

> The distinction between the 'emotional' and the 'cognitive' brain is fuzzy and context-dependent. Indeed, there is compelling evidence that brain territories and psychological processes commonly associated with cognition, such as the dorsolateral prefrontal cortex and working memory, play a central role in emotion [. . .] emotion and cognition are deeply interwoven in the fabric of the brain, suggesting that widely held beliefs about the key constituents of 'the emotional brain' and 'the cognitive brain' are fundamentally flawed.

Neurological research demonstrates that emotional cues and states can affect elements of cognition, including attention (Holtmann et al. 2013), working memory (Clarke & Johnstone 2013; Iordan, Dolcos & Dolcos 2013), cognitive control (Kalanthroff, Cohen & Henik 2013), reinforcement learning (Berghorst, Bogdan, Frank & Pizzagalli 2013), and different kinds of mood-congruent information processing (van Dessel & Vogt 2012).

What does this mean for SLA? Many researchers recognize the need for a more complex approach to individual differences. For example, Lowie et al. (2017, p. 132) suggest that "many internal states such as language aptitude, motivation, attitude, personality traits, and other "individual differences" have an effect on the developmental trajectory" of language acquisition. Larsen-Freeman and Cameron (2008) refer to the dynamic interaction between psycholinguistic, sociolinguistic and situational aspects called the learner's internal dynamics, thus indicating that all of these factors affect the learning process. Dörnyei (2009, 2010) refers to the problem of the relationship between cognitive, motivational and emotional processes and their combined impact on human cognitive functioning. He argues that the modular model of individual differences, which includes many distinct factors, does not reflect reality and suggests that it is probably more effective to focus on higher-order features that function as integrated entities (Dörnyei 2010; Dörnyei & Ryan 2015; cf. Serafini 2017). According to this position, Dörnyei recommends the theory of dynamic systems as a paradigm that best describes individual differences. From this perspective, FL aptitude cannot be analyzed in isolation from psychological variables, as dynamic interaction occurs between these factors. Neuroscience provides some empirical support for the existence of such relationships. For example, the dopamine neurotransmitter, which determines both motivation and information retention, has been found to affect psychological and cognitive variables such as working memory, attention, motivation to learn, and learning effectiveness (e.g. Philips, Vacca & Ahn 2008; Schumann 2004; Wong, Morgan-Short, Ettlinger & Zheng 2012).

Researchers speculate that cognitive and affective factors interpenetrate each other during language learning and that success in learning depends, in the same part, on personality variables (e.g., see Biedroń 2012, 2019; Dewaele, Petrides & Furnham 2008; Griffiths 2008; Hu & Reiterer 2009; Moyer 1999; 2007; Reiterer 2018, 2019). Studies of successful language learners have identified a number of features that facilitate learning (see Dörnyei 2005; Ehrman 2008; Ehrman & Oxford 1995; Griffiths 2008) and improve teaching (Oxford & Gkonou 2018). In particular, motivation seems to come to the fore as a psychological trait in high achievers, such as gifted FL learners (Biedroń 2012; Fein & Obler 1988; Moyer 2014) and polyglots. To quote Hyltenstam (2018, p. 192): "It appears that the combination of an extremely strong motivation and high levels of language aptitude is what makes polyglots the Jaguars of second language acquisition". While engaged in the process of FL learning, polyglots employ a variety of strategies and neglect any face-threatening obstacles in order to take advantage of a conversational opportunity. High motivation in combination with efficient self-motivation strategies and a high level of autonomy always accompanies FL learning success (Biedroń 2012).

Recently a new factor, *language learning curiosity* (Mahmoodzadeh & Khajavy 2019), has been introduced in the literature. This construct is an intellectual dimension of seeking novelty with an open mind and a positive attitude. Language learning curiosity indicates an ability to be open to constant learning, relearning, unlearning, and accepting contradictions in one's knowledge, and resembles the psychological construct of openness to experience. Curious individuals are fully engaged in the learning process and willing to accept the possibility of any change in their knowledge. According to Mahmoodzadeh and Khajavy, a person driven by an innate sense of curiosity may not only initiate learning but also make it meaningful. Inquisitive thinking is also associated with a sense of motivation, enjoyment, excitement, and a positive affect in general.

The latest trends in research concerning affective factors relate to the importance of positive and negative emotions in learning a foreign language. Particular importance is attached to positive emotions that can sustain learning motivation

(Dewaele & Li 2018). This approach fits with the trend of positive psychology (e.g., MacIntyre, Gregersen & Mercer 2016), which is gaining increasing popularity among FL researchers and educators. It should be noted that this trend has been criticized by cognitive psychologists as founded on fallacious arguments (Miller 2008; Singal 2021).

5.3 Research in psychological factors and FL aptitude

The original construct of FL aptitude (Carroll & Sapon 1959) has been developed over the last 60 years thanks to major advances in the fields of SLA, cognitive psychology, genetics, and neurolinguistics (see Chapter 4 this volume). Nevertheless, it is usually defined in terms of exclusively cognitive factors (Doughty 2019). Despite the impact on the learning process attributed to psychological factors, they are usually not included in the theory and practice of FL aptitude research. The first and only complete FL aptitude theory that included both personality and motivational (conative) characteristics was Richard Snow's (1987, 1994) *cognitive-affective-conative triad of FL aptitude*, and further extended by Corno et al. (2002). This theory was a precursor to the aptitude-treatment-interaction (ATI) approach as it refers to being equipped to work at a particular kind of task in a particular kind of situation. Within the framework of Snow's theory, FL aptitude is not limited to cognitive abilities. Personality factors such as achievement motivation, freedom from anxiety, positive self-concept, and impulse control are thought to be aptitudes contributing to ultimate FL achievement. Affective constructs in Snow's theory encompass three types of affective variables: traits of temperament, moods, and personality factors adapted from the *Five Factor Model* (Costa & McCrae 1992). Snow's model has always remained on the margins of research in language skills, and a tool to measure such a construct has never been developed. Nonetheless, one of the most influential theories of FL aptitude, Peter Robinson's Aptitude Complex Model (2002), was inspired by Snow's paradigm.

One of the first important studies into the relationship between FL aptitude and psychological variables was conducted by Ehrman and Oxford (1995). They tested the relationships among FL aptitude, learning strategies, learning styles, personality as measured by the Myers-Briggs Type Indicator (MBTI; Myers & Briggs 1976), motivation and anxiety, and proficiency ratings in FL learning of educated adults in intensive training in a wide range of FLs at the U.S. State Department. Their aim was to determine whether FL aptitude and psychological factors influence ultimate attainment in FL learning. As predicted, aptitude measures were most strongly correlated with proficiency, explaining 25% of the variance in FL proficiency. Their findings revealed that among cognitive styles, the highest score was the one for the analytic language learning style. High-average were the scores for spatial, categorization, sequential processing and detail memory language learning styles. The students obtained high scores on persistence, verbal risk-taking, as well as verbal learning preference. All of the subjects reported very high intrinsic motivation. The MBTI used in the study proposes four bipolar personality types, namely extraversion-introversion, sensing-intuiting, thinking-feeling, and judging-perceiving. The dominant features of the participants in the study were introversion, intuition, judging and thinking. The participants reported low levels of anxiety, high levels of self-esteem, and thick ego boundaries. After FL aptitude, affective and motivational factors were found to demonstrate the strongest correlations with FL proficiency.

Sparks and Ganschow (1991, 1995) have proposed an alternative view of the relationship between affect and FL aptitude in which they hypothesize that affective variables are related to students' levels of native language skills and FL aptitude. Since 1991, they have conducted empirical studies using the FL Classroom Anxiety Scale (FLCAS; Horwitz, Horwitz & Cope 1986) and the FL Reading Anxiety Scale (FLRAS; Saito, Garza & Horwitz 1999), all of which have found that students with higher levels of anxiety exhibit significantly lower levels of language learning skills and FL aptitude, and vice versa. Their findings have shown that items on the FLRAS and FLCAS are related to language learning and reading ability (Sparks & Ganschow 1991; Sparks, Ganschow & Javorsky 2000); individual differences in anxiety are strongly related to individual differences in native language skills, FL aptitude, and FL oral/written proficiency (Ganschow, et al. 1994; Ganschow & Sparks 1996; Sparks & Ganschow 1996; Sparks, Ganschow, Artzer, Siebenhar & Plageman 1997, 2004); individual differences in anxiety in high school are related to individual differences in native language skills several years *prior to* beginning FL courses (Sparks & Ganschow 2007; Sparks, Patton, Ganschow & Humbach 2009); individual differences in anxiety in high school explain unique variance in native language skills several years *prior to* beginning FL courses (Sparks & Patton 2013); individual differences in anxiety in high school explain growth in native language skills from $1^{st} - 5^{th}$ grades and growth in native language reading comprehension skills from $5^{th} - 10^{th}$ grades (Sparks & Patton 2013); individual differences in anxiety explain unique variance in the growth of FL word decoding, vocabulary, listening comprehension, spelling, and writing over three years of FL courses (Sparks, Luebbers, Casteñada & Patton 2018; Sparks, Patton & Luebbers 2018); and individual differences in anxiety explain unique variance in the growth of FL reading comprehension beyond that explained by FL word decoding, listening comprehension, and vocabulary (Sparks & Patton 2013, Sparks this volume). Sparks et al. maintain that affective characteristics are a confounding (third) variable in FL outcomes and that FL anxiety instruments like the FLCAS and FLRAS should *not* be related to individual differences in native language skills measured *prior to* FL learning, explain unique variance in native language skills measured *prior to* FL study, explain unique variance in FL aptitude, and explain the growth in FL skills over time. In empirical studies, anxiety instruments, including the FLCAS and FLRAS, have failed to meet any of the aforementioned criteria. Instead, it is likely that anxiety and other affective instruments are proxies for students' language learning ability and their (accurate) self-perceptions of their language learning ability.

Personality factors have been considered to be good candidates for predicting FL learning success. Personality variables in Snow's theory are mapped into five dimensions contained in his Five Factor Model: openness to experience, agreeableness, conscientiousness, extraversion/introversion, and neuroticism. These are distinct and universal factors that can be recognized in all societies and cultures of the world (Costa & McCrae 1992). Each of the five factors consists of a cluster of more specific traits that correlate with each other and constitutes a continuum with two extreme values (McCrae & Costa 2003). Because of its universality and reliability (Peabody & De Raad 2002), this model has been most often used for personality studies in SLA. As Dörnyei predicted: "current research is dominated by only two taxonomies focusing on personality traits, Eysenck's three-component construct [. . .] and the 'Big Five' model", and "At present, the Big Five is gaining momentum to the extent that it seems almost ubiquitous in the current literature" (2005, pp. 12–13). Nevertheless, eighteen years later, we still know very little about the role of personality in FL aptitude. Analyzing research from the last few years, statistical correlations between personality variables and FL achievement have often been disappointing and large discrepancies in results are also evident (Robinson & Ellis 2008). Among the five factors, openness to experience and extraversion are the most often studied by SLA researchers.

The most popular factor in SLA research is openness to experience, defined in terms of originality and flexibility, an appreciation for art, emotion, adventure, creation of unusual ideas, imagination, curiosity, and a variety of experiences. Openness includes a cognitive aspect, which means that people who score high on intelligence tests tend to display high levels of openness to new experiences and intellectual curiosity and flexibility as well as creativity (Corno et al. 2002; Shi, Dai & Lu 2016). Its correlation with verbal intelligence has been estimated at .30 (DeYoung, Quilty & Peterson 2007). According to the results of twin studies, openness is a relatively stable factor that is believed to have a strong genetic component, which explains 40–60% of its variance.

Forsberg Lundell & Sandgren (2013) examined the relationship between the production of collocations, FL aptitude, cultural empathy, and open-mindedness in late L2 French learners. The personality dimensions of cultural empathy and open-mindedness were significantly correlated with collocations and Llama D (phonetic memory) (Meara 2005). As the authors explained, both of these factors involve a cognitive capacity to adopt other people's perspectives and to be tolerant. Biedroń (2011a, 2012) conducted two studies examining openness to experience in gifted versus non-gifted FL learners and found that open-mindedness was higher in the gifted sample (this study is described in the next section).

Extraversion is connected with energy and enthusiasm, and the tendency to seek stimulation and the company of others. Intuitively, this factor may facilitate communicative activity but does not necessarily accompany high aptitude and its impact on FL learning success is unclear. Psychological studies consistently show extroverts' superiority over introverts on short-term and working memory tests (Lieberman 2000). Naiman, Fröhlich, Stern and Todesco (1978) found weak correlations between extraversion scores and FL measures based on written language. On the other hand, extraversion scores have been found to correlate positively with oral fluency measures in an L2, especially in stressful situations (Dewaele & Furnham 1999). Due to their risk-taking ability, extroverts are more willing to use colloquial and emotion words than introverts. Dewaele (2009) found negative, but statistically insignificant correlations between extroversion and FL course marks. The remaining three factors–*agreeableness, conscientiousness* and *neuroticism*–are even less investigated and little can be said about their alleged links to FL aptitude. Most likely, due to their generality, these three factors may interact with cognitive variables in learning a FL in a non-linear way, constituting complex, dynamic interactions and relationships that are difficult to study in quantitative analysis (Dörnyei 2005).

The most often investigated aptitude from the angle of personality factors is near-native pronunciation ability. An important role is attributed to empathy and openness to experience which have a significant impact on success in pronunciation learning (Hu et al. 2013; Rota & Reiterer 2009) and are highly correlated with language ability (Forsberg et al. 2013). Another vital factor in high attainment in FL pronunciation is motivation (Moyer 1999, 2014).

A study on phonetically talented L2 learners conducted by Hu and Reiterer (2009) provided interesting insights into the correlation between phonetic abilities and personality factors. Weak correlations were found between pronunciation talent and extraversion, openness to experience, or neuroticism, whilst a moderate positive correlation was detected for conscientiousness and agreeableness. These results were attributed to the separateness of phonetic aptitude, which does not require social capability, from other aptitudes affecting oral language (Hu & Reiterer 2009).

Moyer (1999, 2007) evaluated the phonological performance of twenty-four highly motivated, advanced FL learners of German whose L1 was English. She found that motivation and corrective feedback on suprasegmental errors accounted for most of the variance in the learners' attainment. Moyer admitted that although it is impossible to decide why some late learners are better at acquiring a native-like accent than others, certain personality factors and behaviours influence greater ultimate attainment. These individuals actively seek practice opportunities, ask for feedback, develop effective language learning strategies, and set learning goals. Affective and cognitive factors such as motivation, positive attitudes and satisfaction with attainment affect learning outcomes (Moyer 2007, 2013). Moreover, quality and quantity of instruction exert great influence on final attainment in pronunciation (Moyer 1999). According to Moyer (2014) the influence of factors traditionally considered important in acquiring perfect pronunciation, i.e., the age of onset and FL aptitude, is overstated. Socio-psychological variables such as identity, motivation, empathy, length of residence and contacts with native users are just as important as innate abilities. Although restrictions related to critical periods are a function of neurological changes, the principle of negative linear correlation of learning outcomes with age ceases to apply around the age of twelve, and the gradual deterioration of learning outcomes of the second language after this period depends on the aforementioned factors (see also Muñoz 2019).

Recent studies into personality factors and FL aptitude have also considered *self-efficacy* (Leisser 2018), and temperament and empathy (Rizvanović 2018). Leisser investigated 39 university students' self-efficacy related to the pronunciation of the near-open front unrounded [æ] and its correlation with their pronunciation quality. The study's results did not clarify the relationship as the participants with higher self-efficacy were perceived as less 'foreign' by native speakers of British English.

Empathy, which has recently attracted the attention of SLA researchers, refers to the ability "to tune into how someone else is feeling, or what they might be thinking" (Baron-Cohen & Wheelwright 2004, p. 193). Empathy is crucial in social interactions because it allows us to understand the intentions and emotions of others and predict their behavior. Guiora, Brannon and Dull (1972) suggested that empathy lays the foundations for language learning, as it involves an adoption of a new identity, which requires a degree of openness and flexibility. Apart from emotional empathy, cognitive empathy known as "empathic accuracy", is also recognized as important for language learning. According to Hodges and Myers (2007, p. 297), cognitive empathy denotes "having more complete and accurate knowledge about the contents of another person's mind, including how the person feels". Next to openness to experience, this factor is most often found to be a significant predictor of phonetic aptitude. Rizvanović (2018) focused on the correlation between LLAMA test scores and empathy, four types of temperament, the five personality traits, and motivation. This study found a negative correlation between extrinsic motivation and LLAMA E (sound-symbol correspondence) and LLAMA compound scores. As far as temperaments are concerned, phlegmatics outperformed other types of temperaments on the LLAMA B (vocabulary learning), D (phonetic memory), and E subtests. The results also suggest that there is a particularly strong correlation between openness and intrinsic motivation and between openness and cognitive empathy. Moreover, openness and intrinsic motivation were negatively influenced by neuroticism. Unlike Forsberg et al. (2013), Rizvanović found weak correlations between empathy and phonetic memory (LLAMA D) and empathy and sound-symbol correspondence (LLAMA E) (cf. Rota & Reiterer 2009). Also, weak correlations were found between conscientiousness and grammar inferencing (LLAMA F) and vocabulary learning (LLAMA B) scores.

When studying the history of tests developed for measuring language predispositions, we find a few attempts to include non-cognitive factors in the battery of tasks. One of the first tests of this type, the PLAB (Pimsleur 1966), contains a motivation component. This is the only test of FL aptitude that includes a factor other than purely cognitive ability. The latest Hi-Lab language aptitude test constructed by Catherine Doughty (Doughty et al. 2010; Doughty 2019) contained a boundary component, a learning style called *tolerance of ambiguity*, in its original version. Ambiguity tolerance is the ability to accept contradictory or incomplete input data in memory. This is an important feature in language learning because data that conflicts with the individual's knowledge may be crucial at a later stage of learning. Ultimately, the author of the test abandoned this factor and justified her decision by citing the high subjectivity of the measurement tool. The final version of the test of the Hi-Lab contains only purely cognitive components.

5.4 Affective factors and talent for language learning

Studies on language-talented individuals show that language learning abilities are most likely innate, but other factors like temperament, personality, motivation, and the environment determine success (see Biedroń & Pawlak 2016, for a review). Some researchers recognized the necessity of examining personality factors in high achievers (Bongaerts, Planken & Schils 1995; Bongaerts, van Summeren, Planken & Schils 1997). Bongaerts, Mennen and Van der Silk (2000) and Moyer (1999, 2007) tested highly motivated and advanced FL learners, who overlapped with native speaker controls with respect to their pronunciation skills. The researchers found that some specific personality factors might, in connection with exceptional aptitude, contribute to these outstanding FL abilities. In Moyer's study (2007) these factors included, for example, motivation, attitudes and satisfaction with attainment.

Biedroń (2011a) compared two groups of learners—44 talented students of foreign languages (very advanced multilinguals) and 37 students of English philology (level B1-B2) – in their personality factors using the five-factor model cited earlier. The instrument used to measure personality was a Polish adaptation (Zawadzki, Strelau, Szczepaniak & Śliwińska 1998) of the *Revised NEO-Five Factor Inventory*

(Costa & McCrae 1992). The results showed that openness to experience was much higher in talented than less talented students, but no statistically significant differences were found in the other four factors (neuroticism, agreeableness, extraversion and conscientiousness).

In another study with a larger population (44 talented FL learners and 82 English philology students), Biedroń (2012) found that openness as a differentiating factor turned out to be marginally significant; however, next to conscientiousness, openness was the dominant characteristic of people achieving significant successes in FLs. Although gifted L2 learners achieved the highest scores on openness and conscientiousness, these variables placed them in the average range. A high score on openness means that the subjects could be creative, imaginative, curious, flexible, novelty-seeking, untraditional, and interested in art, whereas a high score on conscientiousness indicates that they could be systematic, efficient, organized, responsible, reliable, persevering, and self-disciplined. All of these characteristics may exist in gifted L2 learners, but their level is moderately high. Moreover, no statistically significant differences in personality factors between the gifted and non-gifted L2 learners were observed, although both openness and conscientiousness were lower in the non-gifted sample. A regression analysis in which openness explained a small, but statistically significant part of the variance in FL aptitude confirmed the impact of this factor on language learning ability.

Additionally, in Biedroń's study (2012) the following psychological factors were tested in both groups: styles of coping with stress measured by the *Coping Inventory for Stressful Situations CISS* (Endler & Parker 1990), adapted by Szczepaniak, Strelau and Wrześniewski (1996); locus of control measured by *Delta Questionnaire* by Drwal (1995); emotional intelligence measured by *Emotional Intelligence Questionnaire INTE* by Schutte et al. (1998), a Polish adaptation by Ciechanowicz, Jaworska and Matczak (2000); and second language tolerance of ambiguity measured by *Second Language Tolerance of Ambiguity Scale* (Ely 1995). On the CISS questionnaire measuring styles of coping with stress, all of the participants' styles of coping fell within the average range; however, the task-oriented coping style dominated the participants' responses. Moreover, five subjects recorded over 70 points (high) on the task-oriented style, whereas none achieved such a high score on the avoiding and emotional-oriented styles. The task-oriented coping response is one that leads to problem resolution by purposeful confrontation, cognitive restructuring, or changing the situation, which suggests that gifted L2 learners do not avoid confrontation in a stressful situation, but try to constructively solve the problem. This method of problem-solving is connected with the controllability dimension, the subjectively perceived coping ability and the subjective perception of academic stress. By the same token, in the INTE questionnaire measuring emotional intelligence, the subjects' emotional intelligence (4.7) was average, according to the test's norm. The only extreme result was obtained in the Delta questionnaire measuring locus of control (Rotter 1966). Their mean score was 2.9 on a scale of 0 to 14. On this test, low scores (1–3) indicate the internality of control and high scores (8–10) externality of control. In this study, the participants were internally controlled, which means they tend to ascribe the results of their actions to themselves rather than to external, uncontrollable factors. Ambiguity tolerance was higher in the gifted sample and the difference with the non-gifted group was close to significant.

In Biedroń's study, an interesting tendency observed in the group of non-gifted L2 learners was a number of significant correlations between FL aptitude and personality factors and learning styles. For example, MLAT 1 and MLAT 5 correlated negatively with neuroticism ($r = -.32$) and ($r = -.34$), respectively; MLAT 2 with extraversion ($r = -.29$), whereas MLAT 5 correlated positively with conscientiousness ($r = .39$). One plausible interpretation is that, unlike FL aptitude in the gifted L2 learners, FL aptitude in the non-gifted L2 learners may be more affected by non-cognitive factors, that is, the level of performance on a test task may be mediated by certain personality characteristics. The subtests including the memory component (MLAT 1 and 5) were negatively affected by neuroticism, which is connected with negative affectivity and high anxiety levels. Multiple regression analyses revealed that among the psychological factors openness to experience, conscientiousness, extraversion, neuroticism, the task-oriented style of coping with stress, and tolerance of ambiguity were weak predictors of FL aptitude. However openness to experience, conscientiousness, the task-oriented style of coping with stress, and tolerance ambiguity were positively linked to FL aptitude, whilst extraversion and neuroticism were negatively linked to aptitude. Quantitative and qualitative analyses conducted by Biedroń (2012) showed that talented people are highly motivated, internally controlled and persistent in pursuing the goal, and consequently autonomous. In addition, their psychological profiles show high variation. It is likely that, according to giftedness theories (e.g. Gagné 2005), language talent develops according to a trajectory determined by the talent profile, temperament and personality traits, and environmental factors, whose unique combination results in successful learning.

Erard (2012, 2019) and Hyltenstam (2016, 2018) have conducted studies with polyglots, i.e., individuals achieving high levels of competence in several languages. On the basis of dozens of cases with both empirical and anecdotal data, a cognitive-affective profile of an individual with outstanding linguistic talent emerges. The polyglots themselves believe that they are good observers and followers not only of an accent but also of body language and behavior, which determines their high adaptability. When it comes to learning styles, polyglots seem to be guided by intuition as well as tend to systematize, which means that they choose to organize and categorize the material they absorb. They like patterns, discover rules, and both anticipate and look for exceptions. Their main character traits are self-confidence, motivation, perseverance, and diligence. Most likely, they have the ability to engage in a specific experience called *flow* (Csikszentmihalyi 1990) and actively look for this kind of experience. Flow is a state of self-forgetfulness experienced by people who reach their peak of ability or exceed their limits and involves experiencing spontaneous joy resulting from being completely absorbed in the activity in which they are involved.

One of the most important characteristics found to be associated with polyglots is high motivation (Hyltenstam 2016). Polyglots are very devoted to their passion, which often absorbs them completely and can be typical for talented people. Most polyglots are autodidacts, who are able to adapt to any type of teacher's course and style because they acquire the language themselves. Therefore, they are extremely inventive people who discover new techniques and methods to improve the efficiency of the language learning process. Polyglots also use a wide range of materials, including self-designed ones, to facilitate their learning of languages (see Erard 2012). Personality factors typical for polyglots include openness to experience, high adaptability, curiosity, creativity, confidence, discipline, perseverance, and diligence. They are also individuals with a high level of autonomy. Interestingly, Erard (2019) divided his subjects into two subgroups, one group (A) that claimed to have learned six or more languages and reported that learning languages was easier for them (n = 157) and another group (B) that reported knowing eleven and more languages (n = 17). He administered a survey to determine the respondents' attitude towards their aptitude, that is, the reason to which they attribute their ease of learning multiple languages. In group A, over 50 % selected their inner talent as a significant factor, 60% indicated motivation was important, and 90% reported "liking languages". These results were equal to or higher for the 11+ polyglots in group B. However, the respondents in group B chose factors unrelated directly to languages, e.g., family background, education, and intelligence, less frequently than group A. Moreover, the factor of effort was found to be more decisive by group B. In sum, hyperpolyglots tend to attribute their success to personality characteristics, and not only to cognitive traits or environmental factors.

Lastly, Susanne Reiterer (2019) reported the results of a number of studies conducted in the last decade in the field of phonetic and speech imitation aptitude. The studies revealed that both phonetically gifted children and adults manifest a number of psycho-cognitive characteristics, which include stronger singing abilities and general musicality, as well as auditory working memory. Two personality factors were also found to be important, namely openness to experience and empathy (cf. Forsberg et al. 2013).

5.5 Conclusions and pedagogical implications

Research into the role of psychological factors in FL aptitude shows that there are no systematic or consistent findings in this type of analysis. The dominant models and tests of FL aptitude do not take into account psychological factors, and many aptitude researchers assume that they are of marginal importance. In addition, there appears to be an increasing distance between qualitative research in the field of positive psychology and quantitative research in cognitive factors, which negatively affects the development of the field.

There is a clear need for more systematic research that explores relationships among psychological and cognitive variables. Likewise, there is a demonstrable need for studies with large populations. Most research to date has been conducted with small samples, which does not give a full picture of intercorrelations between large numbers of variables. There is also a need for qualitative or mixed, dynamic and longitudinal research (Serafini 2017), taking into account variability in time. A 'micro' approach that is focused on the investigation of poorly studied factors in different learning conditions could also increase the potential of answering important questions about the interplay of psychological and cognitive factors. The advent of neurological research in language research may hold the potential to add to our knowledge of individual differences in language learning.

Understanding the complex relationships between cognitive factors such as FL aptitude, which by their nature are not easily amenable to training, and factors susceptible to dynamic changes such as motivation, learning strategies, or language anxiety, has a significant didactic dimension. FL teachers equipped with professional knowledge could more effectively adapt the teaching method to a student's profile, focusing on what can be changed, e.g., learning strategies or beliefs, in line with the assumptions of positive psychology. But, it should also be borne in mind that certain traits, such as personality or temperament, are poorly modifiable, especially in a short time. In practice, this means that we cannot expect a full commitment to communicative activities from a taciturn and shy introvert. High motivation, contrary to conventional wisdom, is not a guarantee of success in language learning unless it is accompanied by a reasonable degree of effort and, at minimum, average language aptitude. Similarly, language anxiety could be the result of a student's overall low self-esteem but also self-awareness of his/her low level of language skills. In these situations, raising motivation and reducing anxiety will not alleviate the language learning problem. The same can be said about positive psychology. No amount of "positive thinking" will make up for low language abilities. Despite its popularity, proponents of positive psychology have not presented data showing that their methods increase language learning achievement. Nonetheless, it is important for the teacher to help students achieve as much success as they can in learning a language. Finally, the teacher's active participation in creating a friendly atmosphere in the classroom may stimulate more positive emotions in students, which could increase their motivation to learn.

Recommended Readings

Reiterer, Susanne M. 2018. *Exploring language aptitude: Views from psychology, the language sciences, and cognitive neuroscience*. Springer- Nature.
    The chapters in this volume were mostly based on the research work by Susanne Reiterer and her colleagues in their investigation of individual difference factors such as working memory, intelligence, personality, self-concept, bilingualism and multilingualism, education, musicality, and gender. As its subtitle indicates, a distinctive feature of the volume is its multidisciplinary perspectives.

Biedroń, Adriana. 2011. Personality factors as predictors of foreign language aptitude. *Studies in Second Language Learning and Teaching, 1(4)*, 467–489.
    The study addresses personality predictors of foreign language aptitude. Specifically, it focuses on the Five Factor model, which includes Openness to Experience, Conscientiousness, Extraversion, Agreeableness, and Neuroticism traits differentiating gifted and non-gifted foreign language learners.

Biedroń, Adriana & Mirosław Pawlak. 2016. New conceptualizations of linguistic giftedness. *Language Teaching 49/2*, 151–185.
    This state-of-the-art paper focuses on the issue of linguistic giftedness, somewhat neglected in the SLA literature, and attempts to reconceptualize, expand, and update this concept in response to the latest developments in the fields of psychology, linguistics, and neurology.

References

Arnold, Jane & Henry D. Brown. 1999. A map of the terrain. In Jane Arnold (ed.), *Affect in language learning*, 1–25. Cambridge: Cambridge University Press.

Baron-Cohen, Simon & Sally Wheelwright. 2004. The Empathy quotient: An investigation of adults with Asperger syndrome or high functioning autism, and normal sex differences. *Journal of Autism and Developmental Disorders, 34*, 163–175.

Berghorst, Lisa H., Ryan Bogdan, Michael J. Frank & Diego A. Pizzagalli. 2013. Acute stress selectively reduces reward sensitivity. *Frontiers in Human Neuroscience, 7*, 133.

Biedroń, Adriana. 2011a. Personality factors as predictors of FL aptitude. *Studies in Second Language Learning and Teaching, 1(4)*, 467–489.

Biedroń, Adriana. 2011b. Near-nativeness as a function of cognitive and personality factors. Three case studies of highly able FL learners. In Mirosław Pawlak, Ewa Waniek-Klimczak & Jan Majer (eds.), *Speaking in contexts of instructed FL acquisition*, 99–116. Clevedon: Multilingual Matters.

Biedroń, Adriana. 2012. *Cognitive-affective profile of gifted adult FL learners*. Słupsk: Wydawnictwo Naukowe Akademii Pomorskiej w Słupsku.

Biedroń, Adriana. 2019. Language aptitude: Insights from L2 exceptional learners. In Zhisheng Wen, Peter Skehan, Adriana Biedroń, Shaofeng Li & Richard Sparks (eds.), *Language aptitude: Advancing theory, testing, research and practice*,168–184. New York/ London: Routledge.

Biedroń, Adriana & Mirosław Pawlak. 2016. New conceptualizations of linguistic giftedness. *Language Teaching, 49(2)*, 151–185.

Bongaerts, Theo, Susan Mennen & Frans Van der Silk. 2000. Authenticity of pronunciation in naturalistic second language acquisition. The case of very advanced late learners of Dutch as a second language. *Studia Linguistica, 54*, 298–308.

Bongaerts, Theo, Brigitte Planken & Erik Schils. 1995. Can late starters attain a native accent in a foreign language? A test of the Critical Period Hypothesis. In David Singleton & Zsolt Lengyel (eds.), *The age factor in second language acquisition*, 30–50. Clevedon: Multilingual Matters.

Bongaerts, Theo, Chantai van Summeren, Brigitte Planken & Erik Schils. 1997. Age and ultimate attainment in the pronunciation of a foreign language. *Studies in Second Language Acquisition, 19*, 447–465.

Carroll, John B. & Stanley M. Sapon. 1959/2002. *Modern Language Aptitude Test (MLAT)*. New York, NY: The Psychological Corporation.

Ciechanowicz, Anna, Aleksandra Jaworowska & Anna Matczak. 2000. *Kwestionariusz Inteligencji Emocjonalnej INTE. Podręcznik [Emotional Intelligence questionnaire INTE. Manual]*. Warszawa: Pracownia Testów Psychologicznych PTP.

Clarke, Robert & Tom Johnstone. 2013. Prefrontal inhibition of threat processing reduces working memory interference. *Frontiers in Human Neuroscience, 7*, 228.

Clore, Gerald L., Alexander J. Schiller & Adi Shaked. 2018. Affect and cognition: three principles. *Current Opinion in Behavioural Sciences,19*, 78–82.

Corno, Lyn, Lee J. Cronbach, Haggai Kupermintz, David F. Lohman, Ellen B. Mandinach, Ann W. Porteus & Joan E. Talbert. 2002. *Remaking the concept of aptitude: Extending the legacy of Richard E. Snow*. Mahwah, NJ: Lawrence Erlbaum.

Costa Paul T. Jr. & Robert R. McCrae. 1992. *Revised NEO Personality Inventory (NEO-PI-R) and NEO Five-Factor Inventory (NEO-FFI). Manual*. Odessa, FL: Psychological Assessment Resources.

Csikszentmihalyi, Mihály. 1990. *Flow. The psychology of optimal experience*. New York: Harper Perennial.

Damasio, Antonio. 1994. *Descartes' error: Emotion, reason and the human brain*. New York, NY: Avon.

De Bot, Kees & Szilvia Bátyi, S. 2017. Editorial. *Studies in Second Language Learning and Teaching, 7(1)*, 13–17.

DeYoung, Colin G., Lena C. Quilty & Jordan B. Peterson. 2007. Between facets and domains: 10 aspects of the Big Five. *Journal of Personality and Social Psychology, 93*, 880–896.

Dewaele, Jean-Marc. 2009. Individual differences in second language acquisition. In William C. Ritchie & Tej K. Bhatia. (eds.), *The new handbook of second language acquisition*, 323–346. Bingley, United Kingdom: Emerald.

Dewaele, Jean-Marc & Adrian Furnham. 1999. Extraversion: The unloved variable in applied linguistic research. *Language Learning, 49*, 509–544

Dewaele, Jean-Marc, Konstantinos V. Petrides & Adrian Furnham. 2008. Effects of trait Emotional Intelligence and sociobiographical variables on communicative anxiety and FL anxiety among adult multilinguals. A review and empirical investigation. *Language Learning, 58(4)*, 911–960.

Dewaele, Jean-Marc & Mateb Alfawzan. 2018. Does the effect of enjoyment outweigh that of anxiety in FL performance? *Studies in Second Language Learning and Teaching, 8(1)*, 21–45.

Dewaele, Jean-Marc & Chengchen Li. 2018. Editorial. *Studies in Second Language Learning and Teaching, 8(1)*,15-19.
Doughty, Catherine J. (2019). Cognitive Language Aptitude. *Language Learning, 69(S1)*, 101-126.
Doughty, Catherine J., Susan G. Campbell, Meredith A. Mislevy, Michael M. Bunting, Anita R. Bowles & Joel T. Koeth. 2010. Predicting near-native ability: The factor structure and reliability of HiLab. In Matthew T.Prior, Yukiko Watanabe & Sang-Ki Lee (eds.), *Selected proceedings of the 2008 Second Language Research Forum*, 10-31. Somerville, MA: Cascadilla Proceedings Project. Retrieved from www.lingref.com, document #2382
Dörnyei, Zoltan. 2005. *The psychology of the language learner*. Mahwah, NJ: Lawrence Erlbaum.
Dörnyei, Zoltan. 2009. *The psychology of second language acquisition*. Oxford: Oxford University Press.
Dörnyei, Zoltan. 2010. The relationship between language aptitude and language learning motivation: Individual differences from a dynamic systems perspective. In Ernesto Macaro (ed.), *Continuum companion to second language acquisition*, 247-267. London: Continuum.
Dörnyei, Zoltan & Stephen Ryan. 2015. *The psychology of the language learner revisited*. New York, London: Routledge.
Drwal, Radosław Ł. 1995. Adaptacja kwestionariuszy osobowości. *Wybrane techniki i zagadnienia [Adaptation of personality questionnaires. Selected techniques and issues]*. Warszawa: Wydawnictwo Naukowe PWN.
Ehrman, Madline E. 2008. Personality and good language learners. In Carol Griffiths (ed.), *Lessons from good language learners*, 83-99. Cambridge: Cambridge University Press.
Ehrman, Madline E. & Rebeca L. Oxford. 1995. Cognition plus: correlates of language learning success. *Modern Language Journal, 7(1)*, 67-89.
Ely, Christopher M. 1995. Second language tolerance of ambiguity scale. In Joy Reid (ed.), *Learning styles in EFL/ESL classroom*, 2167-217. Boston, MA: Heinle & Heinle/Thomson International.
Endler, Norman S. & James D. Parker. 1990. *Coping inventory for stressful situations (CISS)*. Manual. Toronto: Multi-Health Systems.
Erard, Michael. 2012. *Babel no more. In search for the world's most extraordinary language learners*. New York, NY: Free Press.
Erard, Michael. 2019. Language aptitude: Insights from hyperpolyglots. In Zhisheng Wen, Peter Skehan, Adriana Biedroń, Shaofeng Li & Richard Sparks (eds.), *Language aptitude: Advancing theory, testing, research and practice*, 153-168. New York/ London: Routledge.
Fein, Deborah & Loraine K. Obler. 1988. Neuropsychological study of talent: A developing field. In Loraine K. Obler & Deborah Fein (eds.), *The exceptional brain*, 3-15. New York, London: The Guilford Press,
Forsberg Lundell, Fanny & Maria Sandgren. 2013. High-level proficiency in late L2 acquisition: Relationships between collocational production, language aptitude and personality. In Gisela Granena & Michael H. Long (eds.), *Sensitive periods, language aptitude, and ultimate L2 attainment*, 231-255. Amsterdam: John Benjamins.
Gagné, Françoys. 2005. From gifts to talents: The DGMT as a developmental model. In Robert, J. Sternberg & Janet E. Davidson (eds.), *Conceptions of giftedness*, 98-120. New York, NY: Cambridge University Press.
Ganschow, Leonore & Richard Sparks. 1996. FL anxiety among high school women. *Modern Language Journal, 80*, 199-212.
Ganschow, Leonore, Richard L. Sparks, Reed Anderson, James Javorsky, Sue Skinner & Jon Patton. 1994. Differences in anxiety and language performance among high, average, and low anxious college FL learners. *Modern Language Journal, 78*, 41-55.

Gregersen, Tammy & Peter D. MacIntyre. 2014. *Capitalizing on language learners' individuality. From premise to practice*. Bristol: Multilingual Matters.

Griffiths, Carol (ed.). 2008. *Lessons from good language learners*. Cambridge: Cambridge University Press.

Guiora, Alexander Z., Robert C. L. Brannon & Cecelia Y. Dull. 1972. Empathy and second language learning. *Language Learning*, *22*, 111–130.

Hodges, Sara D. & Michael W. Myers. 2007. Empathy. In Roy F. Baumeister & Kathleen D. Vohs (eds.), *Encyclopedia of social psychology*, 296–298. Thousand Oaks, CA: Sage.

Holtmann, Jana, Maike C. Herbort, Torsten Wüstenberg, Joram Soch, Sylvia Richter, Henrik Walter, Stefan Roepke & Björn H. Schott. 2013. Trait anxiety modulates fronto-limbic processing of emotional interference in borderline personality disorder. *Frontiers in Human Neuroscience*, *7*, 54.

Horwitz, Elaine, Michael Horwitz & Joann Cope. 1986. FL classroom anxiety. *Modern Language Journal*, *70*, 125–132.

Hu, Xiaochen, Hermann Ackermann, Jason A. Martin, Michael Erb, Susanne Winkler & Susanne M. Reiterer. 2013. Language aptitude for pronunciation in advanced second language (L2) Learners: Behavioural predictors and neural substrates. *Brain and Language 127 (3)*, 366–376.

Hu, Xiaochen & Susanne M. Reiterer. 2009. Personality and pronunciation talent in second language acquisition. In Grzegorz Dogil & Susanne M. Reiterer (eds.), *Language talent and brain activity. Trends in applied linguistics*, 97–130. Berlin, New York, NY: Mouton de Gruyter.

Hyltenstam, Kenneth. (ed.). (2016). *Advanced proficiency and exceptional ability in second language*. Boston/Berlin: Mouton de Gruyter.

Hyltenstam, Kenneth. 2018. Polyglotism: A synergy of abilities and predispositions. In Kenneth Hyltenstam, Inge Bartning & Lars Fant (eds.), *High-level language proficiency in second language and multilingual contexts*, 170–196. Cambridge: Cambridge University Press.

Iordan, Alexandru D., Sanda Dolcos & Florin Dolcos. 2013. Neural signatures of the response to emotional distraction: a review of evidence from brain imaging investigations. *Frontiers in Human Neuroscience*, *7*, 200.

Kalanthroff, Eyal, Noga Cohen & Avishai Henik. 2013. Stop feeling: inhibition of emotional interference following stop-signal trials. *Frontiers in Human Neuroscience*, *7*, 78.

LeDoux, Joseph. 1996. *The emotional brain*. New York, NY: Simon & Schuster.

Leisser, Daniel. 2018. On the role of self-efficacy as a possible component of language aptitude in the acquisition of British [æ]. In Susanne M. Reiterer, (ed.), *Exploring language aptitude: Views from psychology, the language sciences, and cognitive neuroscience*, 75–101. Cham, Switzerland: Springer.

Larsen-Freeman, Diane & Lynne Cameron. 2008. Research methodology on language development from a complex system perspective. *Modern Language Journal*, *92(2)*, 200–213

Lieberman, Matthew D. 2000. Introversion and working memory: Central executive differences. *Personality and Individual Differences*, *28*, 479–486.

Long, Michael H. 2013. Maturational constraints on child and adult SLA. In Gisela Granena & Michael H. Long (eds.), *Sensitive periods, language aptitude, and ultimate L2 attainment*, 3–41. Amsterdam: John Benjamins.

Lowie Wander, Marijn van Dijk, Huiping Chan & Marjolijn Verspoor. 2017. Finding the key to successful L2 learning in groups and individuals. *Studies in Second Language Learning and Teaching*, *7(1)*, 127–148.

MacIntyre, Peter D., Tammy Gregersen & Sarah Mercer. 2016. *Positive psychology in SLA*. Bristol: Multilingual Matters.

Mahmoodzadeh, Masoud & Gholam H. Khajavy. 2019. Towards conceptualizing language learning curiosity in SLA: An empirical study. *Journal of Psycholinguistic Research, 48,* 333–351.

McCrae Robert & Paul Costa. 2003. *Personality in adulthood: A five-factor theory perspective* (2nd ed.). New York: Guilford Press.

Meara, Paul. 2005. Llama Language aptitude test. Swansea: Lognostics. Retrieved from http://www.lognostics.co.uk/tools/llama/llama_manual.pdf

Miller, Alistair. 2008. A critique of positive psychology – or 'the new science of happiness'. *Journal of Philosophy of Education 42,* 591–608.

Moyer, Alene. 1999. Ultimate attainment in L2 phonology. *Studies in Second Language Acquisition, 21,* 81–108.

Moyer, Alene. 2007. Empirical considerations on the age factor in L2 phonology. *Issues in Applied Linguistics, 15(2),* 109–127.

Moyer, Alene. 2013. *Accent and the individual – foreign accent – the phenomenon of non-native speech.* Cambridge. Cambridge University Press.

Moyer, Alene. 2014. What's age got to do with it? Accounting for individual factors in second language accent. *Studies in Second Language Learning and Teaching. Special issue: Age and more, 4(3),* 443–464.

Myers, Isabel B. & Kathrine Briggs. 1976. *The Myers Briggs type indicator.* Farm G. Palo Alto, CA: Consulting Psychologists Press.

Muñoz, Carmen. 2019. A new look at "age": Young and old L2 learners. In John Schwieter & Alessandro Benati (eds.), *The Cambridge handbook of language learning (Cambridge handbooks in language and linguistics,* pp. 430–450. Cambridge: Cambridge University Press.

Naiman, Neil, Maria Fröhlich, Heiko H. Stern & Angie Todesco. 1978. *The good language learner.* Toronto: Ontario Institute for Studies in Education.

Okon-Singer, Hadas, Talma Hendler, Luiz Pessoa & Alexander J. Shackman. 2015. The neurobiology of emotion-cognition interactions: fundamental questions and strategies for future research. *Frontiers in Human Neuroscience, 9,* 58.

Oxford, Rebeca & Christina Gkonou. 2018. Interwoven: Culture, language, and learning strategies. *Studies in Second Language Learning and Teaching, 8(2),* 403–426.

Pavelescu, Liana M. & Bojana Petrić. 2018. Love and enjoyment in context: Four case studies of adolescent EFL learners. *Studies in Second Language Learning and Teaching, 8(1),* 73–101.

Pawlak, Mirosław & Adriana Biedroń. 2019. Verbal working memory as a predictor of explicit and implicit knowledge of English passive voice. *Journal of Second Language Studies, 2 (2). Special issue: Aptitude-treatment interaction in second language learning.* 276–299.

Peabody, Dean & Boele De Raad. 2002. The substantive nature of psycholexical personality factors: A comparison across languages. *Journal of Personality and Social Psychology, 83(4),* 983–997.

Phillips, Anthony G., Giada Vacca & Soyon Ahn. 2008. A top-down perspective on dopamine, motivation and memory. *Pharmacology Biochemistry and Behavior, 90(2),*236–49.

Pimsleur, Paul. 1966. *Pimsleur Language Aptitude Battery.* New York, NY: Harcourt Brace Jovanovich.

Reiterer, Susanne M. 2018. (ed.). *Exploring language aptitude: Views from psychology, the language sciences, and cognitive neuroscience.* Cham, Switzerland: Springer.

Reiterer, Susanne M. 2019. Neuro-psycho-cognitive markers for pronunciation/ speech imitation as language aptitude. In Zhisheng Wen, Peter Skehan, Adriana Biedroń, Shaofeng Li & Richard Sparks (eds.), *Languag(e aptitude: Advancing theory, testing, research and practice,* 277–279. New York/ London: Routledge.

Rizvanović, Nejra. 2018. Motivation and personality in language aptitude. In Susanne M.Reiterer (ed.), *Exploring language aptitude: Views from psychology, the language sciences, and cognitive neuroscience*, 101–119. Cham, Switzerland: Springer.

Robinson, Peter. 2002. Learning conditions, aptitude complexes and SLA: A framework for research and pedagogy. In Peter Robinson (ed.), *Individual differences and instructed language learning*, 113–133. Philadelphia, PA: John Benjamins.

Robinson, Peter & Nick C. Ellis. 2008. Conclusion: Cognitive linguistics, second language acquisition and L2 instruction – issues for research. In Peter Robinson & Nick C. Ellis (eds.), *Handbook of cognitive linguistics and second language acquisition*, 489–545. New York and London: Routledge.

Rota, Giuseppina & Susanne M. Reiterer. 2009. Cognitive aspects of pronunciation talent. In Grzegorz Dogil & Susanne M. Reiterer (eds.), *Language talent and brain activity*, 67–112. Berlin: Mouton de Gruyter.

Rotter, Julian B. 1966. Generalized expectancies of internal versus external control of reinforcements. *Psychological Monographs, 80(609)*, 1–28.

Saito Yoshiko, Thomas J. Garza & Elaine K. Horwitz. 1999. FL reading anxiety. *Modern Language Journal, 83(2)*, 202–218.

Schumann, John H. 2004. The neurobiology of aptitude. In John Schumann (ed.), *The neurobiology of learning: Perspectives from second language acquisition*,7–23. Mahwah, NJ: Lawrence Erlbaum.

Schutte, Nicola S., John M. Malouff, Lena E. Hall, Donald J. Haggerty, Joan T. Cooper, Charles J. Golden & Liane Dornheim. 1998. Development and validation of a measure of emotional intelligence. *Personality and Individual Differences, 25*, 167–177.

Serafini, Ellen J. 2017. Exploring the dynamic long-term interaction between cognitive and psychosocial resources in adult second language development at varying proficiency *The Modern Language Journal, 101*, 369–390.

Shackman, Alexander J. & Tor D. Wager. 2019. The emotional brain: Fundamental questions and strategies for future research. *Neuroscience Letters, 693*, 68–74.

Shi, Baoguo, David Yun Dai & Yongli Lu. 2016. Openness to experience as a moderator of the relationship between intelligence and creative thinking: A study of Chinese children in urban and rural areas. *Frontiers in Psychology, 7*, 641.

Singal, Jesse. 2021. *The quick fix: Why fad psychology can't cure our social ills*. New York: Farrar, Straus and Giroux.

Snow, Richard E. 1987. Aptitude complexes. In Richard E. Snow & Marshall Farr (eds.). *Aptitude, learning and instruction, cognitive process analyses of aptitude* (Vol. 3), 11–34. Hillsdale, NJ: Erlbaum Associates.

Snow, Richard E. 1994. Abilities in academic tasks. In Robert J. Sternberg & Richard K. Wagner (eds.), *Mind in context: Interactionist perspectives on human intelligence*, 3–37. New York, NY: Cambridge University Press.

Sparks, Richard L. & Leonore Ganschow. 1991. FL learning differences: Affective or native language aptitude differences? *Modern Language Journal, 75(1)*, 3–16.

Sparks, Richard L. & Leonore Ganschow. 1995. A strong inference approach to causal factors in FL learning: A response to MacIntyre. *Modern Language Journal, 79(2)*, 235–244.

Sparks, Richard L. & Leonore Ganschow. 1996. Teachers' perceptions of students' FL skills and affective characteristics. *Journal of Educational Research, 89*, 172–185.

Sparks, Richard L. & Leonore Ganschow. 2007. Is the FL Classroom Anxiety Scale measuring anxiety or language skills? *FL Annals, 40*, 260–287.

Sparks, Richard L., Leonore Ganschow, Jon Patton, Marjorie Artzer, David Siebenhar & Mark Plageman. 1997. Language anxiety and proficiency in a foreign language. *Perceptual and Motor Skills, 85(2)*, 559-562.
Sparks, Richard L., Leonore Ganschow, Marjorie Artzer, David Siebenhar & Mark Plageman. 2004. FL teachers' perceptions of students' academic skills, affective characteristics, and proficiency: Replication and follow-up studies. *FL Annals, 37*, 263-278.
Sparks, Richard L., Leonore Ganschow & James Javorsky. 2000. Déjà vu all over again: A response to Saito, Horwitz, and Garza. *Modern Language Journal, 84(2)*, 251-255.
Sparks, Richard L., Julie Luebbers, Martha Casteñada & Jon Patton. 2018. U.S. high school students and FL reading anxiety: Déjà vu all over again all over again. *Modern Language Journal, 102(3)*, 533-556.
Sparks, Richard L. & Jon Patton. 2013. Relationship of L1 skills and L2 aptitude to L2 anxiety on the FL Classroom Anxiety Scale. *Language Learning, 63(4)*, 870-895.
Sparks, Richard L., Jon Patton, Leonore Ganschow & Nancy Humbach. 2009. Long-term relationships among early first language skills, second language aptitude, second language affect, and later second language proficiency. *Applied Psycholinguistics, 30(4)*, 725-755.
Sparks, Richard L., Jon Patton & Julie Luebbers. 2018. L2 anxiety and the FL Reading Anxiety Scale (FLRAS): Listening to the evidence. *FL Annals, 51*, 1-25.
Szczepaniak, Piotr, Jan Strelau, J. & Kazimierz Wrześniewski. 1996. Diagnoza stylów radzenia sobie ze stresem za pomocą polskiej wersji kwestionariusza CISS Endlera i Parkera [The assessment of styles of coping with stress by means of the Polish version of Endler and Parker's CISS inventory]. *Przegląd Psychologiczny, 1*, 187-210.
Van Dessel, Pieter & Julia Vogt. 2012. When does hearing laughter draw attention to happy faces? Task relevance determines the influence of a crossmodal affective context on emotional attention. *Frontiers in Human Neuroscience, 6*, 294.
Wong, Patrick, Kara Morgan-Short, Marc Ettlinger & Jing Zheng. 2012. Linking neurogenetics and individual differences in language learning: The dopamine hypothesis. *Cortex, 48*, 1091-1102.
Zawadzki, Bogdan, Jan Strelau, Piotr Szczepaniak & Magdalena Śliwińska. 1998. *Test osobowości NEO FFI. Podręcznik [NEO FFI personality inventory. Manual]*. Warszawa: Pracownia Testów Psychologicznych PTP.
Zychowicz, Katarzyna, Adriana Biedroń & Mirosław Pawlak. 2017. Polish Listening Span: A new tool for measuring verbal working memory. *Studies in Second Language Learning and Teaching, 7*, 601-618.

Part II: **Memory, Attention and Noticing**

6 Phonological and Executive Working Memory

Zhisheng (Edward) Wen

Abstract: Working memory (WM) is our cognitive ability to simultaneously maintain and manipulate a limited amount of information in our brain to complete some mental tasks. This chapter explores its role in second language learning, processing and long-term proficiency development. Toward this goal, it will first provide an overview of major theoretical perspectives and models of WM in cognitive psychology and neuroscience that have been applied and implemented in current SLA/bilingualism research. These culminate in an integrated account of WM conception and assessment procedures in language and SLA research. In addition, the chapter also calls for a paradigm shift in future WM-SLA research from the current focus on examining WM components to exploring finer-grain WM and executive functions and subprocesses through more ecologically valid assessment procedures. Theoretical and pedagogical implications for L2 pedagogy and instructional design are also discussed.

Keywords: working memory, attention control, executive functions, the multi-component model, the embedded-processes model, the phonological/executive model, WM-SLA nexus

6.1 Introduction

The concept of working memory (WM) is believed to have first appeared in the book by Miller, Galanter & Pribram (1960). The term distinguishes itself from the much-older sister terms of short-term memory (STM) and long-term memory (LTM). WM is best understood not just as a memory store but as the *limited cognitive capacity* that allows us to temporarily store and manipulate a small amount of information in our immediate consciousness in the service of completing some mental tasks (Baddeley 1986; Cowan 2005). Examples of WM functioning abound in our daily life. WM is at work when we keep dialing telephone numbers from our memory or when we are calculating the results of arithmetic equations mentally (Baddeley 2003, 2018; Carruthers 2013, 2015). It may sometimes seem paradoxical that despite its limited capacity in maintaining and processing information, WM could exert such pervasive effects and consequences in essential facets of human cognition (Carruthers 2015), and is said to constitute 'the hub of cognition' (Haberlandt 2007).

The ever-growing body of theoretical and empirical investigations into the concept of WM and its potential effects on human cognition has subsequently given rise to multiple theoretical perspectives and more than a dozen WM models (Miyake and Shah 1999; Logie, Camos, and Cowan 2021; Schwieter and Wen 2022; Wen et al. 2022). Among the multiple sub-disciplines of cognitive sciences (such as those identified in the hexagon by Miller, 2003) that have all shown intense interest in the concept of WM, the three central pillar domains of psychology, linguistics, and neuroscience have all been involved since its inception (Baddeley 2021, 2022). WM-inspired research in language has spanned across all key domains not just in native or first language (Gathercole and Baddeley 1993; Baddeley 2003), but also made inroads into second or additional language acquisition and processing (Schwieter and Wen 2022; Wen 2016; Wen, Mota, and McNeill 2015). The results of empirical studies have converged to show positive, albeit moderate, overall WM effects on L2 learning processes and outcomes (Linck et al. 2014; see also Wen and Li 2019). Recent studies have also pointed to the bilingual, multilingual, or cross-linguistic effects of an enhanced WM capacity (Grundy and Timmer 2017). Despite increasing sophistication in cognitive psychology regarding WM conceptualizations, the construct has not been adequately implemented and measured in language sciences and SLA until recently (Bunting and Wen 2022; Wen 2012, 2016; Wen and Schwieter 2022).

To reflect on these latest developments in WM conceptions and measurement and to further explore their theoretical and pedagogical implications for nuanced SLA and bilingualism research, the present chapter will first review major theoretical perspectives and models of WM in cognitive psychology and neuroscience. Then, the next section will depict the popular assessment procedures of WM from cognitive psychology and neuroscience that have been widely adopted in current SLA/bilingualism research. Such reviews culminate in a reconceptualization of the WM construct in language and SLA research, augmented with general guidelines and practical tips for assessment procedures. Overall, it is hoped that future WM-SLA research and practice will benefit from these integrated reviews. Following the developments in cognitive psychology and neuroscience, the chapter also calls for future WM-SLA studies to gradually shift the current focus from examining WM components to investigating the finer-grained WM functions and subprocesses with more ecologically valid assessment procedures. The ultimate goal is to tap into the underlying WM mechanisms and to explain how WM has evolved into a 'language learning device' (Baddeley et al. 1998; Lu and Wen 2022) that constrains and shapes first and second language evolution, acquisition, processing, and development. The future of WM-SLA will hinge on its pedagogical implications for L2 pedagogy and instructional design.

6.2 Theoretical Perspectives and Models

The Seminal Multi-component Model

Since its inception in the early 1960s, the concept of WM has garnered enormous attention that has been boosted significantly by the WM research team led by Alan Baddeley and his colleagues at the Medical Research Center (MRC) at Cambridge University (Baddeley 2018). These early-day efforts led to the seminal tri-partite WM model by Baddeley and Hitch (1974), the classic model that continues to serve as the standard representation inspiring all ensuing research into WM in related fields of psychology, linguistics, neuroscience, and beyond. In this classic model, also known as the structural or multi-component model (sometimes nicknamed the M-model), the construct of WM is fractionated into two modality-specific buffer components plus a supervisory attentional system, i.e., the central executive (Baddeley 1986). The two buffer stores include the phonological loop that deals with sound-based information from the input or during the output of information (see Baddeley and Hitch 2019 for an updated review) and the visuo-spatial sketchpad, or scratchpad, which processes visual and spatial information. Cognitive resources allocated between these two specific storage buffers are coordinated and regulated by a supervisory attentional system, i.e., the central executive (See Baddeley, Hitch, and Allen 2019, 2021 for updated reviews).

Later, to accommodate the storage of information from other modalities not yet accounted for by the original tri-partite model, Baddeley (2000) added a fourth component to the model, i.e., the episodic buffer, which serves to integrate all information into multimodal episodes interacting with long-term memory (LTM). As Baddeley later emphasized (2012, 2022), the episodic buffer has brought the multicomponent model closer to the more recent embedded processes model developed by Cowan (1999), thus narrowing the differences between the two key models that are widely cited in language and SLA research.

Alternative WM Models and Controversies

Starting in the 1980s, researchers from multiple subdisciplines of cognitive science have also investigated the nature of WM functions and applications and the implications for human cognition. Intensive research endeavors from diverse research camps have led to the propagation of a dozen other 'alternative' models of WM (Logie, Camos, and Cowan 2021; Miyake and Shah 1999; Schwieter and Wen 2022). Besides Baddeley's classic model (2015) which is actively pursued in language sciences and SLA research, several other WM models are also making their way into first and second language acquisition and processing research (Schwieter and Wen 2022). These WM models include, among others, the long-term WM model (Ericsson and Kinstch 1995) which emphasizes the importance of long-term knowledge structure and its retrieval mechanism, thus having implications for reading comprehension (Adams and Delaney 2022). Another model that has gained increasing credence among SLA researchers is Cowan's embedded processes model (1999, 2022), which conceptualizes WM as the limited-capacity 'focus of attention' within the broader activated long-term memory. Finally, the executive or attention control view developed by Engle and colleagues (Engle 2002, 2018; Burgoyne and Engle 2020) has also inspired investigations in language and bilingual processing (e.g., Dong and Li 2020).

On the one hand, controversies and debates remain among these diverse theoretical models of WM including its definition, the source of its limited capacity, the degree of modularity, the role of attention, and the relationship with long-term memory (e.g., Baddeley 2012; Cowan 2017; Adams et al. 2018). On the other hand, despite these seemingly disparate discrepancies, there are commonalities and agreements between the WM models and research camps (Miyake and Shah 2021). Recent years have begun to witness some concerted efforts among different WM theorists to negotiate generally agreed-upon benchmarks for understanding and conceptualizing the WM construct that transcends diverse perspectives and models (Oberauer et al. 2018). To that effect, the recent 'adversary collaboration' project involving three WM laboratories across the UK, Europe, and the US has produced encouraging results (Logie et al. 2021). These efforts can serve as a good example for further collaboration among WM camps in multiple disciplines working towards the common goal of understanding and applying WM theories and implications for human cognition.

Unifying characterizations of WM

Drawing on these converging insights, general characterizations of the WM construct can be tentatively identified in the hope of accommodating its defining features across the theoretical camps and research paradigms (see also Wen and Schwieter 2022; cf. Logie et al. 2021). The most important characterization, WM has *limited capacity*, remains a central insight though its underlying source and its manifestations of *flexibility* remain controversial and elusive (e.g., Conway et al. 2007; Bochacourt and Buschman 2019; Kruijne et al. 2021). The limitations of WM represent the signature feature of the WM construct (Carruthers 2013), distinguishing itself from long-term memory. Notwithstanding, the flexibility of WM comes in many forms (Cowan 1999). For example, one form can refer to the limited mental storage capacity of units that can be held in our mind consciously, which normally range between 4 to 7 units, based on Miller's (1956) original projection and Cowan's recent ramifications (2001). Such limitations can also refer to the short-lived traces left in our consciousness, which normally last between 2 to 15 seconds (unless rehearsed purposefully). These WM limitations are akin to the so-called *now-or-never* bottleneck effects in human cognition (Christiansen and Chater 2016). Though the underlying source and manifestations of the limited WM capacity are still debatable (Conway et al. 2007), such limitations are purported to play a fundamental role in constraining and shaping language design and processing as well as permeating and impacting multiple levels of linguistic domains to varying degrees, ranging from phonological, morphological, syntactic and discourse complexities and processing (Chafe 1994; O'Grady 2017; Lu and Wen 2022).

The latest development in conceptualizing WM is Engle and colleagues' reinforced interpretation of their early executive attention view (Engle 2002; Kane and Engle 2004; Von Bastian et al. 2020), which has now gradually given way to the emerging construct of *attention control* as the cornerstone of high-level cognition (Burgoyne and Engle 2020). According to Burgoyne and Engle (2020), their emphasis on attention control stems from the close relationship between WM and fluid intelligence, the common ground for both of which is their dependence on attention control. The authors argue that the account of WM being replaced by attention control manifests advantages over the inherent view of WM as the number of items, which is now becoming a 'misnomer'. To that effect, it is attention control measured by such simple but challenging tasks (e.g., Stroop-like and antisaccade tasks) that drive WM capacity's power to predict a wide range of high-level cognition and real-world behavior (p. 625).

In short, the evolving WM conceptions in cognitive psychology and neuroscience have witnessed a broadening of research paradigms from an early focus on multiple WM components to the current enthusiasm over finer-grained executive and control functions (Wen et al 2022). In line with these new developments, the language science and bilingualism fields have gradually adjusted their applications and implementations of WM. Interpreted this way, these new insights from language-related research have served as catalysts for refining the WM models (Baddeley 2022). Given the fact that the number of bilingual and multilingual speakers is increasing, a conceptual framework that further integrates these evolving WM components and functions in alignment with specific bilingualism/multilingualism learning domains and skills should pave the ground for framing future explorations of WM effects on L2 learning and processing (Wen et al. 2015; Wen and Li 2019; Wen and Schwieter 2022).

An Integrated Model of WM for language and SLA

Towards this goal of integrating WM and SLA, Wen (2015, 2016, 2019) draws on insights from cognitive psychology, neuroscience, and language science to propose the integrated Phonological/Executive (P/E) model as an overarching theoretical framework for conceptualizing and measuring WM in SLA/bilingualism research. The key tenet of the P/E model lies in its demarcation of phonological WM (PWM) and executive WM (EWM) as well as the grouping of the simple vs. complex WM span tasks for measuring each component, respectively. More importantly, the model incorporates both the structural view of WM (consisting of PWM vs EWM) and the functional views that depict fractionated and finer-grained mechanisms and executive functions embedded within each component. More specifically, the model argues that PWM, approximated by simple memory span tasks such as the digit span, the letter span, and/or the nonword repetition span, subsumes phonological short-term storage and articulatory rehearsal mechanism. On the other hand, EWM can be further operationalized as subsuming three executive functions, namely memory updating, task-switching, and inhibitory control.

Building on previous investigations of WM effects on SLA/bilingualism, the P/E model further posits the specific and testable links between PWM and EWM as they relate to specific SLA domains (lexis, phrases or chunks, and grammatical structures or constructions) and L2 sub-skills of listening, speaking, reading, writing, and interpreting. PWM is assumed to underpin the sound-based and chunking-based aspects of language and SLA domains, thus impacting upon such *acquisitional and developmental* domains of lexical knowledge, collocation knowledge, and grammatical structures or constructions. On the other hand, EWM is postulated to subserve real-time and offline *processing-oriented* aspects of L2 sub-skills such as listening, reading, speaking, writing, and bilingual interpreting. In addition, it is argued that the contributions of PWM and EWM will change dynamically as participants' L2 proficiency progresses (Wen and Jackson 2022).

More recently, Wen (2019) claims that the P/E model holds great promise in not just predicting but also explaining the SLA processes and learning outcomes, rendering it a promising central component of foreign language aptitude (see also Miyake and Friedman 1998; Wen, Biedron, and Skehan 2017). In a recent paper, Wen and Skehan (2021) further delineate the functioning of WM components (PWM and EWM) in tandem with the putative cognitive processes and mechanisms subserving the linguistic knowledge acquisition and control processes (e.g., noticing, pattern identification, corrective feedback, etc.) aligned with the three developmental stages of second language acquisition postulated in Skehan's (2016, 2019) 'Staged' model of language aptitude. Specifically, the authors postulate that WM and language aptitude are both equally important at the *input processing stage*, while they exert greater influence at *the central processing* and *output processing stages*. More importantly, extant research has suggested that language aptitude plays a bigger role in pattern identification and complexification of language acquisition, while WM impacts the corrective feedback stage to a greater extent (also see Li 2017; Mackey 2020).

Caveats besetting WM implementations in language and bilingualism

Notwithstanding the developments of WM conceptions in cognitive psychology and neuroscience (Oberauer et al. 2018), some caveats concerning the conceptualization of the WM construct and its association with language or SLA still merit caution among language and bilingualism researchers (cf. Juffs 2017; Schwering and MacDonald 2020). For example, a direct caveat concerning current WM–SLA research practice was advanced by Juffs (2017) in his recent commentary responding to Pierce, Genesee, Delcenserie & Morgan (2017) that featured the relationship between PWM and early language input and development among both typical and nontypical developmental learners. Juffs argues that the evidence presented by Pierce et al. (2017) suggests that PWM may be an epiphenomenon (i.e., a by-product) arising out of individual differences (IDs) in the robustness and richness of phonological representations in language development, which renders the concept of PWM redundant. Juffs also offered suggestions as to how researchers might test this proposal experimentally or in a corpus of child language to dissociate the relationship between phonology and PWM (cf. Service 1992).

Also, Schwering and MacDonald (2020) have claimed that WM does not pose as a viable *determinant* construct in language processing but rather as an *emergent* property that is parasitic on language comprehension and production (see also Schweppe et al. 2021). These doubts arise from the theoretical ramifications of the underlying mechanism of the *serial order recall* tests, which can be interpreted as tapping into long-term memory knowledge base rather than limited WM capacity (Jones and Macken 2015, 2018). Obviously, more empirical studies are needed to sort not only the parallels and non-parallels between WM and language(s) but also the mechanisms underlying their interactions (cf. Duff and Piai 2020) from both a linguistic and a comparative- or cross-linguistic perspective so that language-level analysis can inform the psychological concept of WM (e.g., Jackson et al. 2021).

6.3 WM Measures and Assessment Paradigms

Paradigms of WM span tasks

Alongside the efforts made to theorize and implement WM in empirical studies, cognitive psychologists have also constructed an array of WM span tasks that aim to approximate the multiple facets of WM functions such as storage and processing. In line with the two major research traditions across the Atlantic (Wen 2016), these WM span tasks have taken different forms for which two broad categories can be identified (Conway et al. 2005). On the one hand, there are *simple* storage-focused WM span tasks that are widely used by most cognitive psychologists following the British tradition (e.g., Baddeley and Gathercole, etc) such as the digit span and letter span tasks. Between these two, Chincotta and Underwood (1997) suggested that digit span is more effective when visually presented items comprise Arabic numerals (7, 3, 9, etc.) than when they are presented as words (seven, three, nine, etc.). The latest and the most widely adopted simple memory span task in current SLA studies nowadays is the nonword recognition or nonword repetition span task, which has now become a standard test of phonological (short-term) memory (Gathercole et al. 1994; Gathercole 2006).

On the other hand, most WM researchers in North America seem to be interested in adopting more *complex* memory span tasks that tap into the *dual storage-plus-processing* functions of WM. The most representative and popular formats in this latter category are the domain-specific reading span task as constructed by Daneman and Carpenter (1980) and its scoring-refined version advocated by Waters and Caplan (1996). Then, there is the domain-general operation span task that is meant to be language-independent (Turner and Engle 1989). In addition, the N-back task designed by Kirchner (1958) is widely used in cognitive neuroscience and WM training programs and it has recently made its way into language and bilingualism research (Wen, Juffs & Winke 2021).

Table 1 provides an overview of major formats and scoring procedures of some of these well-established WM span tasks that are also frequently implemented in language and SLA/bilingualism studies (Conway et al. 2005; see also Leeser and Sunderman 2016; Wen 2016; Wen, Juffs, and Winke 2021). Broadly, these tasks can be categorized into three groups: storage-only *simple* memory span tasks, *complex* dual-processing tasks, attention control, or executive functions tasks.

Despite the popularity of these WM span tasks in cognitive psychology, language sciences, and SLA and the encouraging predictive power reported in studies implementing these WM span tasks (with $r = .25$ as reported by Linck et al., 2014 in their meta-analysis of 79 empirical studies), many theoretical and methodological issues remain unresolved in WM-SLA studies (Wen, Juffs, and Winke 2021). As most WM measures had been designed in cognitive science and constructed based

Table 1: Major Formats and Procedures of WM Span Tasks.

Category I. Simple memory span tasks

– *The Digit Span Task (Forward and backward)*
The Digit Span subtest of the WM index (WMI) includes three formats: Digit Span Forward (DSF), Digit Span Backward (DSB), and the new Digit Span Sequencing (DSS). Among these, DSF measures short-term memory, not WM, while DSB and DSS measure auditory WM (Holdnack 2019). For example, in the DSF, participants are requested to recall and recite a string of digits presented by the examiner, e.g., 2, 3, 9, 1; in the DSB, they are requested to recall and recite a string of digits backward (e.g., 24, 3, 7, 12; Response: 12, 7, 3, 24).

– *The Nonword Repetition Span Task*
In a standard version of the non-word repetition span task (e.g. Gathercole *et al.* 1994), non-words are generally formed from a string of letters that do not exist in the given language but still conform to its phonotactic rules (e.g. *acklar* and *veincort*; Cheung 1996). This task usually includes two implementation procedures, one based on recognition only while the other is based on recognition plus repetition (Gathercole 2006; Gathercole *et al.* 1994).

Category II. Complex memory span tasks

The Reading Span Task
One of the most widely used formats of WM measures by North America-based cognitive psychologists is Daneman and Carpenter's (1980) *reading span task*, in which subjects read aloud increasingly longer sets of sentences and then recall the final words (usually a noun) of all the sentences in their original presentation order. For example, at the two-sentence level, participants are asked to read aloud the following sentences (cited from Miyake 2001):
(1) Due to his gross inadequacies, his position as director was terminated abruptly.
(2) It is possible, of course, that life did not arise on the earth at all.

At the end of this trial, participants are expected to recall the two sentence-final words, *abruptly* and *all*. Later, Waters and Caplan (1996) improved the scoring procedures of the reading span task by taking into account the response latency, accuracy of sentence judgment and the recall of the final words.

The Speaking Span Task
Later, Daneman and Green (1986) developed a spoken version of the reading span task, which became known as the *speaking span test* that is 'modeled after the reading span test in that it taxes processing while simultaneously imposing a storage task' (Daneman and Green 1986: 11). The fundamental difference between the reading span and the speaking span tests was modality in that the former taxes comprehension processes while the latter taxes production processes.

Table 1 (continued)

The Operation span tasks
Turner and Engle (1989) devised the *operation span task*, in which one of the two competing processes is not language-based. The two processes of this task are (a) mathematical operations and (b) memorizing words. For example (cited from Engle 2002):
    Is (8/4) – 1 = 1? Bear
    Is (6 X 2) – 2 = 10? Dad
    Is (10X2) – 6 = 12? Beans

In the operation span task, subjects are expected to work out a simple mathematical operation while maintaining the final word for later recall. The difference between the reading span task and the operation span task is that the former comprises reading and word recall while the latter includes mathematical operations and word recall. A significant correlation has been found between the two measures.

The N-back Task
One of the most popular experimental paradigms for neuroscientific studies of WM (e.g., functional magnetic resonance imaging, event-related potentials, etc.) has been the N-back task originally developed by Kirchner in 1958 (as cited in Gajewski et al. 2018). In this task, participants are usually presented with a series of visual stimuli and then asked to indicate whether the currently presented stimulus is the same as the one presented *n* trials previously. (Owen et al. 2005)

Category III. Attention control and executive function tasks

The running memory span task
Postle (2003) considers the running span as an *updating* task of WM. In a standard running memory span (Pollack, Johnson, and Knaff 1959), each list continues for an unpredictable number of items, after which items from the end of the list are to be recalled. For example, in a 4-item recall condition such as "4, 8, 3, 9, 5, 2, 1, 7, 6, 3, 8, 5", participants would see "4, 8, 3, 9, 5, 2, 1, 7, _, _, _, _". The participants are requested to fill in the blanks from left to right with digits by using the computer's numerical keypad. They would press the "enter" key following each digit, or leave a blank and advance to the next item. Responses could be edited before but not after pressing "enter". (Bunting, Cowan, and Saults 2006).

The mental set-shifting task
Mental set-shifting or task switching (Monsell 2003) is a set of executive function paradigms that measure the cognitive flexibility to unconsciously shift attention between one task and another. For example, in task switching, participants need to judge visually presented stimuli made of colors and shapes (pressing the keyboard button to indicate their choice). The color–shape task switch is assumed to tap several executive control processes including mental set shifting (e.g., Xie 2014).

Table 1 (continued)

The inhibitory control task
The inhibitory control task can be administered through E-prime. For example, in the retrieval-induced inhibition paradigm (e.g., Anderson et al. 1994; as cited in Darcy et al. 2016), participants need to memorize six words of three different categories (vegetables, occupations, or animals) presented visually on the screen. They are then allowed to practice only half the items from two categories (e.g., *tomato, nurse*) by typing them several times on the screen. This will likely increase the level of activation of the practiced items, thus causing inhibition of the unpracticed items which serve as control items. Participants will then be tested on the recognition of the practiced items as well as the unpracticed items with (a) those from the two practiced categories (inhibited items) and (b) those from the unpracticed category (control items).

---

on monolinguals, many issues remain to determine whether they are equally valid and reliable for bilinguals who are speaking at least one other language other than their own (Leeser and Sunderman 2016; Lesser and Herman 2022; Wen 2016; Wen, Juffs, and Winke 2021). In the next section, I will first problematize both the WM construct and its assessment procedures by highlighting several of the thorny issues that have affected WM conceptualization and measurement in cognitive science and language/SLA research. Then, based on these insights and drawing on the latest developments in cognitive science, I propose some general principles as quick tips for adopting and administering these WM span tasks effectively in future SLA studies (see also Wen 2016; Wen, Juffs, and Winke 2021). These principles and tips are included in Table 2.

Table 2: General principles and guidelines for measuring WM in SLA.

- The selection of the *simple* memory span task (e.g., the nonword repetition span task) or the *complex* memory span task should take into account of participants' age and L2 proficiency level (Juffs 2006);
- Future SLA research should aim to differentiate hierarchical factors likely to influence the outcomes of WM measures, including information type, encoding modality, and encoding language (Cai and Dong 2012);
- Future SLA studies should take into account the three possible effects of WM, namely the main effects, the interaction effects, and the threshold effects (Wen 2016);
- In scoring a WM span task, a 'total performance score' in addition to the 'maximum set size score' should be adopted and/or reported to aim at finer-grained variance between WM and SLA. Indeed, SLA researchers should carefully review the works by Conway et al. (2005) and Linck et al. (2014) to understand how their scoring choices may affect the empirical findings of their SLA research;
- As with any empirical study, the raw data from the WM tests should be published in an open-source data repository (e.g., IRIS) so that secondary researchers may reanalyze the WM data to explore the results further (Wen, Juffs, and Winke 2021).

It seems only in recent years that SLA researchers have begun to consider developmental and dynamic factors during the implementation of WM span tasks (Sagarra 2017; Jackson 2020; Wen, Juffs, and Winke 2021; Lesser and Herman 2022). These factors include consideration of participants' age, educational level, and L2 proficiency (Juffs 2006). For example, should the age of very advanced L2 learners (those who have reached native-like proficiency) be taken into account? That is, among L1 or L2 learners, would a *simple* memory span task be more appropriate for measuring PWM among young learners, whereas a complex memory span task should be used to measure adult learners' WM capacity (Wen 2016)? However, for other proficiency groups of L2 learners (i.e., those of low or intermediate proficiency), the age factor becomes less critical and is simply reduced to the L2 proficiency or SLA developmental stages. In other words, it is possible that the effects of WM (as witnessed at the beginning and intermediate stages of SLA) can be expected to gradually diminish at this very advanced level (at this stage, WM–SLA is not very different from WM–L1).

Overall, as demonstrated by Cai and Dong (2012), several internal and external factors may be related to the domain-generality/domain-specificity debate about the WM measures and theories. More importantly, their structural equation modeling (SEM) showed that a multitude of these internal and external factors are likely to influence the WM span results and that these influences are hierarchical in nature with each factor carrying a distinct explanatory power. For example, from relatively strong to relatively weak, the list of factors shows that the effects of the 'information types' of the WM measures (verbal memory span task versus non-verbal memory span task) are greater than the effects of the 'encoding modalities' (listening span task versus reading span task versus speaking span task, etc.), which are in turn greater than those of the 'encoding languages' (i.e., whether the test is conducted in participants' L1 or L2). In this sense, it becomes imperative to disentangle the different hierarchical factors that are proportionately influencing the outcomes of WM measures to be implemented in SLA (e.g., information type, encoding modality, and encoding language; Cai and Dong 2012).

When accompanied by more empirical evidence, a list of factor weightings similar to those of Cai and Dong (2012) should provide useful insights on constructing WM span tasks of greater reliability and validity. These considerations are likely to prove valuable not only in the SLA field but also in illuminating WM research in cognitive psychology. As Linck et al. (2014) have cautioned in their meta-analysis, a minor change in research design and methodology may significantly affect the results of WM effects in SLA research. Therefore, it is conceivable that breakthroughs in the under-researched WM assessment procedures will be critical for the future development of the WM–SLA enterprise (Wen 2012, 2016; Wen, Juffs, and Winke 2021).

6.4 Research Findings and Empirical Evidence

As discussed above, WM has also been found by numerous empirical studies to be closely related to language evolution, acquisition, processing, and development, thus underpinning and shaping many key representational and processing aspects of phonology, morphology, syntax, semantics, pragmatics, and discourse (e.g., Chafe 1994; Lu and Wen 2022; O'Grady 2017). Indeed, evidence from empirical studies in both language sciences and cognitive psychology converged on the pivotal role WM plays in a broad range of language domains and learning activities (Gathercole and Baddeley 1993; Baddeley 2003; Schwieter and Wen 2022; Wen 2016). As a whole, WM has been found to be particularly related to the acquisition and development of novel phonological forms and vocabulary learning trials (Cheung 1996), sentence parsing and processing (Juffs and Rodriguez 2014), reading comprehension (e.g., meta-analyses by Daneman and Merikle 1996; Peng et al. 2018), and language production (Acheson and MacDonald 2009; Hartsuiker and Barkhuysen 2006).

A close examination of the majority of empirical studies investigating the relationship between WM and language/SLA reinforces the classical and component-oriented view advocated by Baddeley and colleagues (Baddeley 2003; Gathercole and Baddeley 1993). Among these multicomponent-oriented studies, a significant proportion investigated the role of the phonological component of WM (i.e., phonological WM, or PWM for short) in specific domains of language acquisition and development. Given its instrumental role in acquiring, sustaining, and consolidating the phonological forms of language, PWM has been positioned as the '*language learning device*' (Baddeley et al. 1998; Papagno 2022). Empirical evidence has pointed to the significant impact of PWM on lexical knowledge, grammatical knowledge, and collocational knowledge in language acquisition and processing as well as in L2 learning domains and skills processing (Linck et al. 2014; Wen et al. 2015). In contrast, other WM components in the original tri-partite model have received much less attention in language and bilingualism studies (Baddeley 2015, 2022).

Despite the popularity of Baddeley's multicomponent model of WM in language and SLA research, a recent trend in both cognitive science and language sciences is the paradigm shift and research focus from Baddeley's structural view to the functional views held by most North America-based WM theorists such as

Cowan's embedded processes model (1999, 2021) and Engle's executive and attention control model (2002, 2018). Unlike previous studies that focused on PWM, these empirical studies have probed individual differences in the central executive of WM and examined their consequences for language comprehension activities such as sentence processing and reading comprehension. In terms of research methods, these studies are discarding the *simple* versions of WM measures advocated by Baddeley and colleagues and subscribe instead to the dual-processing assessment paradigms of WM, such as Daneman and Carpenter's (1980) reading span task, and its domain-general version of the operation-span task (Turner and Engle 1989).

Inspired partly by theoretical insights of WM in cognitive psychology and encouraged by the positive findings of the relationship of WM to native language acquisition, an increasing number of cognitive-oriented SLA studies have also pointed to the specific role of WM in L2 learning and processing (e.g., Harrington and Sawyer 1992; Ellis 1996, 2012; Juffs and Harrington 2011; Williams 2012; Sagarra 2013; Wen 2012, 2016; Wen et al. 2015; Wen and Li 2019). To some extent, results from most empirical SLA studies have largely replicated the positive effects of WM on selective L2 learning processes and outcomes (e.g., see Linck et al. 2014; Grundy and Timmer 2017 for meta-analyses of this body of studies). For example, WM has been found to modulate the acquisition and processing of L2 vocabulary (e.g., Cheung 1996), collocations and formulaic sequences or chunks (Foster et al. 2014; Wen 2018), L2 morpho-syntactic constructions or grammatical structures (Martin and Ellis 2012), as well as some cognitive processes implicated in L2 interactions and performance such as noticing of L2 corrective feedback (Mackey et al. 2002; Mackey 2012).

Other SLA researchers have conceptualized the WM construct by following the executive and cognitive control-oriented views of WM (such as that of Cowan and Engle) to explore the relationship between IDs in WM and L2 learning activities and sub-skills processing. This body of empirical studies has corroborated the modulating effects of executive aspects of WM (EWM) on some online and offline cognitive processes during reading comprehension (Daneman and Merikle 1996; Peng et al. 2018), sentence processing, and production (Acheson and MacDonald 2009). In light of these empirical findings, EWM is best conceived as a *language processing device,* or a *language processor* (Lu and Wen 2022; Wen 2016, 2019).

The executive component of WM, namely EWM, is usually measured by dual-processing memory span tasks such as the reading span (Daneman and Carpenter 1980; Waters and Caplan 1996) and the operation span measures (Turner and Engle 1989;). As measured by these *complex* memory span tasks, WM is found to be especially relevant to cognitive processes during L2 sub-skills learning, cognitively demanding aspects of L2 listening comprehension, speech performance, reading comprehension, writing, and bilingual interpreting (Linck et al. 2014). Overall, given the positive effects of WM on SLA in predicting and explaining the L2 learning process and product (with $r = 0.25$ by Linck et al. 2014), proposals have been made to incorporate WM as a central component of language aptitude (Miyake and Friedman 1998; Wen and Skehan 2011, 2021).

Regarding EWM, a new trend in conceptualizing and transforming these executive aspects of WM is taking shape. New emerging paradigms target the sub-processes-oriented executive functions and their independent or combined impacts on human cognition such as language processing. Though the literature on executive functions is sufficient for an independent chapter if not a whole volume, I introduce the 'unity and diversity' framework proposed by Miyake and Friedman (2012; see also Friedman and Miyake 2017) as it is arguably the most widely cited model by language and SLA researchers. Specifically, this framework envisages three core executive functions, namely information updating, task-switching, and inhibitory control (see also Friedman and Robbins 2022). Though terminological confusion sometimes arises between WM and executive functions (Jurado and Rosselli 2007), I subscribe to Baddeley's fractionated view of WM (2002) in which the central executive encapsulates these executive functions.

Recent years have witnessed comparable enthusiasm towards empirical investigations into the potential individual and combined effects of EFs on language and bilingualism/SLA (e.g., Poarch 2018; Jiao et al. 2021). In terms of executive functions and bilingualism/SLA, the number of studies is growing, though still relatively small compared with those exploring the WM-SLA nexus. Jiao et al. (2021) explored the role of inhibitory control among Chinese-English bilinguals. Michel et al. (2019) used eye-tracking technology to investigate the finer-grained distinctions between updating and inhibitory control as they relate to task-based performance. Despite these emerging patterns, a clear portrayal of the independent and joint potential impacts of EFs on nuanced SLA domains and skills is yet to be drawn. More theoretical and empirical studies are needed to elucidate their underlying mechanisms and assessment procedures before their impacts and implications for language processing and bilingual development can be explained more precisely.

6.5 Pedagogical Implications

It is surprising and somehow unfortunate that despite over 30 years of increasingly intensive research into WM and SLA issues since the early study by Harrington and Sawyer (1992), very few studies have examined the experimental and pedagogical applications of WM training within L2 education. This lack of WM training studies in SLA stands in sharp contrast with the enormous body of empirical research investigating WM training implications and the debate concerning its validity for intelligence. Tullo and Jaeggi (2022) synthesized 19 meta-analyses that examined whether WM training was effective in demonstrating improvements in proximal (near transfer) and distal (far transfer) domains of learning. The results pointed to strong evidence indicating WM training produces consistent small to moderate near-transfer effects; however, the findings are mixed for the translation of benefits to more distal domains. Of course, the inconclusive results of WM training transfer effects may largely be due to the diverse methodologies implemented in these WM training studies (see also Pergher et al. 2020). Tullo and Jaeggi (2022) suggested that future research in WM training would benefit from (a) the investigation of WM training moderators as a primary objective, (b) the evaluation of efficacy using longitudinal designs, and (c) the examination of efficacy using combined and targeted approaches.

In sharp contrast to the enormous body in cognitive training, we could find only two empirical studies conducted by Hayashi and colleagues (Hayashi 2019; Hayashi et al. 2016) that have investigated WM training effects on L2 learning. For example, Hayashi (2019) investigated both the near-transfer effects of retention and the far-transfer effects among a group of Japanese learners of English as a Foreign Language (EFL). Two major findings were reported, namely a) WM training (Cogmed based) effects, though restricted to a small number of trained tasks, could be sustained for as long as 6 months post-training, and b) no significant training effects were reported for four measures of L2 proficiency domains (listening, reading, speaking, and writing). Given these emerging patterns, the study called for more investigations to probe into the far-transfer effects of WM training by also addressing and refining the limitations concerning study design and task selection. Towards this end, the author also proposes that future empirical studies could follow the modular view of WM (as articulated in the MOGUL approach by Truscott 2017) as a framework to target both the weak aspects of participants' L2 knowledge and learning and their associated WM capacity within the modular mind (e.g., Baddeley 2017).

6.6 Conclusions and Future Directions

In light of the insights presented above, I propose some general principles as guidelines for conceptualizing and measuring WM in future SLA research (Wen, 2016).
- In terms of conceptualizing WM, it is argued that a distinction should be made between a nomothetic approach versus an idiographic approach (Cowan et al. 2008). In the first case, the construct of WM can be hypothesized as a *primary* memory subsystem consisting of multiple components and functions. From the perspective of the idiographic approach, Cowan et al. have suggested conceiving three types of limits in WM: *capacity limits* (in the number and size of chunks that can be held in WM), *energy limits* (controlled attention), and *time limits* (related to decay in WM). How each of these WM limits affects various first and L2 learning domains and skills are promising areas for future SLA research exploring WM effects.
- In terms of methodology, I argue for adopting a *developmental* and *hierarchical* view for implementing WM span tasks in future SLA studies targeting L2 learners of different ages and across L2 proficiency levels (Wen, Juffs, and Winke 2021). Above all, it seems imperative to disentangle the different contributions of hierarchical factors (e.g., information type, encoding modality, and encoding language; Cai and Dong 2012) influencing the outcomes of WM measures to be implemented in SLA.
- In terms of implementing WM span tasks, future research may need to consider shifting from the currently popular component-oriented WM span tasks (Baddeley's conception) to finer-grained functional and subprocesses-oriented assessment procedures (Table 3). In particular, future research can be directed towards multiple executive functions such as updating as measured by the running memory span task (Bunting et al. 2006), task switching, and inhibitory control (e.g., Doughty 2019; Indrarathne and Kormos 2018).
- In terms of the scoring procedure of the WM span, it is recommended that WM be treated as a continuous variable rather than a dichotomous variable (Miyake 2001). In other words, the 'total performance score' rather than the 'maximum set size score' should be adopted as the scoring procedure for the WM span tasks in future WM–SLA studies (see also Wen, Juffs, and Winke 2021).

To conclude, WM research has witnessed a shift of paradigms from the early 'structural' components-oriented view towards the 'functional' view of the WM conceptions. More effort can be directed towards applying state-of-the-art technologies (such as eye-tracking, event-related potentials, functional magnetic resonance imaging, etc.) to specify the core cognitive mechanisms and executive

Table 3: Theorizing and Measuring WM in SLA: From components to subprocesses and executive functions.

WM Components	Measures of WM Components	WM Subprocesses and Executive Functions	Measures of WM Subprocesses and Executive Functions
PWM	Simple (storage-only) memory span tasks (e.g., digit span, nonword repetition span, etc.)	Phonological short-term store	Serial recall task (e.g., digit span, letter span, nonword span, etc.)
		Articulatory rehearsal mechanism	Articulatory suppression
EWM	Complex (storage plus processing) memory span tasks (e.g., reading span, operation span, etc.)	WM updating	Running memory span/keep track task
		Task switching	Task-switching numbers/the plus-minus task
		Inhibitory control	Antisaccade/Stroop/Go-Nogo
		Attention control	Burgoyne et al. 2022

functions underlying the *maintenance, access,* and *control* of the two or even more languages residing in the bilingual/multilingual brain (Altarriba and Isurin 2013). Indeed, future WM-SLA studies can be designed to aim at finer-grained WM effects in SLA. In this regard, additional types of WM effects should be considered because WM effects can take different forms such as threshold effects, main effects, and interactional effects (see also Wen 2016). Failure to record a positive relationship of a certain effect should not be taken as conclusive evidence for the null effects of WM in that the lack of evidence may be due to research design or methodological pitfalls (cf. Calvo, Ibáñez, and García 2016). There is also burgeoning research interest in probing the bilingualism effects on WM and/or executive control (Grundy and Timmer 2017; Calvo, Ibáñez, and García 2016; Lukasik et al. 2018). Regarding pedagogy and instruction, within task-based language teaching (TBLT), though the positive effects of WM have been postulated (Wen 2016; Skehan 2015, 2022), how task characteristics and conditions can be designed to overcome WM limitations in task performance (Ellis et al. 2020) or to reduce WM load merits further investigation.

Recommended Readings

Miyake, Akira & Priti Shah. 1999. *Models of working memory: Mechanisms of active maintenance and executive control*. New York: Cambridge University Press.
    A classic collection of the most important working memory models in cognitive psychology and neuroscience. Chapter contributors are mostly proponents of the representative models and they need to answer six common sets of questions raised by the editors regarding the definition, conceptualization and research paradigm of working memory.

Wen, Zhisheng (Edward). 2016. *Working memory and second language learning: Towards an integrated approach*. Bristol: Multilingual Matters.
    A comprehensive account of the different roles of working memory, in particular, its phonological component and executive processes in various aspects of second language acquisition and processing. The Phonological/Executive (P/E) model was put forward and its implications were elaborated for SLA domains and processes, as well as its impacts on task-based performance. The P/E model was also proposed as a central component of language aptitude.

Logie, Robert. H., Valerie Camos, & Nelson Cowan. 2021. *Working memory: State of the science*. Oxford: OUP.
    The volume can be considered as an updated version of Miyake and Shah (1999) in which most of the popular working memory models are reviewed with new and emerging evidence. One interesting insight is that Miyake & Shah (2021) wrote the foreword reviewing the progress being made since their own volume in 1999 and concluded that most of the six themes laid out back then are still relevant and sustained.

Schwieter, John, & Zhisheng (Edward) Wen. 2022. *The Cambridge handbook of working memory and language* (Cambridge Handbooks in Language and Linguistics). Cambridge: Cambridge University Press.
    The latest and the most comprehensive volume deals with working memory in first and second language acquisition, processing, and impairment. The volume starts with an introductory chapter by Alan Baddeley, which is followed by four sections addressing specific issues related to working memory in terms of theoretical models and assessment procedures, theoretical linguistics and language processing, first language acquisition, second language learning, and language disorders, intervention, and training. The enormous volume (40 chapters, almost 1000 pages) concludes with an integrated account of working memory and language by the two editors.

References

Acheson, Daniel J. & Maryellen C. MacDonald. 2009. Verbal working memory and language production: common approaches to the serial ordering of verbal information. *Psychological Bulletin* 135(1). 50–68. https://doi:10.1037/a0014411

Adams, Eryn J., Anh T. Nguyen & Nelson Cowan. 2018. Theories of working memory: Differences in definition, degree of modularity, role of attention, and purpose. *Language, Speech, and Hearing Services in Schools* 49(3). 340–355

Adams, Russell L. & Peter Delaney. 2022. Long-term working memory and language comprehension. In John Schwieter & Zhisheng Wen (eds.), *The Cambridge handbook of working memory and language* pp. 98–119. Cambridge: Cambridge University Press.

Altarriba, Jeanette & Ludmila Isurin. 2013. *Memory, language, and bilingualism: Theoretical and applied approaches*. Cambridge: Cambridge University Press.

Anderson, Michael C, Robert A. Bjork & Elizabeth L, Bjork. 1994. Remembering can cause forgetting: Retrieval dynamics in long-term memory. *Journal of Experimental Psychology: Learning, Memory, and Cognition* 20(5). 1063–1087.

Baddeley, Alan D. 1986. *Working memory*. Oxford: Clarendon.

Baddeley, Alan D. (2000).The episodic buffer: A new component of working memory? Trends in Cognitive Sciences, 4, 417–423.

Baddeley, Alan D. (2012). Working memory: Theories, models and controversies. Annual Review of Psychology, 63, 1–30.

Baddeley, Alan D. 2002. Fractionating the central executive. In Donald T. Stuss & Robert T. Knight (eds.), *Principles of frontal lobe function*, 246–260. Oxford University Press.

Baddeley, Alan D. 2003. Working memory: Looking back and looking forward. *Nature, Reviews Neuroscience* 4(10). 829–839.

Baddeley, Alan D. 2018. *Working memories: Postmen, divers and the cognitive revolution*. Hove: Routledge.

Baddeley, Alan D. 2021. Developing the concept of working memory: The role of neuropsychology. *Archives of Clinical Neuropsychology* 36(6). 861–873.

Baddeley, Alan D. 2022. Working memory and challenges of language. In John Schwieter, & Zhisheng E. Wen (eds.), *The Cambridge handbook of working memory and language* pp. 19–28. Cambridge: Cambridge University Press.

Baddeley, Alan D. & Graham J. Hitch. 1974. Working memory. In Gordon H. Bower (ed.), *The psychology of learning and motivation* Vol. 8. New York: Academic Press.

Baddeley, Alan D. & Graham J. Hitch. 2001. Forward. In Jackie Andrade (ed.), *Working memory in perspective*. Hove, UK: Psychology Press.

Baddeley, Alan D. & Graham J. Hitch. 2019. The phonological loop as a buffer store: An update. *Cortex in press*. https://doi:10.1016/j.cortex.2018.05.015

Baddeley Alan D, Graham J. Hitch & Richard J. Allen. 2019. From short-term store to multicomponent working memory: the role of the modal model. *Memory & Cognition* 47(4),575–588. https://doi:10.3758/s13421-018-0878-5.

Baddeley, Alan D. & Robert H. Logie, 1999. Working memory: The multi-component model. In Akira Miyake & Priti Shah (eds.), *Models of working memory: Mechanisms of active maintenance and executive control*, 28–61. New York: Cambridge University Press.

Bouchacourt, Flora & Timothy J. Buschman. 2019. A flexible model of working memory. *Neuron* 103(1). 147–160.

Bunting, Michael F., Nelson Cowan & John S. Saults. 2006. How does running memory span work? *Quarterly Journal of Experimental Psychology* 59(10). 1691–1700.

Bunting, Michael F., & Zhisheng E. Wen. 2022. Working memory in language and bilingual development. In Robert H. Logie, Zhisheng E. Wen, Suan Gathercole, Nelson Cowan & Randall Engle (eds.), *Memory in science in society* (pp. 301–327). Oxford: OUP.

Burgoyne, Alexander P., et al. "Measuring Individual Differences in Working Memory Capacity and Attention Control and Their Contribution to Language Comprehension." The Cambridge Handbook of Working Memory and Language, edited by John W. Schwieter and Zhisheng

(Edward) Wen, Cambridge University Press, Cambridge, 2022, pp. 247–272. Cambridge Handbooks in Language and Linguistics.

Burgoyne, Alexander P. Randall W. Engle. 2020. Attention control: A cornerstone of higher-order cognition. *Current Directions in Psychological Science* 29(6). 624–630.

Cai, Rendong & Yanping Dong. 2012. Effects of information type, encoding modality, and encoding language on working memory span: Evidence for the hierarchical view In Chinese. *Foreign Language Teaching and Research* 44(3). 376–388.

Cowan, Nelson. (1999). An embedded-processes model of working memory. In Akira Miyake & Priti Shah (Eds.), Models of Working Memory: Mechanisms of active maintenance and executive control (pp. 62-101). Cambridge, U.K.: Cambridge University Press.

Christiansen, Morten H. & Chater, Nick. (2016). The Now-or-Never bottleneck: A fundamental constraint on language. *Behavioral & Brain Sciences, 39*, e62.

Darcy, Isabelle, Joan C. Mora & Danielle Daidone. 2016. The role of inhibitory control in second language phonological processing. *Language Learning* 66(4). 741–773.

Daneman, Meredith and Green, Ian (1986). Individual differences in comprehending and producing words in context. *Journal of Memory and Language, 25*, 1–18.

Gajewski Patrick, Eva Hanisch, Michael Falkenstein, Sven Thönes, & Edmund Wascher. 2018. What does the n-Back task measure as we get older? Relations between working memory measures and other cognitive functions across the lifespan. *Frontiers in Psychology 9*. https://doi:10.3389/fpsyg.2018.02208

Calvo, Noelia, Agustín Ibáñez & Adolfo M. García. 2016. The impact of bilingualism on working memory: a null effect on the whole may not be so on the parts. *Frontiers in Psychology 7*. https://doi:10.3389/fpsyg.2016.00265

Caplan, David. 2016. Working memory and sentence comprehension. In Gregory Hickok & Scott A. Small (eds.), *The Neurobiology of Language*, 633–645. Amsterdam: Elsevier.

Caplan, David., & Gloria S. Waters. 1999. Verbal working memory and sentence comprehension. *Behavioral and Brain Sciences* 22(1). 77–126.

Carpenter, Patricia A., Akira Miyake & Marcel A. Just. 1994. Working memory constraints in comprehension: Evidence from individual differences, aphasia and aging. In Morton A. Gernsbacher (ed.), *Handbook of psycholinguistics*, 1075–1122. San Diego, CA: Academic Press.

Carruthers, Peter. 2013. The evolution of working memory. *Proceedings of National Academy of Sciences* 110 Suppl 2. 10371–10378.

Carruthers, Peter. 2015. *The centered mind: What the science of working memory shows us about the nature of human thought*. Cambridge: Cambridge University Press.

Chafe, Wallace. 1994. *Discourse, consciousness, and time*. Chicago: University of Chicago Press.

Cheung, Him. 1996. Nonword span as a unique predictor of second-language vocabulary learning. *Developmental Psychology* 32(5). 867–873.

Chincotta, Dino & Geoffrey Underwood. 1997. Bilingual memory span advantage for Arabic numerals over digit words. *British Journal of Psychology* 88(2). 295–310.

Cowan, Nelson. 2005. *Working Memory Capacity*. New York and Hove: Psychology Press.

Cowan, Nelson. 2017. The many faces of working memory and short-term storage. *Psychonomic Bulletin & Review 24. 1158–1170.* https://doi:10.3758/s13423-016-1191-6.

Daneman, Meredith & Patricia A. Carpenter. 1980. Individual differences in working memory and reading. *Journal of Verbal Learning and Verbal Behaviour* 19(4). 450–466.

Daneman, Meredith & Philip M. Merikle. 1996. Working memory and language comprehension: A meta-analysis. *Psychonomic Bulletin & Review 3(4)*. 422–433.

Darcy, Isabelle, Joan C. Mora & Danielle Daidone. 2016. The role of inhibitory control in second language phonological processing. *Language Learning* 66(4). 741–773. https://doi:10.1111/lang.12161.

Darcy, Isabelle, Joan C. Mora & Danielle Daidone. 2014. Attention control and inhibition influence phonological development in a second language. *Concordia Working Papers in Applied Linguistics* 5. 115–129.

Đokić, Ratko, Maida Koso-Drljević & Nermin Đapo. 2018. Working memory span tasks: Group administration and omitting accuracy criterion do not change metric characteristics. PLOS ONE 13 (10).e0205169. https://doi:10.1371/journal.pone.0205169

Dong, Yanping & Ping Li. 2020. Attentional control in interpreting: A model of language control and processing control. *Bilingualism: Language and Cognition* 23(4). 716–728. https://doi.org/10.1017/S1366728919000786

Doughty, Catherine J. 2019. Cognitive language aptitude. *Language Learning* 69. 101–126. https://doi.org/10.1111/lang.12322

Draheim, Christopher, Jason S. Tsukahara, Jessie D. Martin, Cody A. Mashburn & Randall W. Engle. 2020. A toolbox approach to improving the measurement of attention control. *Journal of Experimental Psychology: General*. https://doi:10.1037/xge0000783

Duff, Melissa & Vitória Piai (eds.). 2020. *Language and Memory: Understanding Their Interactions, Interdependencies, and Shared Mechanisms*. Lausanne: Frontiers Media SA. https://doi:10.3389/978-2-88966-121-3

Ellis, Nick C. 1996. Sequencing in SLA: phonological memory, chunking and points of order. *Studies in Second Language Acquisition* 18(1). 91–126.

Ellis, Nick C. 2012. Formulaic language and second language acquisition: Zipf and the phrasal Teddy Bear. *Annual Review of Applied Linguistics* 32. 17–44.

Ellis, Rod, Peter Skehan, Shaofeng Li, Shintani Natsuko & Craig Lambert. 2020. *Task-based language teaching: Theory and practice*. Cambridge: Cambridge University Press.

Engle, Randall W. 2001. What is working-memory capacity? In Henry. L. Roediger III & James S. Nairne (eds.), *The nature of remembering: Essays in honor of Robert G. Crowder*, 297–314. Washington, DC: American Psychological Association.

Engle, Randall. W. 2002. Working memory capacity as executive attention. *Current Directions in Psychological Science* 11(1). 19–23.

Ericsson, K. Anders. & Kintsch, Walter. (1995). Long-term working memory. *Psychological Review, 102*, 211–245.

Foster, Pauline, Cylcia Bolibaugh & Agnieszka Kotula. 2014. Knowledge of nativelike selections in an L2: The influence of exposure, memory, age of onset and motivation in foreign language and immersion settings. *Studies in Second Language Acquisition* 36(1). 101–132.

Friedman, Naomi P. & Akira Miyake. 2017. Unity and diversity of executive functions: Individual differences as a window on cognitive structure. *Cortex* 86. 186–204.

Friedman, Naomi P. & Trevor W. Robbins. 2022. The role of prefrontal cortex in cognitive control and executive function. *Neuropsychopharmacol* 47(1). 72–89.

Gathercole, Susan. 2006. Nonword repetition and word learning: The nature of the relationship. *Applied Psycholinguistics* 27(4). 513–543. https://doi:10.1017.S0142716406060383

Gathercole, Susan E. & Alan D. Baddeley. 1993. *Working memory and language*. Hove, UK: Lawrence Erlbaum Associates.

Gathercole, Susan E., Susan J. Pickering, Camilla Knight & Zoe Stegmann. 2004. Working memory skills and educational attainment: Evidence from national curriculum assessments at 7 and 14

years of age. *Applied Cognitive Psychology: The Official Journal of the Society for Applied Research in Memory and Cognition 18(*1). 1–16.
Gathercole, Susan E, Catherine S. Willis, Alan D. Baddeley & Hazel Emslie. 1994. The children's test of nonword repetition: A test of phonological working memory. *Memory* 22(2). 103–127.
Grundy, John G. & Kalinka Timmer. 2017. Bilingualism and working memory capacity: A comprehensive meta-analysis. *Second Language Research* 33(3). *325–340.*
Haberlandt, Karl. (1997). *Cognitive psychology* (2nd ed.). Boston: Allyn & Bacon.
Holdnack, James. A. (2019). The development, expansion, and future of the WAIS-IV as a cornerstone in comprehensive cognitive assessments. In Gerald Goldstein, Daniel N. Allen, & John DeLuca (Eds.), *Handbook of psychological assessment* (pp. 103–139). Elsevier Academic Press.
Joshua Conrad Jackson, Joseph Watts, Johann-Mattis List, Curtis Puryear, Ryan Drabble & Kristen A. Lindquist. 2021. From Text to Thought: How Analyzing Language Can Advance Psychological Science. *Perspectives on Psychological Science.* https://doi:10.1177/17456916211004899
Jackson, Daniel O. (2020). Working memory and second language development: A complex, dynamic future? *Studies in Second Language Learning and Teaching*, 10(1), 89-109. http://dx.doi.org/10.14746/ssllt.2020.10.1.
Jiao, Lu, Liu, Cong, Schwieter, John W., & Chen, Baoguo (2021). Switching between newly learned languages impacts executive control. *Psychophysiology, 58(10),* e13888
Jones, Gary & Bill Macken. 2015. Questioning short-term memory and its measurement: Why digit span measures long-term associative learning. *Cognition* 144. 1–13.
Jones, Gary. & Bill Macken. 2018. Long-term associative learning predicts verbal short-term memory performance. *Memory & Cognition* 46(2). 216–229. https://doi:10.3758/s13421-017-0759-3.
Juffs, Alan. 2006. Working memory, second language acquisition and low-educated second language and literacy learners. *LOT Occasional Papers: Netherlands Graduate School of Linguistics.* 89–104.
Juffs, Alan. 2017. The importance of grain size in phonology and the possibility that phonological working memory is epiphenomenal. *Applied Psycholinguistics* 38(6). 1329–1333.
Juffs, Alan & Michael Harrington. 2011. Aspects of working memory in L2 learning. *Language Teaching* 44(2). 137–166.
Juffs, Alan & Guillermo A. Rodríguez. 2014. *Second language sentence processing.* New York: Routledge.
María Beatriz Jurado & Mónica Rosselli. 2007. The elusive nature of executive functions: A review of our current understanding. *Neuropsychology Review* 17(3). 213–233. https://doi.org/10.1007/s11065-007-9040-z
Haberlandt, Karl. 1997. *Cognitive psychology.* Boston: Allyn & Bacon.
Harrington, Michael & Mark Sawyer. 1992. L2 working memory capacity and L2 reading skill. *Studies in Second Language Acquisition* 14(1). 25–38.
Hartsuiker, Robert J. & Pashiera N. Barkhuysen. 2006. Language production and working memory: The case of subject-verb agreement. *Language and Cognitive Processes* 21(1–3). 181–204.
Hayashi, Yuko. 2019. Investigating effects of working memory training on foreign language development. *The Modern Language Journal* 103(3). 665–685.
Hayashi, Yuko, Taisei Kobayashi & Tsuyoshi Toyoshige. 2016. Investigating the relative contributions of computerised working memory training and English language teaching to cognitive and foreign language development. *Applied Cognitive Psychology* 30(2). 196–213.
Indrarathne, Bimali & Judit Kormos. 2018. The role of working memory in processing L2 input: Insights from eye-tracking. *Bilingualism: Language and Cognition* 21(2). 355–374.
Kirchner, Wayne K. 1958. Age differences in short-term retention of rapidly changing information. *Journal of experimental psychology* 55(4). 352–358. https://doi:10.1037/h0043688

Kruijne, Wouter, Sander M. Bohte, Pieter R. Roelfsema & Christian N. L. Olivers. 2021. Flexible working memory through selective gating and attentional tagging. *Neural Comput*, 33(1). 1–40.

Leeser, Michael & Gretchen Sunderman 2016. Methodological issues of working memory tasks for L2 processing research. In Gisela Grenana, Yucel Yilmaz & Daniel O. Jackson (eds.), *Cognitive individual differences in second language processing and acquisition*, 89–104. Amsterdam: John Benjamins.

Leeser, Michael J. & Herman, E. 2022. Methodological issues in research on working memory and L2 reading comprehension. In John W. Schwieter & Zhisheng E. Wen (eds.), *The Cambridge handbook of working memory and language*. Cambridge University Press.

Li, Shaofeng. 2017. The effects of cognitive aptitudes on the process and product of L2 interaction: A synthetic review. In Laura Gurzynski-Weiss (ed.), *Expanding individual difference research in the interaction approach: Investigating learners, instructors and researchers*, 42–70. Philadelphia: John Benjamins.

Linck, Jared A., Peter Osthus, Joel T. Koeth & Michael F. Bunting. 2014. Working memory and second language comprehension and production: A meta-analysis. *Psychonomic Bulletin & Review* 21(4). 861–883. https://doi:10.3758/s13423-013-0565-2

Lukasik, Karolina M., Minna Lehtonen, Anna Soveri, Otto Waris, Jussi Jylkkä & Matti Laine. 2018. Bilingualism and working memory performance: Evidence from a large-scale online study. *PLoS ONE* 13(11). e0205916. https://doi.org/10.1371/journal.pone.0205916

MacDonald, Maryellen C. & Morten H. Christiansen. 2002. Reassessing working memory: Comment on Just and Carpenter 1992 and Waters and Caplan 1996. *Psychological Review* 109. 35–54.

Mackey, Alison. 2012. *Input, interaction and corrective feedback in L2 learning*. Oxford, UK: Oxford University Press.

Mackey, Alison. 2020. *Interaction, feedback and task research in second language learning*. Cambridge, UK: Cambridge University Press.

Mackey, Alison, Jennifer Philp, Takako Egi, Akiko Fujii & Tomoaki Tatsumi. 2002. Individual differences in working memory, noticing of interactional feedback and L2 development. In Peter Robinson (ed.), *Individual differences and second language instruction*, 181–209. Philadelphia: John Benjamins.

Martin, Katrina. I. & Ellis, Nick C. 2012. The roles of phonological STM and working memory in L2 grammar and vocabulary learning. *Studies in Second Language Acquisition* 34(3). 379–413. https://doi:10.1017/S0272263112000125.

Miller George A, Eugene Galanter, and Karl H. Pribram. (1960). *Plans and the structure of behavior*. New York: Holt.

Miller, George. (2003). The cognitive revolution: A historical perspective. *Trends in Cognitive Science, 7(3)*, 141–144.

Miller, George. (1956). The magical number of seven, plus or minus two: Some limits on our capacity for processing information. Psychological Review, 63/3, 81–97.

Miyake, Aikra & Friedman Noami P. (2012). The nature and organization of individual differences in executive functions: Four general conclusions. *Current Directions in Psychological Science, 21(1)*, 8–14.

Michel, Marije, Kormos, Judit, Brunfaut, Tineke, & Ratajczak, Michael (2019). The role of working memory in young second language learners' written performances. *Journal of Second Language Writing, 45*, 31–45. https://doi.org/(...)6/j.jslw.2019.03.002

Miyake, Akira. 2001. Individual Differences in Working Memory: Introduction to the Special Section [Special Section: Individual Differences in Working Memory]. *Journal of Experimental Psychology: General* 13(2). 163–168.

Miyake, Akira & Naomi P. Friedman. 1998. Individual differences in second language proficiency: working memory as language aptitude. In Alice F. Healy & Lyle E. Bourne Jr. (eds.), *Foreign language learning: Psycholinguistic studies on training and retention* pp. 339–364. Mahwah, N.J.: Lawrence Erlbaum.

Miyake, Akira & Priti Shah. 1999. *Models of working memory: Mechanisms of active maintenance and executive control*. New York: Cambridge University Press.

Monsell, Stephen. 2003. Task switching. *Trends in Cognitive Sciences* 7(3). 134–140.

Oberauer, Klaus et al. (2018). Benchmarks for models of working memory. *Psychological Bulletin*, 144(9):885–958. doi: https://10.1037/bul0000153.

O' Grady, William. 2017. Working memory and language: From phonology to grammar. *Applied Psycholinguistics* 38(6). 1340–1343.

O' Reilly, Randall C & Michael J. Frank. 2006. Making working memory work: A computational model of learning in the frontal cortex and basal ganglia. *Neural Computation* 18(2). 283–328.

Owen, Adrian M, Kathryn M. McMillan, Angela R. Laird & Ed Bullmore. 2005. N-back working memory paradigm: A meta-analysis of normative functional neuroimaging studies. *Human brain mapping* 25(1). 46–59.

Pierce, Lara. J., Genesee, Fred, Delcenserie, Audrey, & Morgan, Gary. (2017). Variations in phonological working memory: Linking early language experiences and language learning outcomes. *Applied Psycholinguistics*, 38, 1265–1302.

Peng, Peng, Marcia Barnes, CuiCui Wang, Shan Li, H. Lee. Swanson, William Dardick & Sha Tao. 2018. A Meta-Analysis on the Relation Between Reading and Working Memory. *Psychological Bulletin* 144(1). 48–76. http://dx.doi.org/10.1037/bul0000124

Pergher, Valentina, Mahsa Alizadeh Shalchy, Anja Pahor, Marc M. Van Hulle, Susanne M. Jaeggi & Aaron R. Seitz. 2020. Divergent research methods limit understanding of working memory training. *Journal of Cognitive Enhancement* 4(1). 100–120. https://doi:10.1007/s41465-019-00134-7

Poarch, Gregory J. 2018. Multilingual Language Control and Executive Function: A Replication Study. *Frontiers in Communication* 3. 46. https://doi:10.3389/fcomm.2018.00046

Pollack, Irwin, Lawrence B. Johnson, & Robert P. Knaff. 1959. Running memory span. *Journal of Experimental Psychology*, 57:137–146.

Postle, Bradley R. 2003. Context in verbal short-term memory. *Memory & Cognition* 31(8). 1198–1207.

Sagarra, Nuria. 2013. Working memory in second language acquisition. In Carol A. Chapelle (ed.), *The encyclopedia of applied linguistics*, 6207–6215. Oxford: Wiley-Blackwell. https://doi:10.1002/9781405198431.wbeal1286

Sagarra, Nuria. 2017. Longitudinal effects of working memory on L2 grammar and reading abilities. *Second Language Research 33(3)*. 341–363. https://doi:10.1177/0267658317690577

Schwering, Steven C & Maryellen C. MacDonald. (2020). Verbal working memory as emergent from language comprehension and production. *Frontiers in human neuroscience* 14. 68. https://doi:10.3389/fnhum.2020.00068

Schwieter, John W & Zhisheng Wen. 2022. *The Cambridge handbook of working memory and language* Cambridge Handbooks in Language and Linguistics. Cambridge: Cambridge University Press.

Segalowitz, Norman & Sarah Frenkiel-Fishman. 2005. Attention control and ability level in a complex cognitive skill: attention-shifting and second language proficiency. *Memory and Cognition* 33(4). 644–653.

Service, Elisabeth. (1992). Phonology, working memory and foreign-language learning. *Quarterly Journal of Experimental Psychology, A 45 (1)*, 21–50.

Sunderman Gretchen & Kroll Judith F. (2009). When study-abroad experience fails to deliver: The internal resources threshold effect. *Applied Psycholinguistics*, 30(1):79–99.

Skehan, Peter. (2016). Foreign language aptitude, acquisitional sequences, and psycholinguistic processes. In Granena, Gisela, Jackson, Daniel O. & Yilmaz, Yucel. (Eds.). *Cognitive individual differences in L2 processing and acquisition* (pp. 17–40). Amsterdam: John Benjamins.

Skehan, Peter. 2015. Working memory and second language performance. In Zhisheng Wen, Mailce Borges Mota & Arthur McNeill (eds.), *Working memory in second language acquisition and processing*, 189–201. Bristol: Multilingual Matters.

Skehan, Peter. 2022. Working memory and L2 speaking tasks. In John W. Schwieter & Zhisheng Wen, (eds.), *The Cambridge handbook of working memory and language* pp. 635–655. Cambridge: Cambridge University Press.

Schweppe Judith, Friederike Schütte, Franziska Machleb & Marie Hellfritsch. 2021. Syntax, morphosyntax, and serial recall: How language supports short-term memory. *Memory & Cognition*. https://doi:10.3758/s13421-021-01203-z

Truscott, John. (2017). Modularity, working memory, and second language acquisition: A research program. *Second Language Research, 33*, 313–323.

Tullo, Domenico & Susanne M. Jaeggi. 2022. Working memory training: meta-analyses and clinical implications. In John W. Schwieter & Zhisheng Wen (eds.), *The Cambridge handbook of working memory and language* pp. 881–906. Cambridge, UK, Cambridge University Press.

Turner, Marilyn L. & Randall W. Engle. 1989. Is working memory task dependent? *Journal of Memory and Language* 28(2). 127–154.

von Bastian, Claudia C., Chris Blais, Gene Brewer, Mate Gyurkovics, Craig Hedge, Patrycja Kałamała, Matt Meier, Klaus Oberauer, Alodie Rey-Mermet, Jeffrey N. Rouder, Alessandra S. Souza, Lea Maria Bartsch, Andrew R. A. Conway, Christopher Draheim, Randall W Engle, Naomi P. Friedman, Gidon T. Frischkorn, Daniel E. Gustavson, Iring Koch, Thomas Redick, Bridget A. Smeekens, Peter S. Whitehead & Elizabeth Wiemers. 2020. *Advancing the understanding of individual differences in attentional control: Theoretical, methodological, and analytical considerations*. PsyArXiv. July 27. doi:10.31234/osf.io/x3b9k.

Waters, Gloria S. & David Caplan. 1996. The measurement of verbal working memory and its relation to reading comprehension. *Quarterly Journal of Experimental Psychology* Section A 49(1). 51–74.

Waters, Gloria S. & David Caplan. 2003. The reliability and stability of verbal working memory measures. *Behavior Research Methods, Instruments, and Computers* 35(4). 550–564.

Wen, Zhisheng, & Jackson, Daniel. (2022). Working memory capacity and functions. In Shaofeng Li, Mostafa Papi and Phil Hiver (eds.), *The Routledge Handbook of Second Language Acquisition and Individual Differences* (pp. 54–66). London & New York: Routledge.

Wen, Zhisheng, Juffs, Alan & Winke, Paula (2021). Measuring working memory. In Paula Winke & Brunfaut Tineke (Eds.). *The Routledge handbook of second language acquisition and testing* (pp. 167–176). London: Routledge.

Wen, Zhisheng. 2012. Working memory and second language learning. *International Journal of Applied Linguistics* 22. 1–22. https://doi:10.1111/j.1473-4192.2011.00290.x

Wen, Zhisheng. 2016. *Working memory and second language learning: Towards an integrated approach*. Bristol: Multilingual Matters.

Wen, Zhisheng. 2018. Using formulaic sequences to measure L2 task performance: The role of working memory. In Mohammad Javad Ahmadian & María del Pilar García Mayo (ed.), *Recent Trends in Task-based Language Teaching and Learning*, 29–51. Berlin: Mouton de Gruyter.

Wen, Zhisheng. 2019. Working memory as language aptitude: The Phonological/Executive Model. In Zhisheng Wen, Peter Skehan, Adriana Biedroń, Shaofeng Li & Richard L, Sparks (eds.), *Language aptitude: Advancing theory, testing, research and practice* pp. 187–214. New York: Routledge.

Wen, Zhisheng, Adriana Biedroń & Peter Skehan. 2017. Foreign language aptitude theory: Yesterday, today and tomorrow. *Language Teaching* 50(1). 1–31. https://doi:10.1017/S0261444816000276

Wen, Zhisheng, Alan Juffs & Paula Winke. 2021. Measuring working memory. In Paula Winke & Tineke Brunfaut (eds.), *The Routledge Handbook of Second Language Acquisition and Language Testing* pp. 167–176. Routledge.

Wen, Zhisheng & Li Shaofeng. 2019. Working memory in L2 learning and processing. In John W. Schwieter & Alessandro G. Benati (eds.), *The Cambridge handbook of language learning*, 365–389. Cambridge: Cambridge University Press.

Wen, Zhisheng, Mailce B. Mota & Arthur Mcneill. 2013. Working memory and SLA: Innovations in Theory and Research" [Special Issue]. *Asian Journal of English Language Teaching* 23. 1–102.

Wen, Zhisheng, Mailce B. Mota & Arthur Mcneill. 2015. *Working memory in second language acquisition and processing*. Bristol, UK: Multilingual Matters.

Wen, Zhisheng & Peter Skehan. 2011. A new perspective on foreign language aptitude: Building and supporting a case for "working memory as language aptitude". *Ilha Do Desterro: A Journal of English language, literatures and cultural studies* 60. 15–44. https://doi:10.5007/2175-8026.2011n60p015.

Wen, Zhisheng & Peter Skehan. 2021. Stages of Acquisition and the P/E Model of Working Memory: Complementary or contrasting approaches to foreign language aptitude? *Annual Review of Applied Linguistics* 41. 6–24. https://doi.org/10.1017/S0267190521000015

Wen Zhisheng, Peter Skehan, Adriana Biedroń, Shaofeng Li & Richard L, Sparks. 2019. *Language aptitude: Advancing theory, testing, research and practice*. New York: Routledge.

Wen, Zhisheng, Teng Feng & Han Lili. 2022. Working memory models and measures in language and bilingualism research: Integrating cognitive and affective perspectives. *Brain Sciences* 12(6). 729. https://doi.org/10.3390/brainsci12060729

Williams, John N. 2012. Working memory and SLA. In Susan M. Gass & Alison Mackey (eds.), *Handbook of second language acquisition*, 427–441. Oxford: Routledge/Taylor & Francis.

Xie, Zhilong. 2014. Second-language proficiency, language use, and mental set shifting in cognitive control among unbalanced Chinese–English bilinguals. *SAGE Open* 4(4). https://doi:10.1177/2158244014563040

7 Consciousness, Attention and Noticing

Zhisheng (Edward) Wen

Abstract: This chapter discusses the three closely related cognitive individual difference constructs, consciousness, attention and noticing. Specifically, it elaborates on their respective theoretical models, hypotheses, and operational frameworks and summarizes key tenets and empirical supports from research in SLA and task-based language teaching (TBLT). In particular, I provide an updated review of Richard Schmidt's *noticing hypothesis* within the broader context of input and output theories of SLA, re-examining its validity against Schmidt's own evidence and support from more recent empirical studies, and investigating its limitations. Then, I move on to discuss the theoretical implications for the two attentional models within TBLT and describe the pedagogical tactics to enhance and nurture noticing in TBLT stages and classroom instructions. Overall, I argue that despite the critical roles of noticing and attention in SLA, they are best seen as *necessary but not sufficient* conditions for L2 learning, playing important roles with other internal and external individual difference factors in modulating the SLA process and outcomes. I conclude the chapter by outlining some possible avenues for future research falling into these lines of inquiry.

Keywords: Consciousness, attention, the Noticing Hypothesis, TBLT, CALF, the Limited Attentional Capacity (LAC) Hypothesis, the Cognition Hypothesis (CH), corrective feedback, recast, noticing the gap, Focus on Form

7.1 Introduction

The role of consciousness and attention has been studied in cognitive psychology for many years, even long before L2 researchers introduced these terms into SLA. Similar to the situation in psychology, their underlying mechanisms and putative roles in L2 learning have been controversial in SLA and language education research. Interest in consciousness and attention was boosted considerably in the early days of SLA research by Krashen (1981), who distinguished between the largely unconscious or naturalistic '*acquisition*' of language versus the mostly conscious or classroom-based '*learning*' (currently known as instructed L2 learning or SLA; e.g., Robinson 2001 & 2002).

Note: This chapter is expanded and updated considerably based on Wen, 2008.

Over time, the relationship between consciousness, attention, and SLA has gradually yielded to controversies and disputes over the relationship between explicit and implicit knowledge (Lichtman VanPatten, 2021; N. Ellis 1994; R. Ellis et al. 2009). There are three well-defined positions regarding their relationships in SLA, best characterized as the 'interface' problems (R. Ellis 2006). Broadly speaking, these positions are:

(a) The *no-interface* position, which views language *acquisition* as essentially natural, unconscious, and implicit; while language *learning* is mostly instructed, conscious or explicit; and that *learning* never becomes *acquisition* (e.g., Krashen 1981);
(b) The *strong interface* position, which argues that conscious understanding of the target language system is necessary for L2 learning, and that explicit knowledge can become implicit knowledge and can be learned through ample practice (e.g., Dekeyser 2007);
(c) The *weak interface* position, which holds that when L2 learners are developmentally ready to learn the target features and if *noticing* and *noticing the gap* become part of the acquisitional processes, explicit knowledge can be converted into implicit knowledge (e.g., N. Ellis 2005; R. Ellis 2006).

Most early SLA researchers would accept the third position, namely that noticing is a *necessary* condition for learning to take place. However, even when this epistemological problem is temporarily resolved, SLA researchers remain divided on their more specific positions for the role of noticing in mediating L2 input and in predicting L2 learning outcomes. For example, it is often the case that L2 learners do not take in all of the input to which they are exposed in the L2 classroom or that is taught to them by L2 instructors (e.g., Dornyei & Ryan 2015). That is, not all *input* becomes *intake or uptake* (Sharwood Smith 1993). The relationships between input, intake, and uptake are listed in Table 1.

Table 1: Differences between input, intake, and uptake.

Input	Intake	Uptake
Processable language.	Processed language.	Learned language.
Accessible language data.	Language noticed, attended to and processed.	Language that has become part of the learners' interlanguage system.

Then, it is natural to ask what makes input become intake, and in turn, intake become uptake? In other words, does attention or noticing play a *necessary* role in the subsequent processing of L2 input data? Or, as some scholars (Schmidt 1990) have suggested, do attention and noticing play a *sufficient or vital* role? Answers to these questions have prompted new rounds of debates in task-based language teaching (TBLT) in more recent years, giving rise to two well-defined theoretical models of attention that are reviewed later in this chapter.

In light of these early debates as well as more recent controversies over the role of noticing in SLA and the latest attentional theoretical models, the current chapter aims to put these closely related cognitive IDs into perspective and re-examine their theoretical claims and supporting evidence for the SLA process and learning outcomes under different learning conditions and contexts. In particular, we will focus on the *noticing hypothesis* by tracing its developments and key tenets, which are then subject to closer scrutiny by examining the emerging evidence within SLA and TBLT. Evidence from both the proponent (Richard Schmidt) and subsequent empirical studies claiming to lend support to these approaches will be reviewed. Next, we will also discuss recent findings synthesized from the increasing body of corrective feedback in TBLT studies within SLA. Then, in the pedagogy section, we will further highlight pedagogical interventions to promote and nurture noticing in L2 classroom instructions and TBLT curriculum design.

7.2 The 'Noticing Hypothesis': Theory and research

(1) Theoretical background and developments

As mentioned above, some SLA researchers have tried to argue for a dissociation between language learning and consciousness (the no-interface position). For example, Velmans (1991) postulated that task demands may appear to involve consciousness due to the need for focal-attentive processing, but in some cases, focal-attentive processes may operate effectively without consciousness being present. Similarly, Tomlin and Villa (1994) viewed the process of attention as being too coarse-grained in SLA and proposed a fine-grained analysis of attention (namely, the attentional functions of *alertness, orientation,* and *detection*) in their model of input processing. These authors claimed that although detection is the level at which acquisition takes place and is most related to awareness, none of the three attentional functions may require awareness to operate. However, as Leow (1997) indicated, the data collection procedure (offline post-exposure questionnaire) used by these researchers to measure the presence or absence of awareness has potential internal validity concerns, especially because it is unable to account for what learners actually paid attention to or became aware of during the experimental exposure.

Additionally, Schmidt (1995) has noted several other methodological problems that plagued these early studies that have been cited as empirical support. For example, he argued that these studies have failed to methodologically establish a complete absence of awareness in language learning. In other words, some participants assigned to the unaware group could have been described as somewhat aware but not completely unaware. Consequently, the categorization of the participants' levels of awareness in the different groups could lead to new interpretations of the same results.

(2) Schmidt's 'noticing' hypothesis

For his own part, Schmidt argued for the opposite point of view: that focal attention is isomorphic with awareness, and consequently, learning cannot take place without awareness. Acknowledging that consciousness is primarily associated with the input side of the nervous system, Schmidt (1990) focused his discussion on the role of consciousness in adult L2 learning on input processing. He equates noticing with attention plus awareness and operationalized noticing as a cognitive operation that takes place both during and immediately after exposure to the input that is available for self-report (1990, p.132).

In his *'noticing hypothesis'*, Schmidt (1990, 1993, 1995, 2001; Schmidt & Frota 1986) has proposed that conscious attention to the form of input (i.e., noticing the gap) plays a *crucial* role in subsequent L2 development. His hypothesis maintains that learners must first demonstrate a conscious apprehension and awareness of some particular form in the input before any subsequent processing or intake of that noticed form can take place. For Schmidt, not all input has equal value and only that input that is noticed then becomes available for intake and effective processing (Skehan, 1998, p.48). Indeed, Schmidt argued strongly against any input converting into intake without being noticed first by the learner. Therefore, his *noticing hypothesis* can also be stated, "what learners notice in input is what becomes intake for learning" (Schmidt 1995, p. 20). In terms of noticing and input process of L2 data, Schmidt was mainly concerned with three issues: (1) the process through which input becomes intake; (2), the degree to which the learner consciously controls the process of intake; and (3), the role of conscious understanding in hypothesis formation (1990, p.138; see also Leow, 2015 & 2018).

To illustrate his position more specifically, Schmidt (1990, p.143) postulates six major factors that influence noticing when learners are processing L2 input data (based on Skehan, 1998). Two of these factors are concerned with the input qualities, including their frequency and saliency (e.g., Ellis & Wulff, 2019). Then, there are two other factors that are concerned with *focused* input: classroom instruction and task demands. The remaining two factors are internal ones that have to do with individual differences (IDs) of the L2 learner per se and include L2 learners' expectations/readiness and their internal processing capacity (such as working memory). Table 2 lists the six factors and their explanations, alongside some supporting scholars and studies.

Table 2: Factors influencing noticing (based on Schmidt, 1990; also see Skehan, 1998; Wen, 2008).

Factors influencing noticing	Explanations	Supporting scholars, arguments, evidence
Frequency of input	more frequently encountered materials are more likely to increase the chance of being noticed by L2 learners	N. Ellis 2002, 2011; Ellis & Wulff, 2019
Perceptual *salience* of input	more salient materials are more likely to be noticed	Ellis 2016; Gass et al. 2017
Instruction	may have a *priming* effect which increases the chance of noticing features in the input	Trofimovich & McDonough 2013
Task demands	are also a powerful determinant of what is noticed and provide one of the basic arguments that what is learned is what is noticed	Ellis 1997
Expectations or readiness of the individual learner	likely to have an effect on his/her noticeability	cf. Ellis et al. 2020
Processing capacity (e.g., working memory) of the individual learner	proves to be an internal factor influencing his/her noticeability	Mackey et al. 2002

An alternative way to understand Schmidt's idea is to incorporate all six factors into the information processing model and connect them with operations of working memory and long-term memory (Gass 1997; Skehan 1998), where noticing plays a mediating role between input and the operation of these two memory systems (Figure 1). All six factors will exert their influence either directly or indirectly upon noticing in L2 input processing. Put another way, before we can claim that "noticing is vital for L2 learning", we need empirical evidence supporting all six factors. Obviously, the SLA field has not yet arrived at this position (Wen 2008). Notwithstanding, the research part of the chapter will critically examine some supporting evidence alongside their critiques for the noticing hypothesis.

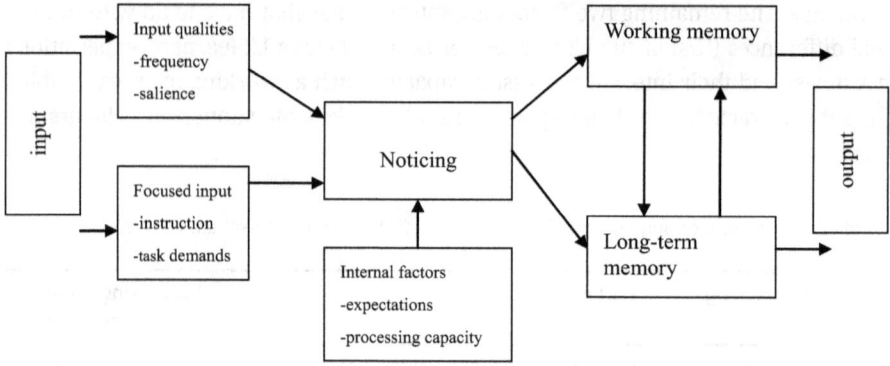

Figure 1: Factors influencing noticing (adapted from Skehan, 1998).

(3) Empirical support for the claims

To justify his own argument, Schmidt primarily drew evidence from a diary study of his own personal attempts to learn Portuguese in Brazil (Schmidt & Frota 1986). In his experience, there were remarkable correspondences between his reports of what he had noticed when Brazilians talked to him and the linguistic forms that he used. He also compared his performance on 21 verbal constructions and found that he had been taught 14 of these. His later analysis appeared to suggest that the presence of forms and frequency in input played some role in learning, although not the whole part. Schmidt based his argument mainly on the evidence that there were many cases in which it was possible to match the new forms and constructions of Portuguese on the tape with comments in his own journal, and more often than not, he could identify the apparent source of innovation as something very specific that someone had previously mentioned to him. In this sense, it is likely that these forms had been present in comprehensible input all along.

Besides citing his own experience of learning Portuguese, Schmidt also referred to several other SLA studies to support his claim, such as: (1) enhanced input designed to draw the learner's attention to specific forms in the input, namely the 'focus-on-form (FonF)' mechanism (Doughty 1991); (2) competition between form and meaning during a language comprehension task (VanPatten 1990); and (3) "uptake" studies, i.e. learners' claims regarding what had drawn their attention and what they had learned during the lesson (Slimani 1992). However, it must be noted that there are several limitations inherent in this evidence when it comes to the role of awareness at the level of noticing. For example, in Schmidt's own example of learning Portuguese, we should acknowledge that scenarios differ when learners process L2 input data in diary entries and natural interactions. Obviously, this example alone is far from enough to claim that L2 learners need to notice before they can learn anything. Even Schmidt himself admitted that 'though it [his own example] provides evidence for a *close connection* between noticing and emergence in production, the study does not show that noticing is sufficient for learning (1990: 141)'. As for the other several studies cited by Schmidt, these investigations did not specifically set out to address the role of consciousness or awareness, and therefore cannot and should not serve as evidence to support his claim. For example, these studies would not be able to explain the role that noticing had played in learners' behavior, and in that sense, could only serve as 'anecdotal evidence' (Leow 1997). Therefore, much more empirical evidence is needed to support the claim that "noticing is vital for L2 learning".

Since then, SLA researchers have conducted a number of empirical studies to investigate the effect of awareness or noticing on L2 learning. The researchers have all mentioned that their findings have provided support for the facilitative role of awareness or noticing in L2 learning behavior, and consequently provide empirical support for Schmidt's argument that "noticing is vital for L2 learning". Major studies falling into this line of argument are briefly sketched in Table 3, followed by critical comments in the next part of the paper.

Table 3: Empirical Studies Supporting the Noticing Hypothesis (based on Wen, 2008).

The Studies	Subjects	Target Forms	Tasks	Data Elicitation Procedures	Major Findings
Alanen (1995)	36 participants (between 18 and 45)	Semi-artificial Finish	1. a reading task 2. a grammatical judgment task	TAPs and Postexposure Tests	Those learners who showed some evidence of having acquired the target structures were the ones who had noticed them and subsequently mentioned them in their TAPs.

Table 3 (continued)

The Studies	Subjects	Target Forms	Tasks	Data Elicitation Procedures	Major Findings
Loew (1997)	28 adult beginning learners of Spanish	stem-changing -*ir* verbs in Spanish	1. a problem-solving task (a crossword puzzle) 2. two postexposure tasks (recognition task & written production task)	TAPs	(a) meta-awareness appeared to correlate with increased usage of hypothesis testing and morphological rule formation, whereas the absence of meta-awareness appeared to correlate with an absence of such processing; and (b) that learners with a high level of awareness performed significantly better than those with a lower level on both the recognition and written production of the targeted forms.
Loew (2000)	32 adult beginning learners of Spanish	stem-changing -*ir* verbs in Spanish	1. a problem-solving task (a crossword puzzle) 2. two postexposure tasks (recognition task & written production task)	TAPs and Retrospective Interviews	Learners who demonstrated awareness of targeted morphological forms were able to take in and produce in writing significantly more of these forms, compared to learners who did not appear to be aware of these forms during exposure.

Table 3 (continued)

The Studies	Subjects	Target Forms	Tasks	Data Elicitation Procedures	Major Findings
Rosa (1999), Rosa & O'Neill (1999)	67 adult beginning learners of Spanish	Spanish conditional	1. a problem-solving task (puzzle task) 2. Multiple choice recognition task	TAPs	Whereas both awareness at the levels of noticing and understanding contributed substantially to a significant increase in learners' ability to recognize the targeted structure, awareness at the level of understanding also had a differential impact on the amount of intake when compared to awareness at the level of noticing.

(4) Further evidence from corrective feedback studies

As claimed by Leow (2020), noticing is the underlying cognitive construct that supports the effectiveness of different types of corrective feedback within TBLT (Mackey, 2020; Chin et al., 2021). Until now, an extensive number of empirical studies have attempted to evaluate the role of noticing in mediating the different types of corrective feedback. In early studies, Gass (1997) found that corrective feedback (CF) triggers noticing the form and/or the meaning and the mismatch between learners' non-target-like form and the target-like form, which eventually leads to grammar restructuring. Long (1996) proposed that conversational interaction can raise learners' awareness of language, resulting in increased attention to form and heightening the inclination for noticing mismatches between the non-target-like form in learner utterances and the target-like form in the modified output.

In classroom-based observational or descriptive studies and classroom-based experimental studies, findings converged to demonstrate the more effective role of explicit learning rather than an implicit type of feedback, i.e., recasts (Li 2017a & 2017b). Other studies have demonstrated that different types of CF may be associated with different levels of noticing (Mackey 2006 & 2020). As noted by Lyster et al.

(2013), more research that conceptually defines the construct of noticing in a more refined manner is warranted. To address this need, Chin et al. (2021) examined the relationships between the type of corrective feedback and the level of noticing, namely whether a more explicit type of CF leads to a higher level of noticing. The study investigated whether more explicit types of corrective feedback prompts lead to a higher level of noticing than recasts, a more implicit type of CF. The findings showed that recasts were able to induce higher levels of noticing the form/target, noticing the gap, and noticing the rule.

That said, no firm conclusions can be reached with regard to the relationship between the type of CF and the level of noticing (Chin et al. 2021) due to the small number of comparative CF noticing studies. Such a limitation is further complicated by a wide array of methodological variations across studies and also in the types of CF, the operationalization of CF, the linguistic target of CF, the noticing elicitation procedures, the noticing categories, and the different instructional contexts. Besides these problems, many current noticing-CF studies also suffer from other limitations that warrant closer scrutiny.

First, many of these noticing-CF studies have a narrow subject base and target forms. Even if we agree that the number of subjects in most cases is relatively adequate (except for Leow's 1997 study that involved only 28 participants), the studies still present a number of other more serious concerns. One concern is that the linguistic backgrounds of the subject base are rather narrow (only Spanish and Finnish) and not representative of the real world of L2 learning. Another concern is that the subjects' linguistic proficiency is so low that their proficiency levels cast doubt on the findings claimed by the researchers that these learners have acquired the (simple morphological, or semi-artificial structures in Alanen's case) target forms simply because they had noticed them previously. Additionally, while these target structures are so prominent and tend to have meaning potential, the effect of saliency was not measured. Another point in Leow's two studies (1997 & 2000) is particularly worth mentioning, viz., these subjects had only been exposed to Spanish for about three weeks (roughly about 7–8 hours of formal exposure in the classroom), but the medium of instruction for these Spanish beginners was Spanish through which ideas, new information, and so forth were exchanged in the oral, aural, and written modes (2000, p.562), all of which may be too challenging for a group of beginners. In both studies, Leow himself admitted that "the findings clearly cannot be extrapolated to other linguistic forms or structures" (1997: 494, 2000: 573), and other researchers have made similar comments at the end of their papers.

Second, there are some methodological issues in these studies, e.g., the data collection procedures and the data analysis procedures that were administered. The data collection procedures were mainly the online elicitation measures of think-aloud protocols (TAPs). Though TAPs have been claimed to be able to outperform offline elicitation measures such as post-exposure questionnaires, they are not as valid and reliable as they may seem (e.g., Revesz 2021). Schmidt's (2001, p.19) comments about Leow's 1997 study indicated, "it is difficult to see how such techniques could show that subjects did not attend to or notice something, since verbal reports (TAPs) (even when concurrent) cannot be assumed to include everything that is noticed". Still, there are several other concerns that need to be addressed in terms of the TAPs used in these studies, i.e., the issue of reactivity effect (Leow & Morgan-Short 2004; Bowles & Leow 2005). Such reactivity effect might result from: (1) the learner's prior knowledge of the target forms due to the fact that these morphological structures are so salient and tend to have meaning-bearing potential; (2) the task demands, i.e., text modes (written or oral), text length, etc.; and (3) multiple exposures (to the input). These concerns were not addressed in all of these studies and we do not have empirical studies in SLA to address them adequately.

(5) Summary

In sum, it can be argued that despite all of the optimistic claims and encouraging results reported by these researchers for the facilitative role of noticing or awareness, they fall short of supporting Schmidt's noticing hypothesis, i. e., that "noticing is vital for L2 data processing". These recent attempts have proved to be both worthwhile and valuable in that they have helped us to gain a better understanding of the cognitive processes underlying L2 learning, to some extent. Most of these studies deserve praise for their high internal validity and robust research design (in particular, Leow's 2000 study and Rosa and O'Neill's study). Still, they have demonstrated that the different degrees of attention paid to L2 input can lead to more or less learning (Simard & Wong 2001), but not in the sense that they are adequate to corroborate that noticing is the 'sufficient' condition for all subsequent L2 data processing.

7.3 Theoretical and Pedagogical implications for instructed SLA

(1) The two theoretical attention models: LAC vs CH

Within the increasingly growing body of TBLT research (e.g., Bygate, 2015; Ellis, et al., 2020), Schmidt's noticing hypothesis in SLA has gradually given way to two emerging *attentional models* representing two epistemological stances on the available cognitive resources (e.g., WM or attention) and their potential consequences for or effects on L2 learners' task-based performance (as normally indexed by the complexity, accuracy, lexis, and fluency framework; Skehan 2009). First of all, there is the *Limited Attentional Capacity (LAC)* Hypothesis proposed by Peter Skehan (e.g., 2014, 2015, 2018, & 2021). In essence, the LAC approach is a bottom-up theoretical model encompassing a series of key tenets or principles (Skehan, 2015, 2018; Ellis et al., 2020, p. 70–72). These principles include:

a) *Principle 1*: The LAC assumes that an individual's WM and attention resources *are limited*, thus likely exerting impacts on L2 processing and performance. This represents the fundamental distinction from Robinson's Cognition hypothesis.
b) *Principle 2*: The LAC claims that the CALF framework provides a viable and useful benchmark to measure L2 task performance as a function of independent variables such as task characteristics and task conditions, and their effects on performance.
c) *Principle 3*: The LAC assumes tasks are constructs that are analyzable and generalizable, although the analytic schemes do not always transfer into actual task performance in straightforward ways.
d) *Principle 4*: The LAC links task performance in tandem with attentional limitations, CALF performance, and task characteristics to the Levelt (1989) model of speaking (as well as its adapted L2 model; De Bot 1992; Kormos 2006) as the basis for making effective predictions.
e) *Principle 5*: The LAC stipulates that task features such as task characteristics (e.g., structured vs. unstructured) and task implementation conditions (pre-task planning, during-task planning, post-task planning, task repetition, etc.) can be manipulated to have measurable impacts on task performance either independently or in combination.
f) *Principle 6*: The LAC stipulates that task difficulty is an inherent quality that needs to be analyzed distinctly for the Conceptualizer and the Formulator in the Leveltian speaking model.

In contrast, the *Cognition Hypothesis* (CH) advocated by Peter Robinson (2011) makes more specific and testable proposals regarding pedagogic issues, such as task sequencing and syllabus design, as well as the role of tasks in promoting feedback and acquisitional processes. These hypotheses and predictions culminate in the triadic componential framework subsuming task complexity, task conditions, and task difficulty (i.e., the SSARC model; Robinson 2011, 2015). Each component is to be elaborated on below.

To begin, *task complexity* mainly concerns the cognitive demands of a task and the extent to which they impact task performance. More importantly, task complexity distinguishes between resource-directing variables such as time perspective, spatial reasoning, intentional reasoning, causal reasoning, etc., and resource-dispersing variables such as providing planning time or not, single vs. dual tasks, task structure, etc.

Next, *task conditions* are concerned mainly with the interactional demands of tasks, including participation variables such as the number and relationships of the tasks, and participant variables such as participants' proficiency level, gender, knowledge, etc.

Then, *task difficulty*, distinguished from Skehan's LAC view, is mainly concerned with learner factors, such as their ability factors (e.g., WM, attention switching, etc.) and affective factors (e.g., task motivation, anxiety, willingness to communicate, etc.) that the participant brings to bear on task performance.

From these descriptions, it is clear that the LAC and CH stem from different epistemological stances on the available cognitive resources, with the LAC assuming limited attentional capacity that will lead to tradeoffs among the different dimensions of the CALF indices, while the CH holds that attentional resources can be contingent and expanded under the right conditions. Such a fundamental distinction in the cognitive underpinnings of task performance gives rise to different hypotheses and predictions in task-based performance and ultimate acquisition. Emerging studies are lending empirical support to both models, although conclusive results remain to be seen. As such, more studies are still needed to further evaluate the validity of their respective claims. (Ellis et al. 2020, p. 87)

(2) Pedagogical implications: nurturing noticing in SLA and TBLT

If noticing is a necessary condition for L2 acquisition, then, a natural question should then become how to nurture noticing (Skehan 2013). Regarding pedagogical implications, every experienced teacher should have realized that consciousness-raising activities (e.g., textual enhancement such as underlining, highlighting, etc.) are *input enhancement* techniques that serve to promote and enhance noticing among students (Sharwood Smith 1993). Within TBLT, Ellis et al. (2020) provide many options in each phase of task completion to nurture noticing, particularly in the form of focus-on form (FonF; also see Benati 2022) activities (which is distinguished from the previous practice of focus on linguistic forms). That is, Focus on form (FonF) promotes noticing. These key FonF options can take place during the pre-task stage, the within-task stage, and the post-task stage. For example, in the main task phase of within-task focus on form, various ways of accomplishing this can be considered, especially with the effective use of corrective feedback (CF), i.e., by providing feedback on errors during task performance.

Meanwhile, the role of noticing can be researched from the teachers' perspective as well. Recently, van den Broek et al. (2022) reviewed EFL teachers' self-reported teaching practices aimed at stimulating students' language awareness or noticing. More specifically, an awareness-raising learning environment includes aspects such as authentic contexts, 'student-centered' discovery and exploration, autonomous learning, and student engagement, while a non-awareness-raising learning environment includes teacher-centered instruction, focusing mostly on outcomes, and often includes working with typical textbook exercises. To determine teachers' implementation of awareness-raising practices, 10 teachers in the Netherlands were interviewed. These teachers reported 41 examples that they claimed to stimulate students' awareness of language. But, approximately half of these examples could be characterized as awareness-raising, i.e., 'student centered'. These integrated multiple topics included authentic contexts and back-and-forth interaction and provided students with the opportunity to reflect on their own and other students' language difficulties, though numerous practices reported as awareness-raising could not be characterized. Therefore, teachers' notion of what constitutes an awareness-raising practice may be incomplete. Future studies should investigate the kinds of support teachers could offer to students and how they could adjust their teaching practices to stimulate students' awareness.

In a similar vein, Jackson (2018 & 2021) has argued that noticing should also be nurtured among teachers, i.e., 'teaching noticing', particularly among pre-service teacher development in TESOL contexts. Emerging key findings show that the amount of noticing reported by novice teachers varies greatly across individuals and that their noticing is often linked to their professional identity and emotion (Jackson, 2018). In addition, Jackson demonstrates that teacher noticing can also contribute to evidence-based reflection by pre-service teachers. Jackson (2021) provides comprehensive discussions demonstrating how teacher noticing can be nurtured to develop rapport with students, encourage their participation, support their language acquisition, and foster self-reflection and guiding observation. It is conceivable that teaching noticing represents a new trend in noticing research in TBLT and SLA.

7.4 Conclusion and future directions

Given the evidence cited here, we conclude that although the facilitative roles of attention and noticing have been generally acknowledged and confirmed by empirical studies, Schmidt's *noticing hypothesis*, i.e., "noticing is vital for L2 learning," remains unresolved. However, as Ellis (see also Ellis 2008, 2015 & 2021) indicated, Schmidt (2001) also distinguished between a *strong* form and a *weak* form of the noticing hypothesis, in which the strong form postulates that there is no learning (whatsoever) without noticing, while the weak form acknowledges that people do not learn much about the things to which they do not attend (Ellis 2008 p. 266). As Truscott (1998) suggests, the problems inherent in the noticing hypothesis can be "eliminated or greatly reduced" if it can be reformulated as noticing "is necessary for L2 learning", playing an important role with other internal and external individual difference factors to modulate the SLA process and final learning outcomes.

As such, further empirical studies must be done to demonstrate the effects of other ID factors such as language aptitude (Chapter 5), working memory (Chapter 6), frequency (N. Ellis 2002 & 2017), saliency (Ellis 2017; Gass et al. 2018), instruction (explicit vs. implicit), and teacher noticing (Jackson 2022) as learners are interacting with L2 input data, L2 interactions, and L2 outputs. Despite the limitations inherent in the noticing hypothesis, this chapter has demonstrated the theoretical and pedagogical implications of noticing for TBLT and SLA. The pedagogical implications of its claims are shedding light on instructional techniques such as consciousness-raising activities, input enhancement, focus on form (FonF), etc., that can be implemented to nurture noticing and to facilitate and promote L2 learning. Future research will be needed to further investigate the functioning mechanisms of these cognitive IDs (e.g., consciousness, attention, noticing) underlying TBLT performance and L2 acquisition and development. The SLA field looks forward to furthering theoretical and methodological advances to nurture noticing that prompts L2 learning success.

Recommended Readings

Bergsleithner, Joara Martin, Frota, Sylvia Nagem & Jim Kei Yoshioka. 2013. *Noticing and Second Language Acquisition: Studies in honor of Richard Schmidt*. Hawai'i: National Foreign Language Resource Center.
    This Festschrift provides an overview and updated view of the theoretical underpinnings of Schmidt's noticing hypothesis, summarizing existing evidence in support or against the hypothesis as well as new empirical studies investigating noticing by using advanced technologies (such as eye-tracking techniques).

Bygate, Martin. 2015. *Domains and directions in the development of TBLT: A decade of plenaries from the international conference*. Amsterdam: John Benjamins.
    This edited volume collects all the keynote plenary talks from the biannual international TBLT conference for over a decade long. In particular, the two papers by Peter Skehan and Peter Robinson based on their plenary talks in 2017 in Hawaii provide detailed accounts of their respective theoretical attentional models that are featured in this chapter (i.e., the LAC and the CH).

Ellis, Rod., Skehan, Peter, Li, Shaofeng., Shintani, Natsuko., & Lambert, Craig. 2020. *Task-based language teaching: Theory and practice*. Cambridge: Cambridge University Press.
  This multi-authored monograph represents the most comprehensive, authoritative, and updated coverage of the theoretical and pedagogical issues related to TBLT. A must-read for all that are interested in TBLT theories and practice.

References

Alanen, Riikka A. 1995. Input enhancement and rule presentation in second language acquisition. In Richard W. Schmidt (ed.), *Attention and awareness in foreign language learning*, 259–302. Honolulu: University of Hawai'i Press.

Benati, Alessandro. (2021). *Focus on form*. Cambridge: Cambridge University Press.

Bergsleithner, Joara Martin, Frota, Sylvia Nagem & Jim Kei Yoshioka. 2013. *Noticing and Second Language Acquisition: Studies in honor of Richard Schmidt*. Hawai'i: National Foreign Language Resource Center.

Bowles, M. Anita & Ronald Leow, 2005. Reactivity and type of verbal report in SLA methodology. *Studies in Second Language Acquisition* 27: 415–440.

Bygate, Martin. 2015. *Domains and directions in the development of TBLT: A decade of plenaries from the international conference*. Amsterdam: John Benjamins.

Carr, Thoma H., & Tim Curran. 1994. Cognitive factors in learning about structured sequences: Applications to syntax. *Studies in Second Language Acquisition* 16: 205–230.

Chin, Choo Siow, Pillai, Stephanie, & Zainuddin, Siti Z. (2021). Recasts, prompts and noticing: A comparative study. *Studies in English Language and Education, 8(2)*, 416–441.

DeKeyser, Robert M. 1997. Beyond explicit rule learning. *Studies in Second Language Acquisition, 192*, 195–221.

De Bot, Kees. (1992). A bilingual production model: Levelt's speaking model adapted. *Applied Linguistics, 13(1)*, 1–24.

Dekeyser, Robert M. 2007. Skill acquisition theory. In Bill VanPatten & Jessica Williams (eds.), *Theories in second language acquisition: An introduction*, 97–113. New Jersey: Lawrence Erlbaum Associates.

Dornyei, Zoltan, & Stephan Ryan. 2015. *The psychology of the language learner revisited*. New York, NY: Routledge.

Doughty, Catherine. 1991. Second language instruction does make a difference: Evidence from an empirical study of SL relativization. *Studies in Second Language Acquisition*, 13: 431–496.

Ellis, Nick C. 1994. *Implicit and explicit learning of languages*. London, England: Academic Press.

Ellis, Nick C. 2002. Frequency effects in language acquisition: A review with implications for theories of implicit and explicit language acquisition. *Studies in Second Language Acquisition*, 24, 143–188.

Ellis, Nick C., (2005). At the interface: Dynamic interactions of explicit and implicit language knowledge. *Studies in Second Language Learning, 27*, 305–352.

Ellis, Nick C. 2011. Frequency-based accounts of SLA. In Susan Gass & Alison Mackey (eds.), *Handbook of Second Language Acquisition*. 193–210. London: Routledge/Taylor Francis.

Ellis, Nick C. 2016. Salience, cognition, language complexity, and complex adaptive systems. *Studies in Second Language Acquisition, 38/2*, 341–351.

Ellis, Nick, & Stephanie Wulff. 2019. Cognitive approaches to second language acquisition. In John Schwieter & Alessandro Benati (eds.), *The Cambridge handbook of language learning* Cambridge Handbooks in Language and Linguistics, 41–61. Cambridge: Cambridge University Press.

Ellis, Rod. (1997). SLA and language pedagogy: An educational perspective. *Studies in Second Language Acquisition, 19*, 69–92.

Ellis, Rod. 2006. Current issues in the teaching of grammar: An SLA perspective. *TESOL Quarterly, 401*, 83–107.

Ellis, Rod. 2008. *The Study of Second Language Acquisition.* 2nd edn. Oxford: Oxford University Press.

Ellis, Rod. 2021. A short history of SLA: Where have we come from and where are we going? *Language Teaching, 542*, 190–205. https://doi.org/10.1017/S0261444820000038

Ellis Rod, Loewen Shawn, Elder Cathy, Erlam Rosemary, Philp Jennifer, and Reinders Hayo (2009) *Implicit and explicit knowledge in second language learning, testing and teaching.* Bristol: Multilingual Matters.

Ellis, Rod., Skehan, Peter, Li, Shaofeng., Shintani, Natsuko., & Lambert, Craig. 2020. *Task-based language teaching: Theory and practice.* Cambridge: Cambridge University Press.

Gass, Susan, Spinner, Patti & Behney, Jennifer. (2018). *Salience in second language acquisition.* New York, NY: Routledge.

Gass, Susan. 1997. *Input, Interaction and the Second Language Learner.* Mahwah, NJ: Lawrence Erlbaum.

Gass, Susan, Ildiko Svetics & Sarah Lemelin. 2003. Differential effects of attention. *Language Learning*, 53, 497–545.

Gass, Susan. M., Patti Spinner & Jennifer Behney. 2017. Salience in second language acquisition and related field. In Susan Gass, Patti Spinner & Jennifer Behney (eds.), *Salience in Second Language Acquisition*, 1–18. New York: Routledge.

Jackson, Daniel O. (2022). *Language Teacher Noticing in Tasks.* Bristol: Multilingual Matters.

Jackson, Daniel O. 2018. Teacher Noticing. *The TESOL Encyclopedia of English Language Teaching*, 1–6. https://doi.org/10.1002/9781118784235.eelt0998

Jackson, Daniel O. 2021. *Language teacher noticing in tasks.* Bristol: Multilingual Matters.

Krashen, Stephan D. (1981). *Second language acquisition and second language learning.* Oxford: Pergamon Press.

Kormos, Judit. (2006). *Speech production and second language acquisition.* Mahwah N.J.: Lawrence Erlbaum.

Leow, Ronald P. 1997. Attention, awareness, and foreign language behavior. *Language Learning*, 47: 467–505.

Leow, Ronald P. 2000. A study of the role of awareness in foreign language behavior. *Studies in Second Language Acquisition*, 22: 557–584.

Leow, Ronald P. 2013. Schmidt's noticing hypothesis: More than two decades after. In Joara Martin Bergsleithner, Frota, Sylvia Nagem & Yoshioka, Jim Kei (eds.), *Noticing and second language acquisition: Studies in honor in Richard Schmidt*, 23–35. Honolulu, HI: University of Hawai'i, National Foreign Language Resource Center.

Leow, Ronald P. 2015. *Explicit learning in the L2 classroom: A student-centered approach.* New York, NY: Routledge.

Leow, Ronald P. 2018. Noticing hypothesis. *The TESOL Encyclopedia of English Language Teaching*, 1–7. Wiley.

Leow, Ronald P. "Attention, Noticing, and Awareness in Second Language Acquisition." The Encyclopedia of Applied Linguistics (2020): 1–7.

Levelt, Willem. J. M. (1989). *Speaking: From intention to articulation.* Cambridge, MA: The MIT Press.

Leow, Ronald P. & Kara Morgan-Short. 2004. To think aloud or not to think aloud: The issue of reactivity in SLA methodology. *Studies in Second Language Acquisition* 26: 35–57.

Li, Shaofeng. 2017a. Cognitive differences and ISLA. In Shawn Loewen & Masatoshi Sato, (eds.), *The Routledge handbook of instructed second language acquisition*, 396–417. NY: Routledge.

Li, Shaofeng. 2017b. The effects of cognitive aptitudes on the process and product of L2 interaction: A synthetic review. In Laura Gurzynski (ed.), *Expanding individual difference research in the interaction approach: Investigating learners, instructors and researchers*, 42–70. Philadelphia: John Benjamins.

Lichtman, Karen & Bill VanPatten. 2021. Was Krashen right? Forty years later. *Foreign Language Annals*, 1–23. https://doi.org/10.1111/flan.12552

Loewen, Shawn. 2018. Focus on form versus focus on forms. In John I. Liontas (ed.), *The TESOL Encyclopedia of English Language Teaching*, Volume V, 2625–3000. Hoboken, NJ: John Wiley & Sons.

Long, Michael. (1996). The role of the linguistic environment in second language acquisition. In W. Ritchie and T. Bhatia (eds), *Handbook of Second Language Acquisition*. San Diego: Academic Press, 413–68.

Lyster, R., Saito, Kazuya, & Sato, Masatoshi. (2013). Oral corrective feedback in second language classrooms. *Language Teaching*, 46(1), 1–40.

Mackey, Alison. 2006. Feedback, noticing and instructed second language learning. *Applied Linguistics*, 273, 405–430. https://doi.org/10.1093/applin/ami051

Mackey, Alison. 2020. *Interaction, feedback and task research in second language learning*. Cambridge, UK: Cambridge University Press.

Mackey, Alison., Jennifer Philp., Takako Egi, Akiko Fujii, & Tomoaki Tatsumi. 2002. Individual differences in working memory, noticing of interactional feedback and L2 development. In Peter Robinson (ed.), *Individual differences and second language instruction*, 181–209. Philadelphia: John Benjamins.

Révész, Andrea. (2021). Methodological Approaches to investigating task-based language teaching: advances and challenges. In Mohammad Ahmadian & Michael Long (Eds.), *The Cambridge handbook of task-based language teaching* (pp. 605–627). Cambridge: Cambridge University Press.

Robinson, Peter. 2001. *Cognition and instructed second language learning*. Cambridge: Cambridge University Press.

Robinson, Peter. 2002. *Individual differences and instructed language learning*. Amsterdam/Philadelphia: John Benjamins.

Robinson, Peter. 2003, 'Attention and memory during SLA', in Catherine Doughty and Michael H. Long (eds.), *Handbook of Second Language Acquisition*, Blackwell, Oxford.

Robinson, Peter. 2005, Aptitude and second language acquisition, *Annual Review of Applied Linguistics* 25, 42–77.

Robinson, Peter. 2010. Situating and distributing cognition across task demands: The SSARC model of pedagogic task sequencing. In Martin Pütz & Laura Sicola (eds.), *Cognitive Processing in Second Language Acquisition: Inside the Learner's Mind*, 243–68. Amsterdam: John Benjamins.

Robinson, Peter. 2011. Second language task complexity, the cognition hypothesis, language learning, and performance. In Peter Robinson (ed.), *Second Language Task Complexity: Researching the Cognition Hypothesis of Language Learning and Performance*, 3–38. Amsterdam: John Benjamins.

Robinson, Peter. 2015. The cognition hypothesis, second language task demands, and the SSARC model of pedagogic task sequencing. In Martin Bygate (ed.), *Domains and Directions in the Development of TBLT*, 87–122. Amsterdam: John Benjamins.

Rosa, Elena M. 1999. *A cognitive approach to task-based research: Explicitness, awareness, and L2 development*. Unpublished doctoral dissertation, Georgetown University, Washington, DC.

Rosa, Elena, & Michael. D O'Neill. 1999. Explicitness, intake, and the issue of awareness: Another piece to the puzzle. *Studies in Second Language Acquisition* 21: 511–556.

Schmidt, Richard W. 1990. The role of consciousness in second language learning. *Applied Linguistics* 11: 129–158.

Schmidt, Richard W. 1993. Awareness and second language acquisition. *Annual Review of Applied Linguistics* 13: 206–226.

Schmidt, Richard W. 1994. Deconstructing consciousness in search of useful definitions for applied linguistics. *AILA Review* 11: 11–26.

Schmidt, Richard W. 1995. Consciousness and foreign language learning: A tutorial on the role of attention and awareness in learning. In Richard W. Schmidt (ed.), *Attention and awareness in foreign language learning*, 1–63. Honolulu: University of Hawai'i Press.

Schmidt, Richard W. 2001. Attention. In Peter Robinson (ed.), *Cognition and second language instruction*, 1–32. New York: Cambridge University Press.

Schmidt, Richard W. & Sylvia N. Frota. 1986. Developing basic conversational ability in a second language: a case-study of an adult learner. In Richard Day (ed.), *Talking to learn*, 237–326. Rowley, Mass.: Newbury House.

Serafini, Ellen J. 2013. *Cognitive and psychosocial factors in the long-term development of implicit and explicit second language knowledge in adult learners of Spanish at increasing proficiency*. Unpublished dissertation, Georgetown University, Washington, DC.

Sharwood Smith, Michael A. 1993. Input enhancement in instructed SLA: Theoretical bases. *Studies in Second Language Acquisition*, 15, 165–179.

Simard, Daphnée & Wynne Wong. 2001. Alertness, orientation, and detection. *Studies in Second Language Acquisition*, 23: 103–124.

Skehan, Peter. 1998. *A cognitive approach to language learning*. New York: Oxford University Press.

Skehan, Peter. (2009). Modelling second language performance: integrating complexity, accuracy, fluency and lexis. *Applied Linguistics, 30/4*, 510–532.

Skehan, Peter. (2018) *Second Language Task-based Performance: Theory, Research, Assessment*. New York: Routledge.

Skehan, Peter. 2013. Nurturing noticing. In Joara Martin Bergsleithner, Frota, Sylvia Nagem & Jim Kei Yoshioka (eds.). *Noticing and second language acquisition: Studies in honor of Richard Schmidt*, 169–180. Honolulu, Ha: University of Hawaii Press.

Skehan, Peter. 2014. *Processing perspectives on task performance*. Amsterdam: John Benjamins.

Skehan, P. 2015. Limited attention capacity and cognition: Two hypotheses regarding second language performance on tasks. In Martin Bygate (ed.), *Domains and directions in the development of TBLT: A decade of plenaries from the international conference*, 123–156. Amsterdam: John Benjamins.

Skehan, Peter. 2021. The psycholinguistics of task-based performance. In Mohammad Ahmadian & Michael Long (eds.), *The Cambridge handbook of task-based language teaching* Cambridge Handbooks in Language and Linguistics, 3–26. Cambridge: Cambridge University Press.

Skehan, Peter. 2022. Performance on second language speaking tasks: supports and impediments. In Alessandro Benati & John W. Schwieter (eds.), *Second Language Acquisition Theory: The legacy of Professor Mike Long*, 211–234. Amsterdam: John Benjamins.

Slimani, Assia. 1992. Evaluation of classroom interaction. In Charles J. Alderson & Alan Bereta (eds.), *Evaluating second language education*, 197–220. Cambridge: Cambridge University Press.

Tomlin, Russell S. & Victor Villa. 1994. Attention in cognitive science and second language acquisition. *Studies in Second Language Acquisition*, 16: 183–203.

Trofimovich Paval & Kim McDonough. 2013. Priming Research. In Carol A. Chapelle (ed.), *The Encyclopedia of Applied Linguistics*. Blackwell Publishing Ltd.

Truscott, John. 1998. Noticing in second language acquisition: A critical review. *Second Language Research* 14: 103–135.

Truscott, John. 2015. *Consciousness and second language learning*. Bristol: Multilingual Matters.

van den Broek Ellen W. R., Helma W. Oolbekkink-Marchand, Ans M. C. van Kemenade, Paulien C. Meijer & Sharon Unsworth. 2022. Stimulating language awareness in the foreign language classroom: exploring EFL teaching practices, *The Language Learning Journal, 50:1*, 59–73, DOI: 10.1080/09571736.2019.1688857

VanPatten, Bill. 1990. Attending to form and content in the input. *Studies in Second Language Acquisition* 12: 287–301.

Velmans, Max. 1991. Is human information processing conscious? *Behavioral and Brain Sciences*, 14: 651–669.

Wen, Zhisheng (Edward). 2008. Is noticing vital for L2 learning? A critical review of Schmidt's 'noticing hypothesis'. *Teaching English in China* 313, 3–8.

Part III: **Learning Strategies, Metacognition and Self-Regulation**

8 Language Learning Strategies

Mark Feng Teng

Abstract: This chapter introduces the historical development of L2 learning strategies. I first reviewed the assessment of language learning strategies by summarizing survey instruments developed by SLA researchers and educational practitioners over the years. Next, I reviewed research findings that shed light on individual differences in strategy use and the factors that result in individual differences in strategy choice and L2 learning performance. These findings highlight the effectiveness of strategy-based instruction on L2 learning. The chapter concludes by highlighting the remaining challenges for instruction and pedagogy related to language learning strategies.

Keywords: Language learning strategies, strategy-based instruction, cognitive strategies, individual differences in strategy choice, assessment of strategies

8.1 Introduction

Assessing individual differences in students' learning is a prominent area of interest in second language acquisition. Individual differences refer to the more-or-less enduring psychological characteristics that distinguish one person from another (Baumeister and Vohs 2007). Factors such as age, motivation, and learning strategies can influence learners' development in another language. According to Oxford (2017), strategies refer to setting goals, determining actions to achieve the goals, and mobilizing resources to execute the actions. Learning strategies are defined as "specific actions, behaviors, steps, or techniques – such as seeking out conversation partners or giving oneself encouragement to tackle a difficult language task – used by students to enhance their own learning" (Scarcella and Oxford 1992: 63). Language learning strategies refer to "the processes and actions deployed by language learners to learn or use a language more effectively" (Rose 2015: 421) or the thoughts and actions operationalized by language learners to carry out "a multiplicity of tasks from the very outset of learning to the most advanced levels of target language performance" (Cohen 2011:7).

In the 1970s, researchers explored the possibilities of gathering data from learners to identify good learner behaviors and then used strategies as the basis for training less effective learners. During the 1980s, work on strategies continued but with a focus on developing questionnaires to assess learners' use of strategies. The notion that learning strategies might assist second and foreign language acquisition is actually quite new. Researchers questioned how L2 learners could use strategies to enhance their language learning. One possible answer is that language learning strategies could help L2 learners in individualized ways to address and deal with their own inner states. "Good" language learners might be doing something special or different from poor language learners, and those strategies could be helpful to less successful language learners. Thus, much emphasis has been placed on the exploration of social, psychological, and affective variables that could either enhance or hamper L2 achievement. In the last few years, there have been extensive attempts to assess language learning strategies and examine the potential of strategy training.

Proponents of language learning strategies suggest that strategies can determine how and how well a learner can learn a second or foreign language. When learners become aware of strategies that fit the L2 task at hand, the strategies may foster active and purposeful self-regulated learning. Learners may also feel more confident and experience lower anxiety for the L2 task. In contrast, learners who fail to identify appropriate strategies for the L2 task at hand may perform poorly, feel less confident, and experience significant anxiety. According to Oxford (1990: 8), strategies "make learning easier, faster, more enjoyable, more self-directed, more effective, and more transferable to new situations". Hence, language learning strategies may enable learners to become more independent in L2 learning.

8.2 Theories

Types of language learning strategies

The description of the strategies used by "good" language learners provided a window for research into the establishment of taxonomies for language learning strategies (LLSs). O'Malley and Chamot (1990) divided LLSs into three major types: cognitive, metacognitive, and social-affective. On the other hand, Oxford (1990) classified LLSs into six broad categories, namely, cognitive, mnemonic, compensatory, metacognitive, affective, and social. Each of the aforementioned strategies is described in the next sections.

Cognitive strategies

Cognitive strategies are learning strategies that can help learners to strengthen associations between new and already-known information (Oxford 1996). The term "cognitive" in its simplest form is the use of the mind (cognition) to complete a learning task. Cognitive strategies help learners regulate thought processes and content to achieve goals or solve problems (Cameron and Jago 2013). These strategies may also increase the efficiency and confidence with which learners complete a learning task. For example, reading comprehension is a complex task. Learners can use a self-directed questioning strategy (a type of cognitive strategy) to think about what they read. Such a strategy can help learners to search the text and combine information, leading them to more actively monitor their own comprehension (Teng 2020). Other academic tasks that utilize cognitive strategies include processing and memorizing information from content, constructing and editing sentences and paragraphs, and paraphrasing and reorganizing information.

Cognitive strategies are based on self-regulation theories of behavior. Cognitive strategies aim to assist learners with scaffolding and the mental structuring of information. Terms used to describe cognitive strategies include procedural facilitators (Bereiter and Scardamalia 1987), procedural prompts (Rosenshine and Meister 1997), and scaffolds (Palincsar and Brown 1984). Typically, cognitive strategies include orienting, repeating (repetition), organizing information, taking systematic notes, summarizing meaning, guessing meaning from context, reasoning inductively and deductively, and using imagery for memorization. These cognitive strategies can help learners to guide their goal-directed behavior. Cognitive strategies are often used for cognitive behavior therapy to direct learners' attentional focus.

The development of cognitive strategies was related to two frameworks, i.e., Vygotsky's Zone of Proximal Development (Vygotsky 1978) and communicative language teaching (Canale and Swain 1980). For example, Vygotsky suggested that learning occurs during interactions with other people (social learning), especially with the help of a more knowledgeable peer or a teacher. The teacher or the capable peer provides scaffolding or assistance, and then the learners gradually pull away when they no longer need assistance for using the strategy. During this process, students can develop cognitive learning strategies or higher thinking skills, e.g., analyzing information and reasoning. Cognitive strategies require learners to conduct hypothesis testing, such as searching for clues from surrounding materials and one's own background knowledge, guessing the meaning of the unknown item, evaluating whether a meaning makes sense, and, if not, locating another appropriate meaning.

Mnemonic strategies

Mnemonic strategies refer to how learners store information for better memory. These strategies can help students to improve their memory for the recall of important information. For example, learners can enhance their understanding and awareness of knowledge by connecting new learning to prior knowledge. Mnemonic methods include recall of information by keywords, sounds (e.g., rhyming), body movement (e.g., total physical response), or location on a page or blackboard (e.g., the locus technique). The rationale is that students can convert difficult or unfamiliar information into more manageable information.

There are some differences between mnemonic strategies and cognitive strategies. Mnemonic strategies can help learners relate one thing to another in a simplistic, stimulus-response manner. Cognitive strategies can better foster deep associations for learners' memory and learning. Mnemonic strategies are useful for learning vocabulary items or grammar rules. For example, mnemonic strategies can help learners streamline the learning process and gain access to broad amounts of information. Access to broad amounts of information means less dependence on working memory.

Considerable emphasis has been placed on the use of mnemonic strategies, e.g., rehearsal strategies, as a means to improve memory of important information. Young learners in the preschool years find it challenging to be engaged in certain activities. They can only transform memory processes into cognitive, purposeful, and voluntary learning only at a later age (Oyen and Bebko 1996). There may be a relation between the manipulation of the learning task and its possible impact on rehearsal use and recall. Increasing learners' interest in the learning task may be the first step to bringing about spontaneous mnemonic strategy use.

Metacognitive strategies

Metacognition is defined as the awareness, analysis, and knowledge that a person has of his/her cognitive (e.g., learning, thinking) processes (Teng & Yue, 2022). The term refers to the cognitive processes used by learners to 'think' about their 'thinking'. Metacognitive strategies are used to help learners plan, control, and evaluate their learning. Learners can rely on metacognitive strategies to develop an appropriate plan for learning and memorizing information. When learners become aware of how they learn, they can use metacognitive strategies to efficiently acquire new information and gradually become capable of becoming independent and autonomous learners (Efklides 2008).

It is essential to foster learners' awareness of metacognitive strategies. First, learners need to become aware of metacognitive strategies because metacognitive strategies can help learners understand the nature of a learning task. For example, metacognitive strategies can help learners to identify available resources, decide on valuable resources, and make plans and goals for a given task. In an empirical study based on five secondary school students, Forbes and Fisher (2018) found that increasing students' awareness and use of metacognitive learning strategies had a positive impact on their confidence and proficiency in speaking. Second, there are potential relationships between metacognitive strategies and language learning outcomes. For example, in a study with 383 grade twelve students from five upper secondary schools, the results showed the indirect effects of self-reported metacognitive strategies on language learning outcomes (Saks and Leijen 2018a). However, as acknowledged by Forbes and Fisher (2018), strategy use is complex in nature, and the strategies that the students chose in their study depended very much on their individual personality. This may be one reason that there are individual differences in language learning aptitude and outcomes.

Compensatory strategies

Compensatory strategies refer to environmental modifications or behavioral strategies to bypass impairment in attention, memory, executive function, and/or other cognitive skills as a means to achieve desired rehabilitation goals (Kurtz 2011). Compensatory strategies are meant to overcome knowledge gaps, communicate in the target language, and develop strategic competence (Oxford 1990). In real-life communication, language learners make use of such strategies if an expression is not known or if something is not well understood. Compensation strategies may also help to overcome limitations in speaking. Learners also need to apply compensatory strategies to understand their learning materials. Such strategies are important for learners from various social and multilingual backgrounds or learners of diverse language proficiency levels.

Compensatory strategies are often necessary to help learners compensate for missing knowledge when using English in oral or written communication. For example, in terms of speaking, learners can use compensatory strategies, e.g., using synonyms, "talking around" the missing word, circumlocution, and gesturing, to suggest the meaning. In terms of writing, learners can use compensatory strategies, such as synonym use or circumlocution, to convey what they want to write. Compensatory strategies are important for those who do not possess the skills to complete the tasks in the proper manner.

Affective strategies

Differences in foreign language learning performance have also been attributed to individual differences in personality, motivation, and anxiety. Such awareness highlights an increased focus on individuals' emotions and feelings. Affective strategies refer to how learners identify their feelings (e.g., anxiety, anger, contentment) and become aware of the learning circumstances or tasks that evoke them (Arnold 1999). Researchers have paid increasing attention to anxiety when learning a foreign language (Horwitz 2010). Oxford (1990) identified three main sets of affective strategies: lowering your anxiety, encouraging yourself, and taking your emotional temperature. In terms of lowering anxiety, learners can use progressive relaxation, deep breathing, or meditation to reduce their anxiety. The strategy of encouraging yourself refers to how learners encourage themselves to be motivated. The strategy of taking your emotional temperature asks learners to assess their feelings, motivations, and attitudes toward learning a new language.

The important role of affect in language learning resonates with the intuitions of second and foreign language teachers. According to Krashen's (1982) affective filter hypothesis, learners who felt anxious or bored in language learning may be because of the existence of an internal barrier. The role of affect in language learning also reflects language learning anxiety, i.e., the fear of communicating in the target language when a judgment of performance is anticipated (Young 1998). Affective strategies can help learners deal with anxiety through actions such as deep breathing, laughter, and positive self-talk ('I know I can do it!', 'I know more than I did before'), and praising oneself for performance can lower anxiety in language learning. Learners who have negative attitudes and beliefs may become demotivated in language learning. In contrast, learners who hold positive attitudes and beliefs can do the reverse (Shao, Pekrun, and Nicholson 2019).

Social strategies

Language learning is both an intellectual and social process as well as an element of social behavior used for communication between people. Thus, it is helpful to understand the importance of social strategies for language learning. Social strategies are helpful for learners to achieve more effective language learning and understand the culture of the language they are learning. Examples of social strategies include asking questions for clarification or confirmation, asking for help, and learning about social or cultural norms. Even though some researchers tend to downplay social strategies (O'Malley and Chamot 1990), social strategies can also be important for communicative language learning. Oxford (1990) delineates three sets of social strategies: asking questions for clarification or verification and correction; cooperating with others (e.g., with peers and proficient users of the new language);

and empathizing with others to develop cultural understanding and becoming aware of others' thoughts and feelings.

8.3 Frameworks and Models

Language learners are encouraged to learn and use a broad range of language learning strategies because language learning could be facilitated if learners become aware of the range of strategies for language learning and use (Shao et al. 2019). One of the efficient ways to build learners' awareness of strategy use is through strategy training. The purpose of strategy training is to help learners become aware of what helps them to learn the target language most efficiently. In terms of language learning strategy training, researchers have probed various models or frameworks that are reviewed here.

Pearson and Dole's (1987) Model

Pearson and Dole (1987) developed a strategy training model for L1 learners. In this model, teachers first instruct learners about the benefits of applying a specific strategy and model the use of strategies. Students then practice the strategies individually and attempt to transfer the strategy to a new learning situation. The final aim is to build students' independent strategy use and promote learner autonomy.

The sequence of strategy training includes the following steps:
– Initial modeling of the strategy by the teacher, including explanations of the strategy's use and importance.
– Initial modeling of the strategy by the teacher.
– Definitions and explanations by the teacher.
– Guided practice with the strategy
– Consolidation, for which teachers help students identify the strategy and decide when it might be used
– Independent practice with the strategy
– Application of the strategy to new tasks

Pearson and Dole's model casts some light on strategy training. In an empirical study (Dole, Brown, and Trathen 1996), the results indicated that readers who received strategy instruction made superior gains in comprehension performance over their peers who received story content or traditional reading instruction. However, Pearson and Dole's model focused only on the training of limited strategies. It is harder to develop students' problem-solving competence in complex and authentic learning tasks. In addition, it may not be easy for teachers to create a classroom climate where students can practice different strategies effectively.

Oxford (1990) Model

Oxford's Model (1990) focuses on explicit strategy awareness, benefits of strategy use, functional and contextualized practice with the strategies, self-evaluation, monitoring of language performance, and suggestions for or demonstrations of the transferability of the strategies to new learning contexts. These strategies are implemented step-by-step in the following procedure:
- Learners are immersed in an authentic language learning task without instructional cues.
- Teachers suggest and demonstrate helpful strategies for greater self-direction and expected benefits.
- Learners practice new strategies with language tasks.
- Learners transfer the strategies to other tasks.
- Learners choose the strategies they will use to complete the language learning tasks.
- Teachers help students understand how to evaluate the success of their strategy use and gauge their progress as responsible and self-directed learners.

Oxford's (1990) model was used as a basis for research on strategy use instruction. Most researchers agree on the importance of explicit strategy instruction (e.g., Shen 2003). Chamot (2005) also pointed out the benefits of explicit learning strategy instruction. Teachers should opt for explicit instruction and integrate the instruction into their regular coursework. One problem with strategy instruction is whether students can transfer strategies learned in one situation to another situation. Early research on learning strategies found that students found it challenging to transfer strategies to new tasks (Seker 2016). To increase the transfer of strategies to new tasks, teachers may need to help students better understand their learning processes (Teng 2016).

Chamot and O'Malley (1994) model

Chamot and O'Malley (1994) developed the Cognitive Academic Language Learning Approach (CALLA). The purpose was to develop students' academic language skills.

This model integrates academic language development, content area instruction, and explicit instruction of learning strategies for language acquisition. This model includes a six-stage problem-solving process.
- Planning. Students plan ways to approach a learning task. The teacher identifies students' current learning strategies, such as recalling prior knowledge and previewing key vocabulary and concepts to be introduced to the lesson.
- Monitoring. Students monitor their performance by paying attention to their strategy use and checking comprehension.
- Problem Solving. Students find solutions to problems they encounter by practicing new strategies.
- Evaluation. Students evaluate the effectiveness of a given strategy and learn to determine the effectiveness of their learning by summarizing or giving self-talk, either cooperatively or individually.
- Expansion: Students transfer strategies to new tasks, combine strategies into clusters and develop a repertoire of preferred strategies.
- Assessment: The teacher assesses students' use of strategies and their impact on performance.

Saks and Leijen (2018b) adapted the strategies from Chamot and O'Malley's (1994) CALLA model and Oxford's (1990) model. Confirmatory factor analysis (CFA) was used to determine whether the model fit the proposed two-factor and six-factor structures. The results found that the six dimensions, i.e., active language use, metacognition, social strategies, compensation strategies, memory strategies, and connecting strategies, showed good model fit. One issue that needs attention is that Chamot and O'Malley's (1994) CALLA model did not consider any of Oxford's affective strategies. It seems essential to explore whether such strategies have any role in supporting language learning. This is of particular importance given that affective strategies are considered theoretically to be highly significant in promoting effective language learning (Oxford and Ehrman 1995).

Cohen's (1998) model

Cohen's (1998) Styles and Strategies-Based Instruction Model (SSBI) is based on a learner-centered approach. This model includes both explicit and implicit integration of strategies into the course content. The teacher's roles included the Teacher as a (1) diagnostician who helps the students identify current strategies and learning styles, (2) language learner who shares his/her own learning experiences and thinking processes, (3) learner-trainer who trains the students on how to use learning strategies, (4) coordinator who supervises students' study plans and monitors difficulties, and (5) coach who provides on-going guidance on students' progress.

Cohen's model prescribes what a teacher should do in English instruction lessons. The model provides more flexibility for teachers to explicitly and implicitly incorporate the language strategies training into the regular classroom program. The feature of the model is to allow students to have more responsibility for learning, become more autonomous, diagnose their strengths and weaknesses, and self-direct their language learning process. Many experimental studies have adopted this model with a focus on the training of cognitive and metacognitive strategies. For example, Cohen (2005) adopted a taxonomy of language learner strategies based on this model to support learners in their efforts to obtain knowledge about speech acts. These strategies have a potentially beneficial role in helping L2 learners reduce the likelihood of pragmatic failure in their performance of speech acts.

Grenfell and Harris's (1999) model

Grenfell and Harris (1999) also developed a model of language learning strategies. The feature of this model is the importance of developing students' metacognitive understanding of the value of learning strategies. The realization comes through the teacher's demonstration and modeling and the students practicing and evaluating the strategies. The goal is to internalize and automatize the strategies and transfer them to new tasks. The procedures are as follows:
(1) Awareness raising. The students complete a task and then identify the strategies they used.
(2) Modeling. The teacher models a new strategy. The teacher then prepares a checklist of strategies for later use.
(3) Practice. The students adopt strategies for different tasks.
(4) Action planning. The students set goals and select appropriate strategies for the attainment of those goals.
(5) Focused practice. The students carry out action plans by selecting appropriate strategies, and the teacher identifies prompts for the students to use.
(6) Evaluation. The teacher and students evaluate the success of the action plan, and set new goals, and the cycle begins again.

In sum, these different models of language learning strategies provide opportunities to assist learners in becoming aware of what helps them to learn the target language. Harris (2003) also highlighted the role of language learning strategy instruction in promoting learner autonomy. Harris compared several models, including O'Malley and Chamot (1994), Oxford (1990), and Grenfell and Harris (1999). Based on the comparison of different models, Harris concluded that learners need to reflect on and make explicit the strategies they are using. Harris also noted that helping learners develop an awareness of common overarching metacognitive strategies and how to scaffold the evaluation process are important issues for consideration.

8.4 Assessment

It is important to diagnose students' potential problems in the use of language learning strategies, locate the possible causes of language deficiencies, and bridge their linguistic gaps. Assessment is not only the evaluation of student's language competence or achievement but also their learning behaviors. Teachers may need to understand the following elements of assessment:
1) Ideal targets of strategic language learning
2) Assessing strategic learning
    a. Types of tools
    b. How to choose tools
    c. How to design tools
3) How to interpret assessment results
4) How to provide feedback
5) How to differentiate instruction based on assessment results

Using self-report questionnaires is the most common assessment method for measuring learning strategies. The advantages of using questionnaires include ease of administration and statistical analyses. Some researchers have argued that questionnaire items cannot generalize across situations and cannot capture the dynamic interplay of person and task essential to self-regulated learning (Kikas and Jõgi 2015). While answering questions, learners may not be able to accurately recall the strategies they use, or their memory reconstructions may be distorted (Veenman 2011). In addition, self-reports have the lowest reliability and validity of all test instruments. Despite these limitations, questionnaires may be able to help teachers assess learners' perceptions, beliefs, or knowledge of strategies. The types of questionnaires include selected-response (fixed format), e.g., true-false, matching, multiple-choice, pick from a list; constructed-response (guided format), e.g., fill-in blanks, short answers, performance, guided interviews; and personal-response (open-ended format), e.g., think-aloud, observation free interviews, diary entries, and narratives.

It is important to have information about the level and quality of students' strategy knowledge and to understand whether students use adequate strategies spontaneously, and if not, why not. Assessment of language learning strategies can help to understand learners' competence and their beliefs in language learning. In an empirical study (Kikas and Jõgi 2015), the assessment of learning strategies was conducted through the concurrent use of questionnaires and cognitive-behavioral learning task methods. The results showed the validity of using a questionnaire to assess language learning strategies.

Teachers can also develop their own tools to diagnose learners' strategic learning. An example of assessing writing strategies is described here.

Example: Assessing writing strategies

Student writers make use of a range of strategies to put their ideas into a written product. In writing, the requirement is to string decoded words together to convey messages or ideas. To do this, students need to think of topic sentences or keywords and organize information to quickly transform ideas into words. Writing requires not only vocabulary and knowledge about topics and linguistic structures but also the use of strategies in making writing activities "self-planned, self-initiated, and self-sustained" (Zimmerman and Risemberg 1997: 73).

For example, when students cannot do well on writing tasks, it is essential to assess their writing strategies. The following figure provides an observation sheet. This assessment tool is designed to create a writing strategy profile for learners, diagnose their writing strategy problems, and customize the writing instructions. In class, when students are required to write an essay or exchange feedback for writing, teachers can focus on whether the students can understand how to use feedback to correct writing errors or enhance their writing competence. Here, three different observations of writing performance are suggested to better understand students' learning process. After three observations, if a student still shows problems in using the feedback for writing, we may assume that the student needs help in learning how to write.

There are some issues to be considered for assessing writing strategies. The assessment of writing strategies involves three steps: 1) being familiar with pedagogical content knowledge for writing, 2) understanding learners' interpretation of assessment outcomes, and 3) providing teacher and peer feedback for writing. The assessment requires the assessor to understand the nature of the writing task and the writing process. In addition, the assessment is also dependent on students' interpretation of their assessment outcomes. Finally, teacher and learner feedback can make a difference in learning to write.

```
┌─────────────────────────────────────────────────────────────────────────┐
│ Student name____                                                        │
│ Tasks                                                                   │
│ □ Collaborative writing on a given topic                                │
│ □ Individual writing on a given topic                                   │
│ □ Book review                                                           │
│ Date of observation                                                     │
│ □ Observation 1 _____ □ Observation 2 _____ □ Observation 3 _____    │
│ Writing strategies                                                      │
│ Making use of peer feedback for writing.                                │
│ Brainstorming ideas and using the ideas as an orientation aid for writing. │
│ Revising the sentences and improving content and style/grammar.         │
│ Trying to understand different genre requirements in writing.           │
│ Synthesizing information for writing through referring to materials.    │
│ Not using it    Developing it    Expert user                            │
│    □               □                 □                                  │
│                                                                         │
│ Diagnosis                                                               │
│ _____          │
│                                                                         │
│ Suggestions                                                             │
│ _____          │
│                                                                         │
│ _____                                                                  │
└─────────────────────────────────────────────────────────────────────────┘
```

Figure 1: An example of assessing writing strategies.

Previous questionnaires assessing language learning strategies

Systematic evaluation of language learning strategies requires the use of valid, reliable, and practical instruments. Among the available tools, questionnaires stand out as tools that can quickly and easily collect data and map out strategy patterns (Oxford 2017). Some of the most often-used questionnaires are included here.

The most cited questionnaire was the Strategy Inventory for Language Learning (SILL) developed by Oxford (1990). This 5-point Likert scale instrument comprises 50 items grouped into six categories: (a) memory strategies (9 items), (b) cognitive strategies (14 items), (c) compensation strategies (6 items), (d) metacognitive strategies (9 items), (e) affective strategies (6 items), and (f) social strategies (6 items). Researchers have applied this instrument in different contexts. For example, Mochizuki (1999) administered the SILL to 44 second-year and 113 first-year language learners at a university in Japan. The results indicated that the students used compensation strategies more frequently than they used affective strategies. In addition, the more proficient students used cognitive and metacognitive strategies more frequently than the less proficient students. Saks and Leijen (2018b) adopted the SILL to measure Estonian learners' use of language learning strategies. The results showed that the original two-factor taxonomy did not provide an acceptable model fit, so an alternative classification, i.e., a different six-factor model, was developed. All goodness of fit statistics fell within the established criteria for the new six-factor model ($\chi2$ = 201.405; df = 103; CMIN/DF = 1.955; CFI =.918; RMSEA =.061). The six factors included active language use (4 items), metacognitive strategies (4 items), social strategies (3 items), compensation strategies (2 items), memory strategies (2 items), and connecting strategies (2 items). Their findings also showed that students who achieved higher scores on the English examination reported using these strategies more frequently than those who achieved lower scores. The authors' six-factor model lacked any of Oxford's affective strategies.

Gu (2018) introduced a new version of the Vocabulary Learning Questionnaire (VLQ) based on his previous studies (see also Gu and Johnson 1996). Gu (2018) piloted two versions of the instrument, a paper version with a 7-point Likert scale and an online version with a 100-point slider bar. The series of validation procedures were based on a total of 682 students in China and resulted in a 62-item instrument. The questionnaire includes two dimensions: metacognitive and cognitive components. Metacognitive dimensions include beliefs about vocabulary learning (10 items) and metacognitive regulation (7 items). Cognitive dimensions include inferencing (7 items), using a dictionary (7 items), taking notes (6 items), rehearsal (9 items), encoding (12 items), and activation (4 items). Only one of the 15 strategies, i.e., Visual Repetition, had an alpha of.638. The remaining strategies were all above.70. The overwhelming majority of strategies were above.80. The Cronbach's alpha of over 0.6 showed acceptable reliability. Subject to EFA, Bartlett's test of sphericity was also acceptable (chi-square = 17672.477, df = 1891, p =.000).

The Metacognitive Awareness of Reading Strategies Inventory (MARSI) is a self-report instrument used to assess learners' awareness of reading strategies (Mokhtari and Reichard 2002). MARSI was developed to elucidate students' use of reading strategies within the context of academic or school-related reading. The MARSI measures three categories of strategies: (1) global reading strategies (GRS), which can be described as strategies aimed at setting the stage for the reading act; (2) problem-solving strategies (PSS), which are perceived as localized, focused problem-solving strategies used in facing the difficulties of understanding textual information; and (3) supportive reading strategies (SRS), which provide the support mechanisms or tools aimed at sustaining responsiveness to reading. After eliminating items with factor loadings lower than.30 in the EFA analysis, GRS contained 13 items, PSS contained 8 items, and SRS contained 9 items. Smith-Keita (2018) used the MARSI with

10th-grade learners and measured the relationship between metacognitive awareness of reading strategies and their achievement with college and career readiness standards for English language arts. The MARSI, including global reading strategies (α =.76), problem-solving strategies (α =.54), and support reading strategies (α =.71), demonstrates sound reliability. The new results provided information about the extent to which students were metacognitively aware of the strategies they used to support themselves as readers. The results showed a moderate, positive relationship between students' metacognitive awareness of the reading strategies they used and their college English language arts achievement scores.

8.5 Research Results and Findings

In this section, the results of studies on students' use of language learning strategies are presented. The findings are organized into themes to better understand the research on this topic.

Individual differences in using language learning strategies and factors that affect strategy choice

Increased attention has been given to examining individual learner differences in the process of learning a second and foreign language. Although an understanding of individual differences has been explored in the discipline of psychology, it is still essential to synthesize what we know and do not know about individual differences in language learning. Every psychological component of the language learning process is a potential source of individual differences in language learners. Understanding individual differences in strategy use is important, as strategies are cognitive steps for learners to acquire, store, and retrieve new information.

Anderson (1991) examined second language readers' individual differences in reading. A total of 28 Spanish-speaking students enrolled in the ESL program completed all phases of the research study. The results showed that when attempting to answer the comprehension questions, high- and low-achieving readers used different kinds of strategies. This finding suggests that strategic reading may be a matter of knowing which strategies to use for understanding a text. The qualitative results showed that compared to learners with high reading proficiency, poorer readers may not understand whether they are successful in applying the strategies.

Sufficient evidence in early research has shown that greater strategy use is related to higher levels of language proficiency (Green and Oxford 1995; Khalil 2005; Lan and Oxford 2003). In an early study, Siegler (1988) examined individual differences in young learners' strategy choices. The focus was on the consistencies in 6-year-olds' strategy choices while performing three tasks: addition, subtraction, and word identification. The children were 21 first-grade boys and 15 first-grade girls attending a middle-class school. The learners completed three tasks and a standardized test measuring mathematics computation, mathematics problem solving, total reading, word recognition, and reading comprehension. Cluster analysis divided the students into three groups: perfectionist, good students, and not-so-good students. The perfectionists appeared to set very high confidence criteria. The good students appeared to set fewer high-confidence criteria. The not-so-good students seemed to set the lowest confidence criteria. The results supported individual differences in first graders' strategy use.

In a recent study, the focus was on exploring the impact of individual differences on the process of second or foreign language writing (Forbes 2019). Drawing upon in-depth qualitative data from writing tasks and stimulated recall interviews, four distinct writer profiles emerged: the strategic writer, the experimenter, the struggling writer, and the multilingual writer. The results also showed the complex and mutually interdependent relationship between strategy use and writing achievement. The findings suggested that the development of strategies may positively influence students' proficiency level, which, in turn, can also impact the extent to which they use strategies and transfer the use of strategies in different contexts.

Overall, strategy use and proficiency may be both causes and outcomes of each other. However, the picture is complicated. Many researchers have questioned the direction of causality in this relationship between proficiency and strategy use (Bremner 1999; Su 2005) and suggested that more proficient learners reported more frequent use of language learning strategies than learners of less proficiency. One reason may be related to the fact that good language learners are willing to take advantage of practice opportunities, persevere in their drive to look for patterns, attend to meaning, monitor the use of language, and develop language as a system (Bruen 2001). Good language learners tend to think in the language, address the affective demands of language learning, and use language as a tool for communication (Wharton 2000). Successful learners know how to choose appropriate strategies, depending on the demands of the learning situation and the language task for which they may use memory strategies that include information organizing, grouping, imagery, and structured review to store information in memory and to recall it when necessary (O'Malley and Chamot 1990). Some research findings did not support the positive relationship between strategy use and proficiency level. For example, Vandergrift (1997) found that similar to successful learners, unsuccessful learners also actively use and apply a number and variety of strategies. Skehan (1989) has explained that the existence of a correlation between two variables does not necessarily suggest causality in a particular direction because poor language learners may not be able to use learning strategies as a result of their weak language skills. These contradictory results should lead us to consider that a certain strategy that may not be effective for all learners, tasks, and learning situations.

What are some factors that may impact the use of language learning strategies? Learners' metacognitive awareness could influence their strategy use. Research findings show that several factors, including the languages they have learned; their language proficiency level; their prior language learning experiences; their feelings; and their aptitude, age, and learning style, can affect their language learning performance as well as their strategy use (Teng and Huang 2019). In addition, research findings have shown the effect of age on language learning strategy use. For example, Devlin (1996) compared the learning strategies employed by 21 mature age (defined as 23 years of age or more) and 104 younger teacher education students (defined as 22 years of age or less). Compared to younger students, mature-age students obtained significantly higher scores on 7 of the 10 Learning and Study Strategies Inventory Scales (Devlin 1996). Mature-age students were better time managers; less anxious about the study; better able to concentrate, process information, and select important ideas from a topic area; more likely to evaluate their level of understanding of a topic; and more knowledgeable of effective examination strategies. Overall, mature-age students had more favorable attitudes towards the study and used more sophisticated language learning strategies than their younger counterparts.

Gender differences may also affect the use of language learning strategies. Hamilton (2008) reported that females used cognitive strategies significantly more often than males. The differences may be associated with women's better awareness of cognitive development, as argued by Hamilton (2008). In a study of adult language learners, Ehrman and Oxford (1989) found that females reported significantly greater use of language learning strategies than male students. For example, female students reported significantly higher use of four strategies: general study strategies, authentic language use strategies, strategies for meaning communication, and self-management strategies. The authors hypothesized that gender differences in language learning strategy use may occur because of women's greater social orientation, stronger verbal skills, and greater conformity to linguistic and academic norms.

Affective variables, including attitudes, motivation, goals, and personality traits, could also influence the use and choice of language learning strategies. For example, students' attitudes were influential in their choice of language learning strategies. Along with attitudes, motivation could determine learners' engagement in language learning (Man, Bui, and Teng 2018). Highly motivated learners demonstrated more varied use of strategies than less motivated learners. In addition, learners with a positive attitude may demonstrate frequent use of strategies for language learning.

Effectiveness of strategy-based instruction on language learning

Learning strategies have been found to be teachable skills. For example, strategy-based instruction can be important for the development of listening (Goh 2017), reading (Teng 2020), and writing (Teng 2016) skills. Based on research findings, strategy-based instruction led to greater strategy use, self-efficacy, anxiety reduction, and increased motivation and confidence for language learning. Strategy-based training can help learners evaluate the effectiveness of different strategies and determine when and how to transfer a given strategy to a new situation. With regard to the effectiveness of strategy-based instruction, learners' cultural backgrounds and beliefs may need to be considered. Basic strategy instruction should address learners' affective and learning-style issues, teach the strategies students need to know and reflect on how to incorporate strategy instruction into regular language learning classrooms. According to the aforementioned research findings, strategy-based instruction should be incorporated as part of the regular language learning class. However, language teachers may feel ill-equipped to conduct strategy-based instruction because they have few opportunities to see or participate in such instruction themselves. In Table 1, I list some ideas about strategy-based instruction.

8.6 Pedagogy and instruction

Next, implications for classroom practice, including the assessment of strategy use, determining learners' individual differences in strategy use, and teaching strategy instruction in the language learning classroom, are presented along with considerations for pedagogy and instruction.

First, teachers and learners can benefit from the assessment of students' language learning strategy use. The assessment of language learning strategies can lead to a greater understanding of their use of learning strategies. Diagnosing strategic learning can provide learners and their teachers with concrete ideas about how to close the language gaps on language assessment tasks. Practical and realistic means of evaluation, e.g., questionnaires, interviews, learner diaries, and

Table 1: Strategy-based instruction in previous studies.

	Procedures for strategy-based instruction
Goh and Taib (2006) Metacognitive instruction for listening	Stage 1: Listen and answer. The listening exercises in six lessons were parallel versions of the listening examination.
	Stage 2: Individual reflection. Questions were written on the board to reflect individually on the completion of their listening exercises. Questions included: What were you listening to? What helped you to understand the text? What prevented you from getting the correct answers? What did you do to understand as much of the text as possible?
	Stage 3: Self-report and group discussion. The learners took turns to read aloud their notes on their reflections. As each learner reported their observations, the others listened and sometimes asked questions or included their own comments.
Teng (2020) Metacognitive instruction for reading	Stage 1: Read and answer. This stage included two parts: Balanced literacy instruction and traditional reading pedagogy. The balanced literacy instruction mainly included instructional strategies involving reading and writing workshops. In terms of traditional reading pedagogy, students first read a text and answered three to five multiple-choice comprehension questions.
	Stage 2: Reflect Student's role: (1) Each student reflected individually on the metacognitive, self-addressed questions. (2) Each student verified his/her cognitive and metacognitive skills based on feedback-corrective processes, including enrichment and remedial help provided by the teacher as necessary.
	Metacognitive prompts: (1) Comprehension Purpose: familiarize students with the articulation of the main ideas in the text. *What was the text about?* *What were the purposes of this text?* *What specific points did I find important in this text?*

Table 1 (continued)

	Procedures for strategy-based instruction
	(2) Connection Purpose: guide students in contemplating the similarities and differences between an immediate text and previously read texts *What were the similarities and differences between this and those I have read in the past?*
	(3) Strategy Purpose: allow students to reflect on appropriate strategies for the exercise *What strategies were appropriate for completing this text reading in time?* *What strategies were useful for grasping the gist of this text?* *What strategies were useful for inferring unknown words?*
	(4) Reflection Purpose: guide students in evaluating their reading process during or at the end of the exercise *Did my strategies for reading make sense?* *Did I focus on all the details of the text?* *Did I consider all relevant information while determining the purpose of this text?* *What prevented me from achieving the correct answers?* *What did I do to understand as much of the text as possible?*
	Stage 3: Report and discuss Participants randomly formed five-member groups for the final stage of reporting and discussion. In each group, students took turns reading their reflection notes aloud while the other students listened and took notes. Students may ask questions or offer comments.
Teng (2016) Metacognitive instruction for writing	Meta-cognitive self-addressed questions in writing: Knowledge of cognition (i) What is writing all about? Take some notes. (ii) What factors will influence our performance in writing? (iii) What strategies can be accessed efficiently for developing a good writing sample? Explain your reasoning. (iv) How should we proceed to develop a solution and in which way can we apply the strategies from previous learning experiences? Quote some. (v) When and why can we use knowledge or strategies to improve our writing?

Table 1 (continued)

	Procedures for strategy-based instruction
	Regulation of cognition
	(i) What background knowledge do you have about planning, monitoring, and evaluating English writing tasks?
	(ii) Do I set reasonable goals for this writing?
	(iii) How should we plan the content of the essay before writing? Quote some, for example, what to write about, what views on the topic were, how to support their views, and how to present information.
	(iv) What strategies should we use to plan the language content of the essays
	(v) How should we organize the content for writing? Quote some, for example, how to organize ideas, language use, etc.
	(vi) How should we monitor a writing task? For example, what are the similarities and differences between the task at hand and the tasks that we have solved in the past?
	(vii) How should we evaluate a writing task? For example, does the writing make sense? Can I write differently? Did I consider all the relevant information?

classroom observations, can help teachers to conduct strategy assessments. Strategic assessment can also help teachers to pair language learning instruction with learners' needs. An understanding of students' language learning strategy preferences can also help teachers to understand students' specific needs. Such understanding can assist teachers with the systematic adoption of strategy instruction and improvement of their language instruction. These assessment tools should be used to supplement rather than supplant existing assessment measures.

Second, an area for future research on individual differences in learning strategies is to determine why some learners use certain strategies while other learners do not (or cannot). Researchers may need to understand learners' individual learning styles. However, there is a lack of reliable and valid measurement instruments for the assessment of learning styles. Teachers find it difficult to provide more appropriate assistance to students who experience problems in the foreign language classroom, which is different from other classrooms, as learners have limited foreign language input. It will be meaningful for future studies to explore the interaction between individual learning styles and strategy use. An understanding of individual differences in strategy use can help teachers and researchers to gain a clear perspective of what individual students are learning while engaged in language learning activities. Continued research and its application to the classroom could assist language learners in enhancing their understanding of strategy use and increasing their ability to use the language in varied situations. Another educational implication is that it might be useful to teach young learners, particularly lower-achieving students, to use backup strategies. The instruction for children in learning how to execute backup strategies affords them more opportunities for retrieval accuracy in inferring meaning while reading (Teng 2020).

Third, strategy-based instruction should provide sufficient practice to help learners integrate strategies into the regular language learning program. Strategy-based instruction should be geared to learners' various needs. Affective factors should be considered in designing and conducting strategy training. However, negative attitudes can make strategy training ineffective. Learners need to develop a positive view of strategy instruction and determine their personal goals for language learning. Additional factors, such as language learning experiences, gender differences, and cognitive development, may also be crucial for the development of strategy training (Arnold 1999). One issue for educators to consider is how teachers can become sensitive to individual differences in language learning. Assessments of strategies can help to guide strategy training. Teachers can use one or more techniques, e.g., diaries, observations, and interviews, to assess learners' current use of learning strategies. Teachers can also try to understand students' goals, motivations, attitudes, and personality types through informal discussions.

Finally, teachers should consider how to adapt strategy-based instruction to the needs of their classrooms. Given the different requirements of strategy instruction formats, helpful steps include attending training sessions, reading the information in published materials, and consulting strategy specialists. Strategy-based instruction can also be the basis for conducting intervention studies. In assessing strategic learning, teachers should consider the progress of each individual. It may be an extra burden on the part of the teacher to develop learning opportunities that attend to the different learning preferences of their students. Assessment should also involve checking the use of language learning strategies and their relationship with learners' individual language proficiency. Strategic learning is an incremental process rather than a rapid process.

In terms of pedagogy and instruction, educators may need to consider other critical issues. Language teachers must become aware of the importance of language learning strategies. The first step is for teachers to discover how to instruct strategies for students of linguistically diverse backgrounds. There are challenges in strategy-based instruction considering students' individual differences in language proficiency, learning motivation, institutional practices, and cultural beliefs. There are some practical concerns regarding how training can be most effectively accomplished. As described by Skehan (1991), several lines of inquiry, such as whether strategy-based instruction is integrated with a regular coursebook or is separate, whether students should be informed of the purposes of training, and whether there are benefits in linking language strategy training to content courses, need to be considered. More research is needed to identify which strategies or strategy categories are most susceptible to training. It is also important to investigate the length of time needed to achieve satisfactory results from strategy training. Some learners may not be influenced by strategy training. Some good learners may be the ones for whom the use of effective strategies is possible, while for poorer learners, strategies may not be helpful or cannot be learned. Further research is required to help learners engage in strategy-based learning. The key issue is to deliver techniques that enable learners to achieve independence in their language-learning efforts.

Overall, all learners use strategies. Some learners are more open to choosing the right strategy for the right occasion. Some learners depend on their teachers to provide feedback for the specific use of strategies. Thus, strategy training may need to aim at improving the decision-making capacities of learners from different cultural backgrounds. Educators may even need to consider cultural norms for strategic learning. If certain language learning strategies are not in line with cultural norms, e.g., cooperative strategies that highlight active communication, teachers may need to learn how to help students conquer problems related to cultural differences. Research is burgeoning in the area of language learning strategies. Researchers need to update theory and conduct investigations to help classroom practitioners better understand their students and provide strategy-based instruction tailored to the diverse needs of students.

Recommended Readings

Gu, Yongqi & Robert Keith Johnson. 1996. Vocabulary learning strategies and language learning outcomes. *Language Learning, 46*(4), 643–679.
 This is a well-cited study attempting to establish the vocabulary learning strategies used by EFL students and the relationship between their strategies and outcomes in learning English.

Goh, Christine & Yusnita Taib. 2006. Metacognitive instruction in listening for young learners. *ELT Journal, 60*(3), 222–232.
 This study aims to delineate young learners' strategy use in listening. The results provide insights into the factors that influence young learners' listening and strategy use.

Teng, Feng. 2020. The benefits of metacognitive reading strategy awareness instruction for young learners of English as a second language. *Literacy, 54*, 29–39.

This study aims to understand young learners' strategy use in reading. The findings articulate the knowledge factors that influence young learners' reading. The results provide insights into the nature and demands of reading and metacognitive knowledge in improving reading comprehension.

References

Anderson, Neil J. 1991. Individual differences in strategy use in second language reading and testing. *The Modern Language Journal* 75(4). 460–472.

Arnold, Jane. 1999. Visualization: language learning with the mind's eye. In Jane, Arnold (ed.), *Affect in language learning*, 260–278. Cambridge: Cambridge University Press.

Baumeister, Roy F & Kathleen D. Vohs. 2007. Self-regulation, ego depletion, and motivation. *Social and Personality Psychology Compass* 1(1). 115–128.

Bereiter, Carl & Marlene Scardamalia. 1987. *The psychology of written composition*. New York, NY: Lawrence Erlbaum Associates, Inc.

Bremner, Stephen. 1999. Language Learning Strategies and Language Proficiency: Investigating the Relationship in Hong Kong. *Canadian Modern Language Review* 55(4). 490–514.

Bruen, Jennifer. 2001. Strategies for Success: Profiling the effective learner of German. *Foreign Language Annals* 34(3). 216–225.

Bui, Gavin, Laura Man & Mark Feng Teng. 2018. From second language to third language learning: Exploring a dual-motivation system among multilinguals. *Australian Review of Applied Linguistics* 41(1). 63–91.

Cameron, Linda D & Lana Jago. 2013. Cognitive strategies. In Marc D. Gellman & J. Rodney Turner (eds.), *Encyclopedia of behavioral medicine*, 26. Springer, New York, NY.

Canale, Michael & Merrill Swain. 1980. Theoretical bases of communicative approaches to second language teaching and testing. *Applied Linguistics* 1(1). 1–47.

Chamot, Anna Uhl. 2005. Language learning strategy instruction: Current issues and research. *Annual review of applied linguistics* 25. 112–130.

Chamot, Anna Uhl & J. Michael O'Malley. 1994. *The CALLA handbook: Implementing the cognitive academic language learning approach*. Reading, MA: Addison Wesley.

Cohen, Andrew D. 1998. Strategies in learning and using a second language. Routledge.

Cohen, Andrew D. 2005. Strategies for learning and performing L2 speech acts. *Intercultural Pragmatics* 2(3). 275–301.

Cohen, Andrew D. 2011. *Strategies in learning and using a second language*. Harlow: Longman/Pearson Education.

Devlin, Marcia. 1996. Older and Wiser? A comparison of the learning and study strategies of mature age and younger teacher education students. *Higher Education Research & Development* 15(1). 51–60.

Dole, Janice A, Kathleen J. Brown & Woodrow Trathen. 1996. The effects of strategy instruction on the comprehension performance of at-risk students. *Reading Research Quarterly* 31(1). 62–88.

Dornyei, Zoltan & Stephen Ryan. 2015. *The psychology of the language learner revisited*. New York: Routledge.

Efklides, Anastasia. 2008. Metacognition: Defining its facets and levels of functioning in relation to self-regulation and co-regulation. *European Psychologist* 13(4). 277–287.

Ehrman, Madeline & Rebecca L. Oxford. 1989. Effects of sex differences, career choice, and psychological type on adults' language learning strategies. *Modern Language Journal* 73(1). I-13.
Forbes, Karen. 2019. The role of individual differences in the development and transfer of writing strategies between foreign and first language classrooms. *Research Papers in Education* 34 (4). 445–464.
Forbes, Karen & Linda Fisher. 2018. The impact of expanding advanced level secondary school students' awareness and use of metacognitive learning strategies on confidence and proficiency in foreign language speaking skills. *The Language Learning Journal* 46(2). 173–185.
Goh, Christine & Yusnita Taib. 2006. Metacognitive instruction in listening for young learners. *ELT Journal* 60(3). 222–232.
Goh, Christine. 2017. Cognition, metacognition, and L2 listening. In Eli Hinkel (ed.), *Handbook of Research in Second Language Teaching and Learning, Volume III*, 214–228. New York: Routledge Taylor & Francis.
Green, John M & Rebecca L. Oxford. 1995. A closer look at learning strategies, L2 proficiency, and gender. *TESOL Quarterly* 29(2). 261–297.
Grenfell, Michael & Vee Harris. 1999. *Modern languages and learning strategies: In theory and practice*. London: Routledge.
Gu, Yongqi. 2018. Validation of an online questionnaire of vocabulary learning strategies for ESL learners. *Studies in Second Language Learning and Teaching* 8(2). 325–350.
Gu, Yongqi & Robert Keith Johnson. 1996. Vocabulary learning strategies and language learning outcomes. *Language Learning* 46(4). 643–679.
Hamilton, Colin. 2008. *Cognition and sex differences*. London, England: Palgrave Macmillan
Harris, Vee. 2003. Adapting classroom-based strategy instruction to a distance learning context. *TESL-EJ* 7(2). 1–19.
Horwitz, Elaine K. 2010. Foreign and second language anxiety. *Language Teaching* 43(2). 154–167.
Hyland, Ken. 2015. Researching language learning strategies. In Brian Paltridge & Aek Phakiti (eds.), *Research methods in applied linguistics*, 421–438. New York: Bloomsbury.
Khalil, Aziz. 2005. Assessment of language learning strategies used by Palestinian EFL learners. *Foreign Language Annals* 38(1). 108–117.
Kikas, Eve & Anna-Liisa Jõgi. 2015. Assessment of learning strategies: self-report questionnaire or learning task. *European Journal of Psychology of Education* 31(4). 579–593.
Krashen, Stephen D. 1982. *Principles and practice in second language acquisition*. Oxford: UK: Pergamon Press.
Kurtz, Matthew M. 2011. Compensatory strategies. In Jeffrey S. Kreutzer, John DeLuca & Bryan Caplan (eds.), *Encyclopedia of clinical neuropsychology*. New York: Springer. (pp.657)
Lan, Rae & Rebecca L. Oxford. 2003. Language learning strategy profiles of elementary school students in Taiwan. *IRAL* 41. 339–379.
Mokhtari, Kouider, & Reichard, Carla. 2002. Assessing students' metacognitive awareness of reading strategies. Journal of Educational Psychology, 94(2), 249–259.
Mochizuki, Akihiko. 1999. Language learning strategies used by Japanese university students. *RELC Journal, 30*(2), 101–113.
O'Malley J., Michael & Anna Uhl Chamot. 1990. *Learning strategies in second language acquisition*. Cambridge: Cambridge University Press.
Oxford, Rebecca L. 1990. *Language learning strategies: What every teacher should know*. Boston: Heinle & Heinle.
Oxford, Rebecca L. 2017. *Teaching and researching language learning strategies: Self-regulation in context* (2nd ed.). New York: Routledge.

Oxford, Rebecca. (Ed.). 1996. Language learning strategies around the world: Cross-cultural perspectives (No. 13). Natl Foreign Lg Resource Ctr.

Oxford, Rebecca L & Madeline E. Ehrman. 1995. Adults' language learning strategies in an intensive foreign language program in the United States. *System* 23(3). 359–386.

Oyen, Anne-Siri & James M. Bebko. 1996. The effects of computer games and lesson contexts on children's mnemonic strategies. *Journal of experimental child psychology* 62(2). 173–189.

Palinscar, Aannemarie Sullivan & Ann L. Brown. 1984. Reciprocal teaching of comprehension fostering and comprehension monitoring activities. *Cognition and Instruction* 1(2). 117–175.

Pearson, P. David & Janice A. Dole. 1987. Explicit comprehension instruction: A review of research and a new conceptualization of learning. *Elementary School Journal, 88(2)*, 151–65.

Rose, Heath. 2015. Researching language learner strategies. In Brian Paltridge & Aek Phakiti (eds.), Research methods in applied linguistics: A practical resource (pp.421–437). New York: Bloomsbury Publishing.

Rosenshine, Barak & Carla Meister. 1997. Cognitive strategy instruction in reading. In Steven A. Stahl & David A. Hayes (eds.), *Instructional models in reading*, 85–107. New York, NY: Lawrence Erlbaum Associates, Inc.

Saks, Katrin & Äli Leijen. 2018a. Cognitive and metacognitive strategies as predictors of language learning outcomes. *Psihologija* 51(4). 489–505.

Saks, Katrin, Äli Leijen. 2018b. Adapting the SILL to measure Estonian learners' language learning strategies: the development of an alternative model. *The Language Learning Journal* 46(5). 634–646.

Scarcella, Robin C & Rebecca L. Oxford. 1992. *The Tapestry of language learning: The individual in the communicative classroom*. Boston, MA: Heinle & Heinle Publishers.

Şeker, Meral. 2016. The use of self-regulation strategies by foreign language learners and its role in language achievement. *Language Teaching Research* 20(5). 600–618.

Shao, Kaiqi, Reinhard Pekrun & Laura J. Nicholsonc. 2019. Emotions in classroom language learning: What can we learn from achievement emotion research? *System* 86. 102121.

Shen, Hwei-Jiun. 2003. The role of explicit instruction in ESL/EFL reading. *Foreign Language Annals* 36(3). 424–433.

Skehan, Peter. 1989. *Individual differences in second-language learning*. London: Edward Arnold.

Skehan, Peter. 1991. Individual differences in second language learning. *Studies in Second Language Acquisition* 13(2). 275–298.

Siegler, R. (1988). Strategy choice procedures and the development of multiplication skill. Journal of Experimental Psychology: General, 117, 258–275.

Siegler, Robert S. 1998. Individual differences in strategy choices: Good students, not-so-good students, and perfectionists. *Child Development* 59(4). 833–851.

Smith-Keita, Davida. 2018. *The relationship between metacognitive awareness of reading strategies use and 10th grade students' college and career readiness achievement in English language arts*. Unpublished doctoral thesis. University of Mississippi, USA.

Su, Min-hsun Maggie. 2005. A study of EFL technological and vocational college students' language learning strategies and their self-perceived English proficiency. *Electronic Journal of Foreign Language Teaching* 2(1). 44–56.

Teng, Feng, & Yue, Mei. 2022. Metacognitive writing strategies, critical thinking skills, and academic writing performance: A structural equation modeling approach. Metacognition and Learning.

Teng, Feng. 2016. Immediate and delayed effects of embedded metacognitive instruction on Chinese EFL students' English writing and regulation of cognition. *Thinking Skills & Creativity* 22. 289–302.

Teng, Feng. 2020. The benefits of metacognitive reading strategy awareness instruction for young learners of English as a second language. *Literacy* 54(1). 29–39.

Teng, Feng & Jing Huang. 2019. Predictive effects of writing strategies for self-regulated learning on secondary school learners' EFL writing proficiency. *TESOL Quarterly* 53(1). 232–247.

Vandergrift, Laurens. 1997. The comprehension strategies of second language (French) listeners: A descriptive study. *Foreign Language Annals* 30(3). 387–409.

Veenman, Marcel V. J. 2011. Learning to self-monitor and self-regulate. In Richard E. Mayer & Patricia A. Alexander (eds.), *Handbook of research on learning and instruction*, 197–218. New York: Routledge.

Vygotsky, L.S & Michael Cole. 1978. *Mind in society: The development of higher psychological processes*. Cambridge, MA: Harvard University Press.

Wharton, Glenn. 2000. Language learning strategy use of bilingual foreign language learners in Singapore. *Language Learning* 50(2). 203–243.

Young, Dolly Jesusita. 1998. *Affect in foreign language and second language learning*. New York: McGraw Hill.

Zimmerman, Barry J & Rafael Risemberg. 1997. Becoming a self-regulated writer: A social cognitive perspective. *Contemporary Educational Psychology* 22. 73–101.

9 Metacognition

Mark Feng Teng

Abstract: Metacognition is a type of individual difference. In the field of educational psychology, metacognition has been explored for decades with the consensus that it plays a role in learners' academic achievement. Increasing attention has also been paid to metacognition in the field of second language learning. Through an overview of educational psychology and second language acquisition studies, this chapter explores the construct of metacognition and provides a theoretical basis for metacognition in second language learning. The chapter highlights the importance of metacognition as a tool for language learning and teaching. This chapter also introduces key instruments for assessing metacognition, and presents research findings that support metacognitive instruction for improving listening, reading, and writing outcomes. Research suggests that students should be aware of how they can activate their existing knowledge to enhance the language learning process, build an awareness of their knowledge gaps and set goals for bridging these gaps. Language teachers play a key role in supporting their students in developing metacognitive awareness through modeling metacognitive strategies. Most importantly, language teachers themselves should be metacognitively aware of their own teaching to help students' language learning.

Keywords: Metacognition, metacognitive knowledge, metacognitive regulation, metacognitive experiences, assessing metacognition

9.1 Introduction

Metacognition is a type of individual difference that can be both trait-like and state-like (Sato 2022). Researchers have found that metacognition plays a role in L2 development (Efklides 2006). L2 learners who possess a high level of awareness of metacognition may better understand the challenges in L2 learning, possess a strong deep-seated belief towards L2 learning, and take self-initiated actions towards realizing goals for developing L2 (Wenden 1998). Metacognition can also have a longitudinal effect on EFL learners' vocabulary learning (Teng, 2021) and reading and writing performance (Teng & Zhang 2021). An understanding of the role of metacognition in L2 learning can be a much-needed contribution to the field of second language acquisition. This chapter explains the connections between theory, research, and classroom practice for metacognition and endeavors to shed light on ways to promote learners' metacognitive awareness.

9.2 Theories & Models

Most researchers attribute the notion of metacognition to Flavell (1976, 1979), who is known for the theory of mind approach and described metacognition as "one's knowledge concerning one's own cognitive processes and products or anything related to them" (1976: 232). He implies that metacognition is the application of the theory of mind to cognitive tasks. Theory of mind refers to the ability to "attribute mental states, such as beliefs, desires, and intentions, to self and others" (Lockl and Schneider 2006: 16). Boekaerts (1997: 165) added that metacognition is not only a theory of mind but also a "theory of self, theory of learning and learning environments". Flavell (1979) further described metacognition as learners' awareness of their cognitive and executive processes in seeking efforts to regulate any aspect of their cognitive activities. He suggests that metacognition includes three domains, metacognitive knowledge, metacognitive experiences, and metacognitive strategies, and further conceptualized metacognition as having four components: metacognitive knowledge, metacognitive experience, goals, and the activation of strategies. Flavell (1985) organized the construct into two dimensions, i.e., knowledge of metacognition and regulation of metacognition, to capture its cognitive nature and regulation of knowledge. Many research studies operationalize metacognition according to this conceptualization.

Metacognition has been widely acknowledged as an essential tool for lifelong learning in all contexts, including multilingual societies, and researchers have given increasing attention to how metacognition is connected with good language learners (Anderson 2008). Research shows that metacognitive knowledge positively influences the quality and effectiveness of academic learning (Schraw 1998; Wenden 1998), self-regulated learning (Wenden 2002), learner autonomy (Victori and Lockhart 1995), and academic success (Zimmerman and Bandura 1994). Fairbanks et al. (2010) argued that teachers who understand the importance of metacognition for learning are better able to support their students' development.

Studies on metacognitive development in the 1970s were mostly concerned with children's metamemory, i.e., their knowledge about person, task, and strategy variables. Since then, researchers in the theory of mind have explored children's initial metacognitive knowledge, that is, knowledge about the existence of mental states, including desires and intentions. Knowledge about the theory of mind has allowed researchers to concentrate on task-related cognitive processes for improving task performance and monitoring improvement. Metacognition is thus described as "knowledge about knowledge", "thoughts about thoughts", or "reflections about actions" (Weinert 1987: 8).

Metacognition is different from cognition. Metacognition refers to the scientific study of an individual's thinking about his or her own cognition. Cognition explores learners' memory, attention, understanding of language, reasoning, learning, problem solving, and decision making. Metacognition, which studies an individual's cognitive process, is multidimensional in nature. Metacognition provides "domain-general knowledge and regulatory skills that enable individuals to control cognition in multiple domains" (Schraw 2001: 7). We can also interpret metacognition as an individual's awareness of and reflection on his/her knowledge, experiences, emotions, and learning in all domains. Flavell (1979) also considers cognitive activities to be different from metacognitive activities. The latter involves learners' planning, reflecting, monitoring, and evaluating their own learning processes, while the former involves a need to learn, understand, remember, process new information, and engage in more complex mental activities such as planning and executing tasks.

Flavell (1979) suggested that person, task, and strategy knowledge comprised metacognitive knowledge. Wenden (1998) described person knowledge as an individual's knowledge about his/her cognitive processes or awareness and understanding of his/her strengths and weaknesses in certain knowledge or skill areas. Any possible factors, including age, language aptitude, and motivation, may impact a person's knowledge. Wenden also described task knowledge as the knowledge essential to the understanding of task purpose and demands. Likewise, strategy knowledge concerns strategies that are likely to be effective for individuals to achieve task goals. Other researchers follow a framework in which metacognitive knowledge is divided into three types according to their processes, i.e., declarative, procedural, and conditional knowledge (e.g., see Paris, Cross, and Lipson 1984). Declarative knowledge refers to factual knowledge about oneself and one's skills, intellectual resources, affective factors, and processing abilities. The process of acquiring declarative knowledge is also called metalinguistic awareness, which refers to "one's ability to consider language not just as a means of expressing ideas or communicating with others but also as an object of inquiry" (Gass and Selinker 2008: 359). Learners who have built metalinguistic awareness can foster language awareness, which in turn fosters metalinguistic awareness. Language awareness refers to "explicit knowledge about language, and conscious perception and sensitivity in language learning, language teaching, and language use" (Svalberg 2012: 376). Explicit knowledge about language learning processes is part of declarative metacognitive knowledge.

Procedural knowledge determines how an individual decides to implement a task through the deployment of appropriate strategies (Paris et al. 1984). An example of procedural knowledge is learning to swim. When learning to swim, no matter what the instructor said, a learner often struggles to grasp the task until s/he has practiced a few times. Once practiced and learned, the task quickly became implicit knowledge, the type of knowledge that is hard to explain, as it is subconsciously stored in the mind. Conditional knowledge is how an individual decides when, where and why to use specific strategies for completing relevant tasks. Conditional knowledge is especially important for the effective selection of strategies and allocation of resources (Schraw 1998). In second language learning, conditional knowledge allows the learner to be a guide to determine when and how strategies can be used for completing a task.

In line with Flavell, Efklides (2008) also suggests metacognition comprises three domains, i.e., metacognitive knowledge, metacognitive experiences, and metacognitive strategies. In her view, metacognitive experiences refer to individuals' awareness of and what they feel when processing information for a task (Efklides 2006). In particular, the feeling and judgments of knowing, effort expenditure, solution correctness, difficulties, familiarity, and confidence are all domains in metacognitive experiences. Metacognitive experiences are thought to be the basis for an individual to become aware of task performance. Efklides (2006) included metacognitive knowledge and metacognitive experiences as the monitoring function and metacognitive skills as the control of cognition. Metacognitive experiences were originally juxtaposed with metacognitive knowledge by Flavell (1981). Learners undergo metacognitive experience as they engage in learning activities, and learners' subjective and affective experiences influence their metacognition (Efklides 2001). For example, learners' emotions, either positive (e.g., satisfaction or confidence) or negative (e.g., boredom and anxiety), may impact their willingness to use the strategy in the future. Such experiences may in turn affect their metacognitive knowledge. Metacognitive experience is an important component in the context of classroom instruction, where learners experience a variety of emotions.

Metacognitive skills were also described as metacognitive regulation by Shimamura (2000). Metacognitive skills included planning, conflict resolution, error detection, and inhibitory control. Metacognitive control refers to the modification of one's current thoughts through strategies such as editing, drafting, idea generation, word production, translation, and revision (Kuhn 2000). Metacognitive skills also included orientation strategies, planning strategies, cognitive processing strategies, monitoring strategies, and evaluation strategies (Veenman and Elshout 1999). Brown (1987) suggested that metacognitive regulation is somewhat different from metacognitive skills; that is, metacognitive regulation is defined as how individuals identify distracting internal and external stimuli to sustain effort over time for executive functions. In particular, Schraw (1998) suggested that metacognitive regulation entails three skills: planning, monitoring, and evaluating. Planning refers to an individual's ability to select and allocate strategies and resources for completing relevant tasks, whereas monitoring is an individual's ability to observe, check, and appraise the performance of a particular task. Evaluating is the individual's ability to assess his/her regulatory processes and learning products. Schraw and Dennison (1994) added debugging strategies and information management strategies as two essential metacognitive strategies. Debugging strategies refer to an individual's ability to modify comprehension and performance errors. Information management strategies refer to an individual's skills in processing, organizing, elaborating, and summarizing information for a particular task. Figure 1 presents an understanding of metacognition.

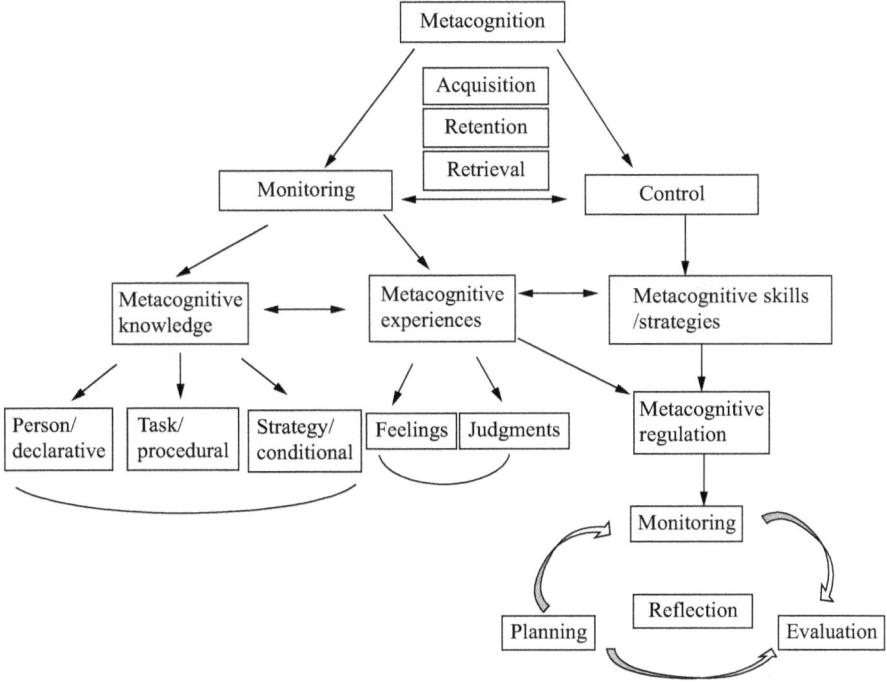

Figure 1: Multifaceted elements of metacognition.

This framework was developed by Teng, Qin, and Wang (2022) to illustrate the field's thinking about metacognition. First, metacognition consists of two aspects: monitoring and control of cognition, as described by Flavell (1979), who delineated metacognition as serving two basic functions, namely, the monitoring and control of cognition. Metacognition is thus a conscious process through which an individual is consciously aware of the monitoring and control processes. The three major stages, i.e., acquisition, retention, and retrieval, are between the control and monitoring levels. Second, metacognition is multifaceted and includes three basic domains: metacognitive knowledge, metacognitive experiences, and metacognitive skills. The three domains are interrelated. Third, the monitoring function involves metacognitive knowledge and metacognitive experiences. The control function includes metacognitive skills and strategies, e.g., planning, monitoring, and evaluating. Reflection is a fundamental part of the plan-monitor-evaluate process. Finally, metacognition is an individual phenomenon that reflects the development of knowledge and the regulation of metacognition. Metacognitive knowledge, metacognitive experiences, and metacognitive skills are interrelated.

9.3 Assessment

To measure learners' metacognitive awareness, researchers have used various types of instruments, including self-report questionnaires, observations, think-aloud protocols, and interviews (Winne and Perry 2005). For example, metacognition can be investigated via stimulated recalls and by retrospectively asking learners what they were thinking at the time of task performance (Bui and Kong 2019). In a review of 123 studies on the assessment of metacognition, Dinsmore, Alexander, and Loughlin (2008) found that one of the most popular types of instruments was the self-report questionnaire. Self-report questionnaires are cost-effective, amenable to large-scale studies, and typically easy to administer and score. Despite the lower reliability of self-report instruments, this tool has received much attention from researchers. This research is reviewed here.

Metacognitive Awareness Inventory (MAI)

The Metacognitive Awareness Inventory (MAI) developed by Schraw and Dennison (1994) is an influential instrument for assessing adolescents' and adults' metacognitive awareness. This instrument includes 52 items that are subsumed into eight factors that measure knowledge of cognition (17 items) and regulation of cognition (35 items). The knowledge dimension includes items addressing declarative, procedural, and conditional knowledge. The regulation dimension includes items addressing planning, information management strategies, monitoring, debugging strategies, and evaluation. The authors' research using the instrument showed support for the two-component view of metacognition. The MAI has been found to be a reliable initial test of metacognitive awareness for older students and can also be used to assess lower-performing students who frequently display comprehension monitoring deficiencies.

Magno (2010) created two structural equation models, one specifying the MAI as the eight theorized factors (e.g., declarative knowledge, procedural knowledge, conditional knowledge, planning, monitoring, evaluating, information management strategy, debugging strategy). The eight factors were further classified as knowledge and regulation factors. He claimed that the eight-factor model is a better fit for assessing metacognition than the two-factor model. Overall, the findings lent support to the validity of MAI. Harrison and Vallin (2018) examined the MAI using empirical factor-structure evidence to conduct four confirmatory factor analyses. The first analysis yielded the unidimensional model, which specified the 52 items, and the second analysis was a two-factor model similar to Schraw and Dennison's (1994) Exploratory Factor Analysis (EFA) model. The third model comprised a knowledge factor (17 items) and a regulation factor (35 items). The fourth model included eight factors. The findings support the reliability of MAI.

The Strategy Inventory of Language Learning (SILL)

The Strategy Inventory of Language Learning (SILL) is a 50-item instrument developed by Oxford (1990) that aims to assess language learners' strategy use, including memory, cognitive and metacognitive, compensation, affective, and social strategies. SILL is based on the observation that successful language learners tend to use good strategies more often than less successful learners and that awareness of strategies is a predictor of language learning performance. SILL equips teachers with the strategy profile of their students and uncovers the kinds of strategies that learners resort to when learning English as a second or foreign language. Oxford and Burry-Stock (1995) described the psychometric quality of the 50-item ESL/EFL SILL in terms of utility, reliability, and validity. Ardasheva and Tretter (2013) included two stages to evaluate the assessment tool with 1,057 students: instrument calibration and instrument validation. The first stage of the assessment was to validate the original 50 SILL items. The second stage was to validate a simplified 28-item survey. Data analyses were based on EFA and CFA. The results validated the 50-item ESL/EFL measure of language learning strategies and supported the validity of the modified version of 28 items. Heo, Stoffa, and Kush (2012) used the SILL with 104 Korean immigrant students in the U.S. The data were assessed with an EFA. The findings supported a good model fit, indicating that the hypothesized factor model fits the sample of participants. These findings add to a growing body of evidence suggesting that SILL primarily consists of a single factor, which should be best described as a general language learning strategy.

Metacognitive Awareness Listening Questionnaire (MALQ)

The Metacognitive Awareness Listening Questionnaire (MALQ) was developed by Vandergrift, Goh, Mareschal, and Tafaghodtari (2006) to assess second language

(L2) listeners' metacognitive awareness and perceived use of strategies while listening to oral texts. The MALQ is a 21-item instrument that covers five distinct factors: problem solving, planning and evaluation, mental translation, person knowledge, and directed attention. The development of the MALQ used Flavell's (1979) model of metacognitive knowledge, i.e., person, task, and strategy knowledge. Students can use the MALQ to determine their current level of metacognitive awareness and to chart the development of their strategy use and listening comprehension awareness over time. The MALQ may also be used for metacognitive training to help learners become skilled listeners who self-regulate their metacognitive comprehension processes automatically. Teachers can also use the MALQ as a diagnostic or consciousness-raising tool for understanding students' metacognitive awareness in listening comprehension.

Ehrich and Henderson (2019) collected information on MALQ's psychometric properties with 229 male Korean adolescent speakers of English using Rasch modeling for scale validity. The results showed that except for personal knowledge, all other subscales had sound reliability. The authors proposed that optimal performance for MALQ was attained by using a 4-point Likert scale. MALQ has also been used in empirical experimental studies. For example, Xu (2017) used structural equation modeling to examine the mediating effect of metacognitive listening awareness on the relationship between a student's motivation (expectancy, importance, interest, listening anxiety) and listening test scores with 560 Chinese first-year undergraduate students. The results demonstrated that metacognitive listening awareness did not mediate the relationship between importance and listening test score. However, metacognitive listening awareness mediated the relationship between expectancy and listening test score, interest and listening test score, and listening anxiety and listening test score.

Metacognitive Awareness of Reading Strategies Inventory (MARSI)

The Metacognitive Awareness of Reading Strategies Inventory (MARSI) was developed by Mokhtari and Reichard (2002) to assess 6th- through 12th-grade students' metacognitive awareness and perceived use of reading strategies while reading academic or school-related materials. MARSI includes three factors, the first of which is the Global Reading Strategies factor, which contains 13 items focused on reading strategies toward a global analysis of the text. The second factor is Problem-Solving Strategies, which contains 8 items measuring strategies for solving problems when text becomes difficult to read. The third factor is Support Reading Strategies, which contains 9 items measuring the use of outside reference materials, taking notes, and other support strategies. MARSI provides feedback for assessing the degree to which a student is or is not aware of the cognitive processes for reading. The results can provide information for students to increase their awareness of their own comprehension processes and help teachers to understand students' strategy use in reading.

Mokhtari, Dimitrov, and Reichard (2018) revised MARSI to assess 1,164 students' awareness of reading strategies when reading school-related materials. They conducted a confirmatory factor analysis of the MARSI instrument that reduced the number of strategy statements from 30 to 15. Cronbach's alpha coefficient for internal consistency reliability of the 15-item scale was .85. The results indicated that regardless of gender and ethnicity, the students assigned the same meanings to the reading strategy statements in the inventory. The results also showed a significant correlation between students' reading scores and their use of global reading, problem-solving, and support reading strategies.

Writing Strategies for Self-Regulated Learning Questionnaire (WSSRLQ)

The Writing Strategies for Self-Regulated Learning Questionnaire (WSSRLQ) developed by Teng and Zhang (2016) includes 40 items and nine factors: goal-oriented monitoring and evaluating, idea planning, peer learning, feedback handling, interest enhancement, emotional control, motivational self-talk, text processing, and course memory. The WSSRLQ can be used as a self-evaluation tool for students to appraise their degree of awareness of writing strategies to reflect on their writing strategy use when developing writing skills in EFL contexts. The instrument provides insights into the understanding of self-regulated writing strategies from cognitive, metacognitive, social-behavioral, and motivational regulation perspectives.

Teng and Huang (2019) applied the WSSRLQ in a Chinese secondary school context with 682 students. One reason for its use with secondary school students is that they tend to adopt fewer SRL strategies than students in universities, where examination-oriented teaching and learning are common. The two purposes of the study were to identify the role of self-regulated writing strategies on EFL students' writing proficiency and to examine whether the use of strategies would vary for individual students. The results showed that students' self-regulated writing strategies influenced their writing performance. The results supported the validity of a higher-order self-regulation model that focuses on cognition, metacognition, social behavior, and motivational regulation (e.g., see Zimmerman 2011). In line with Kizilcec et al. (2017), students' individual differences affected their use of SRL strategies. For example, age, gender, English learning experience, time commitment to writing, familiarity with writing topics, examination experience, school prestige, and interest in learning English all played a role in influencing students' reported use of self-regulated writing strategies (Teng and Huang 2019).

Metacognitive Academic Writing Strategies Questionnaire (MAWSQ)

Teng, Qin, and Wang (2022) developed the MAWSQ through five processes: item generation, reference consultation, initial piloting, psychometric evaluation, and exploratory factor analysis (EFA). The MAWSQ mainly includes two main components: metacognitive knowledge and metacognitive regulation. In terms of metacognitive knowledge, three categories, i.e., declarative knowledge, procedural knowledge, and conditional knowledge, were established. With regard to metacognitive regulation, five categories, i.e., planning, monitoring, evaluating, debugging, and information management, were outlined. Confirmatory factor analysis (CFA) results demonstrated an eight-factor correlated model of metacognitive strategies for EFL academic writing with standardized regression weight, as well as a one-factor second-order model of metacognitive strategies for EFL academic writing. The results also supported the role of different subcategories of MAWSQ in predicting EFL learners' academic writing performance.

9.4 Research Results and Findings

Wenden (1987) was the first to consider metacognition in the context of second language acquisition. Following Wenden (1987), intervention studies examined the effectiveness of teachers' pedagogical approaches with a focus on enhancing learners' metacognition for their learning outcomes. Well-designed intervention studies include two or more independent learner groups in a pre- and post-test design. Here, studies on applying metacognitive strategies for language learning are reviewed.

Metacognition and listening

Vandergriff and Goh (2012) proposed an instructional framework for teaching metacognitive skills for listening. Their framework has three components: knowing, sensing, and doing. The three components are operationalized as drawing on previous knowledge (schema), processing knowledge during listening, and employing self-regulating strategies during and after listening. During the learning process, peer interaction is important. A pedagogical sequence comprises planning, goal setting, predicting, monitoring, evaluation, reflection, and problem solving. The authors argue that metacognitive instruction in the classroom benefits low-proficiency learners. Learners at an early stage in their acquisition would benefit the most from a metacognitive approach to listening.

Some theories have described how to incorporate metacognitive instruction for listening comprehension. For example, Vandergrift (2004) proposed a metacognitive cycle to help learners integrate the use of metacognitive strategies while listening. The cycle includes five stages: planning/predicting, first verification, second verification final verification, and reflection. In the planning/predicting stage, students attempt to know the topic and text type and predict the types of information and possible words they may hear. The related metacognitive strategies in this stage were planning and directed attention. In the first verification stage, students verify initial hypotheses, correct them as needed, and note additional information. The metacognitive strategies in this stage include monitoring, planning, and selective attention. At the second verification stage, students verify points of disagreement, make corrections, and understand details. This stage also includes class discussions and reflections for students to understand the meaning of certain words or parts of the text. Metacognitive strategies at this stage include monitoring, problem solving, and evaluation. At the final verification stage, students listen for information that they could not decipher earlier in the class discussion. Metacognitive strategies in this stage include selective attention and monitoring. At the reflection stage, learners adopt strategies to compensate for what they did not understand and identify goals for the next listening activity. The main metacognitive strategy at this stage was the evaluation strategy.

Goh (2008) also proposed two kinds of learning activities for listening based on key principles for successful metacognitive instruction (Veenman, Van Hout-Wolters, and Afflerbach 2006). The first activity is integrated experiential listening tasks. These tasks enable learners to experience social-cognitive processes of listening comprehension. These activities are mainly used to assist learners in using course books or materials prepared by teachers. The focus is on the extraction of information and the construction of meaning. The incorporation of listening activities with metacognitive prompts can help learners to become aware of various cognitive processes in L2 listening. Students can also learn to apply metacognitive knowledge to their listening development beyond the classroom and to explore their own self-concept as listeners, employ appropriate strategies during listening, and discern factors that may influence their listening performance. The second type of activity is guided reflections for listening. This activity aims to draw out learners' implicit knowledge about L2 listening and encourage them to construct new knowledge to understand their listening experiences. Through reflections, learners can think back to previous events and plan ahead to manage their own learning. In a qualitative study, Goh (1998) observed the use of cognitive and metacognitive strategies by 16 university students. The data from verbal reports during a listening task as well as written diary entries revealed that high-ability listeners used metacognitive strategies more than low-ability listeners.

Studies have also provided support for the use of metacognitive strategies for listening. For example, Goh and Taib (2006) developed eight process-based listening lessons for primary school students. The lessons followed a three-stage sequence: listen and answer, reflect, report and discuss. The findings showed that after eight lessons, the learners demonstrated some metacognitive knowledge of listening. All of the students reported a deeper understanding of what is required to improve listening comprehension. Students also became more confident when completing listening tasks and used better strategic knowledge to cope with difficulties in listening comprehension. The weaker students benefited the most from the designed process-based lessons. Vandergrift (2005) conducted a study in which 57 French adolescent learners completed a metacognitive awareness listening questionnaire, a motivation questionnaire, and a listening comprehension test. The results showed that the more intrinsically motivated the listener, the greater the tendency to report more frequent use of metacognitive listening strategies. The results also support an increasingly strong relationship between students' reported use of metacognitive listening strategies and more self-determined forms of motivation for listening.

Based on the aforementioned studies, learners' beliefs and knowledge of listening appear to play an important role in listening comprehension. The findings support the hypothesis that metacognitive instruction can offer learners opportunities to develop listening comprehension skills. Instruction on relevant listening strategies may also have an impact on the development of students' self-efficacy for improving English listening proficiency. However, instruction on metacognitive listening strategies should be tailored to the needs of the students. One important issue is to build students' awareness of self-evaluation. Students' ability to self-evaluate may boost their self-efficacy since their motivation to carry out self-assessment and problem solving was a result of the metacognitive listening strategy instruction. The studies also provided some evidence that language educators can design appropriate evidence-based curricula, particularly for learners with different language proficiency levels. Given that contextual, learner, and cultural factors may influence learners' knowledge and willingness to adopt metacognitive strategies for achieving L2 listening comprehension, Goh (2018) depicted metacognition as involving mental activities for "directly attending to input, processing it in working memory, and storing the processed knowledge and understanding in long-term memory for retrieval and use" (p. 1). There were gaps between metacognitive instruction and processing for L2 listening, for which metacognitive instruction should involve the learner's conscious awareness of their cognitive activities to make sure that their L2 knowledge retrieval is more accurate and faster and they know what to do to facilitate their learning in future tasks (Sato 2022).

Metacognition and reading

It is commonly acknowledged that learners need pedagogical support to develop strategies for meaningful reading. In particular, learners' metacognitive knowledge of the strategy use in learning to read can build confidence for learners to improve their reading efficiency (Lehtonen 2000). As argued by McLeod and McLaughlin (1986), reading is "not merely a passive process of extracting meaning from the printed page, but rather an active and interactive process in which the reader uses knowledge of the language to predict and create meaning based on the text" (p.114). Readers who have clearer metacognitive awareness of a reading task may adopt various strategies to process and extract text meaning than those who do not.

In one study with 10 EFL students in a Chinese university, Zhang (2001) used a semi-structured interview guide to elicit learners' metacognitive knowledge of strategy use according to Flavell's (1987) metacognition framework. Students' metacognitive knowledge of EFL reading was classified into three categories: person, task, and strategy. The data coding was based on the audio recordings of the participants from semi-structured interviews. Zhang found that the participants' use of metacognitive reading strategies varied across EFL proficiency levels. For example, learners with higher reading scores showed a clearer awareness of reading strategies, while learners with lower reading scores were less able to use different reading strategies. Comprehension monitoring was found to be one of the most important and useful strategies for readers. Zhang's study supported the role of metacognition in reading comprehension.

Studies have also identified a strong correlation between metacognitive instruction and reading ability. For example, metacognitive skills are stronger in individuals with stronger reading skills, and metacognitive instruction improves reading skills. Zhang, Gu, and Hu (2008) focused on 18 primary school students. The results suggested that learners can be guided toward cultivating their own metacognitive strategies for reading comprehension. The young readers demonstrated flexible and appropriate use of reading strategies. However, the strategies varied according to language proficiency, and grade-level higher proficiency students applied a repertoire of strategies when reading. For example, they activated prior knowledge, made connections with the text, noticed the text structure, asked questions about the text, determined contextual information, and summarized what they had read. Students also reported what they were thinking when reading. These findings offer ways that teachers can assist their students in understanding the important aspects of the reading process. When learners become aware of the nature and demands of learning to read, they may be in a better position to self-regulate their own reading by choosing comprehension strategies that enhance their understanding of the text.

Teng (2020a) examined the effectiveness of metacognitive reading strategy instruction with Hong Kong English language learners' reading comprehension. Data were collected from a total of 25 primary school 5th-grade students through notes the learners took during reading, post-reading reflection reports, teacher-facilitated group discussions, and two types of reading tests. These young participants were taught a combination of strategies meant to gradually cultivate a degree of reading independence. The intervention was conducted in three stages: read and answer, reflect, report and discuss. The findings revealed that the learners reported 20 metacognitive knowledge factors that positively influenced reading. For example, compared to students in a control group, the students receiving the intervention also achieved higher scores in reading comprehension. The findings support the hypothesis that metacognitive knowledge can help participants to identify when, why, and how to adapt strategic choices to plan, monitor, and evaluate their reading processes.

The aforementioned studies suggest that metacognitive strategic knowledge may help learners to think about their learning processes. In these studies, helping EFL readers to think about their reading processes encouraged them to deploy strategic knowledge that enhanced reading efficacy. Teachers' initiatives to facilitate learners' use of effective reading strategies are an important step in helping students to improve their reading comprehension skills, and reading instruction should incorporate metacognitive instruction. Teng (2020a) recommends that teachers instruct students in multiple methods, including reflection, teacher modeling, reading and writing workshop approaches, and integrated activity sequences (e.g., reporting and discussing thought processes) that focus alternately on text and process. Such instruction may help readers to increase their awareness of key aspects of the reading process, develop a range of skills and strategies for reading, and ensure that metacognitive instruction in reading remains fresh and innovative. It is helpful for learners to be able to evaluate the content of the text and to form an awareness of its value and quality. A combination of creative methods (e.g., reading and writing workshops, reflections, group discussions, and metacognitive strategy instruction) can be used to facilitate students' independent exploration of content knowledge and their ability to cope with the problems they encounter while reading.

Metacognition and writing

The role of metacognition and self-regulation has been widely acknowledged with respect to writing (Graham, Harris, MacArthur, and Santangelo 2018; Harris, Graham, Brindle, and Sandmel 2009; Teng and Huang 2019; Teng 2020b). Hacker, Keener, and Kircher (2009) have argued that writing is "applied metacognition" (p. 160). As discussed earlier, metacognition is divided into two main sub-components: a knowledge component and an executive regulation component. These two components are also related to writing. For example, in the writing process, the knowledge component is the basis for student writers to make decisions about how to approach a writing task environment. The regulation component enables them to consciously regulate the writing process by managing cognitive loads and adopting relevant regulation strategies (Harris et al. 2009). In particular, planning, monitoring, and evaluation processes have been identified as major regulation components that play an important role in student writers' writing sub-processes, as suggested in previous cognitive models of writing (e.g., see Bereiter and Scardamalia 1987; Flower and Hayes 1981; Hayes 1996; Kellogg 1996).

Several researchers have studied how to make improvements in English learners' writing through metacognitive instruction. For example, Larkin (2009) investigated the effects of metacognition on the writing abilities of 172 sixth-grade students enrolled in five different primary schools in England. The researcher observed 25 periods of writing lessons and noted her reflections and interpretations. The analysis of data from 25 hours of video-based observation, teacher reflections, and notes showed that young learners could engage in metacognitive talk and use metacognition intentionally in the co-construction of written texts. Nguyen and Gu (2013) examined metacognitive strategy training for improvement in writing performance with 130 third-year English-major students in a Vietnamese EFL context. The researchers designed nine lessons of metacognitive strategy training for the learners that included planning, monitoring, and evaluating. Three groups were involved – one group of strategy-based instruction and two control groups. The participants receiving metacognitive strategy instruction significantly improved their ability to plan, monitor, and evaluate a writing task better than their counterparts in the two control groups.

Teng has conducted several studies on the use of metacognitive studies for writing. In one study, 120 students were divided into three groups: a cooperative learning condition with embedded metacognitive instructions (COOP+META), a cooperative learning condition (COOP), and a no-treatment control group (Teng, 2016). The quantitative results showed that the COOP+META group students demonstrated the highest mean scores in writing a comparison and contrast essay, followed by the COOP condition and the control group. Qualitative results showed that students in the COOP+META group deployed varied strategies for the regulation of cognition. In particular, this group was able to plan, monitor, and evaluate their writing process more often than the other groups. In another study, Teng (2019a) assigned a total of 120 students into three groups: group feedback guidance (GFG), self-explanation guidance (SEG), and a control group (CG). Learners in the GFG and SEG groups received metacognitive instruction, but learners in the GFG condition focused on providing and receiving feedback in writing, while learners in the SEG focused on self-constructing explanations or arguments. The results showed that the GFG group outperformed the SEG and CG groups in terms of English writing as measured by an immediate and delayed writing test. An analysis of the groups' journal entries showed that learners in the GFG group displayed better awareness of writing task perception and stronger self-regulation of writing and used metacognitive strategies more often than the other groups.

In other studies, Teng (2019b) also explored the different effects of text structure and self-regulated strategies on young ESL learners' writing quality in Hong Kong. The study included three conditions – text structure instruction (TSI), self-regulated strategy instruction (SRSI), and a control group. Each condition consisted of 20 one-hour sessions. Measures included a written summary and essay. The results showed that compared with traditional instruction, the TSI and SRSI groups each exhibited better writing outcomes. Some new findings revealed that instruction in self-regulated strategies enhanced learners' writing quality, and instruction in text structure enhanced learners' summary of main ideas. In a recent empirical study (Teng 2020b), a total of 144 Chinese primary school students were divided into four groups: self-regulated strategy development plus collaborative modeling of text structure, collaborative modeling of text structure only, self-regulated strategy development only, and traditional instruction. Outcome measures included content comprehension, summarization of main ideas, and essay writing. The results showed that the combination of self-regulated strategy development and collaborative modeling of text structure was particularly effective in increasing students' content comprehension and writing quality. Teng's (2020b) results suggest that writing is a complex process requiring students to master task-specific strategies and develop metacognitive awareness for regulating and controlling strategy use.

These studies support the claim that metacognitive instruction can be effective in enhancing metacognitive skills and improving the writing performance of students in different settings. Writing is a complex socio-cognitive activity that can be supported by metacognitive instruction (Larkin 2009). The complexity lies in the fact that writing is a recursive and cognitive process (Kress 1982). Empirical findings also support cognitive writing models. For example, in line with the Hayes model, writing is a hierarchically and recursively organized process in which greater cognitive demands on working memory are necessary when some processes interrupt other processes (Hayes 1996). Text generation is a problem-solving and goal-oriented process, and student writers need to modify their goals as the writing task progresses. The complexity of writing also lies in the need to transform ideas into written form. Based on Scardamalia and Bereiter's (1987) work, writing includes two models: the knowledge-telling model and the knowledge-transforming model. The knowledge-telling model explains the writing processes of immature writers and why they can only capture the writing processes without goal-directed planning. The knowledge-transforming model explains mature writers' composing processes, which involve an ability to take control of the writing process.

Hence, writing is a developmental process starting from writing down thoughts retrieved from long-term memory to a much more complex process of transforming these thoughts and ideas into a new knowledge structure (Teng and Huang 2019). Student writers need to employ different metacognitive skills, such as planning, evaluating, problem solving, and revising, to attain their writing task goals. The ultimate goal of effective writing incorporates important features such as (a) facilitation of self-planning, self-monitoring, and self-evaluation of the writing process; (b) instruction of specific drafting, editing, and revising strategies; and (c) a dialogic approach to the presentation and modeling of text structure knowledge.

9.5 Pedagogy and Instruction

The studies cited earlier provide evidence that metacognitive instruction can be effective for listening (Goh and Taib 2016), reading (Zhang 2001), writing (Teng 2019ab), and both reading and writing (Teng 2020b). Instruction of cognitive skills and text structure may provide teachers with direction to help students reshape their writing classroom community, enhance their capabilities for learning and using strategies, and improve their cognitive capabilities and motivation for learning to read and write. The findings highlight the importance of pedagogy and instruction for learners. In terms of pedagogy for metacognitive instruction, certain principles are important issues for consideration. Learners' activation of prior knowledge, reflections on what they know and want to learn, and active engagement in making goals for monitoring and evaluating the learning process and product are all important issues for instruction. Here, Anderson's (2002) five components for understanding students' roles when engaged in metacognitive instruction could be followed. These components for learners include 1) preparing and planning for learning; 2) building conscious decisions in selecting and using learning strategies; 3) monitoring and keeping track of strategy use; 4) orchestrating and coordinating various strategies for learning; and 5) building awareness of strategy use. Teachers should thus target different components of metacognitive knowledge (person, task, and strategy) and focus on the aspects of writing that would enhance learners' metacognition.

The pedagogy for metacognitive instruction also requires teachers' awareness of their roles in metacognitive instruction, including the ability to reflect on their own pedagogy, knowledge, and practices. Teachers' explanations and modeling of learner strategies play an important role in metacognitive instruction, and they often find themselves in unpredictable settings. For example, teachers meet students with varying abilities and motivation, so they need to be reflective in evaluating learners' individual differences in the learning process, particularly in a constantly changing environment. If the focus of metacognitive instruction is on learners' awareness in planning, implementing, monitoring, and evaluating their learning, then teachers should also build awareness to plan, implement, monitor, and evaluate their teaching (Svalberg 2007). Hiver and Whitehead (2018) provide several suggestions for teachers' roles in metacognitive instruction. First, language teachers should be proficient in their own language(s) and be able to serve as language models for their learners. Second, language teachers should try to build metalinguistic knowledge of the target language(s) to be cognizant of their own linguistic choices. Third, language teachers should promote learners' intercultural competence, i.e., the conscious monitoring and adjustment of one's own thinking and interaction with other people. Finally, language teachers should try to understand how languages are learned and how they can foster learners' active control in learning by assigning an active role to learners.

Even so, teachers still face challenges related to pedagogy and instruction for metacognition. For example, teachers may have restricted knowledge in implementing metacognitive training to enhance learners' metacognitive awareness or may not believe that curriculum changes will lead to more efficient learning. They may not have sufficient knowledge of and training related to metacognitive knowledge and may not have the autonomy to develop materials for metacognitive instruction. Obviously, if teachers do not believe in the effectiveness of a metacognitive approach to teaching, they may not be willing to implement the instructional model. One powerful way to help language teachers develop greater metacognitive thought and action in their practice is through productive mentoring partnerships. Such a program can provide teachers with a support network to reflect critically on their teaching and to increase the adaptability essential for teaching metacognitive strategies. In addition, teachers should pay attention to learners' emotions and cognition in a complex learning environment. For example, teachers' awareness of students' affective responses (e.g., enjoyment during the tasks) or negative responses (e.g., anxiety about the task demands) would encourage learners to control metacognitive knowledge (e.g., interest in doing more tasks).

It is also equally important to examine L2 learners' metacognition in relation to their behavioral patterns in the classroom, e.g., motivation. Learners may lack the motivation to take an active role in their own learning. Although learners' prior linguistic knowledge is a prerequisite for language learning, most may not be aware of their existing knowledge about language (Hiver and Whitehead 2018). Students could be engaged in various activities that can help them to understand their language learning skills. Students should also be given more opportunities to activate their prior knowledge and to reflect on old and new knowledge. Teachers and students can work as a team to reflect on the language learning process, and metacognitive strategies can be transferred to new language learning contexts. For instance, Haukås (2015) compared L2 and L3 learners' strategy use and found that the teacher needs to help learners to be aware of the potential transfer possibilities of techniques or strategies. Likewise, learners may not utilize their metacognitive knowledge for first- or second-language writing due to low English proficiency levels (Schoonen et al. 2003). This is why some learners find it hard to deal simultaneously with higher-order processes, for example, the activation of metacognitive knowledge (McCutchen 1996).

Finally, educators will also need to consider students' language proficiency level as a factor that may influence the effectiveness of metacognitive instruction on learners' reading comprehension (Zhang et al. 2008) and writing (Ma and Teng 2021). As argued by Sparks and Ganschow (2001), students' level of L1 achievement impacts their levels of L2 aptitude and L2 proficiency. As a result, Sparks and Ganschow (1993, 1995) suggested that it could be problematic to link inefficient use of language learning strategies with poor foreign language outcomes because poor language learners with low L1 achievement may not be those who are able to become metacognitively aware and use the necessary strategies. Likewise, Skehan (1991) reported the possibility that "good learners are ones for whom the use of effective strategies are possible, while for poorer learners they are not" (p. 288). Thus, learners of higher proficiency levels may be more likely to employ their use of reading and writing strategies when performing those tasks (Zhang 2001). Some high-proficiency learners may even go beyond text comprehension to synthesize the information they have understood. In contrast, low-proficiency learners may encounter problems in comprehending text information and be excessively reliant on bottom-up decoding of words when reading and spelling of words when writing rather than on the comprehension of text and production and generation of ideas.

Thus, teachers will need to make metacognitive instruction even more explicit for low-proficiency learners. Problems in L2 learning are likely to arise because of difficulties in L1 skills and the processing difficulties related to the learning of L2 phonological (sound)/orthographic (symbol) relationships, syntax (grammar), and semantic (meaning) skills. If possible, teachers should combine the instruction of metacognitive strategies and linguistic and schematic knowledge to reconstruct clues, interpret meaning, summarize information, and make inferences when reading and writing. With explicit instruction, some learners who fail to comprehend a text or write correctly and efficiently may rely on different strategies to make an overall reconstruction of a coherent meaningful chunk for a reading or writing assignment. Teachers should particularly help low-proficiency learners to orchestrate their strategy use to arrive at a reasonable level of text comprehension and written production.

Recommended Readings

Efklides, Anastasia. 2008. Metacognition: Defining its facets and levels of functioning in relation to self-regulation and co-regulation. *European Psychologist* 13(4). 277–287.
    This is a well-established study presenting a comprehensive understanding of metacognition in the field of educational psychology.

Sato, Masatoshi. 2022. Metacognition. In Shaofeng Li, Phil Hiver & Mostafa Papi (eds.), *The Routledge handbook of second language acquisition and individual differences*, 95–108. New York, NY: Routledge.
    This is a recommended reference for readers to understand metacognition in the field of second language and foreign language learning. Sato summarized metacognition in different language learning skills, including reading, listening, and writing.

Teng, Feng, Chenghai Qin & Chuang Wang. 2022. Validation of metacognitive academic writing strategies and the predictive effects on academic writing performance in a foreign language context. *Metacognition and Learning* 17. 167–190.
    This is a recommended reference for understanding metacognition in the field of EFL writing. This study delineated effective writing strategies based on the understanding of metacognitive knowledge and regulation.

References

Anderson, Peter. 2002. Assessment and development of executive function (EF) during childhood. Child Neuropsychol, 8(2), 71–82.
Anderson, Neil J. 2008. Metacognition and good language learners. In Carol Griffiths (ed.), *Lessons from good language learners*, 99–110. Cambridge: Cambridge University Press.
Ardasheva, Yuliya & Thomas R. Tretter. 2013. Strategy inventory for language learning–ELL student form: Testing for factorial validity. *The Modern Language Journal* 97(2). 474–489.
Bereiter, Carl & Marlene Scardamalia. 1987. *The psychology of written composition*. New York: Routledge.

Blair, Clancy & C. Cybele Raver. 2012. Child development in the context of adversity: Experiential canalization of brain and behavior. *American Psychologist* 67(4). 309–318.
Boekaerts, Monique. 1997. Self-regulated learning: A new concept embraced by researchers, policy makers, educators, teachers, and students. *Learning and Instruction* 7(2). 161–186.
Brown, Ann L. 1987. Metacognition, executive control, self-regulation, and other more mysterious mechanisms. In Franz E. Weinert & Rainer H. Kluwe (eds.), *Metacognition, motivation, and understanding*, 65–116. Hillsdale, New Jersey: Lawrence Erlbaum Associates.
Bui, Gavin & Amy Kong. 2019. Metacognitive instruction for peer review interaction in L2 writing. *Journal of Writing Research* 11(2). 357–392.
Dinsmore, Daniel L, Patricia A. Alexander & Sandra M. Loughlin. 2008. Focusing the conceptual lens on metacognition, self-regulation, and self-regulated learning. *Educational Psychology Review* 20(4). 391–409.
Efklides, Anastasia. 2001. Metacognitive experiences in problem solving. In Anastasia, Efklides, Julius Kuhl & Richard M. Sorrentino (eds.), *Trends and prospects in motivation research*, 297–323. New York: Springer.
Efklides, Anastasia. 2006. Metacognition and affect: What can metacognitive experiences tell us about the learning process? *Educational Research Review* 1(1). 3–14.
Efklides, Anastasia. 2008. Metacognition: Defining its facets and levels of functioning in relation to self-regulation and co-regulation. *European Psychologist* 13(4). 277–287.
Ehrich, John F & Dunstan B. Henderson. 2019. Rasch Analysis of the Metacognitive Awareness Listening Questionnaire (MALQ). *International Journal of Listening* 33(2). 101–113.
Fairbanks, Colleen M, Gerald G. Duffy, Beverly S. Faircloth, Ye He, Barbara Levin, Jean Rohr & Catherine Stein. 2010. Beyond knowledge: Exploring why some teachers are more thoughtfully adaptive than others. *Journal of Teacher Education* 61 (1–2). 161–171.
Flavell, John H. 1971. First discussant's comments: What is memory development the development of? *Human Development* 14(4). 272–278.
Flavell, John H. 1976. Metacognitive aspects of problem solving. In Lauren B. Resnick (ed.), *The nature of intelligence*, 231–235. Hillsdale: Lawrence Erlbaum Associates.
Flavell, John H. 1979. Metacognition and cognitive monitoring: A new era of cognitive developmental inquiry. *American Psychologist* 34(10). 906–911.
Flavell, John H. 1981. Cognitive monitoring. In Patrick W. Dickson (ed.), *Children's oral communication skills*, 35–60. New York: Academic Press.
Flavell, John H. 1985. *Cognitive development* (2nd ed.). Englewood Cliffs, N.J.: Prentice-Hall.
Flavell, John H. 1987. Speculations about the nature and development of metacognition. In Franz E. Weinert & Rainer H. Kluwe (eds.), *Metacognition, Motivation and Understanding*, 21–29. Hillsdale, NJ: Erlbaum.
Flower, Linda & John R. Hayes. 1981. A cognitive process theory of writing. *Composition and Communication* 32(4). 365–87.
Gass, Susan M, Jennifer Behney & Luke Plonsky. 2008. *Second language acquisition: An introductory course* (5th ed). New York: Routledge.
Goh, Christine C. M. 1998. How ESL learners with different listening abilities use comprehension strategies and tactics. *Language Teaching Research* 2(2). 124–147.
Goh, Christine C. M. 2008. Metacognitive instruction for second language listening development: Theory, practice and research implications. *RELC Journal* 39(2). 188–213.
Goh, Christine C. M. 2018. Metacognition in second language listening. In John Liontas (ed.), *The TESOL encyclopedia of English language teaching*, 1–7. John Wiley & Sons.

Goh, Christine C. M & Yusnita Mohd Taib. 2006. Metacognitive instruction in listening for young learners. *ELT Journal* 60(3). 222–232.

Goh, Christine & Taib, Yusnita. 2016. Metacognitive Instruction in Listening for Young Learners. ELT Journal, 60(3), 222–232.

Graham, Steve, Karen R. Harris, Charles MacArthur & Tanya Santangelo. 2018. Self-regulation and writing. In Dale H. Schunk & Jeffrey A. Greene (eds.), *Handbook of self-regulation of learning and performance*, 138–152. New York: Routledge Publishers.

Hacker, Douglas J, Matt C. Keener & John C. Kircher. 2009. Writing is Applied Metacognition. In Douglas J. Hacker, John. Dunlosky, & Arthur C. Graesser (eds.), *Handbook of metacognition in education*, 154–172. New York: Routledge.

Harris, Karen R, Steve Graham, Mary Brindle & Karin Sandmel. 2009. Metacognition and Children's Writing. In Douglas J. Hacker, John. Dunlosky & Arthur C. Graesser (eds.), *Handbook of metacognition in education*, 131–153. New York: Routledge.

Harrison, George M & Lisa M. Vallin. 2018. Evaluating the metacognitive awareness inventory using empirical factor-structure evidence. *Metacognition and Learning* 13(1). 15–38.

Haukås, Åsta. 2015. A comparison of L2 and L3 learners' strategy use in school settings. *Canadian Modern Language Review* 71(4). 383–405.

Hayes, John R. 1996. A new framework for understanding cognition and affect in writing. In C. Michael Levy & Sarah Ransdell (eds.), *The science of writing: Theories, methods, individual differences, and applications*, 1–27. Mahwah, NJ: Erlbaum.

Heo, Misook, Rosa Stoffa & Joseph C. Kush. 2012. Factor analysis of the ESL/EFL Strategy Inventory for Language Learning: Generation 1.5 Korean immigrant college students' language learning strategies. *Language, Culture and Curriculum* 25(3). 231–247.

Hiver, Phil & George E. K. Whitehead. 2018. Teaching metacognitively: Adaptive inside-out thinking in the language classroom. In Åsta Haukås, Camilla Bjørke & Magne Dypedahl (eds.), *Metacognition in Language learning and teaching*, 243–262. New York: Routledge.

Kellogg, Ronald T. 1996. A model of working memory. In C. Michael Levy & Sarah Ransdell (eds.), *The science of writing*, 57–72. Mahwah: Lawrence Erlbaum Associates.

Kizilcec, René F, Mar Pérez-Sanagustín & Jorge J. Maldonado. 2017. Self-regulated learning strategies predict learner behavior and goal attainment in Massive Open Online Courses. *Computers & Education* 104. 18–33.

Kress, Gunther. (1982). *Learning to write*. London: Routledge & Kegan Paul Ltd.

Kuhn, Deanna. 2000. Metacognitive development. *Current Directions in Psychological Science* 9(5). 178–181.

Larkin, Shirley. 2009. Socially mediated metacognition and learning to write. *Thinking Skills & Creativity* 4(3). 149–159.

Lehtonen, Tuula. 2000. Awareness of strategies is not enough: How learners can give each other confidence to use them. *Language Awareness* 9(2). 64–77.

Lockl, Kathrin & Wolfgang Schneider. 2006. Precursors of metamemory in young children: The role of theory of mind and metacognitive vocabulary. *Metacognition and Learning* 1(1). 15–31.

Ma, Maggie & Mark Feng Teng. 2021. Metacognitive knowledge development of students with differing levels of writing proficiency in a process-oriented course: An action research study. In Barry Lee Reynolds & Mark Feng Teng (eds.), *Innovative approaches in Teaching writing to Chinese speakers*, 92–117. Berlin: DeGruyter Mouton.

Magno, Carlo. 2010. The role of metacognitive skills in developing critical thinking. *Metacognition and Learning* 5(2). 137–156

McCutchen, Deborah. 1996. A capacity theory of writing: Working memory in composition. *Educational Psychology Review* 8 (3). 299–325.

McLeod, Beverly & Barry McLaughlin. 1986. Restructuring or automaticity? Reading in a second language. *Language Learning* 36(2). 109–123.

Mokhtari, Kouider & Carla A. Reichard. 2002. Assessing students' metacognitive awareness of reading strategies. *Journal of Educational Psychology* 94(2). 249–259.

Mokhtari, Kouider, Dimiter M. Dimitrov & Carla A. Reichard. 2018. Revising the metacognitive awareness of reading strategies inventory (MARSI) and testing for factorial invariance. *Studies in Second Language Learning and Teaching* 8(2). 219–246.

Nguyen, Le Thi Cam & Yongqi Gu. 2013. Strategy-based instruction: A learner-focused approach to developing learner autonomy. *Language Teaching Research* 17(1). 9–30.

Oxford, Rebecca L. 1990. *Language learning strategies: What every teacher should know*. Boston: Heinle & Heinle.

Oxford, Rebecca L & Judith A. Burry-Stock. 1995. Assessing the use of language learning strategies worldwide with the ESL/EFL version of the Strategy Inventory for Language Learning (SILL). *System* 23(1). 1–23.

Paris, Scott G, Cross David R. & Marjorie Y. Lipson. 1984. Informed strategies for learning: A program to improve children's reading awareness and comprehension. *Journal of Educational Psychology* 76(6). 1239–1252.

Sato, Masatoshi. 2022. Metacognition. In Shaofeng Li, Phil Hiver & Mostafa Papi (eds.), *The Routledge handbook of second language acquisition and individual differences*, 95–108. New York, NY: Routledge.

Schmidt, Kristin, Julia Maier & Matthias Nückles. 2012. Writing about the personal utility of learning contents in a learning journal improves learning motivation and comprehension. *Education Research International* 2012. 1–10.

Schoonen, Rob, Amos van Gelderen, Kees de Glopper, Jan Hulstijn, Annegien Simis, Patrick Snellings & Marie Stevenson. 2003. First language and second language writing: The role of linguistic knowledge, speed of processing, and metacognitive knowledge. *Language Learning* 53(1). 165–202.

Schraw, Gregory. 1998. Promoting general metacognitive awareness. *Instructional Science* 26(1). 113–125.

Schraw, Gregory. 2001. Promoting general metacognitive awareness. In Hope J. Hartman (ed.), *Metacognition in learning and instruction: Theory, research and practice*, 3–16. London: Springer.

Schraw, Gregory & Rayne Sperling Dennison. 1994. Assessing metacognitive awareness. *Contemporary Educational Psychology* 19(4). 460–475.

Shimamura, Arthur P. 2000. Toward a cognitive neuroscience of metacognition. *Consciousness and Cognition* 9(2). 313–323.

Skehan, Peter. 1991. Individual differences in second language learning. *Studies in Second Language Acquisition* 13(2). 275–298.

Sparks, Richard L. 1995. Examining the Linguistic Coding Differences Hypothesis to explain individual differences in foreign language learning. *Annals of Dyslexia* 45(1). 187–219.

Sparks, Richard L & Leonore Ganschow. 1993. Searching for the cognitive locus of foreign language learning problems: Linking first and second language learning. *Modern Language Journal* 77(3). 289–302.

Sparks, Richard L & Leonore Ganschow. 2001. Aptitude for learning a foreign language. *Annual Review of Applied Linguistics* 21. 90–111.

Svalberg, Agneta. 2012. Language awareness in language learning and teaching: A research agenda. Language Teaching, 45 (3), 376–388.

Svalberg, Agneta M-L. 2007. Language awareness and language learning. *Language Teaching* 40(4). 287–308.

Teng, Feng. 2016. Immediate and delayed effects of embedded metacognitive instruction on Chinese EFL students' English writing and regulation of cognition. *Thinking skills & Creativity* 22. 289–302.

Teng, Feng. 2019a. Tertiary-level students' English writing performance and metacognitive awareness: A group metacognitive support perspective. *Scandinavian Journal of Educational Research*. https://doi:10.1080/00313831.2019.1595712

Teng, Feng. 2019b. A comparison of text structure and self-regulated strategy instruction for elementary school students' writing. *English Teaching: Practice and Critique* 18(3). 281–297.

Teng, Feng. 2020a. The benefits of metacognitive reading strategy awareness instruction for young learners of English as a second language. *Literacy* 54(1). 29–39.

Teng, Feng. 2020b. Young learners' reading and writing performance: Exploring collaborative modeling of text structure as an additional component of self-regulated strategy development. *Studies in Educational Evaluation*. https://doi:10.1016/j.stueduc.2020.100870

Teng, Feng & Jing Huang. 2019. Predictive effects of writing strategies for self-regulated learning on secondary school learners' EFL writing proficiency. *TESOL Quarterly* 53(1). 232–247.

Teng Feng (2021). Exploring awareness of metacognitive knowledge and acquisition of vocabulary knowledge in primary grades: a latent growth curve modelling approach. Language Awareness. doi.org/10.1080/09658416.2021.1972116

Teng Feng & Zhang, Lawrence Jun (2021). Development of children's metacognitive knowledge, reading, and writing in English as a foreign language: Evidence from longitudinal data using multilevel models. British Journal of Educational Psychology, 91(4), 1202–1230.

Teng, Feng, Chenghai Qin & Chuang Wang. 2022. Validation of metacognitive academic writing strategies and the predictive effects on academic writing performance in a foreign language context. *Metacognition and Learning* 17. 167–190.

Teng, Lin Sophie & Lawrence Jun Zhang. 2016. A questionnaire-based validation of multidimensional models of self-Regulated learning strategies. *The Modern Language Journal* 100(3). 674–701.

Vandergrift, Larry. 2004. Listening to Learn or Learning to Listen? *Annual Review of Applied Linguistics* 24. 3–25.

Vandergrift, Larry. 2005. Relationships among motivation orientations, metacognitive awareness and proficiency in L2 listening. *Applied Linguistics* 26(1). 70–89.

Vandergrift, Larry & Christine C. M. Goh. 2012. *Teaching and learning second language listening: Metacognition in action*. New York: Routledge.

Vandergrift, Larry, Christine C. M. Goh, Catherine J. Mareschal & Marzieh H. Tafaghodtari. 2006. The metacognitive awareness listening questionnaire: Development and validation. *Language Learning* 56(3). 431–462.

Veenman, Marcel & Jan J. Elshout. 1999. Changes in the relation between cognitive and metacognitive skills during the acquisition of expertise. *European Journal of Psychology of Education* 14(4). 509–523.

Veenman, Marcel V. J, Bernadette H. A. M. Van Hout-Wolters & Peter Afflerbach. 2006. Metacognition and learning: Conceptual and methodological considerations. *Metacognition and Learning* 1(1). 3–14.

Victori, Mia & Walter Lockhart. 1995. Enhancing Metacognition in Self-Directed Language Learning." *System* 23(2). 223–34.

Weinert, Franz Emanuel. 1987. Introduction and overview: Metacognition and motivation as determinants of effective learning and understanding. In Franz E. Weinert & Rainer H. Kluwe (eds.), *Metacognition, motivation, and understanding*, 1–16. Hillsdale, NJ: Lawrence Erlbaum.

Wenden, Anita L. 1987. Metacognition: An expanded view on the cognitive abilities of L2 learners. *Language Learning* 37(4). 573–597.

Wenden, Anita L. 1998. Metacognitive knowledge and language learning. *Applied Linguistics* 19(4). 515–537.

Wenden, Anita L. 2002. Learner development in language learning. *Applied Linguistics* 23(1). 32–55.

Winne, Philip H & Nancy E. Perry. 2005. Measuring self-regulated learning. In Monique Boekaerts, Paul R. Pintrich, & Moshe Zeidner (eds.), *Handbook of self-regulation*, 531–566. Burlingtton: Elsevier Academic Press.

Xu, Jian. 2017. The mediating effect of listening metacognitive awareness between test-taking motivation and listening test score: An expectancy-value theory approach. *Frontiers in Psychology*. https://doi:org/10.3389/fpsyg.2017.02201

Zhang, Lawrence Jun. 2001. Awareness in reading: EFL students' metacognitive knowledge of reading strategies in an acquisition-poor environment. *Language Awareness* 10(4). 268–288.

Zhang, Lawrence Jun, Peter Yongqi Gu & Guangwei Hu. 2008. A cognitive perspective on Singaporean primary school pupils' use of reading strategies in learning to read in English. *British Journal of Educational Psychology* 78(2). 245–271.

Zimmerman, Barry J. 1989. A social cognitive view of self-regulated academic learning. *Journal of Educational Psychology* 81(3). 329–339.

Zimmerman, Barry J. 2011. Motivational sources and outcomes of self-regulated learning and performance. In Barry J. Zimmerman & Dale H. Schunk (eds.), *Handbook of self-regulation of learning and performance*, 49–64. Mahwah, NJ: Lawrence Erlbaum.

Zimmerman, Barry J & Albert Bandura. 1994. Impact of self-regulatory influences on writing course attainment. *American Educational Research Journal* 31(4). 845–862.

10 Self-Regulation

Mark Feng Teng

Abstract: The notion of self-regulation derived from educational psychology in the 1970s. The application of self-regulation to second language learning contexts has gained an interdisciplinary status in the past 20 years. This perspective prompted us to rethink how students can make progress in language learning. Self-regulation is important in second language acquisition because it is the "engine" that helps students manage their strategic learning. Although self-regulation has developed into a mature phase in educational psychology, it has not generated a profound influence in the field of SLA. This chapter aims to provide a theoretical basis for understanding self-regulation in second language learning by reviewing key models of self-regulation, examining conceptual and methodological issues of self-regulation, and summarizing research findings to determine the role of self-regulation in second language acquisition. Finally, this chapter discusses some challenges involved in developing a self-regulated capacity for second language learning.

Keywords: Self-regulation, learner agency, assessing self-regulation, self-reflection, agentive behaviors

10.1 Introduction

The initial introduction of self-regulation to SLA is attributed to Dörnyei (2005), who proposed a shift of focus of SLA from what is learned to how a new language is acquired. Self-regulation (SR), or self-regulated learning (SRL), is a core conceptual framework designed to understand learners' cognitive, motivational, and emotional engagement. Based on Bandura's (1977, 1986) social cognitive theory, Zimmerman (1986) defined self-regulated learners as students who are metacognitively, motivationally, and behaviorally active participants in their own learning process. The emphasis of SRL was on how students think, perform, and reflect on their learning process. Zimmerman (2005) described a self-regulated learning process as three phases: forethought, performance, and self-reflection. Forethought refers to careful consideration of self-motivational beliefs, including how to set goals and use cognitive learning strategies (e.g., organization, elaboration). During the performance stage, learners apply self-observational metacognitive strategies to monitor their learning process. During the self-reflection stage, learners initiate their self-judgment and self-reaction processes by comparing their performance against specific standards.

The concept of self-regulated learning (SRL) refers to three classes of regulation: covert (personal), behavioral, and environmental (Zimmerman and Risemberg 1997). Covert self-regulation refers to the "adaptive use of cognitive or affective strategies" to help students reduce anxiety in learning. Behavioral self-regulation pertains to "the adaptive use of a motoric performance strategy" to maintain positive behaviors for learning. Environmental self-regulation refers to "the adaptive use of a context-related strategy" to cope with distracting environmental events (Zimmerman and Risemberg 1997: 77). A learner who can exert strategic control over the three classes of regulation can be described as a self-regulated learner (Zimmerman 1989). Hence, SRL includes three parameters: personal processes, environmental events, and behavioral attributes. The three parameters enable a learner to identify a topic, set goals to become familiar with the topic, adopt strategies to examine the topic, and evaluate and modify relevant strategies for a deeper understanding of the subject matter (Zimmerman and Schunk 2001). Overall, self-regulation entails taking control of one's own learning and behavior (Ziegler, Stoeger, and Grassinger 2011), for which learners are required to coordinate multiple aspects of executive function, such as attention, working memory, and inhibitory control, along with the motor or verbal functions to guide self-directed learning amid distractions (McClelland et al. 2007).

Self-regulated learners often exhibit a high sense of self-efficacy because self-regulation depends on the coordination of various cognitive processes that help them to manage learning behaviors (McClelland and Cameron 2012). Self-regulated learners have also been found to be cognizant of their strengths and weakness in academic learning (Pintrich and Schunk 2002) and control their cognitive processes through planning resources, setting goals, monitoring, and evaluating their own understanding (Pintrich 2000). Zimmerman (2013) argued that self-regulated learners can draw upon different dimensions of SRL strategies to determine how they can control their beliefs, behaviors, and external environments in the learning process. Such self-initiated controls allow students to regulate "learning strategies as well as internal and external learning resources (e.g., motivation and learning environment)" (Ziegler, Stoeger, and Grassiner 2011: 76). Hence, self-regulation is a process by which learners try to "plan, monitor, and evaluate" their learning by regulating their "thoughts, feelings, and actions" (da Silva Marini and Boruchovitch 2014: 323). In the L2 learning context, I define self-regulation as the ways that learners systematically activate and sustain their cognitions, motivations, and behaviors toward their goals in learning a target language. Self-regulation in learning a second language is a dynamic and cyclical process comprising the systematic use of task-relevant strategies, goal-directed activities, and self-oriented feedback.

10.2 Theories and Models

Zimmerman's SRL models from the socio-cognitive perspective

Zimmerman developed three different SRL models. The first model is known as the Triadic Analysis of SRL. This model delineates the interactions of environment, behavior, and a person's level of self-regulated learning (Zimmerman 1989). According to Zimmerman (1986), this model was based on Bandura's (1986) social cognitive theory. This model, described by Zimmerman (1989) as "triadic reciprocality" (p.330), delineated how SRL could be envisioned within Bandura's triadic model of social cognition. According to this model, a distinction should be made among personal, environmental, and behavioral determinants of self-regulated learning. For example, self-regulated learning is determined not only by personal perceptions of efficacy but also by environmental and behavioral events in a reciprocal fashion. This reciprocal formulation also suggests that individuals' self-regulatory responses or behaviors can influence both the environment and personal self-efficacy perceptions. This model reflects Bandura's (1986) triadic formulation, for which human behavior is a product of self-generated and external influence. For example, self-efficacy belief serves as a sort of thermostat that regulates strategic efforts to acquire knowledge and skill through a cybernetic feedback loop. This model links individuals' self-regulatory processes to specific social learning or behaviorally enactive experiences. Such reciprocal formulation locates two key processes, self-efficacy perceptions and strategy use. Through the two processes, self-regulated learning is realized.

The second model represented the cyclic phases of SRL (Zimmerman 2000). This model explains the interrelation of forethought, the performance of volitional control, and self-regulation (Zimmerman and Campillo 2003). Zimmerman's model explains metacognitive and motivational processes and is organized into three phases: forethought, performance, and self-reflection. The forethought phase is for students to analyze the task, set goals, and plan how to reach them. During this process, a number of motivational beliefs influence the activation of learning strategies. The performance phase is for learners to execute the task. During this process, learners monitor how they are progressing and use a number of self-control strategies to keep themselves cognitively engaged and motivated for specific tasks. The self-reflection phase is for the learners to assess how they have performed the task. These attributions are the source of self-reactions that may positively or negatively influence learners' behaviors to approach the task.

The third model was based on the second model. Zimmerman and Moylan (2009) revised the second model by including metacognitive and volitional strategies in the performance phase, self-motivation belief in the forethought phase, and self-reaction in the self-reflection phase. According to this model, self-regulated learners are proactive self-regulated individuals who can focus on and engage in productive forethought and self-reflect on their learning. The three-phase model explains the links between students' processes and outcomes (forethought phase), strategy automatization (performance control phase), and motivational reactions to outcomes (self-reflection phase). The key feature of this model is the intersection of metacognitive and motivational measures, which prompts consideration of a number of methodological and conceptual issues. One issue concerns the assessment of self-regulation. A second issue concerns how proactive learners can be developed.

Boekaerts' Dual Processing Self-Regulation Model

Boekaerts' dual processing self-regulation model (Boekaerts and Niemivirta 2000) attempts to conceptualize when, why, and how students self-regulate their learning in the classroom. Boekaerts and Cascallar (2006) used this model to explain why some students' self-regulation systems work in some domains but not in other domains. They explained that some students who want to reach a goal may adopt agentic actions in the growth pathway, while other students who mainly care about their well-being may focus more on cues that signal unfavorable learning conditions, e.g., drawbacks. They named these the growth and well-being pathways. However, I want to argue that learners may have an aptitude for language but do not have the aptitude for math, or vice versa, so any self-regulation system works for language class but not well for math class. Boekaerts and Cascallar (2006) viewed goals as the "knowledge structures" that guide their behavior. For instance, students who perceive the task as threatening to their well-being may have negative cognitions and emotions. They may try different strategies to protect the ego from damage. On the other hand, those students who perceive the task as congruent with their goals and needs may feel stimulated to strengthen their competence, thus triggering positive cognitions and emotions and moving onto the growth pathway. Boekaerts (2011) added that students are not fixed on one of two pathways. For example, students who are in the growth pathway may move to the well-being pathway when they detect cues that they regard as frustrating to them. To ensure students' development of self-regulated capacity, this model suggests several implications, e.g., increasing students' knowledge and skills, preventing threats to the self and loss of resources, ensuring students' commitments to the growth pathway, and preventing students from becoming trapped on the well-being pathway.

Winne and Hadwin's SRL model from a metacognitive perspective

The focus of Winne and Hadwin's SRL model is on the metacognitive perspective. Self-regulated learning is a process of managing learning via the use of metacognitive strategies (Winne and Hadwin 1998, 2008). Their model has been widely used in computer-supported collaborative learning (Winne, Hadwin, and Gress 2010). According to Winne and Hadwin's model (Winne and Hadwin 1998, 2008), academic learning is powered by SRL across four linked phases that are open and recursive in a feedback loop. The four linked phases are (a) task definition, i.e., students' comprehension and awareness of knowledge in performing a task; (b) goal setting and planning, i.e., students' ability to set up goals and a plan to achieve them; (c) enacting study tactics and strategies, i.e., relevant actions needed to reach those goals; and (d) adaptations to metacognition, i.e., understanding students' decisions to make long-term changes in their motivations, beliefs, and strategies. Winne and Hadwin (1998) also proposed that SRL deploys five different facets of tasks, which were (a) conditions, i.e., resources available to a person and the constraints inherent to a task or environment (e.g., the context, time); (b) operations, i.e., the cognitive processes, tactics, and strategies, including searching, monitoring, assembling, rehearsing and translating; (c) products, i.e., the information produced by operations (e.g., new knowledge); (d) evaluations, i.e., feedback about the fit between products and standards that are either generated internally by the student or provided by external sources (e.g., teacher or peer feedback); and (e) standards, i.e., criteria against which products are monitored.

Pintrich's SRL model from the perspective of motivation

In contrast to Winne and Hadwin's SRL model, which connects SRL and metacognition, Pintrich (2000) proposed an SRL model from the perspective of motivation. According to Pintrich's (2000) model, SRL consisted of four phases: (1) Forethought, planning, and activation; (2) Monitoring; (3) Control; and (4) Reaction and reflection. Each phase includes four different areas of regulation: cognition, motivation/affect, behavior, and context. That combination of phases and areas offers a comprehensive picture to understand prior content knowledge activation, efficacy judgments, and self-observations of behavior and offers several features. First, Pintrich (2000) described the regulation of cognition as judgments of learning and feelings of knowing. Second, Pintrich (2004) explained that SRL capacity is dependent on students' regulation of motivation and affect. Third, the regulation of behavior reflects the social cognitive theory introduced by Bandura (1997) and the Triadic model introduced by Zimmerman (1989). Finally, self-regulation means students have to "monitor, control and regulate the (learning) context" (Pintrich, 2000, p. 469).

10.3 Assessment

Over the past few years, attention has been directed to self-regulation interventions tailored to second language acquisition, e.g., writing (Teng 2016) and reading (Zhang 2008). The intervention programs emphasized the importance of teaching self-regulation strategies. The instruction of self-regulation strategies highlights the assessment of self-regulation. SRL has properties as an aptitude and an event (Winne 1997). An aptitude describes a relatively enduring attribute of a person who predicts future behavior. An event is similar to a snapshot that "freezes activity in motion, a transient state embedded in a larger, longer series of states unfolding over time" (Winne and Perry 2000: 532). In terms of measuring SRL as an aptitude, the common protocols included questionnaires, structured interviews, or teacher ratings. In terms of measuring SRL as an event, the measures included the use of hypermedia and think-aloud protocols (Greene, Robertson, and Costa 2011), structured personal diaries (Schmitz and Wiese 2006), error detection tasks (Baker and Zimlin 1989), observations (Turner 1995), behavioral traces on work products (Perry and Winne 2006), and clickstream data (Li, Baker, and Warschauer 2020). Among the various measures, surveys and structured interviews are the common approaches to assessing self-regulation (Winne and Perry 2000).

Survey

Self-report questionnaires are commonly used, perhaps because they are relatively easy to design, administer, and score. In this chapter, I briefly introduce five self-report questionnaires, which include the Motivated Strategies and Learning Questionnaire (MSLQ) (Pintrich and De Groot 1990), the Learning and Study Strategies Inventory (LASSI) (Weinstein, Schulte, and Hoy 1987), Study Process Questionnaire (SPQ) (Biggs 1987), Strategy Inventory for Language Learning (SILL) (Oxford 1990), and Self-regulatory Writing Strategy Questionnaire (SRWSQ) (Teng, Wang, and Zhang 2022). These questionnaires usually require learners to respond to several Likert scale statements that reflect their learning behavior by either predicting their behavior in future learning or recalling their behavior during previous learning. However, there is a caveat about the low reliability of self-report measures.

Motivated Strategies and Learning Questionnaire (MSLQ)

Pintrich and his colleagues developed the MSLQ with the purpose of assessing college students' motivational orientations toward the use of different learning strategies. The instrument includes 81 items and 15 sub-scales. The 15 sub-scales were divided into two categories, i.e., motivation and learning strategies. The motivation category includes a value section with three subscales – intrinsic goal orientation, extrinsic goal orientation, and task value – as well as an expectancy section that consists of three subscales – control of learning beliefs, self-efficacy for learning and performance, and test anxiety. The learning strategies category also includes two sections. A cognitive and metacognitive strategies section includes five subscales: rehearsal, elaboration, organization, critical thinking, and metacognitive self-regulation. A resource management strategies section has four subscales: time and study environment, effort regulation, peer learning, and help-seeking. The measure of the items is based on a seven-point scale from "not at all true of me" (1) to "very true of me" (7).

Learning and Study Strategies Inventory (LASSI)

The LASSI (Weinstein et al. 1987) includes 77 items and aims to measure the use of learning and study strategies related to skill, will, and self-regulation components of strategic learning. The focus is on both covert and overt thoughts, behaviors, attitudes, and beliefs that relate to successful learning and that may be altered through educational interventions. The instrument includes 10 subscales that cover 80 items. One useful application of this questionnaire is for the diagnosis and evaluation of learning strategies. The 10 subscales are divided into three major components: skill, will, and self-regulation. The skill component includes information processing, selecting main ideas, and test strategies. The Will component includes attitude, motivation, and anxiety. The self-regulation component encompasses concentration, time management, self-testing, and study aids. Items include declarations (e.g., I try to interrelate themes into what I am studying) and conditional relations (e.g., When work is difficult, I either give up or only study the easy parts). Students respond using a five-point scale: "not at all typical of me," "not very typical of me," "somewhat typical of me," "fairly typical of me," and "very much typical of me."

Study Process Questionnaire (SPQ)

Based on the idea of the "approach to learning" (Marton and Säljö 1976), Biggs (1987) proposed the "student approaches to learning" (SAL) theory, which was defined as "a composite of a motive and an appropriate strategy" (p.10). SAL theory has become a meta-theory for conceptualizing teaching and learning. This theory includes two directions: phenomenography and constructivism. The main assertion of this theory states that each learning motive is expressed through a corresponding learning strategy and that congruency between students' motives and strategies is essential to their conceptions of learning and their overall attitude toward future learning. For example, students with achieving motives who employ surface strategies would be unlikely to feel satisfied with the outcome of their learning.

The Study Process Questionnaire (SPQ) (Biggs 1987) was developed based on SAL theory. The 80 items, which are presumed to be relevant to approaches in academic learning, constituted three levels of factors. In level one, ten unidimensional scales (pragmatism, achievement neuroticism, test anxiety, rote learning, class dependence, internality, achievement motivation, openness, meaning, and organization) were developed to measure the study process domain and constitute the first-order factor structure of the SPQ. The level two higher-order factors were the three different levels of factor structures of the instrument, i.e., the three approaches (deep, surface, and achieving). Each approach included three motives (deep motive, surface motive, and achieving motive) and three strategies (deep strategy, surface strategy, and achieving strategy) subscales. These motives and strategies are regarded as the second level of the SPQ factor structure. Finally, the deep, surface, and achieving approaches to learning combine to form two higher-order (level three) factors (deep-achieving and surface-achieving).

Strategy Inventory for Language Learning (SILL)

The Strategy Inventory for Language Learning (SILL) developed by Oxford (1990) is probably the most widely cited measurement tool for language learning strategies. The instrument includes two versions: a 50-item and an 80-item version. The 50-item questionnaire is for non-English speakers who are learning English and includes six categories: memory (9 items), cognitive (14 items), compensation (6 items), metacognitive (9 items), affective (6 items) and social strategies (6 items). The learners rate items on a five-point scale. The 80-item version is designed for native English speakers learning a new language. The 80 items of the SILL are divided into six subscales: remembering more effectively using your mental processes, compensating for missing knowledge, organizing and evaluating your learning, managing your emotions, and learning with others. The two versions are based on a five-point Likert scale.

Self-regulatory Writing Strategy Questionnaire (SRWSQ)

The Self-regulatory Writing Strategy Questionnaire (SRWSQ) developed by Teng, Wang, and Zhang (2022) is the most recent measurement tool for understanding young learners' self-regulatory writing strategies. Items in SRWSQ pertain to how learners perceive their use of strategies related to knowledge (e.g., their strengths and weaknesses) and regulation (e.g., planning, monitoring, and evaluating) in writing. Confirmatory factor analysis (CFA) confirmed six factors for the 30-item questionnaire. The six factors are writing planning, goal-oriented monitoring, goal-oriented evaluation, emotional control, memorization strategies, and metacognitive judgment. Learners' metacognitive awareness is orchestrated through a repertoire of general and specific writing strategies for coping with EFL writing. The six factors cluster under a single common latent factor, which accounts for the six subcategories. The first factor (writing planning) is composed of six writing strategies: global discourse planning (item 3), local lexical planning (item 2), time management (item 1), materials preparation (item 4), and planning based on feedback (items 5 and 6). The second factor (goal-oriented monitoring) includes six writing strategies, such as course learning monitoring (item 11), lexical-level processing (item 12), monitoring learning progress (items 9 and 10), and adjusting strategies (item 8). The third factor (goal-oriented evaluation) contains six writing strategies: (1) assessment of language use and content (items 12 and 16), knowledge and skills (item 15), evaluation of previous learning (items 13 and 14), and organization (item 17). Items related to emotional control measure learners' efforts to control emotions and negative feelings when learning to write (items 19, 20, 21, and 22). Items on memorization strategies refer to learners' working memory capacity in retaining sentences (item 23), course materials (item 24), and vocabulary knowledge (items 25 and 26). The sixth factor is metacognitive judgment, which investigates learners' perceived capability to execute metacognitive control in the learning-to-write process. It measures learners' belief in linguistic knowledge (item 29), initiatives in learning to write (items 27 and 28), and writing strategies (item 30).

Strategic interviews

Interviews are an effective way to assess self-regulation. Through structured interviews, researchers can utilize a fixed set of questions to explore learners' past events or behaviors, current behaviors, or prospective behaviors based on future or hypothetical situations or scenarios. Zimmerman and Martinez-Pons (1986) developed the Self-Regulated Learning Interview Scale (SRLIS). During an interview using the SRLIS, students are required to prepare for six distinct academic situations, such as preparing for a test at home, writing an essay, or completing math assignments. Their responses to the hypothetical scenarios are coded into distinct self-regulation strategy categories, including rehearsal, seeking social information, or transformation strategies. The SRLIS is different from self-report surveys because it utilizes questions that are both context-specific and task-specific. The questions may prompt the learners to describe the behaviors or strategies they exhibited when completing specific tasks or assignments. The questions may also prompt learners to make judgments about the prospective behaviors they might display in a given situation. In contrast, items in a survey may stimulate learners to report how typical a set of prescribed behaviors apply to them. Despite the potential of strategic interviews, Zimmerman (2008) questioned the use of such a method because it does not assess learners' actual behavior or cognition that occurs during a particular task or activity.

Overall, despite the availability of these instruments, assessing self-regulation is still challenging. It is not possible to use only one instrument to measure the complex and dynamic nature of the self-regulation process. In addition, self-regulation is context-dependent. Factors that include students' values and motives, task demands, and classroom climate can affect learners' judgment of their self-regulation. The mainstream measures mostly require learners to recall their knowledge to rate their use of specific learning strategies, their beliefs about and attitudes toward learning, their methods of study, or their efforts to plan and take control of study time. Such recall or anticipatory knowledge may not reflect the participants' use of self-regulated strategies. In SLA contexts, we may need to assign learners to different real-time tasks, e.g., writing an essay or reading a text, to stimulate them to recall their knowledge or strategy use under challenging circumstances.

10.4 Research Results and Findings

Research on self-regulation has witnessed exponential development in the past decade. In a recent study (Müller and Seufert 2018), 52 students received instruction on self-regulation prompts for 30 minutes in a hypermedia learning setting. The research design was based on the between-subject factor group (prompt vs. no-prompt), the within-subject factor learning session (first, second session), and the time within the session (before, during, after). The dependent measures were learners' perceived self-efficacy (before, during, and after each learning session) and learning performance (recall, comprehension, transfer) after each session. The results showed that prompted learners outperformed learners without prompts and that prompted learners tended to report higher overall self-efficacy. The importance of self-regulation in academic learning has been recognized in other studies (e.g., see review by Blankson and Blair 2016; Cornoldi, Carretti, Drusi, and Tencati 2015). For example, learners who plan time, set reasonable goals, select appropriate strategies, and allocate resources for a writing task achieve better writing performance (Teng 2016). During this process, learners need to assess strategies, monitor task performance and evaluate whether they have performed well.

Panadero (2017) compared different SRL models and suggested the importance of intervention according to the different models. Teachers should recognize those students who are not motivated to perform a task. Table 1 summarizes some key references that support the above-reviewed SRL models.

Table 1: Research findings on the reviewed models.

Models	Supported references	Research purpose	Research findings
Zimmerman's SRL models	Cleary and Zimmerman (2001); Kitsantas and Zimmerman (2002)	Explore and compare differences in the basketball experts, non-experts, and novices' self-regulatory forethought and self-reflection processes	Experts have more domain-specific declarative knowledge than novices; Within the forethought phase, all self-regulatory processes were related significantly; findings revealed sequential relationships between forethought and self-reflection processes hypothesized according to a cyclical dynamic model of self-regulation.

Table 1 (continued)

Models	Supported references	Research purpose	Research findings
Boekaerts' Dual Processing Self-regulation Model	Crombach et al., 2003	An online motivation questionnaire was used to explore the effect of prospective cognitions and emotions on learning intention.	A confirmatory factor analysis revealed that seven of the eight presupposed factors could be distinguished empirically. The internal structure of the tested model was invariant over the four tasks stemming from different academic subjects and seemed stable over a half-year period.
Winne and Hadwin's SSRL model	Järvelä et al., 2013	Explore the challenges individuals and groups experienced during collaborative group work, students' experiences in collectively regulating challenges in collaborations and the comparison of collaborative learning outcomes between groups with varying degrees of emerging shared regulation.	Progressive regulation was observed when the groups were not collectively able to define their strategies or the consistent strategy statements aligned with the challenges experienced; weak shared regulation was seen when the students were not able to progressively identify challenges and activate regulating strategies for their task progress; Progressive shared regulation among the three groups contributes to strong or improving collaborative learning results while weak shared regulation results in weak or improving collaborative learning results;
Pintrich: SRL models from the perspective of motivation	Pandarero et al., 2015	Explore the relationship between individual self-regulated learning (SRL), socially shared regulation of learning (SSRL), and group performance plus the effect of an intervention promoting SSRL	MSLQ developed by Pintrich is an individual SRL questionnaire that emphasizes cognitive and metacognitive skills in addition to motivation. MSLQ was a predictor for group goal planning, as well as a predictor for the strategies students used to overcome challenges.

Researchers in the 1990s explored techniques for gathering data from semi-structured interviews. For example, O'Malley and Chamot (1990) identified seven aspects of executive control (planning, directed attention, selective attention, self-management, self-monitoring, problem identification, and self-evaluation) used by foreign language learners through interviews and think-aloud data. In later research, questionnaires were also used to induce learners to reflect on their previous learning experiences. In earlier research (Politzer and McGroarty 1985), questionnaires were devised to assess how often individual learners used particular strategies in, e.g., classrooms, self-study, and interaction. While the research showed little relationship between questionnaire-based measures and language learning outcomes, such findings were contradicted in later studies. For instance, Teng and Huang (2019) argued that learners' use of self-regulated writing strategies significantly influenced their writing performance. In addition, they noted that learners' language proficiency also influenced their use of self-regulated writing strategies. However, theorists and researchers agree that enough evidence has not been generated to substantiate a positive relationship between learners' strategic behaviors and their language learning results (Cohen and Macaro 2007). In addition, the claim that good learners always use more self-regulated strategies than less proficient learners is insufficient to date. As suggested by Chamot and Kupper (1989), what may distinguish good and bad learners is not so much the number of strategies employed but rather prior language study, type and degree of difficulty of the task, and motivation. All learners, regardless of their language proficiency level, adopt strategies, but the difference between good and poor learners may be that good learners know how to choose the right strategy for the right occasion. Can training be provided to enhance the decision-making capacities of learners?

A growing trend among self-regulated strategy researchers is to explore different ways the body of knowledge about self-regulated language learning can be integrated into classrooms to benefit second or foreign learners (Chamot 2005). Despite extensive and impressive attempts to examine the application of strategy training, studies on strategy intervention or training for different language skills are limited. Oxford (1989) provided a guidebook on language learning strategies for teachers' use in which strategies were categorized as indirect and direct. Direct strategies included memory, cognitive, and compensatory strategies, while indirect strategies included metacognitive, affective, and social strategies. Oxford also provided guidance for teachers when using strategies for training students. For example, she provided techniques for gathering information on learning strategies and reported concerns on the part of learners when strategy training was used. Thompson and Rubin (1996) taught listening strategies for an academic year. Significant improvements in listening comprehension were detected for learners who received training on self-regulated listening strategies. Ikeda and Takeuchi (2003) conducted reading strategy instruction for eight weeks. The results supported the potential of reading strategy training for Japanese university students' reading enhancement. In a study of writing strategy intervention among Chinese students (Teng 2016), students who received training on metacognitive strategies registered significant gains in writing over a semester-long period.

Even so, few successful strategy intervention studies related specifically to SLA have not yet been found. There are a number of practical concerns in learner strategy research. One basic question concerns how training can be most effectively accomplished. For example, should instruction in strategies be integrated with a regular coursebook or be separate? Should strategy training be taught to the students? Skehan (1991) highlighted the fact that "despite the enormous energies and talent that have gone into developing strategy training materials, there has been relatively little evidence of a gain-score nature to indicate the effectiveness of such training" (p.287). He also mentioned that there is a lack of systematic work to identify which strategies or strategy categories are most susceptible to training, determine the length of training time needed to achieve significant and enduring learning results, discover which types of presentation techniques are effective for training, and determine whether all learners, e.g., low- or high-language-proficiency learners, are equally influenced by strategy training. Thirty years have passed since Skehan's arguments. However, research that addresses these four issues is still limited. Research of this nature will be required to determine the type of strategies, length of time, and delivery techniques that benefit all L2 learners and how this training does so.

10.5 Pedagogy and Instruction

From an SRL perspective, learners are regarded as active participants in the learning process. Learners are assumed to be agents in constructing their own meanings, goals, and strategies from the information available in the "external" environment as well as information in their own minds (the "internal" environment) (Pintrich 2004). An SRL perspective assumes that learners can potentially monitor, control, and regulate certain aspects of their own cognition, motivation, and behavior as well as some features of their environments. However, it is unlikely that learners can or will monitor and control their cognition, motivation, or behavior at all times or in all contexts. From an SRL perspective, we must acknowledge that learners' efforts at self-regulation can be impeded because of biological, developmental, contextual, and individual constraints. This argument also highlights a learning style approach, for which individual differences in SRL can be more stable or less controllable due to contextual variation. Teacher and student interactions around learning strategies are expected to boost students' understanding of the importance of self-regulated learning. Teachers do so by enabling learners to plan, organize, and evaluate their learning processes. Their systematic engagement with students in such metacognitive endeavors reinforces students' abilities to take control of their learning. The issue of how language educators can increase student levels of self-regulation in language learning is of central importance.

The challenge in teaching self-regulation is how to engage learners in information elaboration and organization (van de Pol et al. 2019). One effective approach is to support learners. Support consists of eliciting metacognitive strategies (planning, monitoring, regulating, elaboration, organization) through the use of prompts (Teng 2016, 2019ab). Nückles et al. (2020) proposed the use of journal writing to facilitate self-regulated learning because journal writing allows writers to freely develop their ideas about the subject matter and to select the aspects of a learning episode on which to focus. Schmidt et al. (2012) examined the effects of prompting learners to reflect on the personal relevance of their learning content. They argued that the use of prompts increased both students' acceptance of journal writing and their motivation. Hence, students should be guided to identify a topic, set reasonable goals, adopt appropriate strategies, and evaluate and modify these strategies as a deeper understanding of the subject matter is developed. The understanding of subject matter knowledge requires a dynamic interaction with and sensitivity to the influences of one's personal, behavioral, and environmental events.

However, language teachers are not yet prepared to teach students to become self-regulated language learners. Various studies have been conducted to tap into the subprocesses in students' self-regulated learning without creating a complete picture. For example, Nguyen and Gu (2013) and Teng (2016) attempted to explore the effectiveness of instructing metacognitive strategies for EFL writing. Despite the positive findings of the two studies, some questions need further consideration. For example, their studies focused on semester-long, strategy-based instruction. The focus was on the role of various affective, cognitive, and motoric subprocesses in self-regulated learning. Teaching such a wide range of strategies for language learners in a longitudinal way was challenging. Their findings did not support the short-term effectiveness of strategy training for learners with lower proficiency levels. Strategy-based instruction seemed to be more difficult for those who struggled with learning. Although these abilities may improve over time, the question remains: are some learners naturally better regulated than others and is self-regulation teachable? More evidence is needed to answer these important questions.

Some researchers have claimed that self-regulatory processes are teachable and can lead to increases in students' academic learning performance and their motivation for academic learning (Schunk and Zimmerman 1998). Boekaerts (2011) claimed that the pursuit of task goals was driven by learners' values, needs, and personal goals. We may need to consider learners' emotions and provide relevant support in activating the well-being pathway through bottom-up strategies, such as volitional strategies and emotion-regulation strategies. However, we may have to acknowledge that the self-regulatory processes, for example, goal setting and self-monitoring, are generally too covert, and teachers may not be aware of the many overt manifestations of these processes. Although self-regulated learners often seek help from others to improve their academic learning (Zimmerman 2002), we may still need to consider that it is challenging to instruct self-regulatory processes such as goal setting, strategy use, and self-evaluation.

In terms of assessment, previous studies have focused more on the investigation of learners' strategy use through the use of questionnaires. For example, Rubin (1975) examined learners' different strategies for different aspects of language learning, including vocabulary learning strategies, cognitive strategies, and social strategies. Dörnyei (2005) categorized strategies into five types, i.e., commitment control strategies, metacognitive control strategies, satiation control strategies, emotion control strategies, and environmental control strategies. Research on self-regulation seems to be centered on looking at the initial driving forces, while research on strategy use examines the outcome of these forces. The understanding that no single assessment tool can effectively capture learners' self-regulation in its entirety should be acknowledged. Learners' regulatory thoughts and actions occur in real time. A multidimensional assessment approach that provides more useful information for future contextualized, individualized interventions for learners who struggle with second language learning seems essential. For example, a multidimensional assessment approach can possibly include various types of self-reports, direct observations, and perhaps teacher and/or parent ratings.

At the same time, many conceptual and methodological issues need to be considered when developing, adapting, or adopting self-report questionnaire instruments to assess self-regulated learning. Self-report instruments can be valid and reliable; however, limitations in their use are well documented. For example, while self-report questionnaires can assess learners' attitudes or propensities to use self-regulatory strategies, self-report questionnaires are limited in capturing the actual events or ongoing dynamic processes of self-regulation (Winne and Perry 2000). Other process-oriented measures, such as stimulated recall, traces, observations, or other experimental methods, may tap into the need for capturing actual events. However, those measures may have less practical utility. This may be one reason why self-report questionnaires are still widely used in research on self-regulated learning. In particular, two issues need special attention. First, teachers need guidance in learning how to use instruments for assessing SRL. Second, they need instruction on how well measurement protocols work across the age spectrum.

As discussed above, SRL has dual qualities as both an aptitude and an event. SRL is a process influenced by environmental plus mental factors and potentials. Learners' metacognitive monitoring and metacognitive control may change as they deal with different task demands. We may consider the combined use of self-report questionnaires, structured interviews, teacher judgments, think-aloud measures, error detection tasks, trace methods, and observations of performance to tap into different components of conditions, cognitive operations, and event-related change. Some may contend that using several measures at the same time is impractical. At the very least, determining which measurement protocol is helpful for the research purpose is fundamental. Future work is necessary to determine how measures of SRL as an aptitude or event can be coordinated to characterize the full spectrum of SRL. Assessing self-regulation merits special emphasis in future work. While the main focus of studies has been placed on measuring self-regulation as an aptitude, few studies have been conducted that measure self-regulation as an event. In addition, protocols are needed for collecting longitudinal measurements that span multiple brief episodes, e.g., across grade levels. Future research also needs to evaluate learners' self-regulation across the age spectrum. Due to the challenges in measuring self-regulation across the age spectrum, what we know about measurement protocols and developmental trajectories is still limited.

We may also recognize the issue of definitional fuzziness of the language-learning-strategy classification systems. Previous studies have been highly concentrated on language learning strategies but have failed to create an overall picture of different dimensions of self-regulation. We may need to explore the possibility of qualitative research, which could provide insights into this line of research. The criticisms still resonate in language learning strategy research today as the concept of self-regulation continues to make inroads into strategy research. The criticisms call for a movement for a clearer definition of strategic learning. The qualitative method may be essential to explore strategy use and examine strategic learning, both in terms of learners' self-regulation of the learning task and the cognitive and behavioral strategies they employ. Thus, self-regulation and strategy use can be explored to discover whether educational psychology theory remains malleable to new findings in second language acquisition.

Finally, SRL models are related to other research areas, e.g., emotion regulation, positive psychology, and collaborative learning. Although this chapter has reviewed several key SRL models, a crucial aspect is a lack of criteria and standards to set goals, monitor, and evaluate. Although Winne and Hadwin (1998) attempted to describe how students constantly monitor their activities against standards and use tactics to perform tasks, very little connection to emotions was made. Researchers can utilize interdisciplinary approaches to better understand various SRL models and comprehend how to apply the models to their research goals for second language acquisition. Researchers and teachers should also consider how a repertoire of models can help them tailor their interventions more effectively. These future advances should promote knowledge and understanding of individual differences in self-regulated capacity and second language acquisition.

Recommended Readings

Oxford, Rebecca L. 1990. *Language learning strategies: what every teacher should know*. Boston: Heinle & Heinle Publishers.
  This is a well-established monograph for understanding language learning strategies. Teachers can gain knowledge on the different language learning strategies that can benefit learners.

Winne, Philip. H. & Allyson F. Hadwin. 2008. The weave of motivation and self-regulated learning. In Dale H. Schunk & Barry J. Zimmerman (eds.), *Motivation and Self-Regulated Learning: Theory, Research and Applications*, 297–314. New York, NY: Lawrence Erlbaum Associates.
  This is a recommended reference for understanding self-regulation. This paper also delineates the interaction between motivation and self-regulation.

Zimmerman, Barry J. & Risemberg, Rafael. 1997. Becoming a self-regulated writer: A social cognitive perspective. *Contemporary Educational Psychology* 22. 73–101.
  This is a very classical study in understanding self-regulation in writing. The key feature is a social cognitive model of writing, which is composed of three fundamental forms of self-regulation: environmental, behavioral, and covert or personal.

Teng, Feng, Chuang Wang & Lawrence Jun Zhang. 2022. Assessing self-regulatory writing strategies and their predictive effects on young EFL learners' writing performance. *Assessing Writing* 51. 100573.
  This is a recommended recent study in documenting young learners' self-regulation in writing. Students' use of self-regulated writing strategies varies according to grade levels and gender. The six strategy factors (i.e., writing planning, goal-oriented monitoring, goal-oriented evaluation, emotional control, memorization, and metacognitive judgment) predicts writing performance.

References

Baker, Linda & Zimlin Laurie. 1989. Instructional effects on children's use of two levels of standards for evaluating their comprehension. *Journal of Educational Psychology* 81(3). 340–346.
Bandura, Albert. 1977. Self-efficacy: Toward a unifying theory of behavioral change. Psychological Review, 84(2), 191–215.
Bandura, Albert. 1986. *Social foundations of thought and action: A social cognitive theory*. Englewood Cliffs, NJ: Prentice-Hall.
Bandura, Albert. 1997. *Self-efficacy: The exercise of control*. New York, NY: W. H. Freeman and Company.

Biggs, John B. 1987. *Student Approaches to Learning and Studying*. Camberwell, Vic.: Australian Council for Educational Research.
Blanksona, A. Nayena & Clancy Blairb. 2016. Cognition and classroom quality as predictors of math achievement in the kindergarten year. *Learning & Instruction* 41. 32–40.
Boekaerts, Monique. 2011. Emotions, emotion regulation, and self-regulation of learning. In Barry J. Zimmerman & Dale H. Schunk (eds.), *Handbook of self-regulation of learning and performance*, 408–425. New York, NY: Routledge.
Boekaerts, Monique & Eduardo Cascallar. 2006. How far have we moved toward the integration of theory and practice in self-regulation? *Educational Psychology Review* 18(3). 199–210.
Boekaerts, Monique & Markku Niemivirta. 2000. Self-regulated learning: Finding a balance between learning goals and ego-protective goals. In Monique Boekaerts, Paul R. Pintrich & Moshe Zeidner (eds.), *Handbook of self-regulation*, 417–451. San Diego, California: Academic.
Chamot, Anna. Uhl. 2005. Language learning strategy instruction: Current issues and research. *Annual Review of Applied Linguistics* 25. 112–130.
Chamot, Anna. Uhl & Lisa Kupper. 1989. Learning strategies in foreign language instruction. *Foreign Language Annals* 22(1). 13–24.
Cleary, Timothy J & Barry J. Zimmerman. 2001. Self-regulation differences during athletic practice by experts, non-experts, and novices. *Journal of Applied Sport Psychology* 13(2). 185–206.
Cohen, Andrew D & Ernesto Macaro (eds.). 2007. *Language learner strategies: Thirty years of research and practice*. Oxford: Oxford University Press.
Cornoldi Cesare, Barbara Carretti, Silvia Drusi & Chiara Tencati. 2015. Improving problem solving in primary school students: The effect of a training programme focusing on metacognition and working memory. *British Journal of Educational Psychology* 85(3). 424–439.
Crombach, Marjo J, Monique Boekaerts, & Marinus J. M. Voeten. 2003. Online measurement of appraisals of students faced with curricular tasks. *Educational and Psychological Measurement* 63(1). 96–111. https://doi:10.1177/0013164402239319
da Silva Marini, Janete Aparecida & Evely Boruchovitch. 2014. Self-regulated learning in students of pedagogy. *Paidéia* 24. 323–330.
Dörnyei, Zoltán. 2005. *The psychology of the language learner: Individual differences in second language acquisition*. Mahwah, NJ: Lawrence Erlbaum.
Greene, Jeffrey Alan, Jane Robertson & Lara-Jeane Croker Costa. 2011. Assessing self-regulated learning using think aloud methods. In Barry J. Zimmerman & Dale H. Schunk (eds.), *Handbook of self-regulation of learning and performance*, 313–328. New York, NY: Routledge.
Ikeda, Masato & Osamu Takeuchi. 2003. Can strategy instruction help EFL learners to improve their reading ability? An empirical study. *JACET Bulletin* 37(1). 49–60.
Järvelä, Sanna, Hanna Järvenoja, Jonna Malmberg & Allyson F. Hadwin. 2013. Exploring socially shared regulation in the context of collaboration. *Journal of Cognitive Education and Psychology* 12(3). 267–286.
Li, Qiu jie, Rachel Baker & Mark Warschauer. 2020. Using clickstream data to measure, understand, and support self-regulated learning in online courses. *The Internet and Higher Education*. https://doi:10.1016/j.iheduc.2020.100727
Marton, Ference & Roger Säljö. 1976. On qualitative differences in learning – I: Outcome and process. British Journal of Educational Psychology 46(1). 4–11.
McClelland, Megan M. & Claire E. Cameron. 2012. Self-regulation in early childhood: Improving conceptual clarity and developing ecologically valid measures. *Child Development Perspectives* 6(2). 136–142.

McClelland, Megan M, Claire E. Cameron, Carol M. Connor, Cathleen L. Farris, Abigail M. Jewkes & Frederick J. Morrison. 2007. Links between behavioral regulation and preschoolers' literacy, vocabulary, and math skills. *Developmental Psychology* 43(4). 947–959.

Müller, Nadja M & Tina Seufert. 2018. Effects of self-regulation prompts in hypermedia learning on learning performance and self-efficacy. *Learning and Instruction* 58. 1–11.

Nguyen, Le Thi Cam Yongqi Gu. 2013. Strategy-based instruction: A learner-focused approach to developing learner autonomy. *Language Teaching Research* 17(1). 9–30.

Nückles, Matthias, Julian Roelle, Inga Glogger-Frey, Julia Waldeyer & Alexander Renkl. 2020. The Self-regulation-view in writing-to-learn: Using journal writing to optimize cognitive load in self-regulated learning. *Educational Psychology Review*. https://doi:10.1007/s10648-020-09541-1

O'Malley, J. Michael & Anna Uhl Chamot. 1990. *Learning strategies in second language acquisition*. Cambridge: Cambridge University Press.

Oxford, Rebecca L. 1989. *Language learning strategies: What every teacher should know*. Rowley, MA: Newbury House.

Oxford, Rebecca L. 1990. *Language learning strategies: what every teacher should know*. Boston: Heinle & Heinle Publishers.

Panadero, Ernesto. 2017. A review of self-regulated learning: Six models and four directions for research. *Frontiers in Psychology*. https://www.frontiersin.org/articles/10.3389/fpsyg.2017.00422/ful

Panadero, Ernesto, Paul A. Kirschner, Sanna Järvelä, Jonna Malmberg & Hanna Järvenoja. 2015. How Individual Self-Regulation Affects Group Regulation and Performance: A Shared Regulation Intervention. *Small Group Research* 46(4). 431–454.

Perry, Nancy E & Philip H. Winne. 2006. Learning from learning kits: gStudy traces of students' self-regulated engagements with computerized content. *Educational Psychology Review* 18(3). 211–228.

Pintrich, Paul R. 2000. The role of goal orientation in self-regulated learning. In Monique Boekaerts, Paul R. Pintrich, & Moshe Zeidner (eds.), *Handbook of self-regulation*, 451–502. San Diego, CA: Elsevier Academic Press.

Pintrich, Paul R. 2004. A conceptual framework for assessing motivation and self-regulated learning in college students. *Educational Psychology Review* 16(4). 385–407. https://doi:10.1007/s10648-004-0006-x

Pintrich, Paul R & Dale H. Schunk. 2002. *Motivation in education: Theory, research, and applications*. Upper Saddle River, NJ: Merrill-Prentice Hall.

Pintrich, Paul R & Elisabeth Vialpando De Groot. 1990. Motivational and self-regulated learning components of classroom academic performance. *Journal of educational psychology* 82(1). 33–40.

Politzer, Robert L & Mary McGroarty. 1985. An exploratory study of learning behaviors and their relationship to gains in linguistic and communicative competence. *TESOL Quarterly* 19(1). 103–123.

Rubin, Joan. 1975. What the good language learner can teach us. *TESOL Quarterly* 9. 41–51.

Schmitz, Bernhard & Bettina S.Wiese. 2006. New perspectives for the evaluation of training sessions in self-regulated learning: Time-series analyses of diary data. *Contemporary Educational Psychology* 31(1). 64–96.

Schunk, Dale H & Barry J. Zimmerman. (eds.). 1998. *Self-regulated learning: From teaching to self-reflective practice*. New York: Guilford Press.

Schmidt, Kristin, Julia Maier & Matthias Nückles. 2012. Writing about the personal utility of learning contents in a learning journal improves learning motivation and comprehension. *Education Research International*. 1–10.

Skehan, Peter. 1991. Individual differences in second language learning. *Studies in Second Language Acquisition* 13(2). 275–298.

Teng, Feng. 2016. Immediate and delayed effects of embedded metacognitive instruction on Chinese EFL students' English writing and regulation of cognition. *Thinking skills & Creativity* 22. 289–302.

Teng, Feng. 2019a. Tertiary-level students' English writing performance and metacognitive awareness: A group metacognitive support perspective. *Scandinavian Journal of Educational Research*.

Teng, Feng. 2019b. A comparison of text structure and self-regulated strategy instruction for elementary school students' writing. *English Teaching: Practice and Critique 18*(3). 281–297.

Teng, Feng & Jing Huang. 2019. Predictive effects of writing strategies for self-regulated learning on secondary school learners' EFL writing proficiency. *TESOL Quarterly* 53(1). 232–247.

Teng, Feng, Chuang Wang & Lawrence Jun Zhang. 2022. Assessing self-regulatory writing strategies and their predictive effects on young EFL learners' writing performance. *Assessing Writing* 51. 100573.

Thompson, Irene & Joan Rubin. 1996. Can strategy instruction improve listening comprehension? *Foreign Language Annals* 29(3). 331–342.

Turner, Julianne C. 1995. The influence of classroom contexts on young children's motivation for literacy. *Reading Research Quarterly* 30. 410–441.

Weinstein, Claire E, Schulte, Ann C & Darcie R. Palmer. 1987. *LASSI: Learning and Study Strategies Inventory*. Clearwater, FL: H. & H.

Winne, Philip. H. 1997. Experimenting to bootstrap self-regulated learning. *Journal of Educational Psychology* 89(3). 1–14.

Winne, Philip. H., & Allyson F. Hadwin. 1998. Studying as self-regulated engagement in learning. In Douglas J. Hacker, John Dunlosky, Arthur C. Graesser (eds.), *Metacognition in Educational Theory and Practice, 277–304*. Hillsdale, NJ: Erlbaum.

Winne, Philip. H and Nancy E. Perry. 2000. Measuring self-regulated learning. In Monique Boekaerts, Paul R. Pintrich, & Moshe Zeidner (eds.), *Handbook of self-regulation*, 532–568. Orlando, Florida: Academic Press.

Winne, Philip. H, Allyson F. Hadwin & Catherine Gress. 2010. The learning kit project: software tools for supporting and researching regulation of collaborative learning. *Computers in Human Behavior 26.* 787–793. https://doi:10.1016/j.chb.2007.09.009

van de Pol, Janneke, Anique B. H. de Bruin, Mariëtte H.van Loon & Tamara van Gog. 2019. Students' and teachers' monitoring and regulation of students' text comprehension: effects of metacomprehension cue availability. *Contemporary Educational Psychology* 56. 236–249.

Zhang, Lawrence Jun. 2008. Constructivist pedagogy in strategic reading instruction: Exploring pathways to learner development in the English as a second language (ESL) classroom. *Instructional Science* 36(2). 89–116.

Ziegler, Albert, Heidrun Stoeger & Robert Grassinger. 2011. Actiotope model and self-regulated learning. *Psychological Test and Assessment Modeling* 53(1). 141–160.

Zimmerman, Barry J. 1986. Becoming a self-regulated learner: Which are the key subprocesses? *Contemporary Educational Psychology* 11(4). 307–313. https://doi:10.1016/0361-476X(86)90027-5

Zimmerman, Barry J. 1989. A social cognitive view of self-regulated academic learning. *Journal of Educational Psychology 81(3).* 329–339.

Zimmerman, Barry J. 2000. Attaining self-regulation: a social cognitive perspective. In Monique Boekaerts, Paul R. Pintrich, & Moshe Zeidner (eds.), *Handbook of self-regulation*, 13–14. San Diego, CA: Academic Press.

Zimmerman, Barry J. 2002. Becoming a self-regulated learner. *Theory Into Practice* 41(2). 64–70.

Zimmerman, Barry J. 2005. Attaining self-regulation: A social cognitive perspective. In Monique Boekaerts, Paul R. Pintrich, & Moshe Zeidner (eds.), *Handbook of self-regulation*, 13–39. San Diego, CA: Academic Press.

Zimmerman, Barry J. 2008. Goal-setting: a key proactive sources of self-regulated learning. In Dale H. Schunk & Barry J. Zimmerman (eds.), *Motivation and Self-Regulated Learning: Theory, Research and Applications*, 267–296. Hillsdale,

Zimmerman, Barry J. 2013. From cognitive modeling to self-regulation: A social cognitive career path. *Educational Psychologists 48 (3)*. 135–147.

Zimmerman, Barry J & Dale H. Schunk (eds.). 2001. *Self-regulated learning and academic achievement: Theoretical perspectives* (2nd ed.). Mahwah, NJ: Erlbaum.

Zimmerman, Barry J & Magda Campillo. 2003. Motivating self-regulated problem solvers. In Judy E. Davidson & Robert J. Sternberg (eds.), *The nature of problem solving*, 233–262. New York, NY: Cambridge University Press.

Zimmerman, Barry & Moylan, Adam. 2009. Self-regulation: Where metacognition and motivation intersect. In D. J. Hacker, J. Dunlosky, & A. C. Graesser (Eds.), Handbook of metacognition in education (pp. 299–315). Routledge/Taylor & Francis Group.

Zimmerman, Barry J & Manuel Martinez-Pons. 1986. Development of a structured interview for accessing student use of self-regulated learning strategies. *American Educational Research Journal* 23(4). 614–628.

Zimmerman, Barry J & Rafael Risemberg. 1997. Becoming a self-regulated writer: A social cognitive perspective. *Contemporary Educational Psychology* 22. 73–101.

Part IV: **L2 Skills, Learning Difficulties, and Anxiety**

11 L2 Reading and Writing Skills

Richard L. Sparks

Abstract: Reading and writing are important for L2 acquisition and are rooted in oral language proficiency. Reading exposes students to more new (and rare) vocabulary, grammar, and language structures in the target language than will oral language exposure. In order to read the target L2, an individual must be able to both decode (read) words and comprehend the meaning of the text. The Simple View of Reading (SVR) model has been found to explain the bulk of the variance in the cognitive skills necessary for both word decoding and language comprehension in both L1 and L2. Likewise, the Simple View of Writing (SVW) model has been found to explain the cognitive components of written language. In this chapter, the author will describe the SVR and SVW models, examine the relationship between listening comprehension and reading comprehension and between writing and oral language, and explain how to assess English reading and writing skills using available standardized testing measures. The chapter concludes by discussing pedagogical methods for teaching English skills to L2 learners.

Keywords: Simple View of Reading, Simple View of Writing, Second language reading and writing, word decoding, reading comprehension, dyslexic, hyperlexic

11.1 Introduction

Reading comprehension has been hypothesized to be a unitary construct. If a student could read a text and successfully answer multiple choice questions or restate facts, s/he was thought to be a good comprehender. Likewise, writing was thought to be a straightforward process of putting one's thoughts on paper. However, studies conducted by L1 and L2 researchers have found that reading comprehension and writing involve complex cognitive processes (see Chen, Dronjic, and Helms-Park 2015; Oakhill, Cain, and Elbro 2014; Graham 2020). Two models, the Simple View of Reading (SVR) (Gough and Tunmer 1986; Hoover and Gough 1990) and the Simple View of Writing (SVW) (Juel, Griffith, and Gough 1986), have been proposed by researchers to explain the cognitive processes necessary for successful reading and writing. Studies over 30 years have shown that cognitive skills explain the bulk of the variance in L1 reading and writing ability. For reading, word decoding and oral language (listening) comprehension have been found to make independent contributions to reading comprehension (see Foorman et al. 2015; Hoover and Tunmer 2020; Kim 2020; Language and Reading Research Consortium 2015). In writing, skills related to transcription and ideation (text generation) have been shown to explain L1 writing ability. L1 researchers have also found that: a) reading and writing are closely related skills, b) oral language (listening) comprehension is strongly predictive of reading comprehension, and c) discourse-level oral language is strongly related to writing ability (Kim and Schatschneider 2017).

The purpose of this chapter is to examine the cognitive skills that have been found to be necessary for learning to read and write English using the findings from research with the SVR and SVW models. The literature review first describes the *theories* underlying the two models. Then, the author examines the *evidence* that supports the utility of the models for explaining the development of L1 and L2 reading and writing skills, and examines the intimate connections between reading and writing, reading comprehension and oral language (listening) comprehension, and oral language (expression) and writing. Next, he describes a procedure for the *assessment* of English reading and writing skills using available standardized measures and presents several measures that can be used for the assessment of English reading, writing, and oral language skills. The chapter concludes with a discussion of *pedagogical* strategies for teaching English skills based on the models.

11.2 Simple View of Reading Model

The SVR posits that the primary task in learning to read is determining how print maps onto spoken language and that the two most important skills are word recognition (decoding) and language (listening) comprehension. Word decoding requires knowledge of the speech sounds in spoken words and the system by which those speech sounds are represented by print. It is well-established that word decoding skills are dependent on the acquisition of phonological awareness, letter-sound knowledge, orthographic and morphological knowledge, and rapid naming (see Kilpatrick 2015). Language (listening) comprehension represents the linguistic processes used for the comprehension of oral language at both the word level and for connected text and includes learning vocabulary in the target language. In recent studies, researchers have also found that background knowledge has a direct effect on reading comprehension after controlling for adult participants' word decoding, listening comprehension, and oral vocabulary (Talwar, Tighe, and Greenberg 2018). The SVR model also proposes that decoding and language comprehension make independent contributions to reading skills, a finding that has been replicated in numerous studies over many years (e.g., see Hoover and Tunmer 2020; Wagner et al. 2015). Figure 1 depicts the SVR model.

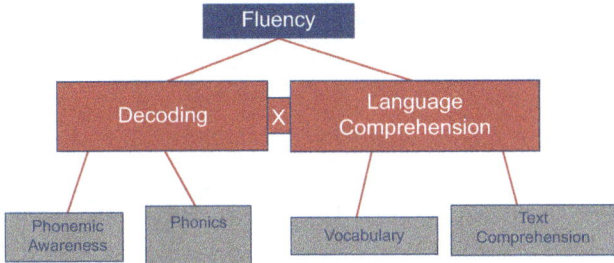

Figure 1: Simple View of Reading Model.

Gough and Tunmer (1986) hypothesized that the SVR model would help classroom teachers to identify the types of readers whom they encounter. Since the SVR proposes that reading skills can result only from the product of word decoding and language comprehension, the model posits that will be four types of readers in classroom settings. *Good* readers will exhibit both average to above-average word decoding and average to above-average oral language comprehension. The SVR model posits there will be three different types of poor readers. *Mixed* poor readers display both poor word decoding and poor oral language comprehension skills. *Hyperlexic* poor readers have good word decoding skills accompanied by deficits in oral language comprehension. *Dyslexic* poor readers have good (oral) language comprehension, but exhibit a deficit in word decoding skills caused by deficits in phonological processing that will result in poor reading comprehension because they are unable to read enough words to comprehend the written text.[1] Studies over several years have validated the types of reader profiles proposed by the SVR model (Catts, Adolf, and Weismer 2006; Foorman et al. 2015; Tunmer and Chapman 2012). Figure 2 depicts the four types of readers in the SVR model.

In L1 reading research, strong empirical support has been offered for the accuracy of the SVR model in predicting students' reading skills (Aouad and Savage 2009; Carver 1998; Joshi and Aaron 2000). Although the bulk of studies supporting the SVR model had been conducted with English-speaking children (Nakamato, Lindsey, and Manis 2007), there are an increasing number of studies conducted by reading researchers with speakers of other languages. These studies have supported the SVR model with languages including Chinese (Joshi et al. 2012), Hebrew

---

[1] Gough and Tunmer use the terms *dyslexic* and *hyperlexic* to characterize readers who display specific profiles of decoding and comprehension skills, *not* to reference disability diagnoses. For example, in the SVR model, a poor reader can display a dyslexic reader profile (weak decoding, good oral language comprehension) but may not be classified with dyslexia (reading disability).

	Decoding	
	Poor	Good
Language Comprehension — Good	Dyslexia Specific decoding deficit	No deficits
Language Comprehension — Poor	Garden Variety Decoding and comprehension deficits	Hyperlexia Specific language comprehension deficit

Figure 2: Types of Readers Proposed by the SVR Model.

(Joshi et al. 2015), Italian (Bonifacci and Tobia 2017); Norweigan (Høien-Tengesdal and Høien 2012), French (Megherbi, Seigneuric, and Ehrlich 2006), and Dutch (Verhoeven and van Leeuwe 2012). [See also Joshi (2018) for a review of the SVR model in different orthographies.] In recent studies, Kim (2017, 2020) has found that word decoding and oral language (listening) comprehension explain most of the variance for reading comprehension in L1 (English) and L2 (Korean) populations. These studies and others have found that word decoding skill explains more variance in the early stages of learning to read, and that the contribution of oral language (listening) comprehension increases in the later grades (e.g., see Francis et al. 2005; García and Cain 2014). Recent studies have found that both word decoding and language comprehension skills also contribute to L2 reading comprehension. For example, Jeon and Yamashita (2014) conducted a meta-analysis of L2 reading comprehension correlates and found that L2 grammar knowledge ($r = .85$), L2 vocabulary ($r = .79$), L2 listening comprehension ($r = .77$), and L2 word decoding ($r = .56$) skills were the strongest predictors of L2 reading comprehension.

Studies conducted by the author and his colleagues have examined how the cognitive components in the SVR model explain the L2 reading skills of monolingual English U.S. high school L2 learners. In contrast to learning to read their native language, these monolingual students were learning to read and speak an L2 (Spanish) simultaneously, beginning quite a number of years after they had learned to speak and comprehend as well as read and write their L1. In one study, Sparks (2015) administered standardized measures of Spanish word decoding, reading comprehension, listening comprehension, and vocabulary normed with native Spanish speakers, i.e., *Batería III Woodcock-Muñoz Pruebas de aprovechamiento*, to students (n = 165) completing first and second year Spanish courses and found that the majority displayed good Spanish word decoding skills but poor Spanish reading comprehension and poor Spanish vocabulary knowledge. In another study with these participants, Sparks and Patton (2016) found that Spanish word decoding and Spanish listening comprehension explained 67% of the variance in Spanish reading comprehension, while Spanish vocabulary added an additional 3% unique variance.

In a study with a larger group of secondary level participants enrolled in Spanish (n=293 in first year, n=268 in second year, n=51 in third year), Sparks and Luebbers (2018) administered the *Batería III Woodcock-Muñoz* and obtained results similar to the aforementioned study, i.e., stronger word decoding than comprehension. In still another study, findings revealed little difference between the students' Spanish reading comprehension and Spanish listening comprehension skills, even after two to three years of classroom instruction (Sparks, Patton, and Luebbers 2019). Sparks et al. hypothesized that students achieved low scores in Spanish reading comprehension and listening comprehension ($<1^{st}$ percentile) largely because they had acquired very low levels of Spanish vocabulary ($<1^{st}$ percentile). Similar to studies cited earlier, findings showed that the correlation between L2 listening and reading comprehension for third year students was strong (r = .76). In the latter study, a path analysis procedure showed that Spanish listening comprehension was the strongest predictor of Spanish reading comprehension, and that Spanish vocabulary added a small amount of unique variance to the prediction of Spanish reading comprehension.

In a new study, Sparks (2019) used hierarchical regression analyses to investigate the contributions of L2 word decoding, L2 listening comprehension, and L2 vocabulary for the prediction of L2 reading comprehension in monolingual U.S. L1 English students studying Spanish. For students completing third year Spanish, results showed that all three variables were significant predictors of Spanish reading comprehension; together, the three variables explained 61% of the variance in Spanish reading comprehension (31% word decoding, 25% listening comprehension, 5% vocabulary). When the Modern Language Aptitude Test (MLAT; Carroll & Sapon, 1959, 2000) was included as a variable in the hierarchical model as a proxy for students' language aptitude, this measure added a small amount of unique variance (2%) to the prediction of third-year Spanish reading comprehension after the contributions of L2 word decoding, listening comprehension, and vocabulary had been partialed.

In sum, these studies with monolingual U.S. L2 learners have found that the cognitive factors proposed by the SVR model–L2 word decoding and L2 listening comprehension–are strong predictors of L2 reading comprehension. In addition, the studies have shown that U. S. secondary level language learners learn to decode L2 (Spanish) words relatively well, but achieve very low levels of reading comprehension, listening comprehension, and vocabulary. These findings with monolingual U.S. L2 learners are similar to findings with L2 learners who have L1s that are different from English, that is, stronger L2 word decoding than L2 reading and oral language comprehension (e.g., see Geva, 2006; Geva and Yaghoub 2006).

11.3 Simple View of Writing Model

In contrast to reading, the study of writing has received less attention from researchers. However, one model of writing has been the focus of writing researchers. In 1986 Juel, Griffith, and Gough proposed the Simple View of Writing (SVW) model. Like the SVR model, the SVW was hypothesized to consist of two components–spelling and ideation. Juel and her colleagues followed children from 1st–4th grades and found that spelling required the skills necessary for word decoding, i.e., phonemic awareness and letter-sound knowledge. They proposed that ideation is the ability to generate and organize ideas, and the term was used broadly to incorporate the generation of creative thoughts and their organization into sentences and text structures (Juel 1988: 438). Although their model seemed simplistic, the authors proposed that the two components were complex and would be found to contain additional subcomponents. Similar to the SVR model in which lower order processes (decoding) would impede the ability to employ higher order processes (comprehension), Juel et al. also hypothesized that poor lower order processes (spelling) would disrupt the development of higher order processes (ideation), that is, until lower order processes were somewhat automatic, attention for the written word would be diverted from higher to lower order processes. The results of their four-year study supported their hypothesis, i.e., poor spelling impeded ideation, and also found that poor readers in 1st grade became poor writers in 4th grade.

Berninger and her colleagues (e.g., see Berninger 2000; Berninger et al. 1994; Berninger and Graham 1998) enhanced the SVW model by proposing that *transcription* is a separate component of writing that consists of spelling and handwriting (keyboarding). Confirmatory factor analysis found that spelling and handwriting have separate factor loadings (Abbott and Berninger 1993), and in a recent meta-analysis Feng et al. (2019) found that handwriting fluency contributes to writing fluency and writing quality. Other researchers have found that lack of accuracy and fluency and poor transcription skills constrained writing ability by interfering with higher order skills such as planning and content generation (e.g., see McCutchen et al. 2000). A more recent meta-analysis examined true- and quasi-experimental intervention studies conducted with K-12 students to determine if teaching handwriting enhanced legibility and fluency and resulted in better writing performance (Santangelo and Graham 2016). When compared to no instruction or non-handwriting instructional conditions, teaching handwriting resulted in statistically greater legibility and fluency, and handwriting instruction produced statistically significant gains in the quality, length, and fluency of students' writing. The findings provided support for an assumption underlying the SVW, i.e., handwriting fluency is a separate component of writing ability. These studies have confirmed that the transcription component of the SVW includes two subcomponents, spelling and handwriting fluency.

Additional research has found that *ideation* (text generation) involves oral language representation (e.g., see Kim et al. 2011; McCutchen 2006) because " . . . preverbal ideas and thoughts have to be encoded into written text, therefore, text generation is operationalized in oral language skills" (Kim and Schatschneider 2017: 36). Other researchers have found that oral language skills such as vocabulary (Coker 2006) and grammar knowledge (Olinghouse 2008) are related to writing skills in young children after accounting for transcription skills (Kim et al. 2014). Likewise, oral discourse was found to be related to writing ability after the variance explained by spelling (Kim et al. 2015) as well as sentence and reading comprehension (Berninger and Abbott 2010) were partialed. These studies have led researchers to suggest that oral language, vocabulary, and grammar knowledge are all important contributors to the ideation component of the SVW.

More recent studies have expanded knowledge of the ideation component in the SVW. In their study with 1st grade children, Kim and Schatschneider (2017) investigated the direct and indirect effects of the component skills for writing. They found that discourse-level oral language, spelling, and handwriting fluency completely mediated the relationships of foundational and higher-order cognitive skills (e.g., self-regulation, inference) and working memory to writing, and that language and cognitive skills had both direct and indirect relations to discourse-level oral language. Their results of their model explained 67% of the variance in writing quality. Another recent meta-analysis examined the SVW for L2 writing and found that transcription skills explained 31.2%, vocabulary 24.8%, and oral language 15.8% of the variance in L2 writing (Graham and Eslami 2020). The authors concluded that the components hypothesized by the SWW may explain the variation in L2 writing ability.

In sum, findings over several years have found that the basic tenets of the SVW, i.e., writing is comprised of *transcription* and *ideation*, are important for explaining writing ability. Since the initial hypothesis was presented in 1986, researchers have included handwriting fluency and spelling in the transcription component and proposed that the ideation component includes text generation (vocabulary, grammar knowledge, oral language) and text organization.

11.4 Understanding the Oral Language Component for Reading and Writing

L1 research has confirmed that oral language proficiency is strongly related to both reading and writing ability. For reading, studies have shown that the correlation between reading comprehension and oral language (listening) comprehension is strong, usually .80 and higher, particularly for adolescents and students in the upper elementary grades (Aaron et al. 2008). Research has also shown that listening comprehension measures can be used as a valid and reliable predictor of reading comprehension (Kintsch and Kominsky 1977; Palmer et al. 1985). The relationships between listening comprehension and reading comprehension have been confirmed by reading researchers over several years (e.g., see Cain, Oakhill, and Bryant 2004; Florit et al. 2009; Lepola et al. 2012). For example, in a recent study with 350 English- speaking 2nd graders, the language and cognitive skills in the model explained 86% of the variance in listening comprehension and 66% of the variance in reading comprehension (Kim 2017). Moreover, the results revealed that word reading (decoding) and listening comprehension completely mediated the relationships of the language and cognitive skills to reading comprehension and explained almost all of the variance in reading comprehension, i.e., the results fit the SVR model.

Studies with English language learners (ELLs) have found that oral language proficiency, particularly vocabulary knowledge, is an important predictor of reading comprehension skills (see Gottardo and Mueller 2009; Lesaux and Kieffer 2010). L2 researchers have found that despite schooling in and exposure to the target language, English vocabulary knowledge of ELL learners often lags far behind their English word decoding skills, in part from living in a home where the target language is not spoken or is not spoken extensively or fluently (Farnia and Geva 2013; Geva and Ramirez 2015). Likewise, L2 reading research has demonstrated strong correlations between L2 reading comprehension and L2 listening comprehension. Tschirner (2016) reviewed research on the relationship between students' proficiency in L2 reading comprehension and L2 listening comprehension. In one study, researchers administered the Test of English for International Communication (TOEIC) to 12,000 examinees in Taiwan, Korea, and Japan and found a significant and strong correlation (r = .76) between their reading comprehension and listening comprehension skills (Liao, Qu, and Morgan 2010). In another study with

Asian English learners using the revised TOEIC, In'nami and Koizumi (2012) also found a strong and significant relationship ($r = .87$) between students' reading comprehension and listening comprehension proficiency. Bozorgian (2012) examined Iranian students' scores on the International English Language Testing System and found that the strongest correlations among language skills were between listening comprehension and reading comprehension proficiency ($r = .74$). In his study with college foreign language majors, Tschirner found strong and significant relationships between reading and listening proficiency in all L2s ($r = .67$). In their study with U.S high school students enrolled in Spanish, Sparks, Luebbers, and Casteñada (2017) found that the correlations between L2 reading comprehension and L2 listening comprehension increased from .40 in first-year Spanish to .51 in second-year Spanish to .76 in third-year Spanish courses. These findings are consistent with the results of a large scale meta-analysis, which found that L2 listening comprehension ($r = .77$) was among the three highest correlates of L2 reading comprehension, the other two correlates being L2 grammar knowledge ($r = .85$) and L2 vocabulary knowledge ($r = .79$) (Jeon and Yamashita 2014).

Like reading, writing skills have also been found to be strongly related to oral language proficiency. In the SVW model, ideation has been measured by learners' oral language proficiency (e.g., see Hayes 2012). As indicated earlier, written text cannot be generated without being translated into oral language using appropriate words, writing the words with correct grammar, and organizing the words in a logical sequence at the discourse level. Research on the importance of oral language in writing has accumulated over several years with students in kindergarten through the middle school level (e.g., see Berninger and Abbott 2010; Juel, Griffith, and Gough 1986; Kim et al. 2011, 2013, 2014). Further evidence for the importance of oral language in writing comes from individuals with language impairments. For example, students with impaired language skills produce written texts with poor grammar, lower vocabulary levels, fewer words and ideas, and poor organization (Dockrell and Connelly 2009; Dockrell, Lindsay, and Connelly 2009). Researchers have also found that the nature of the skills in the SVW, transcription and ideation, change over time. That is, transcription skills constrain ideation (text generation) in the beginning stages of writing development, leaving fewer cognitive resources for generating and translating ideas into oral language. However, as transcription skills improve, text writing fluency increases along with text generation. Thus, text writing fluency (automaticity) will vary at different stages of development. Fluent writers will be able to write organized text with accuracy, speed, and proficiency (Kim et al. 2018).

Researchers have also found that reading and writing are intimately connected. According to shared knowledge theory (Tierney and Shanahan 1991), " . . . readers draw on knowledge while reading that overlaps with the knowledge they draw on while writing, and vice versa" (Graham 2020: 537). That is, although reading and writing are not identical processes, the cognitive systems used by reading, e.g., oral language, vocabulary, grammar, phonemic awareness, are shared by writing. A meta-analysis conducted by Graham and Hebert (2011) revealed that writing about text improved reading comprehension, and that instruction designed to teach writing skills led to improvements in reading comprehension. Another meta-analysis showed that reading instruction not only improved writing skills but also found that more time devoted to reading resulted in better writing skills and secondary level students level students made the largest gains in writing (Graham, Liu, and Bartlett 2018). In his review of research on reading-writing connections, Shanahan (2016) reported that studies have shown 72–85% shared variance for word factors and 65% for text level factors.

The cognitive consequences of poor reading and writing achievement have been examined in L1 research on print exposure (reading volume), where cognitive differences between individuals with different reading levels have been found in vocabulary size, grammar, fund of background knowledge, and a host of language-related skills (Cunningham and Stanovich 1997; Stanovich 1993;). Researchers have found that print contains more rare (high level) vocabulary words, more complex grammatical structures, and more declarative knowledge than (oral) speech (see review by Cunningham and Stanovich 1998). Extensive research with good and poor readers has shown that poor readers read less and are exposed to fewer words, i.e., lower reading volume, than good readers, reducing not only the number of words but also the complexity of the language structures to which they are exposed. Over time, poor reading skills combined with reduced reading volume will have debilitating consequences on poor readers' oral language (speaking, listening) proficiency, and weak oral language proficiency will have negative consequences for writing ability. The consequences of differences in reading skills and subsequent reading volume for L1 have also been found to have long-term consequences for L2 achievement and proficiency (Sparks et al. 2012a, b).

In sum, these findings show that oral language proficiency is strongly related to more and less proficient reading comprehension and written language skills, and that reading and writing skills share similar cognitive abilities. Over time, the exposure to print provided by good reading (and writing) skills has the potential to improve students' oral language expression and listening comprehension in both L1 and L2.

11.5 SVR Model: Assessment of English Reading and Linguistic Skills

Research with the SVR in L1 and L2 has shown that the cognitive skills in two domains–word decoding and oral language (listening) comprehension–explain the bulk of the variance in reading comprehension. Therefore, the assessment of English reading ability requires the selection of tests designed to measure skills in these two domains. In the U.S., there are group-administered, standardized achievement tests available for all levels of elementary and secondary education students as well as college entrance exams. While group measures provide a broad overview of academic achievement, including reading ability, they are not designed to be diagnostic, that is, to identify a learner's strengths and weaknesses in a specific academic skill. For reading, group-administered tests will identify good readers with average to above average overall reading achievement, i.e., both good word decoding and good comprehension, and poor readers with below-average skills in word decoding or comprehension, or both poor decoding and comprehension. However, if an individual achieves low scores on a group-administered test, the locus of the weak reading skills is unclear. For example, if a student achieves an overall reading score in the low average to below average range (10th–20th percentile), the group-administered test will not identify whether the source of the reading problem is poor decoding, poor comprehension, or both, nor will the measure identify whether the weakness is phonics (pseudoword reading), phonemic awareness, vocabulary, background knowledge, or a combination of these skills.

The assessment of word decoding and comprehension and the skills in each of these two domains is best accomplished with individually-administered diagnostic measures. Fortunately, there are many published and readily available testing measures in English designed specifically for the assessment of reading skills. Appendix A includes a list of commonly-used diagnostic tests that measure the skills necessary for efficient functioning in word decoding and language comprehension.[2] These measures have been normed for individuals ranging from kindergarten age through postsecondary education and various stages of adulthood. The tests have been standardized with English-speaking populations in the U.S., and each measure

---

[2] Some of these measures–WJ-IV, WRMT-III, GORT-5, PPVT-5 – have alternate, or equivalent, forms, e.g., Form A and Form B. Alternate forms of the standardized test measure the same skills to the same extent and are standardized on the same population. Alternate forms do not contain the same items. But, the means and variances of the two forms are the same, that is, an individual would be expected to achieve the same score on both forms.

has been shown to have strong validity and reliability.[3] The measures can be used by educators (and researchers) of L1s other than English to assess the English reading achievement of ELLs for diagnostic purposes, that is, to determine an individual's overall achievement in reading and their skills in the two cognitive domains.[4] In most cases, each measure listed in Appendix A can be administered in 5–10 minutes. Once familiar with the measures, an assessment of an individual's word decoding and language comprehension skills can be completed in 30–40 minutes, or less, depending on the examinee's age/grade. A battery for the assessment of reading skills in the domains of word decoding and language comprehension includes those skills in Table 1.

Table 1: Skills for measurement of reading assessment.

Word Decoding	Language Comprehension
Word Reading (real words)	Reading Comprehension
Pseudoword Decoding (nonsense words)	Receptive/Expressive Vocabulary
Phonological Awareness (K-3)	Oral Language (Listening) Comprehension
	Background Knowledge

---

[3] A norm-referenced test reports an individual's performance in relation to a specific group, e.g., the same grade or age. Norms are not standards of performance but instead serve as a frame of reference for test score interpretation. For example, the *Woodcock-Johnson* is an achievement test, not a mastery test with criterion references that determine the level of performance. On a standardized test, the norm, or comparison, group refers to the population for whom the test is intended, in this case, a native English-speaking population. The population sample for the *Woodcock-Johnson* on which the test was normed included a large sample of native English speakers from kindergarten through adulthood. To develop norms for the *Woodcock-Johnson*, the population sample enrolled in each grade was administered the items from each subtest. Each individual in the population obtained a raw score, i.e., the number of correct items, which was converted to a derived score, i.e., a standard score with $M = 100$, $SD = 15$, in order to construct a normal distribution to rank future test takers.

[4] Although it may seem unfair to compare ELL students who would have less experience with English to monolingual English norms on standardized tests, there are three lines of justification. First, converting ELL test-takers' raw scores on the testing measures to z-scores would result only in comparing their scores to others in the same group, i.e., ELLs, a procedure that would yield little or no insight into their English decoding and English reading comprehension skills *in an English-speaking context*. Second, there may be value in meaningful comparisons of ELL's reading skills to monolingual English readers' skills in establishing functional benchmarks for English reading skills for ELLs of a specific age after a targeted period of instruction in English. Third, a monolingual speaker of another L1 will be compared to a monolingual English speaker on a daily basis if s/he lives in the U.S. For monolingual English speakers being assessed in another language, the same reasoning would apply.

After the measures have been scored, an individual's reading profile will be clear, that is, s/he can be identified as a good (strong, average) or poor (weak) reader. Good (strong and average) readers will score in the average to above-average range in both word decoding and language comprehension. Poor readers will score in the low-average to the below-average range. Figure 3 depicts the profile of word decoding and comprehension scores for a good (strong, average) reader. The type of poor reader, i.e., mixed, hyperlexic, dyslexic, will also be clear based on their word decoding and language comprehension scores. For example, the *mixed* poor reader will score in the low average to below average range on the word decoding and language comprehension measures (Figure 4). The *hyperlexic* poor reader will score, at minimum, in the average range on the word decoding measures, but in the low average to below average range on the language comprehension measures (Figure 5). The dyslexic poor reader will score in the low average to below average on the word decoding measures but achieve in the average to above average range on the *oral* language comprehension measures, i.e., listening comprehension, receptive/expressive vocabulary, and background knowledge (Figure 6). However, the dyslexic poor reader's *reading* comprehension score(s) will be similar to his/her scores on the word decoding measure(s), i.e., below average, because the dyslexic cannot read (decode) enough words to comprehend the meaning of the text, i.e., 95% of words in a text must be read correctly for adequate comprehension (see e.g., O'Connor, Swanson, and Geraghty 2010).[5]

For further clarification of readers' strengths and weaknesses, Aaron (1991) proposed a method by which individuals' oral language (listening) comprehension skill can be compared to their reading comprehension skill using standardized tests. The method uses comparable measures of reading comprehension and listening comprehension. The listening comprehension test is read aloud to the examinee, who must listen but cannot see the printed words. [The primary difference between reading comprehension and oral language (listening) comprehension is that reading comprehension requires the individual to decode print.] The level of difficulty between the two texts in, e.g., vocabulary, sentence complexity, passage length, memory demands, must be equivalent under both listening and reading conditions. Aaron used one form of the WRMT-R (III) Passage Comprehension subtest for reading comprehension and its alternate form for oral language (listening)

---

5 Keenan, Betjemann, and Olson (2008) found that some standardized reading comprehension tests measure different skills. For example, decoding skill explains the largest part of the variance in reading comprehension on some tests, while linguistic comprehension explains the largest part of the variance in reading comprehension on other standardized tests. They recommended that evaluators may want to administer more than one type of reading comprehension test, e.g., cloze procedure and open-ended questions.

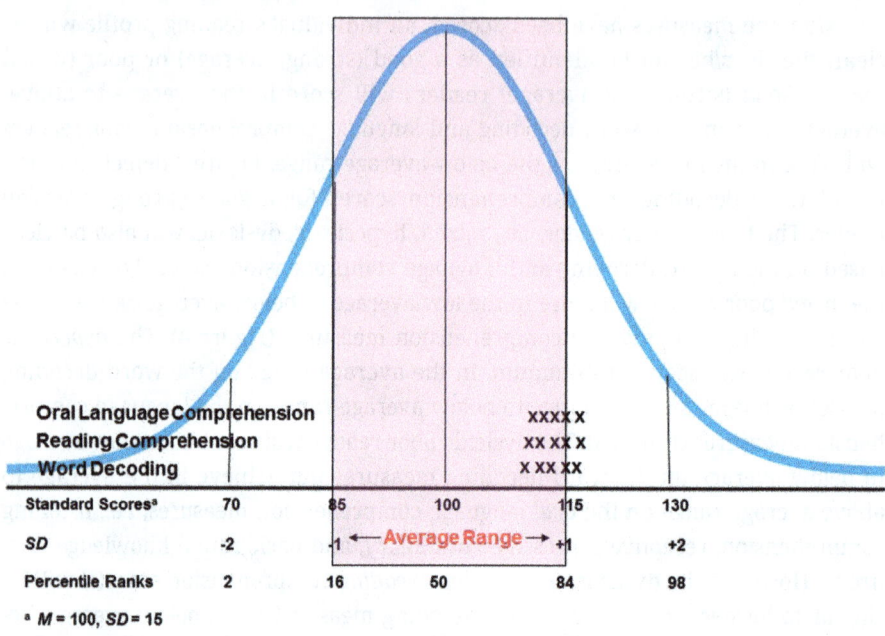

Figure 3: Profile of scores on Word Decoding and Comprehension Measures for Good Reader.

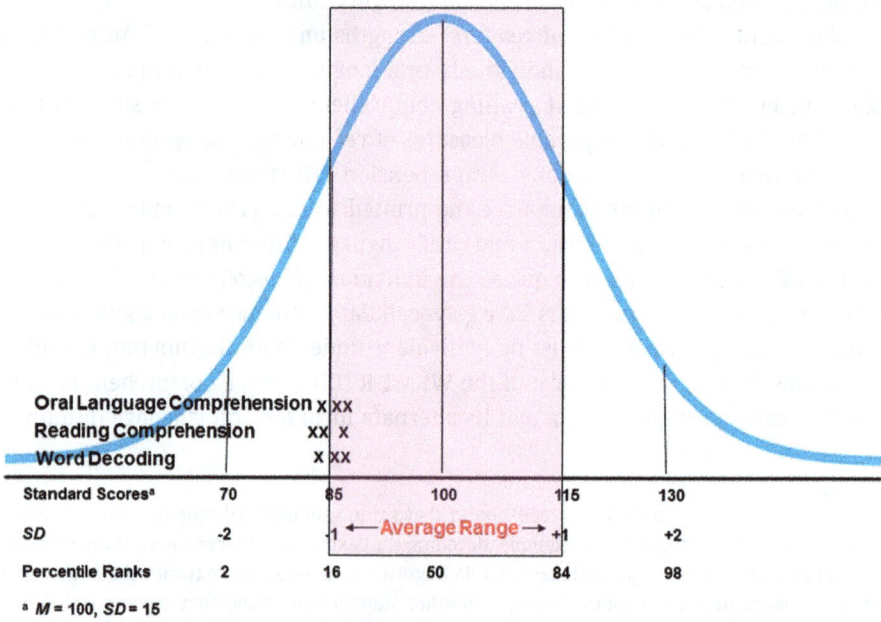

Figure 4: Profile of scores on Word Decoding and Comprehension Measures for Mixed Poor Reader.

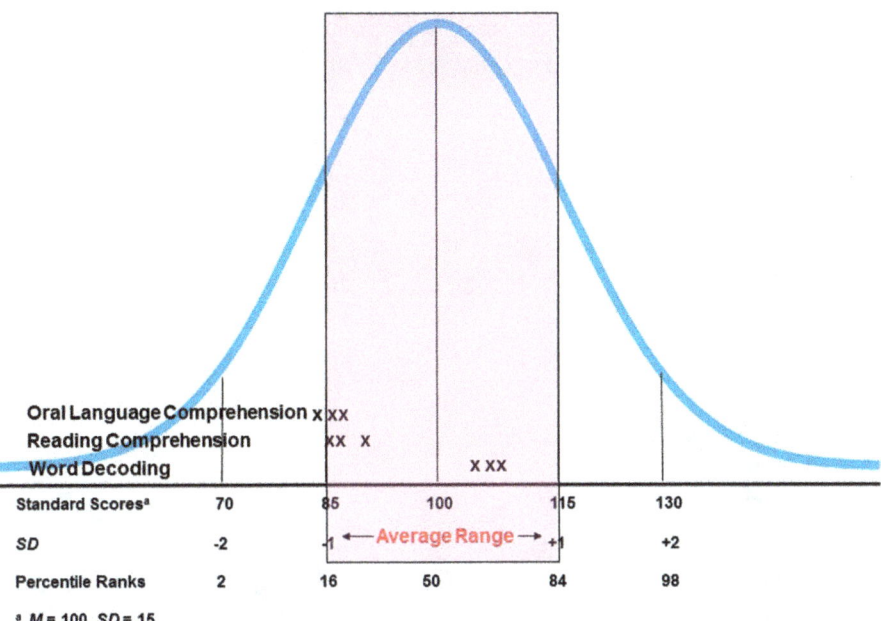

Figure 5: Profile of scores on Word Decoding and Comprehension Measures for Hyperlexic Poor Reader.

comprehension (see Appendix A). (The alternate forms of the WJ-IV Passage Comprehension subtest can also be used for this procedure.) The subtests use a *cloze* format in which the items are composed of 1–2 sentences and increase in language complexity (but not length, so as not to test working memory) as the test progresses. For the reading comprehension version, one form of the WRMT-III Passage Comprehension subtest is administered in the standard fashion. For listening comprehension, the alternate form of the WRMT-III Passage Comprehension subtest is administered by reading the items aloud and asking the examinee to supply the missing word. (Items can also be presented in audio format with headphones.) The items can be repeated upon request. *The only difference between the two subtests is the modality of presentation, i.e., examinee must decode the word in the reading comprehension format, and listen to the words in the listening comprehension format.*

The results of the four reader types on the reading comprehension and listening comprehension measures are depicted in Figures 3–6. *Good* (strong) readers will exhibit similar reading comprehension and listening comprehension scores in the average to above-average range. *Mixed* poor readers will exhibit similar reading and listening comprehension scores, but their scores will be in the low-average to below-average range. *Hyperlexic* poor readers will exhibit stronger reading

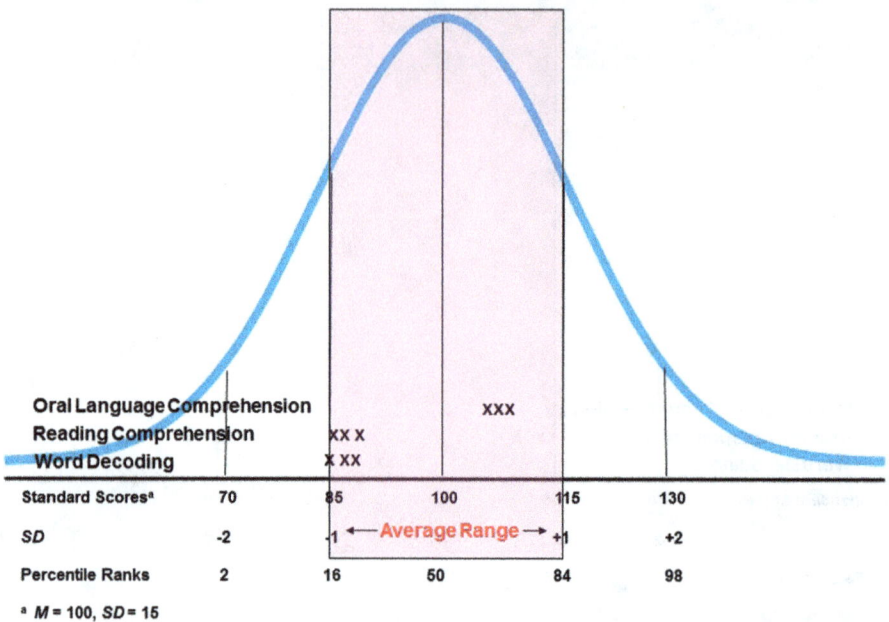

Figure 6: Profile of scores on Word Decoding and Comprehension Measures for Dyslexic Poor Reader.

comprehension than listening comprehension scores because their decoding skills are stronger than their oral language (listening) comprehension skills (i.e., vocabulary, background knowledge). *Dyslexic* poor readers will display stronger listening comprehension than reading comprehension scores because their word decoding skills are so poor they cannot decode enough words to comprehend the written text.

11.6 SVW Model: Assessment of English Writing and Linguistic Skills

Similar to the assessment of reading skills, group measures of writing provide a broad, but limited, overview of writing achievement. Group measures are not designed for diagnostic purposes, that is, to identify learners' strengths and weaknesses. Research into writing skills and the SVW model has found that two components, transcription and ideation, are important for efficient writing ability. A battery for the assessment of writing skills in the two components should include the skills listed in Table 2.

Table 2: Skills for measurement of writing assessment.

Transcription	Ideation
Spelling	Grammar
Handwriting	Vocabulary
Writing Fluency	Text Generation and Organization

The assessment of transcription and ideation skills in the two components is best accomplished with individually-administered diagnostic measures. Like reading, there are published and readily available testing measures in English designed specifically for the assessment of writing skills. Appendix B includes a list of commonly-used diagnostic tests that measure the skills necessary for efficient functioning in writing. Like the reading tests described earlier, these measures have been normed for individuals ranging from primary-age children through secondary and postsecondary education and adulthood. The tests have been standardized with English-speaking populations in the U.S., and each measure has been shown to have strong validity and reliability. The measures can be used by educators (and researchers) of L1s other than English to assess the English writing achievement of ELLs for diagnostic purposes, i.e., to assess an individual's overall achievement in writing and their skills in the two cognitive components. In most cases, each measure listed in Appendix B can be administered in 5–15 minutes. Once familiar with the measures, the assessment of an individual's transcription and writing skills can be completed in 30–40 minutes, or less, depending on the age/grade of the examinee.

11.7 Should Additional Skills be Assessed for Reading and Writing?

In a recent paper, Alderson, Nieminen, and Huhta (2016) suggested that measures of working memory, rapid automatized naming (RAN), and affective measures (motivation, anxiety) could be included in the assessment of L2 reading, or in the case of the present paper, ELL reading and writing skills. In most cases, an individual's scores on measures of spelling and writing will be consistent with his/her scores on measures of reading. As noted earlier, researchers have found that writing and reading skills are strongly correlated (Ahmed, Wagner, and Lopez 2014), and that spelling ability is strongly associated with word and pseudoword decoding skills (Stanovich 2000). Although *working memory* is a "core process" in oral language and reading comprehension, Kilpatrick (2015) has reviewed extensive evidence which has found that working memory plays an associative, not causal, role in reading development, and that working memory cannot be remediated to improve reading skills. While RAN is associated with reading difficulties, there is no known method to improve RAN (deJong and Vrielink 2004), and evidence has shown that improvement in RAN task performance follows an improvement in reading ability (see Torgesen et al. 2010).

Another question is whether *affective* variables should be included in the assessment of reading and writing skills. Researchers have found that students with higher motivation and lower levels of anxiety exhibit stronger L1 skills, L2 aptitude, and L2 achievement (e.g., see Sparks et al. 2018; Sparks, Patton, and Luebbers 2018). But, unlike the cognitive variables responsible for effective reading and writing skills, neither motivation nor anxiety has been found to play a causal role in the development of English reading and writing skills. Instead, students' L1 skills and L2 aptitude have been found to be confounding (third) variables in attempting to attribute causal effects to motivation and anxiety for language learning. Moreover, researchers have not shown that strong motivation or low anxiety for learning to read and write an L2 can compensate for (or overcome) deficiencies in the cognitive variables necessary for skilled reading and writing. Given the aforementioned evidence, affective variables are more likely to be a consequence of good/poor reading and writing ability. However, low achievement in reading and writing will have negative cognitive consequences for both oral and written language development in the target language.

11.8 Pedagogical Implications

The SVR model contends that word decoding and oral language comprehension are separable skills for assessment and instruction, and that good reading comprehension cannot be achieved unless both word decoding and language comprehension skills are strong. Skills in both cognitive domains–word decoding and oral language comprehension–are necessary for efficient reading ability. For pedagogical purposes, the teaching of English reading will be successful when it addresses these skills. The specific types of intervention for poor readers will depend on their assessment profiles. *Mixed* poor readers will need targeted, and additional, instruction in the skills necessary for both word decoding and language comprehension, *hyperlexic* poor readers will need targeted instruction in the skills necessary for language comprehension, and *dyslexic* poor readers will need targeted instruction in the skills necessary for word decoding. The SVR model maintains that improvement in word decoding or language comprehension will improve reading comprehension unless the student has no facility, e.g., vocabulary knowledge, in the target language (Hoover and Gough 1990: 151).

For L2 teachers of English, the primary conclusion from the evidence supporting the SVR model and the assessment of the skills in the cognitive domains outlined earlier is that the development of the skills in both domains is important for ELLs (see Savage 2020). Both word decoding and oral language comprehension are important for reading comprehension, and deficiencies in either domain can result in reading comprehension problems. Geva and Ramirez (2015) maintain that effective teaching involves not only copious teaching, practice, and exposure to the target language, but also maintaining a "developmental outlook" because "over time, one should expect to see a shift in the relative importance of decoding and [oral] language comprehension to the reading comprehension of EL2 learners" (p. 43). Here, they acknowledge the converging evidence which has shown that word decoding skill explains more of the variance in the early stages of learning to read, but as word decoding skill develops, reading comprehension is more closely related to oral language comprehension. Over time, reading comprehension problems will be related to the increase in the demands of academic texts for understanding new (rare) vocabulary and more complex grammatical structures, as well as learning unfamiliar background knowledge.

Similar to the evidence on the SVR provided by reading scientists, the science of writing has yielded scientifically-based instructional recommendations for teaching writing. The SVW has proposed that writing is comprised of two components, transcription and ideation, and the evidence shows that the skills in both components require explicit instruction from classroom teachers. For pedagogical purposes, the teaching of English writing will be successful when it addresses these skills. Graham has conducted several meta-analyses of effective writing instructional procedures over several years (see Graham and Harris 2018; Graham 2020) and found that direct instruction in writing skills produces more positive effects on students' writing ability than less explicit instruction in the foundational skills necessary for writing (Graham and Sandmel 2011). These analyses have shown that students' writing improves when they acquire greater knowledge about writing through the teaching of handwriting (and/or typing), sentence construction, vocabulary, and spelling. This type of instruction helps students become adept at turning ideas into sentences and sentences into print. As students improve their transcription skills, their writing fluency becomes automatic and they can focus less on, e.g., legibility and spelling, and focus more on ideation. Here, students require explicit instruction in grammar and continued instruction in vocabulary. Instruction on the elements of different types of text, reading model text, and providing both timely and constructive feedback will serve to improve the quality of students' writing. Writing skills are strengthened further by teaching the planning, drafting, and revising processes of writing and supporting these processes with clear and specific writing goals, helping students gather and organize writing content, and encouraging peers to compose together. Like most skills, an emphasis on practice and feedback will make a positive difference in students' writing. Graham reported that the aforementioned instructional recommendations resulted in statistically significant and positive effects (ES=.24 to 1.26).

In most cases, young English-speaking children with typically-developing oral language skills have language comprehension that is far superior to their reading comprehension and writing skills because they have not learned to spell or decode printed words. For example by 1st grade, the typical English-speaking child has accumulated a vocabulary of 3–5,000 words. Over the next several years, s/he will acquire new word meanings at the rate of ≈3,000 words per year through 12th grade (see Nagy and Herman 1987). In addition, they will learn new syntactic knowledge, understand more difficult academic language, and acquire a large fund of background (cultural) knowledge. However, ELLs generally encounter English reading and writing instruction without the preceding several years of exposure to spoken English. Instead, they may be learning to speak and comprehend English *at the same time* that they are learning to read and write the language. While they may have experience in learning to decode print in their own language, which is especially valuable if their L1 is an alphabetic orthography, they may have little or no English vocabulary knowledge with which to comprehend the words they learn to read in print or hear in speech. Instead of a vocabulary of 3,000–5,000 English words by 1st grade, ELLs who have lived in a largely monolingual context have little or no English vocabulary to bring to the task of oral language (speaking, listening) or written language (reading, writing). Nation (2001) has distinguished between high-frequency, academic, technical, and low frequency words in L2 text and found that high frequency words account for 80% of the words in the text. However, ELLs learning to read and write English may not have knowledge of these high-frequency English vocabulary words. As a result, ELLs learning to read and write English may learn to decode and spell English words well, but still display significant problems with English reading comprehension, listening comprehension, and oral proficiency skills.

In sum, L2 educators in different countries and cultural contexts for teaching ELLs will have to teach directly the skills required for both reading and writing, and focus intensely on their students' acquisition of vocabulary knowledge in English.

11.9 Conclusion

At this time, the SVR and SVW models are the scientifically-supported developmental models that provide a framework for the assessment and differentiated instruction of the skills necessary for learning to read and write. The models have been investigated rigorously and the skills in the cognitive domains–word decoding and language comprehension for reading and transcription and ideation for writing–have been found to explain the large majority of the variance in reading and writing skills. The models present an opportunity for educators and researchers in L1s other than English to examine their usefulness in assessing and teaching the skills necessary for English literacy.

Appendix A

Testing Measures for the Assessment of English Reading and Linguistic Skills[a]

Test/Subtest	Description
Word Decoding	Ability to read and pronounce increasingly difficult (real) words correctly
WJ-IV ACH Word Identification subtest	
WRMT-III Word Identification subtest	
WIAT-III Word Reading subtest	
TOSWRF-2	
TOWRE-2 Sight Word Efficiency subtest	
Pseudoword Decoding	Ability to read and pronounce increasingly difficult pseudo (nonsense) words correctly that conform to English spelling rules
WJ-IV ACH Word Attack subtest	
WRMT-III Word Attack subtest	
WIAT-III Word Reading subtest	
TOWRE-2 Pseudoword Decoding Efficiency subtest	
Reading Comprehension	
WJ-IV ACH Passage Comprehension subtest	Ability to read increasingly difficult short passages with a modified cloze procedure and identify a missing key word that makes sense within the context
WRMT-III Passage Comprehension subtest	
WIAT-III Reading Comprehension subtest	Ability to read increasingly difficult passages aloud or silently and answer open-ended questions about the passages
GORT-5 Reading Comprehension	Ability to read increasingly difficult passages aloud and answer open-ended questions about the passages

(continued)

Test/Subtest	Description
Listening Comprehension	
WRMT-III Listening Comprehension	Ability to verbally respond to questions after listening to passages read aloud
WJ-IV-OL Listening Comprehension Cluster	
Oral Comprehension subtest	Ability to comprehend a short sentence and supply a missing word using syntactic and semantic clues
Understanding Directions subtest	Ability to listen to a sequence of instructions and follow directions by pointing to objects in a picture
WIAT-III Listening Comprehension Composite	
Receptive Vocabulary subtest	Ability to match a spoken word to a picture that illustrates the word
Oral Discourse subtest	Ability to listen to passages and answer questions verbally
Vocabulary	
WJ-IV-OL Picture Vocabulary subtest	Ability to name common to less frequent objects in environment shown in a picture with the correct English word
Peabody Picture Vocabulary Test-5 (PPVT-5)	Ability to match a spoken word to objects, actions, or concepts presented in a picture (multiple choice format)
Receptive One Word Picture Vocabulary Test-4	Ability to match a spoken word to objects, actions, or concepts presented in a picture (multiple choice format)
Expressive One Word Picture Vocabulary Test-4	Ability to name common to less frequent objects in environment shown in a picture with the correct English word
Background Knowledge	
WJ-IV-ACH Academic Knowledge Cluster	Ability to answer increasingly difficult questions about knowledge of sciences, history, geography, government, economics, art, music, and literature

(continued)

Test/Subtest	Description
Phonological Awareness	
WJ-IV-ACH Sound Awareness subtest	Ability to complete phonological processing tasks (rhyme, syllables, phonemes)
WRMT-III Phonological Awareness subtest	Ability to complete phoneme awareness tasks (deletion, matching, blending)
Comprehensive Test of Phonological Processing-2 (CTOPP-2)	Assesses phonological awareness, phonological memory, rapid naming

[a] WJ-IV-ACH = Woodcock-Johnson-IV Tests of Achievement (Forms A, B, C).
WJ-IV-OL = Woodcock-Johnson-IV Tests of Oral Language
WRMT-III = Woodcock Reading Mastery Test-III (Forms A, B)
WIAT-III = Wechsler Individual Achievement Test-III
TOSWRF-2 = Test of Silent Word Reading Fluency-2 (Forms A, B, C, D)
TOWRE-2 = Test of Word Reading Efficiency-2 (Forms A, B, C, D)
GORT-5 = Gray Oral Reading Test-5 (Forms A, B)

Appendix B

Testing Measures for the Assessment of English Writing and Linguistic Skills[a]

Test/Subtest	Description
Spelling	Ability to write (spell) orally presented words correctly
WJ-IV ACH Spelling subtest	
WIAT-III Spelling subtest	
TWS-5 Spelling	
WRAT-5 Spelling subtest	
TOWL-4 Spelling subtest	
Handwriting/Writing Fluency	
WJ-IV ACH Sentence Writing Fluency subtest	Ability to write simple sentences when presented with a picture stimulus and three words in a 5 minute time limit

(continued)

Test/Subtest	Description
Grammar	
WJ-IV ACH Editing subtest	Ability to identify and correct errors in a written passage, i.e., grammar, punctuation, capitalization errors
WIAT-III Sentence Composition subtest	Ability to combine the information from 2–3 sentences into a single sentence with the same meaning
TOWL-4 Logical Sentences subtest	Ability to edit illogical sentences to make better sense
TOWL-4 Sentence Combining subtest	Ability to integrate several short sentences into one grammatically correct written sentence
Vocabulary	
TOWL-4 Vocabulary subtest	Ability to write sentence with stimulus words
Ideation	
WJ-IV Writing Samples subtest	Ability to compose sentences based on directions, sentences evaluated based on quality of expression
WIAT-III Essay Composition	Ability to write an essay within a 10-minute time limit
TOWL-4 Contextual Conventions and Story Composition Composite	Ability to write a short story in response to a picture stimulus. Story is evaluated relative to the quality of composition and for grammar (and spelling)

[a] TWS-5 = Test of Written Spelling-5
WRAT-5 = Wide Range Achievement Test-5
TOWL-4 = Test of Written Language-4

Recommended Readings

Gough, Philip & William Tunmer. 1986. Decoding, reading, and reading disability. *Remedial and Special Education 7 (1)*. 6–10.
    This classic paper presented the Simple View of Reading (SVR) to the L1 reading field. The SVR holds that reading equals the product of word decoding and oral language (listening) comprehension. It follows that there must be good readers and three types of poor readers resulting from an inability to decode, an inability to comprehend, or both.

Graham, Keith & Zohreh Eslami. 2020. Does the Simple View of Writing explain L2 writing development?: A meta-analysis. *Reading Psychology 41*(5). 485–511.

The meta-analysis examined how components of the Simple View of Writing, transcription and ideation, contribute to writing development for English second-language (L2) learners. The study examined effect sizes (correlations) reported in the literature on the relationship between transcription and ideation for writing. Three separate meta-analyses were run for transcription (spelling/handwriting), oral language, and vocabulary. The results suggested that the components of the Simple View of Writing may explain writing variation in L2 writing.

Sparks, Richard. 2015. Language deficits in poor L2 comprehenders: The Simple View. *Foreign Language Annals 48(4)*. 635–658.

The first paper in the L2 literature showing that L2 readers fit the good and poor reader profiles posited by the authors of the Simple View of Reading model, which proposes that reading comprehension is the product of word decoding and language comprehension. In this study, first- and second-year high school students studying Spanish in U. S. were administered measures of Spanish word decoding, pseudoword decoding, vocabulary, and reading comprehension. The majority of students met the hyperlexic profile (good word decoding, poor reading comprehension). No participant fit the dyslexic profile (poor decoding, good reading comprehension), and none met the good reader profile (good word decoding, good reading comprehension).

Catts, Hugh, Suzanne Adolf & Susan Weismer. 2006. Language deficits in poor comprehenders: A case for the Simple View of Reading. *Journal of Speech, Language, and Hearing Research 49*. 278–293.

Studies examined the language abilities of children with specific reading comprehension deficits ("poor comprehenders") and compared them to typical readers and children with specific decoding deficits ("poor decoders"). Study 1 showed that poor comprehenders had concurrent deficits in language comprehension, but normal abilities in word decoding. Poor decoders were characterized by the opposite pattern of language abilities. Study 2 showed that subgroups had language and word decoding profiles in the earlier grades that were consistent with those observed in the 8th grade. The results supported the Simple View of Reading and presented profiles of the types of readers proposed by the model.

References

Aaron, P. G. 1991. Can reading disabilities be diagnosed without using intelligence tests? *Journal of Learning Disabilities 24 (3)*. 178–186.
Aaron, P.G., R. Malatesha Joshi, Regina Gooden & Kwesi Bentum. 2008. Diagnosis and treatment of reading disabilities based on the component model of reading. *Journal of Learning Disabilities 41(1)*. 67–84.
Abbott, Robert & Virginia Berninger. 1993. Structural equation modeling of relationships among developmental skills and writing skills in primary-and intermediate-grade writers. *Journal of Educational Psychology 85*(3). 478–508.
Ahmed, Yusra, Richard Wagner & Danielle Lopez. 2014. Developmental relations between reading and writing at the word, sentence, and text levels: A latent change score analysis. *Journal of Educational Psychology 106*(2). 419–434.
Alderson, J. Charles, Ari Huhta & Lea Nieminen. 2016. Characteristics of weak and strong readers in a foreign language. *The Modern Language Journal 100 (4)*. 853–879.

Aouad, Julie & Robert Savage. 2009. The component structure of preliteracy skills: Further evidence for the Simple View of Reading. *Canadian Journal of School Psychology* 24(2). 183–200.

Berninger, Virginia. 2000. Development of language by hand and its connections with language by ear, mouth, and eye. *Topics in Language Disorders* 20(4). 65–84.

Berninger, Virginia & Robert Abbott. 2010. Listening comprehension, oral expression, reading comprehension, and written expression: Related yet unique language systems in grades 1, 3, 5, and 7. *Journal of Educational Psychology* 102(3). 635–651.

Berninger, Virginia, Ana Cartwright, Cheryl Yates, H. Lee Swanson & Robert Abbott. 1994. Developmental skills related to writing and reading acquisition in the intermediate grades. *Reading and Writing* 6(2). 161–196.

Berninger, Virginia & Steve Graham. 1998. Language by hand: A synthesis of a decade of research on handwriting. *Handwriting Review* 12. 11–25.

Bozorgian, Hossein. 2012. The relationship between listening and other language skills in International English Language Testing System. *Theory and Practice in Language Studies 2(4)*. 657–663.

Bonifacci, Paolo & Valentina Tobia. 2017. The Simple View of Reading in bilingual language-minority children acquiring a highly transparent second language. *Scientific Studies of Reading* 21(2). 109–119.

Cain, Kate, Jane Oakhill & Peter Bryant. 2004. Children's reading comprehension ability: Concurrent prediction by working memory, verbal ability, and component skills. *Journal of Educational Psychology 96 (1)*. 31–42.

Carroll, John & Stanley Sapon. 1959, 2000. *Modern Language Aptitude Test (MLAT): Manual*. San Antonio, TX: Psychological Corp. Republished by Second Language Testing, Inc. https://lltf.net/aptitude-tests/language-aptitude-tests/modern-language-aptitude-test-2/

Carver, Ronald. 1998. Predicting reading level in grades 1–6 from listening level and decoding level: Testing theory relevant to the SVR of reading. *Reading and Writing: An Interdisciplinary Journal 10*. 121–154.

Catts, Hugh, Suzanne Adolf & Susan Weismer. 2006. Language deficits in poor comprehenders: A case for the Simple View of Reading. *Journal of Speech, Language, and Hearing Research* 49(2). 278–293.

Chen, Xi, Vedran Dronjic & Rena Helms-Park. 2015. *Reading in a second language: Cognitive and psycholinguistic issues*. Oxfordshire, UK: Routledge.

Coker, David. 2006. Impact of first-grade factors on the growth and outcomes of urban schoolchildren's primary-grade writing. *Journal of Educational Psychology* 98(3). 471–488.

Cunningham, Anne & Keith Stanovich. 1997. Early reading acquisition and its relation to reading experience and ability 10 years later. *Developmental Psychology* 33(6). 934–945.

Cunningham, Anne & Keith Stanovich. 1998. What reading does for the mind. *American Educator* 22. 8–17.

de Jong, Peter & Lidy Vrielink. 2004. Rapid automatic naming: Easy to measure, hard to improve (quickly). *Annals of Dyslexia* 54. 65–88.

Dockrell, Julie & Vince Connelly. 2009. The impact of oral language skills on the production of written text. *BJEP Monograph Series II(6), Number 6-Teaching and Learning Writing*. 45–62.

Dockrell, Julie, Geoff Lindsay & Vince Connelly. 2009. The impact of specific language impairment on adolescents' written text. *Exceptional Children* 75(4). 427–446.

Dunn, Douglas. 2019. *Peabody Picture Vocabulary Test-5* (*PPVT-5*). New York: Pearson.

Farnia, Fataneh & Esther Geva. 2013. Growth and predictors of change in English language learners' reading comprehension. *Journal of Research in Reading* 36(4). 389–421.

Feng, Luxi, Amanda Lindner, Xuejun Ji & R. Malatesha Joshi. 2019. The roles of handwriting and keyboarding in writing: A meta-analytic review. *Reading and Writing 32(1)*. 33–63.
Florit, Elena, Maja Roch, Gianmarcoe Altoè & Maria Levorato. 2009. Listening comprehension in preschoolers: The role of memory. *British Journal of Developmental Psychology 27 (4)*. 935–951.
Foorman, Barbara, Sharon Koon, Yaakov Petscher, Allison Mitchell & Adrea Truckenmiller. 2015. Examining general and specific factors in the dimensionality of oral language and reading in 4th–10th grades. *Journal of Educational Psychology 107 (3)*. 884–899.
Francis, David, Jack Fletcher, Hugh Catts & J. Bruce Tomblin. 2005. Dimensions affecting the assessment of reading comprehension. In Scott Paris & Steven Stahl (eds.), *Children's reading comprehension and assessment*, 369–394. Mahwah, NJ: Erlbaum.
García, J. Ricardo & Kate Cain. 2014. Decoding and reading comprehension: A meta-analysis to identify which reader assessment characteristics influence the strength of the relationship in English. *Review of Educational Research 84 (1)*. 74–111.
Geva, Esther. 2006. Second-language oral proficiency and second-language literacy. In Diane August & Tim Shanahan (eds.), *Developing literacy in second-language learners: Report of the National Literacy Panel on Language-Minority Children and Youth*. 123–139. Mahwah, NJ: Erlbaum.
Geva, Esther & Zohreh Yaghoub Zadeh. 2006. Reading efficiency in native English-speaking and English-as-a-second-language children: The role of oral proficiency and underlying cognitive-linguistic processes. *Scientific Studies of Reading 10(1)*. 31–57.
Geva, Esther & Gloria Ramirez. 2015. *Focus on reading*. Oxford, UK: Oxford University Press.
Gottardo, Alexandra & Julie Mueller. 2009. Are first- and second-language factors related in predicting second-language reading comprehension? A study of Spanish-speaking children acquiring English as a second language from first to second grade. *Journal of Educational Psychology 101(2)*. 330–344.
Gough, Philip & William Tunmer. 1986. Decoding, reading, and reading disability. *Remedial and Special Education 7 (1)*. 6–10.
Graham, Keith & Zohreh Eslami. 2020. Does the Simple View of Writing explain L2 writing development?: A meta-analysis. *Reading Psychology 41(5)*. 485–511.
Graham, Steve. 2020. The sciences of reading and writing must become more fully integrated. *Reading Research Quarterly 55 (S1)*. 35–S44.
Graham, Steve & Karen Harris. 2018. Evidence-based practices in writing. *Best Practices in Writing Instruction*. 3–29.
Graham, Steve & Michael Hebert. 2011. Writing to read: A meta-analysis of the impact of writing and writing instruction on reading. *Harvard Educational Review 81(4)*. 710–744.
Graham, Steve, Xinghua Liu, Brendan Bartlett, Clarence Ng, Karen Harris, Angelique Aitken & Joy Talukdar. 2018. Reading for writing: A meta-analysis of the impact of reading interventions on writing. *Review of Educational Research 88(2)*. 243–284.
Graham, Steve & Karin Sandmel. 2011. The process writing approach: A meta-analysis. *The Journal of Educational Research. 104(6)*. 396–407.
Hammill, Donald & Stephen Larsen. 2009. *Test of Written Language-4 (TOWL-4)*. Austin, TX: PRO-ED.
Hayes, John. 2012. Modeling and remodeling writing. *Written Communication 29(3)*. 369–388.
Høien-Tengesdal, Ingjerd & Torleiv Høien-Tengesdal. 2012. The reading efficiency model: An extension of the componential model of reading. *Journal of Learning Disabilities 45 (5)*. 467–479.
Hoover, Wesley & Philip Gough. 1990. The simple view of reading. *Reading and Writing: An Interdisciplinary Journal 2*. 127–160.
Hoover, Wesley & William Tunmer. 2020. The Simple View of Reading: A useful way to think about reading and learning to read. *The Reading League Journal 1(2)*. 35–40.

In'nami, Yo & Rie Koizumi. 2012. Factor structure of the revised TOEIC® test: A multiple-sample analysis. *Language Testing. 29(1)*. 131–152.

Jeon, Eun Hee & Junko Yamashita. 2014. L2 reading comprehension and its correlates: A meta-analysis. *Language Learning 64 (1)*. 160–212.

Joshi, R. Malatesha. 2018. Simple View of Reading (SVR) in different orthographies: Seeing the forest with the trees. *Reading and Dyslexia*. 71–80.

Joshi, R. Malatesha & Aaron, P. G. 2000. The component model of reading: Simple view of reading made a little more complex. *Reading Psychology 21 (2)*. 85–97.

Joshi, R. Malatesha, Xuejun Ji, Zevia Breznitz, Meirav Amiel & Astri Yulia. 2015. Validation of the Simple View of Reading in Hebrew. *Scientific Studies of Reading 19(3)*. 243–252.

Joshi, R. Malatesha, Sha Tao, Aaron, P. G. & Blanca Quiroz. 2012. Cognitive component of Componential Model of Reading applied to different orthographies. *Journal of Learning Disabilities 45 (5)*. 480–486.

Juel, Connie. 1988. Learning to read and write: A longitudinal study of 54 children from first through fourth grades. *Journal of Educational Psychology 80(4)*. 437–447.

Juel, Connie, Priscilla Griffith & Philip Gough. 1986. Acquisition of literacy: A longitudinal study of children in first and second grade. *Journal of Educational Psychology 78(4)*. 243–255.

Keenan, Janice, Benjamin Betjemann & Richard Olson, R. 2008. Reading comprehension tests vary in the skills they assess: Differential dependence on decoding and oral comprehension. *Scientific Studies of Reading 12(3)*. 281–300.

Kendeou, Panayiota, Catherine Bohn-Gettler, Mary Jane White, and Paul Van den Broek. 2008. Children's inference generation across different media. *Journal of Research in Reading 31 (3)*. 259–272.

Kilpatrick, David. 2015. *Essentials of assessing, preventing, and overcoming reading difficulties*. Hoboken, NJ: Wiley.

Kim, Young-Suk Grace. 2017. Why the Simple View of Reading is not simplistic: Unpacking component skills of reading using a direct and indirect model of reading (DIER). *Scientific Studies of Reading 21(4)*. 310–333.

Kim, Young-Suk Grace. 2020. Simple but not simplistic: The Simple View of Reading unpacked and expanded. *The Reading League Journal 1(2)*. 15–21.

Kim, Young-Suk Grace, Stephanie Al Otaiba, Jeanne Wanzek & Brandy Gatlin. 2015. Toward an understanding of dimensions, predictors, and the gender gap in written composition. *Journal of Educational Psychology 107(1)*. 79–95.

Kim, Young-Suk Grace, Brandy Gatlin, Stephanie Al Otaiba & Jeanne Wanzek. 2018. Theorization and an empirical investigation of the component-based and developmental text writing fluency construct. *Journal of Learning Disabilities 51(4)*. 320–335.

Kim, Young-Suk Grace & Heather Pilcher. 2016. What is listening comprehension and what does it take to improve listening comprehension? In Rachel Schiff & R. Malatesha Joshi (eds.), *Handbook of interventions in learning disabilities*, 159–174. New York: Springer.

Kim, Young-Suk Grace, Stephanie Al Otaiba, Cynthia Puranik, Jessica Sidler, Luana Greulich & Richard Wagner. 2011. Componential skills of beginning writing: An exploratory study. *Learning and Individual Differences 21*. 517–525.

Kim, Young-Suk Grace, Stephanie Al Otaiba, Jessica Sidler & Luana Greulich. 2013. Language, literacy, attentional behaviors, and instructional quality predictors of written composition for first graders. *Early Childhood Research Quarterly 28*. 461–469.

Kim, Young-Suk Grace, Stephanie Al Otaiba, Jessica Sidler, Luana Greulich & Cynthia Puranik. 2014. Evaluating the dimensionality offirst grade written composition. *Journal of Speech, Language, and Hearing Research 57(1)*. 199–211.

Kim, Young-Suk Grace & Christopher Schatschneider. 2017. Expanding the developmental models of writing: A direct and indirect effects model of developmental writing (DIEW). *Journal of Educational Psychology 109*(1). 35–50.

Kintsch, Walter & Ely Kozminsky. 1977. Summarizing stories after reading and listening. *Journal of Educational Psychology 69(5)*. 491–499.

Language and Reading Research Consortium. 2015. The dimensionality of language ability in young children. *Child Development 86*. 1948–1965.

Larsen, Stephen, Donald Hammill & Louisa Moats. 2013. *Test of Written Spelling-5 (TWS-5)*. Austin, TX: PRO-ED.

Lepola, Janne, Julie Lynch, Eero Laakkonen, Maarit Silvén &Pekka Niemi. 2012. The role of inference making and other language skills in the development of narrative listening comprehension in 4- to 6-year old children. *Reading Research Quarterly 47(3)*. 259–282.

Lesaux, Nonie & Michael Kieffer. 2010. Exploring sources of reading comprehension difficulties among minority learners and their classmates in early adolescence. *American Educational Research Journal 47(3)*. 596–632.

Liao, Chi-wen, Yanxuan Qu & Rick Morgan. 2010. The relationships of test scores measured by the TOEIC listening and reading test and TOEIC speaking and writing tests. *TOEIC Compendium Study 10*. 1–15.

Martin, Nancy & Rick Brownell. 2010. *Expressive One Word Picture Vocabulary Test-4 (EOWPVT-4)*. Austin, TX: PRO-ED.

Martin, Nancy & Rick Brownell. 2010. *Receptive One Word Picture Vocabulary Test-4 (ROWPVT-4)*. Austin, TX: PRO-ED.

Mather, Nancy, Donald Hammill, Elizabeth Allen & Rhia Roberts. 2014. *Test of Silent Word Reading Fluency-2 (TOSWRF-2)*. Austin, TX: PRO-ED.

McCutchen, Deborah. 2000. Knowledge, processing, and working memory: Implications for a theory of writing. *Educational Psychologist 35(1)*. 13–23.

McCutchen, Deborah. 2006. Cognitive factors in the development of children's writing. *Handbook of Writing Research 8*. 115–30.

McCutchen, Deborah. 2000. Knowledge, processing, and working memory: Implications for a theory of writing. *Educational Psychologist 35(1)*. 13–23.

Megherbi, Hakami, Alix Seigneuric, & Marie-France Ehrlich. 2006. Reading comprehension in French 1st and 2nd grade children: Contribution of decoding and language comprehension. *European Journal of Psychology of Education 21*. 135–147.

Nagy, William & Patricia Herman 1987. Breadth and depth of vocabulary knowledge: Implications for acquisition and instruction. In Margaret McKeown & Mary Curtis (eds.), *The nature of vocabulary acquisition*, 19–35. Mahwah, NJ: Erlbaum.

Nakamoto, Jonathan, Kim Lindsey & Franklin Manis. 2007. A longitudinal analysis of English language learners' word decoding and reading comprehension. *Reading and Writing: An Interdisciplinary Journal 20*. 691–719.

Nation, I. S. P. 2001. *Learning vocabulary in another language*. Cambridge, U. K.: Cambridge University Press.

Oakhill, Jane, Kate Cain & Carsten Elbro. 2014. *Understanding and teaching reading comprehension: A handbook*. Oxfordshire, UK: Routledge.

O'Connor, Rollanda, H. Lee Swanson & Cathleen Geraghty. 2010. Improvement in reading rate under independent and difficult text levels: Influences on word and comprehension skills. *Journal of Educational Psychology 102*(1). 1–19.

Olinghouse, Natalie. 2008. Student-and instruction-level predictors of narrative writing in third-grade students. *Reading and Writing: An Interdisciplinary Journal 21*. 3–26.

Palmer, John, Colin MacLeod, Earl Hunt & Janet Davidson. 1985. Information processing correlates of reading. *Journal of Memory and Language 24*(1). 59–88.

Santangelo, Tanya & Steve Graham. 2016. A comprehensive meta-analysis of handwriting instruction. *Educational Psychology Review 28*(2). 225–265.

Savage, Robert. 2020. The Simple View of Reading: A scientific framework for effective teaching. *The Reading League Journal 1*(2). 41–45.

Schrank, Fredrick, Nancy Mather & Kevin McGrew. 2014. *Woodcock-Johnson-IV Tests of Achievement (WJ-IV ACH)*. Rolling Meadows, IL: Riverside.

Shanahan, Timothy. 2016. Relationships between reading and writing development. In Charles MacArthur, Steve Graham & Jill Fitzgerald (eds.) *Handbook of Writing Research*, 194–207. New York: Guilford.

Sparks, Richard. 2015. Language deficits in poor L2 comprehenders: The Simple view. *Foreign Language Annals 48*(4). 635–658.

Sparks, Richard. 2019. Developmental reading disorders in U.S. high school L2 learners? *Paper presented at the Scientific Studies of Reading Conference*, Toronto, Canada, 19 July, 2019.

Sparks, Richard & Julie Luebbers. 2018. How many US high school students have a foreign language reading "disability"? Reading without meaning and the simple view. *Journal of Learning Disabilities 51*(2). 194–208.

Sparks, Richard, Julie Luebbers & Martha Castañeda. 2017. How well do U.S. high school students achieve in Spanish when compared to native Spanish speakers? *Foreign Language Annals 50* (2). 339–366.

Sparks, Richard & Jon Patton. 2016. Examining the Simple View of Reading (SVR) Model for U.S. high school Spanish students. *Hispania 99*. 17–33.

Sparks, Richard, Jon Patton, Leonore Ganschow & Nancy Humbach. 2012a. Relationships among L1 print exposure and early L1 literacy skills, L2 aptitude, and L2 proficiency. *Reading and Writing 25*(7). 1599–1634.

Sparks, Richard, Jon Patton, Leonore Ganschow & Nancy Humbach. 2012b. Do L1 reading achievement and L1 print exposure contribute to the prediction of L2 proficiency? *Language Learning 62*(2). 473–505.

Sparks, Richard, Jon Patton & Julie Luebbers. 2018. For U.S. students, L2 reading comprehension is hard because L2 listening comprehension is hard, too. *Hispania 101* (2). 183–210.

Sparks, Richard, Jon Patton & Julie Luebbers. 2019. Individual differences in L2 mirror individual differences in L1 skills and L2 aptitude: Evidence for cross-transfer. *Foreign Language Annals 52* (2). 1–29.

Stanovich, Keith. 1993. Does reading make you smarter? Literacy and the development of verbal intelligence. In Hayne Waring Reese (ed.), *Advances in child development and behavior*, 133–180. San Diego, CA: Academic Press.

Stanovich, Keith. 2000. *Progress in understanding reading: Scientific foundations and new frontiers.* New York: Guilford.

Stanovich, Keith, Richard West & Michele Harrison. 1995. Knowledge growth and maintenance across the life span: The role of print exposure. *Developmental Psychology 31*(5). 811–826.

Talwar, Amani, Elizabeth Tighe & Daphne Greenberg. 2018. Augmenting the simple view of reading for struggling adult readers: A unique role for background knowledge. *Scientific Studies of Reading 22*(5). 351–366.
Tierney, Robert & Timothy Shanahan, T. 1991. *Research on the reading–writing relationship: Interactions, transactions, and outcomes*. Mahwah, NJ: Erlbaum.
Torgesen, Joseph, Richard Wagner, & Carol Rashotte. 2010. Computer assisted instruction to prevent early reading difficulties in students at risk for dyslexia: Outcomes from two instructional approaches. Annals of Dyslexia 60(1). 40–56.
Torgesen, Joseph, Richard Wagner & Carol Rashotte. 2012. *Test of Word Reading Efficiency-2 (TOWRE-2)*. Austin, TX: PRO-ED.
Torgesen, Joseph, Richard Wagner, Carol Rashotte, Stephen Burgess & Stephen Hecht. 1997. Contributions of phonological awareness and rapid automatic naming ability to the growth of word-reading skills in second-to fifth-grade children. *Scientific Studies of Reading* (2)*1*. 161–185.
Tschirner, Erwin. 2016. Listening and reading proficiency levels of college students. *Foreign Language Annals 49*. 201–223.
Tunmer, William & James Chapman. 2012. The Simple View of Reading redux: Vocabulary knowledge and the independent components hypothesis. *Journal of Learning Disabilities 45 (5)*. 453–466.
Verhoeven, Ludo & Jan van Leeuwe. 2012. The simple view of second language reading throughout the primary grades. *Reading and Writing: An Interdisciplinary Journal 25*. 1805–1818.
Wagner, Richard, Sarah Herrera, Mercedes Spencer & Jamie Quinn. 2015. Reconsidering the Simple View of Reading in an intriguing case of equivalent models: Commentary on Tunmer and Chapman (2012). *Journal of Learning Disabilities 48*(2). 115–119.
Wagner, Richard, Joseph Torgesen, Carol Rashotte & Nils Pearson. 2013. *Comprehensive Test of Phonological Processing-2 (CTOPP-2)*. Austin, TX: PRO-ED.
Wechsler, David. 2009. *Wechsler Individual Achievement Test (3rd ed.) (WIAT-III)*. San Antonio, TX: Pearson. Torrance, CA: WPS.
Wiederholt, Lee & Brian Bryant. 2012. *Gray Oral Reading Test-5 (GORT-5)*. Austin, TX: PRO-ED.
Wilkinson, Gary & Gary Robertson. 2017. *Wide Range Achievement Test-5 (WRAT-5)*. Torrance, CA: WPS.
Woodcock, Richard. 2011. *Woodcock Reading Mastery Test-III (WRMT-III)*. New York: Pearson.
Woodcock, Richard, Ana Muñoz-Sandoval, Kevin McGrew & Nancy Mather. 2004. *Batería-III Woodcock-Muñoz*. Rolling Meadows, IL: Riverside.

12 L2 Learning Difficulties and Disabilities

Richard L. Sparks

Abstract: Students from primary school through postsecondary education display learning problems in both L1 and L2, and some students display severe deficits in their language learning skills. The term learning *disability* (LD) is used in the U.S. to describe students with specific academic deficits, while other countries use generic terminologies such as learning *difficulties*, learning *differences*, and learning *problems* for these students. It is important to understand differences in terminology used by U.S. and European educators and to be cognizant of differences between the cultural and sociolinguistic contexts for learning L2s. This chapter explains the construct of learning *disability* and examines the definitions and diagnostic criteria used by U.S. professionals in the special education and psychology fields. The author brings an international perspective to the study of learning problems by explaining how differences in terminology, definitions, and diagnosis cause confusion in the identification of students who exhibit severe L2 learning problems. Studies conducted over 30+ years with U.S. L2 learners showing that L2 learning problems are language-based are reviewed. Educators' beliefs about LDs and L2 learning are described and the evidence for the beliefs is examined. The chapter concludes with pedagogical strategies for teaching L2s to students with LDs and other language learning problems.

Keywords: Learning disabilities, learning differences, learning difficulties, L2 learning, pedagogical strategies, specific learning disabilities/difficulties

12.1 Introduction

Students at all levels of education display learning problems. Some students display a severe deficit in one skill (reading), and others exhibit severe deficits in all skills. In the U.S., the term *learning disability* (LD) was adopted to describe learners with specific academic deficits thought to be unexpected based on their average, or better, intellectual ability (potential). Although the umbrella term LD was developed to explain domain-specific deficits, e.g., reading, math, and writing, the use of the term *learning disability* has often been applied to students with a range of learning problems. As a result, the term LD has caused confusion among educators and researchers when distinguishing LD from non-LD students.

In comparison, the study of academic learning problems and LDs in other countries is a more recent development. For example, although European scholars have investigated how children learn to read, spell, and write their L1 (see Joshi and Aaron 2006; Verhoeven and Perfetti 2017), the study of learning problems has lagged behind the U.S., where research began in the 1950s and 60s (see Kauffman, Hallahan, and Pullen 2017). Instead of learning *disabilities*, other countries use generic terms such as learning *differences* and learning *difficulties* to describe students with learning problems. As a result, educators and researchers in the U.S., Europe, and other countries identify very different individuals as LD.[1] For comparison purposes in this chapter, the author focuses on the U.S. and European contexts.

An important difference between the U.S. and Europe is the cultural context for L2s. According to the Pew Research Center (Devlin 2018), learning an L2 for European students is "nearly ubiquitous" because they typically begin studying L2s in primary school, and studying an additional language (L3) is compulsory in more than 20 European countries. But in the U.S., far fewer students participate in L2 education and most do not begin L2 classes until high school. For example, only 20% of U.S. high school students study an L2 in school (Devlin 2018), and only 7–8% of university students enroll in L2 courses (Stein-Smith 2019). The U.S. is largely a monolingual society, so most students in language classes practice the L2 only in the classroom for one hour each day, 180 days per year. Moreover, there are no national standards for achieving L2 proficiency. Both high school and university students may pass L2 courses to fulfill a requirement, but most are not required to achieve a specific level of proficiency in the L2 to pass (Gass, Van Gorp, and Winke 2019). As a result, less than 1% of U.S. adults are proficient in a FL that they learned in school (Friedman 2015).

The primary aims of this chapter are to a) explain the construct of learning *disability* and examine the definitions and diagnostic criteria used by professionals in the special education and psychology fields, b) review research showing that L2 learning problems are, first and foremost, *language* learning problems, c) examine the relationship between LDs and L2 learning problems, and d) explore teaching methods for students with L2 learning problems. In the first section, the author brings an international perspective to the study of learning problems by comparing the terms used for learning problems in the U.S. and Europe and explaining how differences in definitions and diagnosis cause problems in the identification of students who exhibit L1/L2 learning problems. In the second section, he reviews studies over 30 years with U.S. L2 learners, which have shown that L2 learning problems are language-based. Then, he reviews studies in the U.S. with

---

[1] A recent issue of *Learning Disabilities: A Contemporary Journal* reviewed the LD construct in several different countries and found that there are *widely* divergent views on the definition and diagnosis of LD. The consensus view was that the various perspectives were unlikely to be united behind a commonly accepted definition for LD (Grünke and Cavendish 2016).

LD students in L2 courses, outlines educators' beliefs about LDs and L2 learning, explains how the beliefs are falsified by empirical studies, and concludes there is not a unique "disability" for L2 learning. In the final section, he reviews pedagogical strategies proposed to teach L2s to students with LDs and other language learning problems.

12.2 Theory: International Perspectives on Learning Problems

A construct has both a conceptual definition and an operational definition. The conceptual definition is what the construct means in theoretical terms, and the operational definition links the concept to the concrete world by specifying how to identify (measure) the construct. In the U.S., the construct of specific learning disability (LD) was coined in 1963. However, a conceptual definition was not adopted until 1977:

> Specific learning disability means a disorder in one or more of the basic psychological processes involved in understanding or using language, spoken or written, which may manifest itself in an imperfect ability to listen, think, speak, read, write, spell, or do mathematical calculations. The term includes such conditions as perceptual handicaps, brain injury, minimal brain dysfunction, dyslexia, and developmental aphasia. The term does not include children who have learning problems that are primarily the result of visual, hearing, or motor handicaps, mental retardation, emotional disturbance, or of environmental, cultural, or economic disadvantage (U.S. Office of Education, 1977: 65083).

The broad, generic nature of this conceptual definition was problematic, and the LD field struggled to agree on empirically-based diagnostic criteria, i.e., an operational definition, for the LD construct. By the 1980s, the field had coalesced around the idea that individuals with LD have normal intellectual ability, and LD should be viewed as a problem with *academic* skills (Kavale and Forness 1995; Stanovich 1991). An operational definition of LD based on the discrepancy between scores on standardized measures of intelligence (IQ) and academic achievement was adopted. In the U.S., quantifying a discrepancy is straightforward because there are nationally standardized measures of IQ and academic achievement that compare students from kindergarten through adulthood to their same-age (grade) peers in the general population. Even though the discrepancy concept was later falsified (Aaron 1997, Stanovich 2005; Stuebing et al. 2002), the consensus that LD is a problem with academic skills was affirmed. However, some scholars in the field maintained that domain-specific disabilities, i.e., reading disability, math disability, and written language disability, should be treated separately, not under a generic LD construct (see Stanovich 1999).

In Europe, views on learning problems are different than in the U.S. Rather than learning *disability*, terms for learning problems range from specific learning *disorder*s to specific learning *differences* to specific learning *difficulties* (Kormos 2016). European countries have adopted a broad view of learning difficulties extending beyond academic achievement that represent separate diagnostic categories in the U.S. In a recent document published by Erasmus +, the conceptual definition for the specific learning disabilities/difficulties (SpLD) construct is:

> Persons with SpLD all show different intellectual and emotional profiles strengths, weaknesses, learning styles, and life experiences . . . SpLD can be identified as distinctive patterns of difficulties relating to the processing of information, within a continuum from very mild to severe, which may result in restrictions in literacy, language, number, motor function, short term memory, and organizational skills . . . These form what can be seen as the SpLD umbrella: Dyslexia, Developmental Coordination Disorder/Dyspraxia, Dyscalculia, ADHD, High Functioning ASD, Specific Language Impairment, Associated Emotional and Social Difficulties (ESD). Persons with SpLD have average or above-average cognitive abilities (90 or above measured IQ . . . . [www.euspld.com, retrieved on 3/24/20].

The conceptual definition of SpLDs goes beyond the notion of specific academic deficits.[2] According to Kormos, operational definitions (diagnostic criteria) for SpLD used in Europe are both qualitative (input from teachers, parents, and students) and quantitative (test scores). Although some countries have developed standardized measures of single-word reading (e.g., Alouette test in France, Alef-Taf test in Israel), unlike the U.S., standardized tests that compare individuals to their same-age (grade) peers are generally unavailable in most countries (Kormos personal communication, 23 March 2020; Nijakowska personal communication, 24 March 2020).

---

[2] To cite three specific examples, the Diagnostic and Statistical Manual of Mental Disorders (DSM-5) (American Psychiatric Association 2013) include: *Dyslexia* is Specific Learning Disorder in Reading (315.00); *Dyscalculia* is Specific Learning Disorder in Math (315.1), and Coordination Disorder overlaps with *Dyspraxia* and called Developmental Coordination Disorder (315.4). There are three different types of ADHD, four different types of language impairments, and a wide array of social, emotional, and behavioral disorders.

12.3 Measurement: Operational Definitions of Learning Disabilities

12.3.1 Differences, Difficulties, or Disabilities?

The brief descriptions of the U.S. and European context for learning problems reveal considerable variation in the conceptual definitions for the LD and SpLD constructs. Both LD and SpLD include individuals with school learning problems. But in the U.S., LDs are understood largely as academic deficits in individuals with normal intellectual ability (potential). In Europe, SpLD includes individuals with academic deficits, but also students with problems unrelated to academics (e.g., motor coordination).[3] The greater heterogeneity in the conceptual definition for SpLD leads to the following questions: a) How are SpLD students distinguished from non-SpLD students?, and b) How are SpLD students in Europe distinguished from LD students in the U.S.?

The term learning *differences* (SpLD) raises the question, *different from what or whom*? To identify an individual with a learning difference, there must be an operational definition (measurable standard) on which to base the difference. A related question is whether differences refer to intra-individual or inter-individual differences. If the learning difference is intra-individual, then *all* individuals would be different because *everyone* displays learning differences (e.g., strong math skills, and average reading skills). But, if the learning difference is inter-individual (between or among individuals), then a measurable standard (operational definition) from which to judge difference is required. The term learning *difficulties* raises the same question: Difficulty when compared to what or whom? To determine difficulty, there must be a measurable standard (operational definition) on which a judgment of difficulty is based. If not, learning difficulty could encompass *all* individuals because anyone can display difficulties with learning one or more skill(s). Likewise, an individual could display difficulty if his/her skills are consistently in the low average range along the normal distribution. As depicted in Figure 1, an individual could have more difficulty with reading and writing skills than with math skills. In Figure 2, another learner could have difficulty with reading, writing, *and* math skills. In both cases, the student's skills are in the average range. Would these individuals be SpLD (conceptual definition) and by what standard (operational definition)? The adoption

---

[3] To be fair, the disability literature in the U.S. and Europe demonstrates how the notion of "concept creep," or expanding notions of harm (see Haslam 2016), has affected the heterogeneity of both LD and SpLD populations. For example, studies with "dyslexic" populations show that a wide range of criteria is used to include and exclude participants (Lopes et al. 2020).

of an operational definition for SpLD with a measurable standard is difficult because standardized tests comparing individuals to their same-age (grade) peers are generally unavailable in many European countries.

The term learning *disability* (LD) prompts the same question: *Disabled when compared to what or whom*? In the U.S., although the conceptual definition for LD is broad, the operational definition in DSM-5 is written to include only individuals who exhibit *below average* functioning, i.e., a *deficit*, in a domain-specific skill, such as reading. An individual with a deficit, i.e., below average skill, exhibits a *substantial impairment* (minimum 1.0 *SD* below the mean) compared to same-age (grade) peers in the general population on a standardized testing measure. Figure 3 depicts the profile of an individual with a domain-specific deficit and substantial impairment in reading. Here, the operational definition answers the question of comparison to what (a measurable standard) and to whom (same age or grade peers in the general population). Qualitatively, individuals with LD should have a record of poor grades, low scores on group standardized achievement measures, and a record of treatment, e.g., tutoring. But, the individual should also meet the operational definition for LD depicted in Figure 3: a substantial (quantitative) impairment in a domain-specific skill when compared to same-age (grade) peers in the general population on standardized testing measures. Diagnosis and substantial impairment are related, but are separate issues, i.e., a diagnosis (conceptual definition) is not necessarily a disability

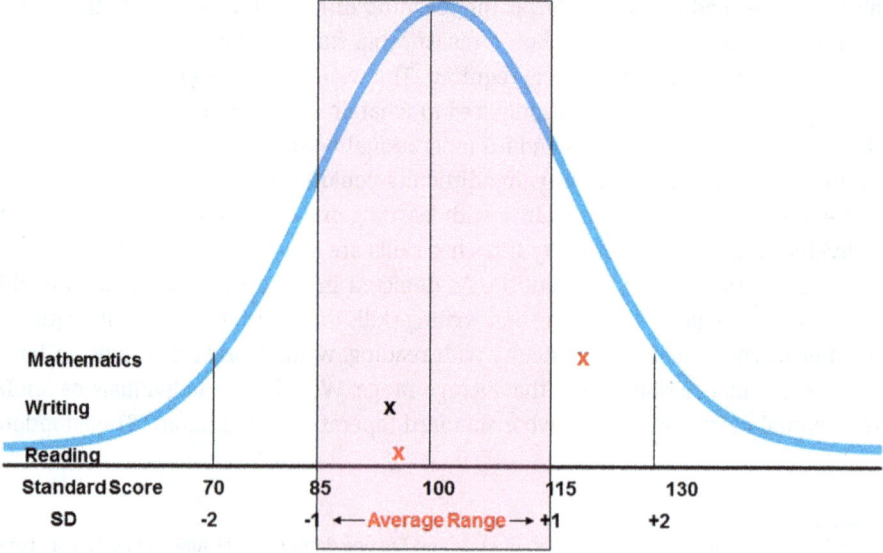

Figure 1: Example of Student with Learning "Difference" with Skills in the Average Range.

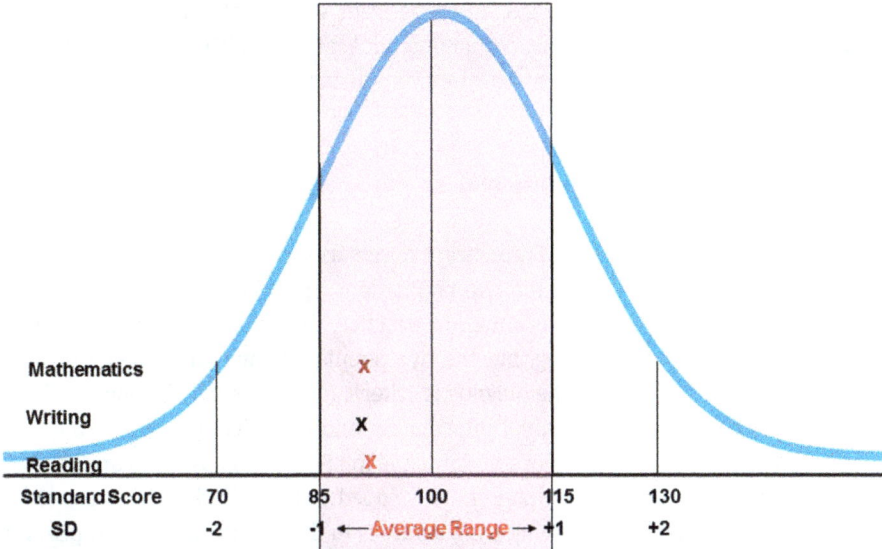

Figure 2: Example of Student with Learning "Difficulties" with Skills in the Average Range.

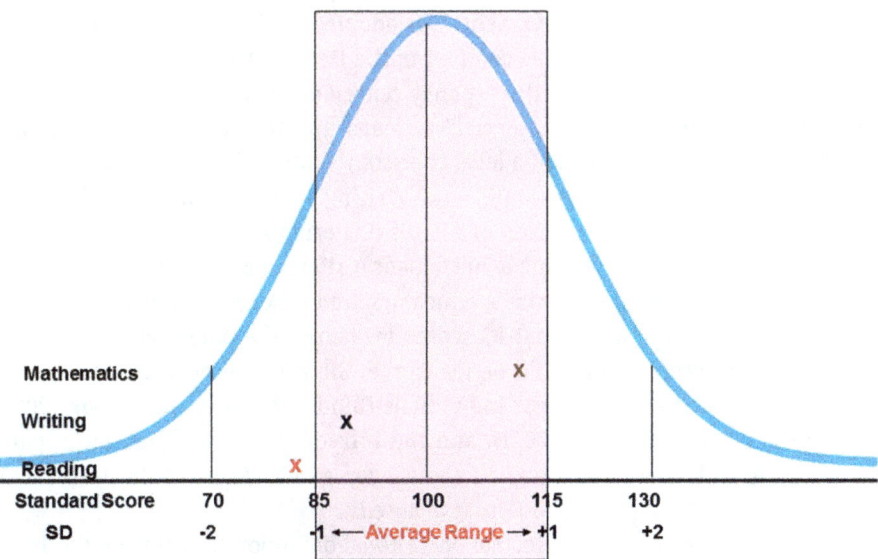

Figure 3: Example of Student with Learning "Disability" with a Deficit (Substantial Impairment) in a Specific Domain.

(substantial impairment). In the U.S., the Americans with Disabilities Act (ADA 1990) and the Americans with Disabilities Amendments Act (ADAAA 2008) have maintained the "average person" standard for determining substantial impairment.

12.3.2 Diagnosis of Learning Disabilities

The inclusive nature of the SpLD construct necessarily creates problems for educators and researchers. In theory, the two populations, SpLD and LD, are similar–both experience issues with school learning. In practice, there may be some overlap in their issues with school learning, but the two populations may also have distinctly different problems. In theory, the diagnostic criteria (operational definition) for SpLD include both subjective (qualitative) information and objective data (test scores). In practice, there are no quantitative standards for the SpLD diagnosis, in part, because most countries (except the U.S.) have not developed standardized tests for academic skills that yield objective data comparing students to their same age (grade) peers in the general population. Inevitably, SpLD populations will represent a wide cross-section of learners with diverse problems.

The broad conceptual definition of LD is also problematic. In the U.S., the discrepancy concept (IQ vs. achievement) was adopted as the operational definition for LD, and the discrepancy was codified in the DSM-IV criterion (American Psychiatric Association 1994). The discrepancy criterion was based largely on the assumptions that IQ showed "potential" to learn and that an individual should perform in all academic skills at a level consistent with his/her IQ score. In theory, DSM-IV criteria for Reading, Math, and Writing Disorders included both IQ-achievement discrepancy criterion of 2.0 *SD*s (Criterion A) and a criterion that required impairments in academic achievement (Criterion B). In practice, Criterion B was mostly ignored by clinicians, educators, and other stakeholders for many reasons including the belief that IQ scores measured the potential to learn, the ease by which discrepancy could be measured, the routine (normal) presence of performance differences in most individuals (Binder, Iverson, and Brooks 2009; Jeffay, Binder, and Zakzanis 2021), and the infrequency of substantial impairments in individuals with average to above-average IQs. Figure 4 illustrates how the discrepancy concept in DSM-IV was *misused*.

Discrepancy remained the formal operational definition for LD from the 1980s to 2013. But, as evidence falsifying the discrepancy concept (see Aaron 1997; Stanovich 2005; Stuebing et al. 2002) and studies showing that differences in individuals' cognitive and achievement profiles are normal (Binder, Iverson, and Brooks 2009) began to accumulate, DSM-5 guidelines discarded discrepancy and adopted rigorous criteria for the operational definition of LD (American Psychiatric Association

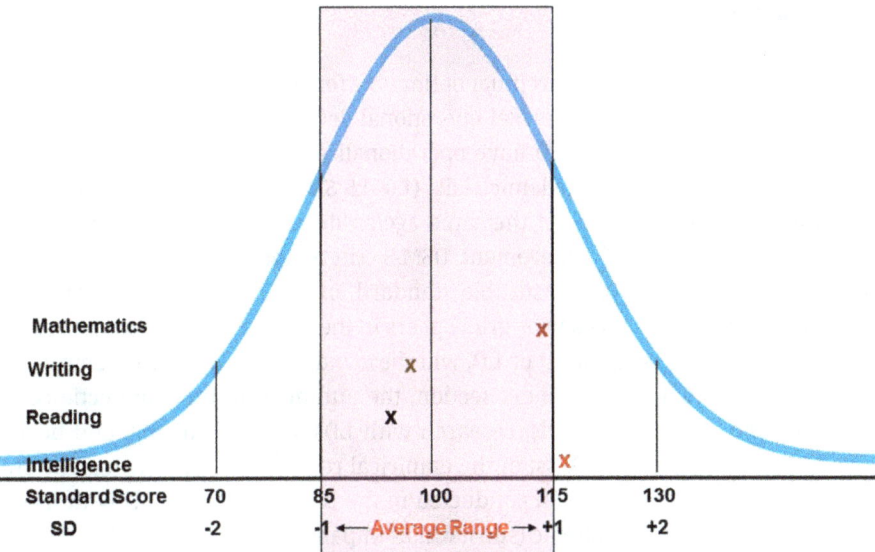

Figure 4: Example of Student with Above Average IQ and Average Academic Achievement without Substantial Impairments in a Specific Academic Domain, Not Meet Criteria for Learning *Disability*.

2013). DSM-5 criteria stipulate that an individual display *substantial impairments* in academic skills of 1.0–1.5 *SD* below the mean score of their same-age peers in the general population on standardized achievement tests of reading, math, or writing *without regard to IQ*, that is, s/he must exhibit, at minimum, below-average achievement (*SS* ≤ 85, ≤ 15th percentile). An individual who exhibits a large IQ-achievement discrepancy but no academic deficits should not be diagnosed as LD.[4] Diagnosticians should consider qualitative information such as the individual's developmental, medical, family, and educational histories, but there should be substantial impairments in an academic domain. To meet the operational definition for proper classification as LD, an individual should display scores on standardized testing measures similar to the profile in Figure 3.

---

[4] In theory, DSM-IV Criterion B, i.e., impairment in academic skills, and DSM-5, i.e., substantial impairments in academic skills, are used for diagnosis of LD. In practice, this criterion is often ignored by U.S. schools and diagnosticians, who still use discrepancy, cite ambiguous "processing deficits" or processing strengths and weaknesses (PSW), use LD to describe non-academic problems, and/or claim clinical (subjective) judgment for diagnosing LD, all of which have been falsified by researchers (e.g., see Fletcher and Miciak 2017; Miciak et al. 2014; Stuebing, Fletcher et al. 2012).

12.3.3 Summary

The inclusive nature of the conceptual definitions for the SpLD and LD constructs is problematic for developing a formal operational definition.,[5,6] But, unlike the SpLD construct, DSM-5 criteria for LD have operationalized substantial impairment as a substantial impairment in academic skills (1.0–1.5 *SD* below the mean) when compared to the average person of the same age/grade in the general population on standardized measures of achievement. DSM-5 criteria for LD answer the questions of *comparison to what* (a measurable standard, or substantial impairment) and *comparison to whom* (same age or grade peers in the general population) for LD.

Whether classified as SpLD or LD, will these individuals have problems learning another language? In the next section, the author examines connections between L1 and L2 learning skills, research with LDs and L2 learning, and beliefs about L2 learning and LDs. Most of the empirical research on L2 learning and students with disabilities has been conducted in the U.S., so the term LD with its operational definition of academic (substantial) impairment is used.

12.4 Research with U.S L2 Learners

For many years, the author and Leonore Ganschow, both of whom are LD and reading disability (dyslexia) specialists in the U.S., pursued a research agenda guided by their Linguistic Coding Differences Hypothesis (LCDH) (Sparks 1995; Sparks and Ganschow 1991, 1993a). The LCDH proposes that the primary causal factors in more and less successful L2 learning are linguistic, high- and low-achieving L2 learners exhibit individual differences (IDs) that are language-related, and these IDs explain their ultimate attainment in L2 skills. They posited that since L2 learning is the learning of *language*, the skills necessary for L2 learning are necessarily language-related. Like Skehan (1998), they take the position

---

5 In a recent paper, Kormos (2017) cites DSM-5 criteria for the conceptual definition, i.e., academic skills must be "substantially and quantifiably below those expected for the individual's chronological age. . ." (p. 67). However, she did not acknowledge the *numerical* criterion for the operational definition in the manual, i.e., the individual's skills must be ". . .at least 1.5 standard deviations [SD] below the population mean for age. . . .standard score of 78 or less. . .which is below the 7th percentile. . .for the greatest diagnostic certainty" (p. 69).

6 Although many of the countries contributing to the special issue on LD (Note 1) acknowledged the use of the DSM-5 criteria for the conceptual definition of LD (p. 65), none appeared to use the quantitative criteria cited in DSM-5 for their operational definition (p. 67, Note 5). In one case, an author noted that a country rejected DSM-5 criteria and stated that the schools or diagnosticians rely on professional (clinical, or subjective) judgment for the diagnosis.

that language is special and qualitatively different from other cognitive skills. The LCDH also built upon John Carroll's (1962) theory of L2 aptitude and his Modern Language Aptitude Test (MLAT; Carroll and Sapon 1959, 2000) by showing that L2 aptitude may be a "residual" of L1 ability. Their model is similar to Cummins' (1979) Linguistic Interdependence Hypothesis (L1 and L2 have a common underlying foundation) and Linguistic Threshold Hypothesis (L2 proficiency attainment is moderated by one's level of attainment in L1).

Since 1991, their studies with U.S. L2 learners have shown that: 1) there are strong relationships among early L1 ability, L2 aptitude, and later L2 achievement, 2) L1 and L2 learning depend on similar language learning components in both languages, 3) L2 achievement is moderated by students' level of L1 ability, 4) there are normal IDs in L1 ability and L2 aptitude, 5) L1 ability and L2 aptitude explain significant variance in L2 proficiency and achievement, and 6) affective differences are linked to differences in L1 ability and L2 aptitude. Their longitudinal studies have found long-term, cross-linguistic transfer of early L1 skills to later L2 aptitude and L2 proficiency. (For a complete review of these studies, see Sparks 2012, 2022.) In addition, Sparks et al. have found that many students experience problems with L2 learning, but the number of LD students in L2 courses who exhibit below average L1 skills is small.

Researchers elsewhere have also found strong relationships between L1 ability and L2 learning, in particular with English Language Learners (ELLs), and have supported the premises of the LCDH. These studies have shown that young students who have L1 literacy problems experience problems with L2 spelling (Lindgren and Kaine 2011), L2 reading accuracy (Borodkin and Faust 2014), L2 reading fluency (Kahn-Horwitz, Shimron, and Sparks 2005; Morfidi et al. 2007), acquisition of L2 vocabulary (Kahn-Horwitz, Shimron, and Sparks 2006), and morphological tasks (Helland and Kaasa 2005). In secondary school environments, studies have shown that students with L1 skill impairments in Polish and Chinese had difficulty learning L2 English (see review by Nijakowska 2010). In a study with Polish high school students, Lockiewicz and Jakulskaa (2016) found that students with dyslexia in L1 exhibited poorer performance in English L2 word reading, reading fluency, and spelling, and L2 vocabulary. They also found a strong relationship between word reading accuracy, reading speed, and spelling between the two languages.

Sparks et al.'s studies with the LCDH and the premise that L2 learning is the learning of *language*, Carroll's theory of L2 aptitude, Cummins' hypotheses, and Skehan's notion that language is special for L2 learning prepared the foundation for studying U.S. students classified as LD in L2 courses.

12.5 Learning Disabilities (LD) and L2 Learning

The false assumptions about discrepancy in LD diagnosis described earlier have been problematic for U.S. educators studying LDs and L2 learning. For example, some educators assumed that LD students will have "special difficulties" with L2 learning (Difino and Lombardino 2004), exhibit "functional limitations" in learning L2s (Ofiesh 2007), and require modified, special sections of L2 courses (Amend et al. 2009). Others accepted the premise of a "disability" for L2 learning, i.e., a "foreign language learning disability," specific to students classified as LD (Grigorenko 2002), and still others recommended course substitutions and waivers for a school's L2 requirement (Shaw 1999). The assumptions were based on case studies of individual learners, case studies of modified classes, personal anecdotes, and advice from educators about accommodations (see Sparks 2006a, 2009). However, these assumptions have not been supported by empirical evidence.

Unfortunately, in the 1990s, it became popular for educators in the U.S. to grant course substitutions for or waivers from the college L2 requirement to students diagnosed as LD. [In the U.S., students are often excused from L2 classes if educators decide they might do poorly, not because they demonstrate some level of proficiency in a L2. In fact, students do not have to achieve a predetermined level of proficiency to pass a L2 course. Instead, they only have to pass the course (Gass, Van Gorp, and Winke 2019).] The first investigation of this practice was undertaken by the author and colleagues with 97 college students, all of whom had been diagnosed as LD and received course substitutions for one university's L2 requirement (Sparks, Philips, and Ganschow 1996). Course substitutions might allow a student to, e.g., complete two semesters of French history or literature courses in English rather than completing French courses. The authors examined students' demographic profiles and found that their college entrance exam scores were in the average range and their graduating college grade point average (GPA) was similar to the student body at this university. Most students (63%) had been referred for evaluation only for *self-reported* problems with L2 learning, and less than half met even a minimum criterion criteria for LD diagnosis. The students' overall intelligence (IQ) and academic achievement scores on standardized testing measures of reading, writing, and math were in the average range, but their MLAT scores were low average to below average. Since most students did not have a discrepancy or a substantial impairment in academic achievement, the authors speculated that the MLAT was used as the sole criterion to classify students as LD and recommend course substitutions, a practice that is in conflict with the purpose of a language aptitude test (see Sparks, Javorsky, and Ganschow 2005). The students' college L2 grades showed that 80% had at least one grade of course withdrawal (W) and 39% had two or more grades of W in L2 courses, but 32% had achieved grades of A, B, C, or D in college L2 courses, and more than half of the grades were A, B, or C. The results suggested that course substitutions for the L2 requirement were based on the improper diagnosis of LD and withdrawal from, but not failure in, L2 courses. Given these findings, Sparks et al. suggested that it is inappropriate to conflate L2 learning problems with the LD construct.

12.6 Myths about L2 Learning and LDs

Although there was no empirical evidence to support the concept, by 2000 the idea of a 'disability' for learning L2s had become acceptable in the U.S., and the use of course substitutions and waivers increased. As a result, several myths about LDs and L2 learning became common. Sparks et al. embarked on a series of studies to examine the profiles of LD students who received course substitutions and those who passed L2 courses. The myths about L2s and LDs and the evidence that falsified them are examined next.[7]

Myth #1: Students classified as LD will exhibit L2 learning problems, fail, or withdraw from L2 courses

Several studies showed that most students classified as LD passed L2 courses, but more non-LD students exhibited L2 learning problems and failed L2 courses. For example, studies showed that 95% of LD students completed, and passed, at least one L2 course in high school and college with average to above-average grades; nonetheless, they received course substitutions in college (Sparks, 2001). At the high school level Sparks, Humbach, and Javorsky (2008) found that 93% of LD students passed L2 courses, and their course grades were not significantly different from low-achieving, non-LD L2 learners in the same courses. At the university level, the majority of LD students who had fulfilled the L2 requirement achieved grades of A, B, and C in L2 courses (Sparks and Javorsky 1999; Sparks et al. 1999a, b; Sparks, Philips, and Javorsky 2002, 2003). Although LD students *could* exhibit difficulties with L2 learning, their performance in L2 courses was similar to low-achieving, non-LD students. The findings refuted the notion that LD diagnosis should be used as the *sine qua non* for determining who will have L2 learning problems.

---

7 Portions of the following section were published in Sparks (2016). Permission was granted by the journal and its publisher for use in this chapter.

Myth #2: Withdrawal from FL courses is evidence of an undiagnosed LD or a "disability" for FL learning.

As noted earlier, Sparks et al. (1996) found that most LD students had previously passed at least one L2 course in both high school *and* college with average or better grades. To determine if there were significant differences in language ability and overall academic achievement between LD students who passed vs. those who withdrew from college L2 courses, Sparks et al. compared students' L1 skills and their college entrance exam scores and found no significant differences between the groups on these measures (Sparks and Javorsky 1999; Sparks et al. 1999a; Sparks, Philips, and Javorsky 2002). Both groups' scores in L1 reading, writing, and math were in the average range. The findings from these studies showed that W grades from college L2 courses were *not*: a) indicative of whether or not LD students possessed the language learning skills to pass L2 courses, b) a marker (signal) for LD, and c) indicative of whether a student had problems in the L2 course. Even if students withdrew from L2 courses, their grades were passing (WP), not failing (WF), when they withdrew.

Myth #3: Students classified as LD in L2 courses exhibit weaker language learning skills and L2 aptitude than low-achieving, non-LD students

Originally, the author hypothesized that LD students enrolled in L2 courses would display poorer L1 skills than low-achieving, non-LD students in L2 courses. However, no significant differences were found between the scores of low-achieving, non-LD students and students classified as LD on all L1 skill measures and in L2 aptitude (MLAT) (see Sparks, Artzer et al. 1998). In another study, Sparks, Humbach, & Javorsky (2008) found no significant differences between high school LD students and low-achieving, non-LD students in L2 courses in L1 reading, language, and writing skills; intelligence (IQ); L2 aptitude; L2 (Spanish) oral and written proficiency and L2 course grades. Moreover, the L1 skills of the LD students were in the average range (see Table 1). Evidence showed no meaningful distinctions between the L1 skills and L2 aptitude of LD students and low-achieving, non-LD students in L2 courses.

Myth #4: Students classified as LD granted course substitutions exhibit low (below average) levels of L1 learning ability different from students classified as LD who pass L2 courses.

Other studies investigated differences between LD students who were–and were not–granted course substitutions for a university's L2 requirement. Findings revealed that LD students with course substitutions exhibited average to above average L1 skills in reading, spelling, writing, and vocabulary. Likewise, studies with LD students who passed L2 courses in college showed that they achieved in

Table 1: Mean scores of secondary level students classified as LD on standardized reading, spelling, writing, vocabulary and verbal memory measures[a].

Study	Reading	Spelling	Writing	Vocabulary/ Language	Verbal Memory
Sparks, Ganschow, Pohlman, Artzer, & Skinner, 1992	90–99	89–102	90–104	96–107	93–109
Sparks, Ganschow, Javorsky, Pohlman, & Patton,1992	94	90	94	–	
Sparks & Ganschow, 1993	95–97	96–97	–	105	103–107
Sparks, Ganschow, Fluharty, & Little, 1996	92–93	88–90	–	99–106	–
Sparks, Artzer, Javorsky et al. 1998	94–98	95	–	100	101
Sparks, Artzer, Patton, et al. 1998	89–102	88–98	–	93–103	96–102
Sparks, Humbach, & Javorsky, 2008	98–100	–	–	96–98	–

[a]Standard scores, $M = 100$, $SD = 15$, Average range $SS = 85$–115.

the average range in L1 skills and on college entrance exams (Sparks and Javorsky 1999; Sparks et al. 1999a, b; Sparks, Philips, and Javorsky 2002, 2003). In addition, these studies found no significant differences between the L1 reading and writing skills, college entrance exam scores, and graduating GPAs of LD students who had passed college L2 courses vs. LD students granted course substitutions (Sparks et al. 1999b). The authors compared the L2 course grades of LD students with the L2 grades of the LD students who passed L2 courses and found the distribution of the two groups' grades was not significantly different. In another study with a larger dataset of students, Sparks et al. (2003) found no significant differences in the two groups' L1 reading and writing skills, L1 vocabulary, college entrance exam scores, graduating college GPAs, and L2 course grades, and that their L1 skills and college entrance scores were in the average range (See Table 2). These findings showed that LD students did not exhibit deficits in the language skills that have been found to be necessary to pass L2 courses and fulfill a school's L2 requirement.

Myth #5: A low score on an L2 aptitude test and/or a discrepancy between IQ and L2 aptitude scores are evidence of LD and/or potential L2 learning problems.

The MLAT has been widely used for selecting students for L2 courses and placing students in different L2 curricular options (Sparks and Ganschow 2001). Through

Table 2: Mean scores of university students classified as LD on standardized reading, spelling, writing, vocabulary and college entrance exam measures[a].

Study	Reading	Spelling	Writing	Vocabulary	ACT[b]
Ganschow, Sparks, Pohlman et al., 1991	100	88	96	–	–
Sparks, Philips, Ganschow, & Javorsky, 1999a	99–107	95	95–97	–	22.3
Sparks & Javorsky, 1999	104–109	97	87	–	23
Sparks, Philips, Ganschow, & Javorsky, 1999b	103–108	–	95–106	–	21.7–23.5
Sparks, Philips, & Javorsky, 2002	96–108	93	95–97	107	21
Sparks, Philips, & Javorsky, 2003	110–116	–	97–103	–	21–24

[a]Standard scores, $M = 100$, $SD = 15$, Average range $SS = 85–115$
[b]Mean = 20.8, $SD = 4.8$, Average range $SS = 16–26$

factor analytic studies, Carroll (1962, 1990) found that four independent variables were predictive of L2 learning: (a) *phonetic coding*, the ability to code and remember auditory phonetic material over time; (b) *grammatical sensitivity*, the ability to handle grammar; (c) *inductive language learning* ability, the ability to infer linguistic forms, rules, and patterns from new linguistic content; and (d) *rote memory*, the capacity to learn phonetic and grammatical associations. Carroll's early studies indicated that the MLAT, which measures the aforementioned variables, was a good predictor of success in learning an L2, and subsequent studies have supported its predictive value (Skehan 1998; Sparks et al. 2009, 2011).

Carroll (1963, 1990) described the purpose of L2 aptitude tests as predicting whether a particular level of language proficiency can be achieved in the time allotted for its study, *not* to predict who can and cannot learn languages. Despite his admonition that the MLAT not be used to "deselect" (waive) students from L2 study, the test has been used for this purpose (e.g., see Reed and Stansfield 2004). But, doing so demonstrates a fundamental misunderstanding of the L2 aptitude concept and uses the MLAT for a purpose for which it was not designed (Sparks, Javorsky, and Ganschow 2005).

There is empirical evidence regarding whether low scores on the MLAT can determine which students can, and cannot, pass L2 courses. In a study with high school students in Spanish courses, Sparks, Humbach, and Javorsky (2008) found no significant differences between the MLAT scores of LD students ($SS = 83.6$, 14th percentile) and low-achieving, non-LD students ($SS = 84.6$, 15th percentile), both of whom scored at least 1.0 SD below the mean. Even so, all but two LD students passed first-year Spanish courses (93% pass rate), while seven low-achieving students failed first-year Spanish (87% pass rate). In three studies with postsecondary

LD students, the author and colleagues found that their mean scores on the MLAT ranged from SS = 79.1–80.2 (8th-10th percentile), over 1.0 SD below the mean. Nonetheless, 92–96% of the students who had completed at least one L2 course in college before receiving course substitutions passed L2 courses, and 63–82% had earned grades of A, B, or C (Sparks and Javorsky 1999; Sparks et al. 1999a; Sparks, Philips, and Javorsky 2002). Moreover, there were *no* significant differences between the MLAT scores of LD students who had passed L2 courses and the LD students who had received only withdrawal grades in L2 courses before receiving course substitutions. Students classified as LD achieved a mean MLAT score well over 1.0 SD *below* the mean (SS = 80.2, or 9th percentile), but 95% of their high school L2 grades were passing. The available evidence has shown that a low score on an L2 aptitude test does not predict failure in L2 courses.

Myth #6: Discrepancy between IQ and academic achievement is evidence of a 'disability' for L2 learning.

In their studies, the author and colleagues showed that students in L2 courses *with* IQ-achievement discrepancies did not exhibit significantly lower scores on L1 achievement and L2 aptitude measures than L2 learners classified as LD *without* IQ-achievement discrepancies (Sparks, Artzer et al. 1998; Sparks and Javorsky 1999). In other studies, they found that postsecondary LD students with and without discrepancies did not exhibit significant differences in their college entrance exam scores, college L2 GPA, graduating college GPA, and MLAT scores (Sparks, Philips, and Javorsky 2002). Likewise, no differences were found in L2 course grades or L2 proficiency between students classified as LD with and without discrepancies (Sparks 2001, 2006a, 2009, 2012). The empirical evidence has shown that the presence of IQ-achievement discrepancies is *irrelevant* for predicting who will experience problems with L2 learning, and that LD students with/without discrepancies perform equally well on L1 achievement and L2 aptitude tests and also in L2 courses.

Myth #7: Students enrolled in L2 classes classified as LD meet the criteria for an LD diagnosis.

An additional myth is that students classified as LD in L2 classes meet the classification criteria for LD. The authors investigated whether postsecondary LD students, most of whom received course substitutions, displayed IQ-achievement discrepancies and/or severe deficits (substantial impairments) in academic skills (reading, writing). In one study, they found that only 24% of students exhibited a substantial impairment, i.e., SS ≤ 85 (≤ 15th percentile), in reading, spelling, or writing, and most scored below average on only a single subtest (Sparks, Philips, and Ganschow 1999a). Most students' scores on standardized measures of academics were, at minimum, in the average range. In a study with another university group of LD students who received course substitutions, Sparks and Javorsky (1999) found that only 43% met even the minimum discrepancy criterion (1.0 *SD*) for LD diagnosis, only 36% (15/42) exhibited a substantial impairment in L1 skills, usually on one subtest, and most L1 achievement scores were in the average range. In another study at a different university with a larger group of LD students granted course substitutions, Sparks, Philips, and Javorsky (2002) found a minority (44%, or 70/158) met the minimum criterion (1.0 *SD* IQ-achievement discrepancy) for LD diagnosis, and a small percentage (16%) displayed substantial impairment in L1 reading, spelling, or writing. Again, most students' L1 achievement skills were in the average range.

These studies found that most college LD students with L2 course substitutions did *not*: a) meet the minimum criteria for LD diagnosis, b) exhibit substantial impairments in academic skills, and c) receive a diagnosis as LD until college when they encountered the L2 requirement. Findings showed that below average L2 learning is best predicted below average by L1 learning skills, but that most U.S. L2 learners exhibit average, or better, L1 skills.[8]

12.7 Pedagogy for Teaching L2s: Evidence-Based Teaching Strategies for Language Learning Problems

Ganschow and Sparks (2001) summarized pedagogical methods for teaching L2s to students with language learning problems. At that time, L2 educators had given little attention to these individuals in L2 classes at any level of education. Prior to 1990, U.S. students with L1 learning problems were usually advised not to enroll in high school L2 courses, and most who did not complete L2 courses did not attend four-year colleges. This situation changed when U. S. college enrollments expanded from 12 million in 1980 to 21 million in 2010 [statistica.com/statistics/183995/us-college-enrollment-and-private-institutions] and LD students enrolled in college. By the 1990s, LD students were often granted course substitutions because educators believed (incorrectly) they would have L2 learning problems and fail L2 courses. As a result, L2 educators (and researchers) had little reason to investigate teaching methods for these students.

In the 1990s, the only pedagogical method proposed for teaching L2s to students with language learning problems came from special educators (Sparks et al. 1991).

---

[8] In these studies, many LD students who received course substitutions displayed academic problems *only* in mathematics, *not* in the language learning skills important for L2 learning success. However, there is no empirical evidence showing that students with severe problems in mathematics will have L2 learning problems.

The multisensory structured language approach (MSL) had been used for many years to teach L1 reading, spelling, and writing to students with L1 learning difficulties (Gillingham and Stillman 1960). This approach directly and explicitly teaches the phonological/orthographic (sound, sound-symbol), syntactic (grammar), and morphological systems of a language, and emphasizes skill development and conscious attention to language structures. The instruction is "multisensory", i.e. students hear, see, and write language elements simultaneously. The concepts of the language are sequenced from easy to difficult, and students master easier concepts before moving to new concepts. Based on the premise that L2 learning is the learning of *language*, Sparks et al. speculated that teaching the components of the target L2 (phonology, phonological/orthographic, grammar, etc.) in a direct, explicit manner, i.e., form-focused instruction, would be beneficial to all L2 learners, but especially students with L1 problems. Through the 1990s, they conducted a series of studies with U.S. high school students, which showed that low-achieving (at-risk, LD) L2 learners enrolled in Spanish and taught with the MSL approach in Spanish made significant gains in their L1 skills and L2 aptitude (MLAT) (Ganschow and Sparks 1995; Sparks et al. 1992; Sparks and Ganschow 1993b), and achieved expected levels of oral and written proficiency in Spanish after two years of L2 classes (Sparks et al. 1997). [To the author's knowledge, the investigations that used this teaching approach are the only studies that show that: a) the scores on a L2 aptitude test, the MLAT, significantly increased on pre-post1 testing after one year of the L2 study, and b) the scores did not decrease on post 2 testing after another year of L2 courses.] In a longitudinal study, Sparks et al. compared the average/high-achieving L2 learners in regular sections of Spanish classes with low-achieving/LD students in special sections of Spanish taught with the MSL approach (Sparks, Artzer et al. 1998). As expected, findings revealed significant differences in the groups' pre- and post-test L1 skills. Unexpectedly, there were no significant differences between the groups' L2 oral and written Spanish proficiency after two years of L2 courses.

More recently, L2 researchers in Europe have conducted studies using the MSL approach with L2 learners classified as dyslexic in L1. In a small study with Polish students learning English, Nijakowska (2008) found that dyslexic students taught with MSL made significant gains in English word reading and spelling. Pfenninger (2015) used the MSL approach in a Swiss context with students identified as dyslexic and non-dyslexic and found that MSL instruction was beneficial for both groups in improving their German L2 and English L3. Nijakowska (2013) has also reported studies demonstrating the effectiveness of this approach.

Some U.S educators developed special sections of L2 classes with modified Spanish, Italian, and Latin curricula for LD students and students with L1 learning problems (Downey and Snyder 2001). They reported success in L2 acquisition for these students. However, at the same time that studies were demonstrating success with the MSL approach and the modified L2 curricula, inclusion for students with disabilities and special needs, including LD students, became the dominant educational paradigm in the U.S. and Europe, and students with all types of disabilities were placed in regular classes alongside their non-disabled peers (see Kormos 2016). Unfortunately, for students in the U.S. classified as LD, course substitution and waivers for the L2 requirement became the norm and a diagnosis of LD, justified or not, constitutes the *sine qua non* for substitutions, waivers, and other accommodations (Sparks 2016).

Unfortunately, knowledge about teaching L2s to students with language learning problems has stagnated. Instead, both L2 and special educators have proposed pedagogical techniques based on theories proposing causes for L2 problems unrelated to language difficulties. For example, some educators have hypothesized that affective characteristics, such as motivation and anxiety, are causal factors in poor L2 learning. However, the notion of affective differences as causal factors in L2s is problematic for several reasons, most notably: a) affective characteristics, such as low motivation and high levels of anxiety, are *not* directly related to language learning, b) low motivation and high levels of anxiety for L2 learning in high school have been linked to significantly lower levels of L1 skills as early as primary school, several years *before* exposure to L2 instruction, c) motivation for and anxiety about L2 learning are strongly related to students' levels of L2 aptitude (MLAT) *prior to* enrolling in L2 classes, and d) research has not demonstrated that L2 achievement can be increased by lowering anxiety or increasing motivation for L2 learning (see Sparks 2022, this volume).

Other L2 educators have speculated that teaching language learning strategies and teaching to students' learning styles are important for successful L2 learning (see Oxford 1990). Although the idea of teaching-learning strategies has been popular for many years, research has not supported their use for increasing L2 proficiency (Dörnyei 2005). Likewise, learning styles theory (auditory vs. visual, analytic vs. holistic) has been *thoroughly* debunked by L1 researchers (e.g., see Pashler et al. 2009), and Sparks (2006b) has cited the lack of evidence generated by L2 researchers supporting the use of styles for teaching L2s.

Largely as a result of the inclusion movement in the U.S. and Europe, the standard practice for assisting poor L2 learners in regular classrooms has been the use of accommodations. Accommodations in classes are modifications and adjustments to the tasks, environments, and usual practices that enable individuals with disabilities to participate in an academic program (U.S. Department of Education 2007). According to the National Center for Education Statistics (Raue and Lewis 2011), LD students are the largest group receiving accommodations in schools. The primary accommodation used by LD students is extended time on tests. Some students are granted the use of a computer with spellcheck for writing, but other students may request a reader or scribe to assist with tests, oral directions, and a separate testing room (Lovett & Lewandowski, 2015). Kormos and Smith (2012) described the use of accommodations and modifications for SpLD students in L2 courses. Accommodations and course modifications have become accepted practice in the U.S. (because of ADA) and in Europe, Australia, and some Canadian provinces [because of the Children and Families Act (2014)]. However, accommodations and course modifications are not designed to assure that students master course material, including the mastery of an L2 in second language classes. Instead, these practices are designed only to allow *participation* in courses with non-disabled peers using accommodations.

In sum, the only evidence-based studies demonstrating success in teaching L2s to students with language learning problems in L1 have been those investigating the MSL approach teaching directly and explicitly the language components of the L2. This approach may be successful because it teaches skills directly related to *language* learning.

12.8 Conclusions

There are differences in the conceptual and operational definitions between the U.S. and Europe for the LD and SpLD constructs. However, one commonality is that educators identify students who experience L2 learning problems, generally. Voluminous research in the U.S. and elsewhere has shown that students with below-average L1 learning skills will exhibit L2 learning problems. Studies with the LCDH have shown that: 1) there are strong relationships between early L1 ability, L2 aptitude, and later L2 achievement, 2) L1 and L2 learning depend on basic language learning components similar in both languages, 3) L2 achievement and proficiency are moderated by students' level of L1 ability, 4) there are normal IDs in L1 ability and L2 aptitude among L2 learners, 5) L1 ability and L2 aptitude explain significant variance in L2 proficiency, and 6) there is long-term, cross-linguistic transfer of early L1 skills to later L2 aptitude and L2 proficiency.

Research with LD students in the U.S. mirrors the aforementioned findings but has not found a "special" relationship between LDs and L2 learning problems or a "unique" disability for L2 learning. Instead, evidence shows that LD students and low-achieving, non-LD students in L2 classes exhibit similar levels of L1 skills and L2 aptitude and achieve similar L2 outcomes. Given these findings, which students should be considered "at-risk" for L2 learning problems? Table 3 presents the testing profiles of several students enrolled in L2 classes. If IQ-achievement discrepancy is *misused*, students A, B, and C would be classified as LD because they exhibit IQ-achievement discrepancies. But, students A and B should not be diagnosed as LD or considered to be "at-risk" for L2 problems because they do not exhibit academic impairments; instead, their L1 skills are in the average to above-average range. Although student C displays an academic impairment in mathematics, s/he is not "at-risk" for L2 learning problems because his/her L1 (language) skills and L2 aptitude are in the average to above-average range. Student D exhibits the *same* (average) levels of reading and writing achievement and the *same* average L2 aptitude score as students A, B, and C, and is also not "at-risk" for L2 problems. Given their L1 skills and L2 aptitude profiles, students A, B, C, and D should exhibit, at minimum, average performance in L2 courses. L2 teachers should be most concerned about students E and F because their L1 skills and L2 aptitude are in the low average to below-average range. Their low levels of L1 skills and L2 aptitude are consistent with the empirical evidence showing that students with deficits (substantial impairments) in L1 (language) skills *and* below average L2 aptitude will likely exhibit problems with L2 learning. The low L1 skills displayed by students E and F should *not* be considered a "disability" for L2 learning. In fact, a diagnosis of a disability is irrelevant to understanding who will exhibit L2 learning problems. Instead, students E and F will exhibit L2 learning problems because they have below-average L1 skills. Figure 5 depicts the students' scores on the IQ, L1 achievement, and L2 aptitude measures.

Table 3: Profiles of Students' IQ, L1 Achievement, and L2 Aptitude Scores.

Standardized Testing Measure [a]	A	B	C	D	E	F
Intelligence						
Full Scale IQ	130	122	115	100	100	90
L1 Academic Achievement						
Reading	100	100	100	100	81	81
Spelling	100	100	100	100	81	81
Written language	100	100	100	100	81	81
Receptive vocabulary	136	116	112	96	101	81
Listening comprehension	123	129	119	104	99	81
Oral expression/vocabulary	120	111	129	102	98	81
Verbal memory	111	109	114	107	102	81
Mathematics	135	128	80	98	100	96
L2 Aptitude						
Modern Language Aptitude Test	102	102	102	102	80	80

[a] All scores are standard scores, $M = 100$, $SD = 15$, Average Range $SS = 85–115$.

Pedagogical recommendations for students who experience L2 problems proffered by L2 (and LD) educators have not been helpful for teaching the skills necessary to

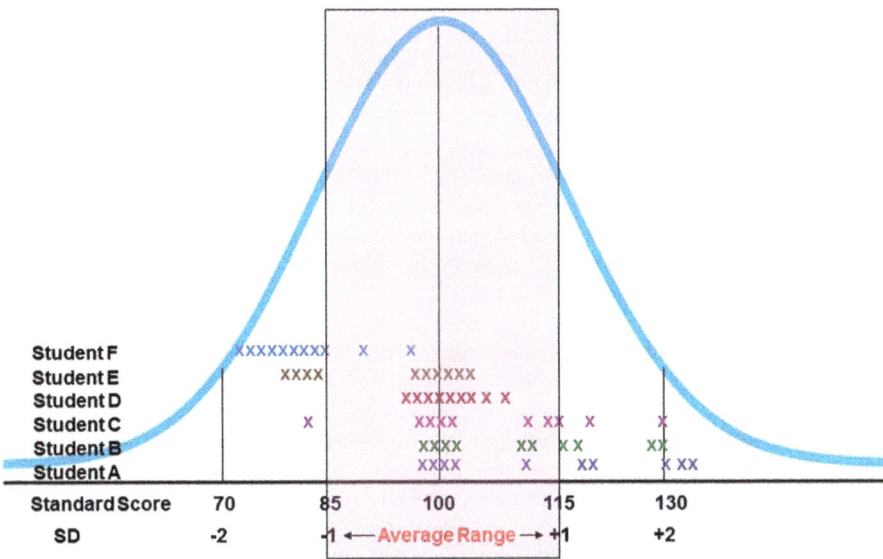

Figure 5: Profiles of Students' IQ, L1 Achievement, and L2 Aptitude Scores.

master an L2. In the U.S. and Europe, the philosophy of inclusion means that students with LDs and other learning difficulties are provided with accommodations and course modifications. The accommodations and modifications may allow them to *participate* with their non-disabled peers in L2 classes, but do *not* ensure they master course material or learn the language. In the U.S., high school and university students classified as LD are regularly provided with course substitutions (waivers) for L2 courses that preclude exposure to the L2. For many years, Sparks et al. have recommended that L2 educators develop methods that focus on teaching the *language* skills necessary to develop proficiency in L2. Instead, L2 educators have proposed pedagogies based on hypotheses about L2 problems that are unrelated to learning a language. Thus far, the only pedagogical approaches found to be helpful for teaching L2s to students with language learning problems (Students E and F) are those that teach directly and explicitly the language skills necessary to become literate and fluent in an L2.

If progress is to be made in the development of teaching methodologies for L2s to students with language learning problems at all levels of schooling, educators in different cultural contexts must agree that L2 learning problems are language-based because L2 learning is the learning of *language*. If L2 problems, and L2 learning generally, are thought of as learning language, then methods that teach directly and explicitly the language skills necessary to become literate and fluent in an L2 will be those that are successful.

Recommended Readings

Grünke, Matthias & Wendy Cavendish. 2016. Learning disabilities around the globe: Making sense of the heterogeneity of the different viewpoints. *Learning Disabilities: A Contemporary Journal 14 (1)*. 1–8.

Learning disability is a globally, widely used, yet very heterogeneously understood term related to academic failure. The concept is used differently in different parts of the world and has been influenced by the ideals, norms, language, historical heritage, political currents, and scientific paradigms that affect education in a given culture. As a result, these various perspectives are not united behind a commonly accepted definition. The paper provides information about how the term learning disability is viewed across societies.

Fletcher, Jack & Jeremy Miciak. 2017. Comprehensive cognitive assessments are not necessary for the identification and treatment of learning disabilities. *Archives of Clinical Neuropsychology 32(1)*. 2–7.

The authors address the controversy about the necessity of cognitive assessment for learning disability (LD) and maintain that the controversy should be adjudicated through empirical research. They review five sources of evidence commonly provided as support for cognitive assessment as part of the LD identification process, highlighting gaps in empirical research and where evidence is insufficient for use of validity of cognitive assessments. They conclude that current evidence does not justify routine cognitive assessment for LD identification. They offer an instructional conceptualization of LD based on documenting low academic achievement, inadequate response to intensive interventions, and a consideration of exclusionary factors.

Sparks, Richard. 2009. If you don't know where you're going, you'll wind up somewhere else: The case of "foreign language learning disability." *Foreign Language Annals 42(1)*. 7–26.

Despite the lack of empirical evidence, the term *foreign language learning disability* (FLLD) became popular in the learning disabilities (LD) and L2 literature. The author contends there is not a unique "disability" for foreign language (L2) learning and suggests instead that L2 skills run along a continuum of very strong to very weak L2 learners. He reviews problems with the definition and diagnostic criteria for LD and cites problems with the development and use of a logically consistent, easily operationalized, and empirically valid definition and diagnostic criteria for the FLLD concept. He details implications for identifying students who L2 problems, addresses policies that permit students to obtain waivers from or course substitutions for L2 requirements, and describes issues hidden from L2 educators by the LD and FLLD concepts.

Kormos, Judit. 2016. *The second language learning processes of students with specific learning difficulties*. New York: Taylor & Francis.

The author presents an in-depth discussion of the L2 learning processes of students with specific learning difficulties (SpLDs), summarizing research in cognitive and educational psychology and integrating them with studies in L2 acquisition (SLA). The reader will note the many differences in how learning disabilities (LDs) are viewed in the U.S. and how SpLDs are viewed in Europe. The book is relevant to those who are interested in the role of specific learning difficulties in learning L2s and those who would like to understand how individual differences in cognitive functioning influence L2 learning. This is a resource for language teachers, students, and researchers in the areas of second language acquisition and applied linguistics.

References

Aaron, P. G. 1997. The impending demise of the discrepancy formula. *Review of Educational Research 67(4)*. 461–502.

Al-Yagon, Michael & Malta Margalit. 2016. Specific learning disabilities: The Israeli perspective. *Learning Disabilities: A Contemporary Journal 14(1)*. 39–51.

Amend, Amanda, Carolyn Whitney, Antonia Messuri & Hideko Furukawa. 2009. A modified Spanish sequence for students with language-based learning disabilities. *Foreign Language Annals 42(1)*. 27–41.

American Psychiatric Association. 1994. *Diagnostic and statistical manual of mental disorders: DSM-IV*. Washington, DC: Author.

American Psychiatric Association. 2013. *Diagnostic and statistical manual of mental disorders: DSM-5*. Washington, DC: Author.

Americans with Disabilities Act (ADA). 1990. Pub. L. No. 101-336, 104 Stat. 328 (1991).

Americans with Disabilities Act (ADA) Amendments Act of 2008. Pub. L. 110-325.42 USCA 12101.

Binder, Laurence, Grant Iverson & Brian Brooks. 2009. To err is human: "Abnormal neuropsychological scores and variability are common in healthy adults. *Archives of Clinical Neuropsychology 24(1)*. 31–46.

Borodkin, Katy & Miriam Faust. 2014. Native language phonological skills in low-proficiency second language learners. *Language Learning 64(1)*. 132–159.

Carroll, John. 1962. The prediction of success in intensive foreign language training. In Robert Glaser (ed.), *Training and research in education*, 87–136. Englewood Cliffs, NJ: Prentice-Hall.

Carroll, John. 1963. A model of school learning. *Teachers College Record 64(8)*. 723–733.

Carroll, John. 1990. Cognitive abilities in foreign language aptitude: Then and now. In Thomas Parry & Charles Stansfield (eds.), *Language aptitude reconsidered*, 11–29. Englewood Cliffs, NJ: Prentice-Hall.

Carroll, John & Stanley Sapon. 1959, 2000. *Modern Language Aptitude Test (MLAT): Manual*. San Antonio, TX: Psychological Corp. Republished by Second Language Testing, Inc. https://lltf.net/aptitude-tests/language-aptitude-tests/modern-language-aptitude-test-2/

Cummins, Jim. 1979. Linguistic interdependence and the educational development of bilingual children. *Review of Educational Research 49(2)*. 222–251.

Department of Health. 2014. The Care Act and whole-family approaches. London: Department of Health.

Devlin, Kat. 2018. "Most European students are learning a foreign language in school while Americans lag." https://www.pewresearch.org/fact-tank/2018/08/06/most-european-students-are-learning-a-foreign-language-in-school-while-americans-lag/

DiFino, Sharon & Linda Lombardino. 2004. Language learning disabilities: The ultimate foreign language challenge. *Foreign Language Annals 37(3)*. 390–400.

Dörnyei, Zoltan. 2005. *The psychology of the language learner*. Mahwah, NJ: Erlbaum.

Downey, Doris & Lynn Snyder. 2001. Curricular accommodations for college students with language learning disabilities. *Topics in Language Disorders 21(2)*. 55–67.

Erasmus+. "What are specific learning disabilities (SpLD)." Retrieved on March 26, 2020. http://euspld.com/spld/

European Commission (EPALE). "Everything you wanted to know about specific learning disabilities/difficulties." Retrieved on March 26, 2020. https://epale.ec.europa.eu/en/resource-centre/content/everything-you-need-know-about-specific-learning-disabilitiesdifficulties.

Fletcher, Jack & Jeremy Miciak. 2017. Comprehensive cognitive assessments are not necessary for the identification and treatment of learning disabilities. *Archives of Clinical Neuropsychology 32(1)*. 2–7.

Friedman, Amelia. 2015. America's lacking language skills. *The Atlantic*, May 10. https://www.theatlantic.com/education/archive/2015/05/filling-americas-language-education-potholes/392876/

Ganschow, Leonore & Richard Sparks. 1995. Effects of direct instruction in Spanish phonology on the native-language skills and foreign-language aptitude of at-risk foreign-language learners. *Journal of Learning Disabilities 28(2)*. 107–120.

Ganschow, Leonore & Richard Sparks. 2001. Learning difficulties and foreign language instruction: A review of research and instruction. *Language Teaching 34(1)*. 79–98.

Gass, Susan, KoenVan Gorp & Paula Winke. 2019. Using different carrots: How incentivization affects proficiency testing outcomes. *Foreign Language Annals 52(2)*. 216–236.

Gillingham, Anna & Bessie Stillman. 1960. *Remedial training for children with specific disability in reading, spelling, and penmanship*. Cambridge, Massachusetts: Educators' Publishers Service.

Grigorenko, Elena. 2002. Foreign language acquisition and language-based learning disabilities. In Peter Robinson (ed.), *Individual differences and instructed language learning*, 95–112. Amsterdam: John Benjamins.

Grünke, Matthias & Wendy Cavendish. 2016. Learning disabilities around the globe: Making sense of the heterogeneity of the different viewpoints. *Learning Disabilities: A Contemporary Journal 14(1)*. 1–8.

Haslam, Nick. 2016. Concept creep: Psychology's expanding concepts of harm and pathology. *Psychological Inquiry 27*. 1–17.

Helland, Turid & Randi Kaasa. 2005. Dyslexia in English as a second language. *Dyslexia(1) 11*. 41–60.

Jeffay, Eliyas, Laurence Binder & Konstantine Zakzanis. 2021. Marked intraindividual cognitive variability in a sample of healthy graduate students. *Psychological Injury and Law 14(3)*. 171–183.

Joshi, R. Malatesha & Aaron, P. G. 2006. *Handbook of orthography and literacy*. Mahwah, NJ: Erlbaum.

Kahn-Horwitz, Janina, Joesph Shimron & Richard Sparks. 2005. Predicting foreign language reading achievement in elementary school students. *Reading and Writing: An Interdisciplinary Journal 18*. 527–558.

Kahn-Horwitz, Janina, Joseph Shimron & Richard Sparks. 2006. Weak and strong novice readers of English as a foreign language: Effects of first language and socioeconomic status. *Annals of Dyslexia 56(1)*. 161–185.

Kauffman, James, Daniel Hallahan & Paige Pullen. 2017. *Handbook of special education*. New York: Routledge.

Kavale, Kenneth & Steven Forness. 1995. *The nature of learning disabilities: Critical elements of diagnosis and classification*. Mahwah, NJ: Erlbaum.

Kormos, Judit. 2016. *The second language learning processes of students with specific learning difficulties*. New York: Taylor & Francis.

Kormos, Judit. 2017. The effects of specific learning difficulties on processes of multilingual language development. *Annual Review of Applied Linguistics 37*. 30–44.

Kormos, Judit & Anne Margaret Smith. 2012. *Teaching languages to students with specific learning differences*. Tonawanda, NY: Multilingual Matters.

Lindgrén, Signe-Anita & Matti Laine. 2011. Cognitive-linguistic performances of multilingual university students suspected of dyslexia. *Dyslexia 17*. 184–200.

Łockiewicz, Marta & Martyna Jaskulska. 2016. Difficulties of Polish students with dyslexia in reading and spelling in English as L2. *Learning and Individual Differences 51*. 256–264.

Lopes, João, Cristina Gomes, Célia Oliveira & Julian Elliott. 2020. Research studies on dyslexia: Participant inclusion and exclusion criteria. *European Journal of Special Needs Education 35(5)*. 1–16.

Lovett, Ben & Larry Lewandowski. 2015. *Testing accommodations for students with disabilities: Research-based practice*. Washington, DC: American Psychological Association.

Miciak, Jeremy, Jack Fletcher, Karla Stuebing, Sharon Vaughn & Tammy Tolar. 2014. Patterns of cognitive strengths and weaknesses: Identification rates, agreement, and validity for learning disabilities identification. *School Psychology Quarterly 29(1)*. 21–37.

Morfidi, Eleni, Aryan Van Der Leij, Peter De Jong, Femke Scheltinga & Judith Bekebrede. 2007. Reading in two orthographies: A cross-linguistic study of Dutch average and poor readers who learn English as a second language. *Reading and Writing 20*. 753–784.

Nijakowska, Joanna. (2008). An experiment with direct multisensory instruction in teaching word reading and spelling to Polish dyslexic learners of English. In Judit Kormos & Edit Kontra (eds.), *Language learners with special needs: An international perspective*, 130–157. Bristol. UK: Multilingual Matters.

Nijakowska, Joanna. 2010. *Dyslexia in the foreign language classroom*. Bristol, ENG: Multilingual Matters.

Nijakowska, Joanna. 2013. Multisensory structured learning approach in teaching foreign languages to dyslexic learners. In Danuta Gabryś-Barker, Ewa Piechurska-Kuciel & Jerzy Zybert (eds.), *Investigations in Teaching and Learning Languages*, 201–215. Springer: Heidelberg.

Ofiesh, Nicole. 2007. Math, science, and foreign language: Evidence-based accommodation decision making at the postsecondary level. *Learning Disabilities Research and Practice 22(4)*. 237–245.

Oxford, Rebecca. 1990. Styles, strategies, and aptitude: Connections for language learning. In Thomas Parry & Charles Stansfield (eds.), *Language aptitude reconsidered*, 67–125. Englewood Cliffs, NJ: Prentice-Hall.

Pashler, Harold, Mark McDaniel, Doug Rohrer & Robert Bjork. 2008. Learning styles: Concepts and evidence. *Psychological Science in the Public Interest 9(3)*. 105–119.

Pfenninger, Simone. 2015. MSL in the digital ages: Effects and effectiveness of computer-mediated intervention for FL learners with dyslexia. *Studies in Second Language Learning and Teaching 5(1)*. 109–133.

Raue, Kimberly & Laurie Lewis. 2011. Students with disabilities at degree-granting postsecondary institutions: First Look. NCES 2011-018. Washington, DC: *National Center for Education Statistics, US Department of Education, Statistical Analysis Report 18*.

Reed, Daniel & Charles Stansfield. 2004. Using the Modern Language Aptitude Test to identify a foreign language learning disability: Is it ethical? *Language Assessment Quarterly 1*. 161–176.

Shaw, Robert. 1999. The case for course substitutions as a reasonable accommodation for students with foreign language learning difficulties. *Journal of Learning Disabilities 32(4)*. 320–328.

Skehan, Peter. 1998. *A cognitive approach to language learning*. Oxford, ENG: Oxford University Press.

Sparks, Richard. 1995. Examining the linguistic coding differences hypothesis to explain individual differences in foreign language learning. *Annals of Dyslexia 45(1)*. 187–214.

Sparks, Richard. 2001. Foreign language learning problems of students classified as learning disabled and non-learning disabled: Is there a difference? *Topics in Language Disorders 21(2)*. 38–54.

Sparks, R. 2006a. Is there a 'disability' for learning a foreign language? *Journal of Learning Disabilities 39(6)*. 544–557.

Sparks, Richard. 2006b. Learning styles: Making too many" wrong mistakes": A Response to Castro and Peck. *Foreign Language Annals 39(3)*. 520–528.

Sparks, Richard. 2009. If you don't know where you're going, you'll wind up somewhere else: The case of "foreign language learning disability." *Foreign Language Annals* 42(1). 7–26.
Sparks, Richard. 2012. Individual differences in L2 learning and long-term L1-L2 relationships. *Language Learning* 62(Supp. 2). 5–27.
Sparks, Richard. 2016. Myths about foreign language learning and learning disabilities. *Foreign Language Annals* 49(2). 252–270.
Sparks, Richard. 2022. *Exploring L1-L2 relationships: The impact of individual differences*. UK: Multilingual Matters.
Sparks, Richard. in press. The Linguistic Coding Differences Hypothesis and L2 learning: A thirty-year retrospective. In Edward Wen, Peter Skehan & Richard Sparks (eds.), *Language aptitude theory and practice: Pushing the boundaries*. Cambridge: Cambridge University Press.
Sparks, Richard, Marjorie Artzer, James Javorsky, Jon Patton, Leonore Ganschow, Karen Miller & Dottie Hordubay. 1998. Students classified as learning disabled (LD) and non-learning disabled students: Two comparison studies of native language skill, foreign language aptitude, and foreign language proficiency. *Foreign Language Annals* 31(4). 531–551.
Sparks, Richard, Marjorie Artzer, Jon Patton, Leonore Ganschow, Karen Miller, Dottie Hordubay & Geri Walsh. 1998. Benefits of multisensory language instruction in Spanish for at-risk learners: A comparison study of high school Spanish students. *Annals of Dyslexia* 48(1). 239–270.
Sparks, Richard & Leonore Ganschow. 1991. Foreign language learning differences: Affective or native language aptitude differences? *Modern Language Journal* 75(1). 3–16.
Sparks, Richard & Leonore Ganschow. 1993a. Searching for the cognitive locus of foreign language learning difficulties: Linking first and second language learning. *Modern Language Journal* 77(3). 289–302.
Sparks, Richard & Leonore Ganschow. 1993b. The effects of a multisensory structured language approach on the native and foreign language aptitude skills of at-risk learners: A replication and follow-up study. *Annals of Dyslexia* 43(1). 194–216.
Sparks, Richard & Leonore Ganschow. 2001. Aptitude for learning a foreign language. *Annual Review of Applied Linguistics* 21. 90–111.
Sparks, Richard, Leonore Ganschow, Marjorie Artzer & Jon Patton. 1997. Foreign language proficiency of at-risk and not-at-risk foreign language learners over two years of foreign language instruction. *Journal of Learning Disabilities* 30(1). 92–98.
Sparks, Richard, Leonore Ganschow, Sylvia Kenneweg & Karen Miller. 1991. Use of an Orton-Gillingham approach to teach a foreign language to dyslexic/learning disabled students: Explicit teaching of phonology in a second language. *Annals of Dyslexia* 41(1). 96–118.
Sparks, Richard, Leonore Ganschow, Jane Pohlman, Marjorie Artzer & Sue Skinner. 1992. The effects of a multisensory, structured language approach on the native and foreign language aptitude skills of high-risk foreign language learners. *Annals of Dyslexia* 42(1). 25–53.
Sparks, Richard, Nancy Humbach & James Javorsky. 2008. Comparing high and low achieving, LD, and ADHD foreign language learners: individual and longitudinal differences. *Learning and Individual Differences* 18(1). 29–43.
Sparks, Richard & James Javorsky. 1999. Students classified as learning disabled and the college foreign language requirement: Replication and comparison studies. *Journal of Learning Disabilities* 32(4). 329–349.
Sparks, Richard, James Javorsky & Leonore Ganschow. 2005. Should the Modern Language Aptitude Test (MLAT) be used to determine course substitutions for and waivers of the foreign language requirement? *Foreign Language Annals* 38(2). 201–210.

Sparks, Richard, Jon Patton, Leonore Ganschow & Nancy Humbach. 2009. Long-term relationships among early L1 skills, L2 aptitude, L2 affect, and later L2 proficiency. *Applied Psycholinguistics 30(4)*. 725–755.

Sparks, Richard, Jon Patton, Leonore Ganschow & Nancy Humbach. 2011. Subcomponents of second-language aptitude and second-language proficiency. *Modern Language Journal 95(2)*. 1–21.

Sparks, Richard, Lois Philips & Leonore Ganschow. 1996. Students classified as learning disabled and the college foreign language requirement: A case study of one university. In Judith Liskin-Gasparro (ed.), *Patterns and policies: The changing demographics of foreign language instruction*, 123–159. Boston, MA: Heinle and Heinle.

Sparks, Richard, Lois Philips, Leonore Ganschow & James Javorsky. 1999a. Students classified as learning disabled and the college foreign language requirement: A quantitative analysis. *Journal of Learning Disabilities 32(4)*. 566–580.

Sparks, Richard, Lois Philips, Leonore Ganschow & James Javorsky. 1999b. Comparison of students classified as learning disabled who petitioned for or fulfilled the college foreign language requirement. *Journal of Learning Disabilities 32(6)*. 553–565.

Sparks, Richard, Lois Philips & James Javorsky (2002). Students classified as LD who received course substitutions for the foreign language requirement: A replication study. *Journal of Learning Disabilities 35(6)*. 482–499, 538.

Sparks, Richard, Lois Philips & James Javorsky. 2003. Students classified as LD who petitioned for or fulfilled the college foreign language requirement – Are they different?: A replication study. *Journal of Learning Disabilities, 36(4)*, 348–362.

Stanovich, Keith. 1991. Discrepancy definitions of reading disability: Has intelligence led us astray? *Reading Research Quarterly 26(1)*. 7–29.

Stanovich, Keith. 1999. The sociopsychometrics of learning disabilities. *Journal of Learning Disabilities 32(4)*. 350–361.

Stanovich, Keith. 2005. The future of a mistake: Will discrepancy measurement make the learning disabilities field a pseudoscience? *Learning Disability Quarterly 28(2)*. 103–106.

Stein-Smith, Kathleen. 2019. Foreign language classes becoming more scarce. *The Conversation*, February 6. https://theconversation.com/foreign-language-classes-becoming-more-scarce-102235

Stuebing, Karla, Jack Fletcher, Lee Branum-Martin & David Francis. 2012. Evaluation of the technical adequacy of three methods for identifying specific learning disabilities based on cognitive discrepancies. *School Psychology Review 41(1)*. 3–22.

Stuebing, Karla, Jack Fletcher, Josette LeDoux, Reid Lyon, Sally Shaywitz & Bennett Shaywitz. 2002. Validity of IQ-discrepancy classifications of reading disabilities: A meta-analysis. *American Educational Research Journal 39(1)*. 469–518.

U.S. Office of Education. 1977. Definition and criteria for defining students as learning disabled. *Federal Register 42:250*, p. 65083. Washington, D.C: U.S. Government Printing Office.

U.S. Office of Education, National Center for Education Statistics. 2007. The condition of education. Digest of Education Statistics, 2007 (NCES 200-022). Washington, DC: Author.

Verhoeven, Ludo & Charles Perfetti (eds.). 2017. *Learning to read across languages and writing systems*. Cambridge, UK: Cambridge University Press.

13 L2 Anxiety: An Affective Factor or a Linguistic Variable?

Richard L. Sparks

Abstract: The idea of a special anxiety unique to learning L2s is popular as an explanation for more and less successful L2 achievement. Language learning (L2) anxiety is thought to cause negative emotions that interfere with speaking, comprehending, reading, and writing a L2. Researchers have developed instruments to measure anxiety for L2s. However, these instruments are confounded by students' L1 skills and L2 aptitude measured years prior to L2 coursework. In this chapter, research on the anxiety hypothesis, anxiety surveys, and empirically-based challenges to the anxiety hypothesis are reviewed. The chapter also presents the results of a new study on the relationship between L2 reading skills and language anxiety. The discussion focuses on the chain of evidence-based results generated over several years showing that L2 anxiety instruments are measuring students' L2 achievement, accurate self-perceptions of their reading and language learning skills, or both. Language skills are posited to be a confounding variable in L2 anxiety research. The chapter concludes by proposing that L2 learning is not contingent on the presence or absence of anxiety and that L2 learners will benefit from pedagogical methods that focus on teaching the language skills necessary for L2 competence.

Keywords: Language anxiety, language learning, language aptitude, FLCAS, FLRAS

13.1 Introduction

A number of theories have been proposed to explain the problems of students who exhibit L2 learning problems ranging from differences in personality, language aptitude, learning and cognitive styles, and affective characteristics. Since the 1980s, a prominent explanation for L2 learning problems has been a special type of anxiety–foreign language (L2) anxiety–that manifests itself only for L2 learning (Horwitz, Horwitz, & and Cope 1986). L2 anxiety is thought to cause negative emotional reactions and lead to problems in speaking, comprehending, reading, and writing the L2 (Gkonou, Daubney, and Dewaele 2017). L2 researchers have also developed surveys to determine the presence of anxiety for L2 learning generally, and L2 reading specifically.

Since the early 90s, Sparks and his colleagues have questioned the claims made by L2 educators about the role of anxiety in language learning (Sparks and Ganschow 1991). Their hypothesis for L2 learning, the Linguistic Coding Differences Hypothesis (LCDH; Sparks 1995, Sparks and Ganschow 1993), is consistent with Cummins' (1979) Linguistic Interdependence Hypothesis, that L1 and L2 have a common underlying foundation, and Linguistic Threshold Hypothesis, that the level of L2 proficiency is moderated by one's level of attainment in L1. The LCDH uses the Assumption of Specificity (AOS; Hall and Humphreys 1982) to propose that individual differences (IDs) in L2 learning must be reasonably related to the L2 task, that is, the underlying causal factors must be language-related and not extend too far into other domains of cognitive functioning. Sparks et al.'s studies have found that L2 anxiety instruments reflect students' L1 skills and L2 aptitude, that is, students with higher anxiety have weaker L1 skills and L2 aptitude, and vice versa (see Sparks, Luebbers et al. 2018; Sparks, Patton, & Luebbers 2018).

The outcome of studies involving L2 anxiety has implications for theory, measurement, research, and pedagogy in L2 education. Although researchers have found negative correlations between students' anxiety on the Foreign Language Classroom Anxiety Scale (FLCAS; Horwitz, Horwitz, and Cope 1986) and the Foreign Language Reading Anxiety Scale (FLRAS; Saito, Garza, and Horwitz 1999) and their L2 achievement, these instruments have also been found to be strongly related to students' L1 ability in primary school and their L2 aptitude, and to explain unique growth in students' L1 skills in elementary school several years prior to L2 coursework. These findings raise questions about whether L2 anxiety instruments are measuring an anxiety for language learning or IDs in language ability.

The purpose of this chapter is to examine the role of anxiety and language skills in L2 proficiency. The literature review examines *theories* about the role of anxiety in L2 learning, the *measurement* of anxiety, and *evidence* that supports and challenges the L2 anxiety hypothesis. Next, the results and findings of a longitudinal *research* study using hierarchical regression analyses to determine whether IDs on the FLRAS would explain unique variance in the growth of L2 reading comprehension skills over three years of L2 courses are presented. Then, the results of L2 anxiety studies are discussed in relation to whether L2 anxiety is an affective variable or a cognitive variable. The chapter concludes by exploring how confusion about the role of anxiety in L2 learning may affect L2 *pedagogy*.

13.2 Review of the Literature

There are two measures that have been featured prominently in the L2 anxiety literature, the Foreign Language Classroom Anxiety Scale and the Foreign Language

Reading Anxiety Scale. In the first two sections of the review, the content of and research with these instruments are examined.[1,2]

13.2.1 L2 Anxiety and the FLCAS: Theory, Measurement, and Research

The notion of L2 anxiety as a constraint in language learning has been examined by a number of researchers. In an early review of the literature on language anxiety, Scovel (1978) found inconsistent results for the relationship between anxiety and L2 learning. His review of studies showed positive relationships, no relationship, or negative relationships between L2 anxiety and L2 achievement, but he speculated that these ambiguous experimental results might be resolved by drawing a distinction between facilitating and debilitating anxiety.

In 1986, Horwitz and her colleagues developed a self-report survey, the Foreign Language Classroom Anxiety Scale (FLCAS) to assess the "degree of anxiety [in a FL] as evidenced by negative performance expectations and social comparisons, psychological symptoms, and avoidance behaviors" (Horwitz 1991: 37). The FLCAS is a 33-item, Likert-type scale designed to measure the anxiety level of L2 learners (Horwitz, Horwitz, and Cope 1986). In preliminary studies, they found that the FLCAS had acceptable internal consistency (r = .93) and test-retest reliability (r = .83) (Horwitz 1991). They also found that there were negative relationships between anxiety on the FLCAS and students' L2 course grades, and determined that anxiety explained approximately 25% of the variance in students' L2 grades. Researchers have used the FLCAS to investigate the relationship between anxiety and several outcome variables. For example, studies have found that there are significant negative correlations between the FLCAS and: 1) L2 course grades (Aida 1994; Arnaiz and Guillén 2012; Zhao, Dynia, and Guo 2013); 2) L2 anxiety levels across L2 proficiency levels (Marcos-Llinás and Garau 2009); and 3) students' L2 listening comprehension and L2 speaking skills (Elkhafaifi 2005; Hewett and Stephenson 2012; Philips 1992). Literature reviews have also reported that "good" language learners report higher levels of anxiety (Horwitz 2010; Tran 2012) and studies with L2 anxiety measures other than the FLCAS have yielded similar results (e.g., see MacIntyre and Gardner 1994a, b; Onwuegbuzie, Bailey, and Daley 1999).

A recent study performed a comprehensive search that identified 97 reports of studies on L2 anxiety and L2 achievement with a total of 105 independent

---

[1] Portions of the following section were published in Sparks, Patton, and Luebbers (2018). Permission was granted by the journal and its publisher for use in this chapter.
[2] Portions of the following section were published in Sparks et al. (2018). Permission was granted by the journal and its publisher for use in this chapter.

samples from 23 countries (Teimouri, Goetze, and Plonsky 2018). The authors conducted a meta-analysis of these studies and found evidence for the negative role of anxiety and nonlinguistic variables on L2 achievement. In another recent study, Zhang (2019) also performed a large meta-analysis with studies involving over 10,000 participants and found that the anxiety-performance correlation remained stable across groups with different L2 proficiency levels. However, the authors of both studies could not analyze the role of IDs in L1 skills and L2 aptitude because most studies they surveyed did not include L1 skills or L2 aptitude measures in their test batteries with the exceptions of Sparks and colleagues (Plonsky, personal communication; Zhang, personal communication). Recent investigations have yielded similar findings and concomitant limitations (Botes, Dewaele, and Greiff 2020; Otier and Al-Otaibi 2019).

13.2.2 L2 Anxiety and the FLRAS: Theory, Measurement, and Research

While the FLCAS proposes an anxiety specific to language learning generally, Saito, Garza, and Horwitz (1999) proposed an anxiety specific to L2 reading. They hypothesized that L2 reading anxiety is ". . . the anxiety that learners experience during the FL [L2] reading process and thus is related to the specific skill of reading" (Zhao, Guo, and Dynia 2013: 765). In their paper, Saito et al. introduced the Foreign Language Reading Anxiety Scale (FLRAS), which was designed to measure an anxiety distinct from general language anxiety measured by the FLCAS. The FLRAS is a 20-item survey that uses a Likert scale to elicit students' self-perceptions of anxiety about L2 reading difficulties compared to other L2 skills. In their pilot study, Saito et al. reported that the FLRAS and the FLCAS shared approximately 41% of the variance, i.e., $r = .64$. Because 59% of the variance was not shared by the instruments, they hypothesized that general anxiety about L2 learning was related to, but distinct from, L2 reading anxiety.

The FLRAS has been administered in several studies. For example, in a study with university students enrolled in Spanish, Brantmeier (2005) found that students at advanced stages of language instruction felt less anxious about reading the target language than they did about speaking and writing the language. In an investigation of elementary and intermediate level English-speaking university students studying Chinese, Zhao, Guo, and Dynia (2013) showed that L2 reading performance was negatively correlated with L2 reading anxiety. In another study with university L2 Spanish students, Sellers (2000) found that low anxious students recalled more passage reading content than students who reported higher levels of anxiety. In most studies conducted with the FLRAS in the U.S. and internationally, results have revealed varying levels of overlap between the FLRAS and the FLCAS as well as negative correlations between the FLRAS and L2 reading achievement (e.g., see Hadidi and Barzegar 2015; Matsuda and Gobel 2004; Matsumara 2001; Zhao, Guo, and Dynia 2013).

More recently, Li (2022) meta-analyzed the overall average correlations between L2 reading anxiety on the FLRAS and two high evidence correlates (language anxiety, reading performance) and two low-evidence correlates (reading self-efficacy, reading strategies). The results showed a moderate correlation between language anxiety and reading problems, and the two low-level correlates had moderate to large effect sizes. However, Li noted that other "equally important" variables such as L1 skills and L2 aptitude could not be analyzed because researchers other than Sparks et al. had not included these variables in their test batteries.

In the next section, we examine evidence that challenges the L2 anxiety hypothesis.

13.3 Challenges to the L2 Anxiety Hypothesis: Theory, Measurement, and Research

Although researchers have found negative relationships between L2 anxiety and L2 performance, others have challenged the implication that anxiety is a causal variable for L2 learning. For example, Sparks and Ganschow (1991) hypothesized that native language (L1) skills and L2 aptitude are confounding variables when considering the role of anxiety for L2 learning and speculated that students who report higher levels of anxiety would be found to demonstrate lower levels of language learning skills. They found that the 33 items on the FLCAS were related to students' receptive and expressive language skills, speed of language processing, and verbal memory ability and critiqued Horwitz et al. (1986) and others for failing to use comparison groups and control for participant's level of L1 skills and/or L2 aptitude (MLAT; Carroll & Sapon, 1959, 2001) in their studies (see Sparks and Ganschow 1995; Sparks and Patton 2013). They also contended that students' responses on the FLCAS and other L2 anxiety surveys reflected their self-perceptions of their language learning skills.

In the 1990s, Sparks et al. investigated these hypotheses in a series of studies with secondary and postsecondary learners using the FLCAS and measures of L1 skills, L2 aptitude, and L2 achievement and proficiency (Ganschow et al. 1994; Ganschow and Sparks 1996; Sparks et al. 1997). In each study, students who reported higher levels of anxiety on the FLCAS exhibited significantly weaker L1 skills and lower L2 aptitude on the MLAT, as well as significantly lower L2 achievement than students with lower levels of anxiety.

Studies with other anxiety instruments have been conducted. Sparks et al. conducted two studies using an author-designed instrument comprised of items related to students' language skills and affective characteristics designed to be completed by participants' L2 classroom teachers. In the first study, results showed that L2 teachers rated students with lower levels of L1 skills and L2 aptitude as having less positive affective characteristics, i.e., higher anxiety, lower motivation (Sparks and Ganschow 1996). Students who scored lower on L1 skill and L2 aptitude measures administered by the authors and were perceived by their teachers as having higher anxiety and achieved lower L2 course grades. In the second study, the students were followed through a second year of L2 courses, administered individualized measures of oral and written L2 proficiency, divided into high-average-low L2 proficiency groups, and compared on the teacher rating scale (Sparks et al., 2004). The findings showed that the average and low proficiency learners were perceived by the L2 teachers as having higher anxiety than the high proficiency L2 learners.

Sparks et al. also conducted a prospective, longitudinal study that followed students over 10 years, from 1st grade through 10th grade. In 1st–5th grades, they administered measures of L1 skills (reading, spelling, vocabulary), and an IQ test; in 9th grade, the MLAT, FLCAS, and an L1 reading comprehension measure; and, at end of 10th grade after two years of L2 courses, measures of L2 reading, writing, spelling, listening comprehension, and speaking proficiency. In one study, Sparks and Ganschow (2007) divided the students into high, average, and low anxiety groups based on their FLCAS scores and compared the groups on the aforementioned L1 and L2 measures. The findings showed that the groups exhibited significant overall differences on all L1 measures and that the low anxious group scored significantly higher than the high anxious group on all L1 measures as early as 2nd grade. The low anxious group also scored significantly higher than the high anxious group on measures of L2 aptitude, L2 proficiency, L2 achievement (course grades), and 10th grade L1 reading comprehension. In another study, the FLCAS was negatively correlated with all L1 measures as early as 1st grade, several years *before* the students had begun L2 courses (Sparks et al. 2009). Sparks et al. observed that if the FLCAS were measuring a "special" anxiety for L2 learning in high school, there would be no *a priori* reason for individual differences in L1 skills among the groups when they were in the primary grades and no plausible explanation for negative correlations between the FLCAS and measures of L1 skills in 1st grade, eight years *before* they were exposed to an L2 in high school.

In another study with these participants, Sparks and Patton (2013) used a full information maximum likelihood procedure (FIML) to investigate whether the FLCAS would explain unique variance in L1 skills and L2 aptitude and predict growth in L1 skills over time. They found that the FLCAS explained: a) significant unique variance in L1 skills from 1st–5th grades, many years *before* the students began the L2 in 9th grade, and b) significant unique variance on the MLAT and in L1 reading comprehension and language skills in 9th grade. Hierarchical regressions showed that the FLCAS explained unique variance in the growth of L1 reading, spelling, and language skills from 1st–5th grades and from elementary school to high school. Sparks et al. contended that if the FLCAS measured a unique anxiety for L2 learning, then IDs in L2 anxiety should not be related to L1 skills *many years prior to* enrolling in L2 courses, nor should the FLCAS predict unique variance in L1 skills or L2 aptitude.

Prior to conducting studies with the FLRAS, Sparks, Ganschow, and Javorsky (2000) critiqued Saito et al.'s studies with the instrument because: a) the FLRAS is comprised of 20 items asking about students' reading skills, leading to uncertainty about whether anxiety or reading is measured, b) the research design did not show participants were equivalent in language ability or level of anxiety, c) participants' L2 reading skills were not measured, and d) participants' L1 reading skill and/or L2 aptitude were not measured or controlled. In response, Horwitz et al. suggested that some individuals are "anxious about L2 learning independent of processing deficits" (Horwitz 2000: 256), but she cited only anecdotal evidence. Sparks et al. speculated that the outcome of studies with the FLRAS would be similar to those with the FLCAS.

In their first study with the FLRAS, U.S. high school L2 students were administered several measures of L1 skills (reading, writing, vocabulary, language analysis), L1 cognitive processing (working memory, metacognitive knowledge), L1 reading-related skills (print exposure, reading attitudes), L2 aptitude (MLAT), and L2 achievement (standardized measures of written and oral language L2 skills), then followed through two to three years of L2 courses (Sparks et al. 2018). They were administered the FLRAS at the end of 1st year Spanish, divided into three anxiety groups, and compared on all L1 measures, the L2 aptitude test, and the L2 achievement measures at the end of 1st, 2nd, and 3rd year Spanish courses. The findings showed that students who reported higher levels of anxiety scored significantly lower than the low anxiety students on all L1 measures and the MLAT, and significantly lower than the average anxiety students on most L2 measures at the end of 1st and 2nd year Spanish courses. The 3rd year Spanish students, all of whom scored in the low or average anxiety range, exhibited significantly stronger L1 achievement, cognitive processing, and reading-related skills, higher L2 aptitude, and stronger L2 achievement than the students who completed only 1st and 2nd year Spanish. The results suggested the FLRAS is likely to be measuring IDs in students' L1 skills and L2 aptitude, not their anxiety about L2 reading.

In another study with this population, Sparks, Patton, and Luebbers (2018) administered the FLRAS and the aforementioned measures of L1 skills, L2 aptitude, and L2 achievement and examined whether the FLRAS would: 1) explain unique variance in L1 achievement, L1 working memory, L1 metacognitive knowledge, L1 print exposure, and L1 reading attitudes, 2) explain unique variance in L2 aptitude, and 3) predict growth in L2 achievement over time. To answer the first two questions, the authors conducted a path analysis procedure which showed that the FLRAS explained unique variance in all of the aforementioned L1 skills and L2 aptitude. To answer the third question, a series of hierarchical regression analyses showed that the FLRAS predicted significant unique growth in L2 reading, spelling, writing, vocabulary, and listening comprehension from 1st to 2nd to 3rd year Spanish courses. Like the earlier studies, results suggested that the FLRAS is likely to be measuring IDs in students' L1 skills and L2 aptitude, their (accurate) self-perceptions of their language learning ability, or both but not an anxiety unique to L2 learning. Figure 1 presents a summary of Sparks et al.'s studies described in this section of the chapter.

Other researchers have also reported that students' scores on the FLCAS are related to their language learning ability. In a study with students whose L1 is Hebrew learning English, Argaman and Abu-Rabia (2002) found that language anxiety appeared to be the consequence, not a cause, of failure to learn English reading and writing. In a study with Taiwanese students learning English, Chen and Chang (2004) found that anxious students had a history of English learning problems and obtained low grades. In a recent investigation that examined the directionality of the association between L2 anxiety and L2 achievement, Alamer and Lee (2021) conducted a longitudinal study with Saudi undergraduates in English courses using a cross-lagged panel analysis. The study examined the causal relationship between L2 anxiety and L2 achievement, each of which was measured at three time points across 17 weeks. The results showed that language achievement preceded language anxiety, that is, the evidence did not support the claim that anxiety negatively affected future L2 achievement. Instead, the findings showed that language achievement predicts anxiety and not the other way around. In another recent study using structural equation modeling, Sparks and Alamer (2022) found that the effect of early L1 skills in elementary school on L2 anxiety in high school was indirect through L2 aptitude and L2 achievement, indicating the impact of L1 skills is better understood through the L2 mediators. The effect of L2 achievement on L2 anxiety was direct, and large in magnitude, and the results remained stable across different ages and invariant across gender. In a study with another group of students, Sparks and Alamer (in press) found that the effect of L1 skills on L2 anxiety in high school was indirect through L2 aptitude, L2 achievement, and L1 metacognitive knowledge, indicating the impact of L1 skills is better understood through these L1 and L2 mediators. In another investigation, Alamer, Sparks, and Alrabai (under review) found that a teaching method which focused on expanding students' vocabulary knowledge in the target L2 decreased language anxiety significantly in an experimental group while vocabulary knowledge remained stable among the control group. All of the aforementioned results suggest that language anxiety is likely to be the consequence of learners' language achievement and level of language aptitude and that language anxiety measures are indirectly measuring students' language learning skills, their self-perceptions of their language skills, or both.

Study	Participants	Anxiety Instrument	Results
Ganschow, Sparks et al., 1994	College students (n = 36)	FLCAS	Significant overall differences among Hi-Ave-Low Anxiety groups and between-group differences on L1 reading and oral language, MLAT tests
Ganschow & Sparks, 1996	High school (n = 154)	FLCAS	Significant overall differences among Hi-Ave-Low Anxiety groups on L1 reading, spelling, vocabulary, MLAT tests; L1 English and L2 course grades; significant differences between Hi-Low Anxiety groups on most measures
Sparks & Ganschow, 1996	High School (n = 168)	Author-designed	L2 teachers rated students with significantly lower L1 and MLAT scores and lower L1 English and L2 grades as having higher levels of anxiety; significant differences in anxiety between Hi-Low L1/L2 skill groups
Sparks, Ganschow, Artzer et al., 1997	High school (n = 60)	FLCAS	Significant overall and between- group differences among Hi-Ave-Low Anxiety groups on L2 reading, writing, speaking, and listening comprehension proficiency measures
Sparks, Ganschow, Artzer et al., 2004	High school (n = 101)	Author-designed	L2 teachers rated students with significantly lower scores on L2 reading, writing, speaking, and listening comprehension proficiency measures as having weaker L1 skills and higher levels of anxiety
Sparks & Ganschow, 2007	High school (n = 54)	FLCAS	Students followed over 10 years. Significant overall differences among Hi-Ave-Low Anxiety groups on all L1 skills and MLAT. Hi Anxiety group scored significantly lower than Low Anxiety group on all L1 measures beginning in 2nd grade. High Anxiety group scored significantly lower than Low Anxiety group on MLAT, all L2 proficiency tests

(continued)

Study	Participants	Anxiety Instrument	Results
Sparks, Patton, Ganschow et al., 2009	High school (n = 54)	FLCAS	Students followed over 10 years. FLCAS in high school was negatively correlated with L1 skills in elementary school many years prior to L2 courses in high school.
Sparks & Patton, 2013	High school (n = 128)	FLCAS	Students followed over 10 years. FLCAS accounted for significant unique variance in L1 skills in elementary school several years *before* the students' engaged in L2 study as well as significant unique variance on the MLAT and L1 skills measured in high school. Hierarchical regressions found that the FLCAS predicted growth in L1 skills (reading, spelling, language) from 1st-5th grades and from 5th grade reading to 10th grade reading.
Sparks, Luebbers, Patton, & Castañeda, 2018	High school, n = 266 completed two years and n = 51, completed three years of L2 courses	FLRAS	Students followed over 3 years and administered L1 skills, L1 cognitive processing (working memory, metacognitive knowledge), MLAT and norm-referenced measures of L2 achievement. Findings showed the Hi Anxiety group scored significantly lower than Low Anxiety group on all L1 and L2 measures, and significantly lower than the Ave Anxiety group on most L1 and L2 measures at end of 1st- and 2nd-year Spanish. 3rd year Spanish students achieved higher scores on MLAT and some L1 skill measures.

(continued)

Study	Participants	Anxiety Instrument	Results
Sparks, Patton, & Luebbers, 2018	High school, $n = 266$ completed two years, and $n = 51$ completed three years of L2 courses	FLRAS	Students followed over 3 years and administered L1 skills, L1 cognitive processing (working memory, metacognitive knowledge), L1 reading-related skills (print exposure), MLAT, and norm-referenced measures of L2 achievement. Path analysis showed that FLRAS explained significant unique variance in most L1 skills and L2 aptitude *prior to* L2 courses. Hierarchical regressions showed that FLRAS explained growth in L2 reading, spelling, vocabulary, writing, and listening from 1st to 2nd to 3rd year Spanish.
Sparks & Alamer, 2022	High school ($n = 54$)	FLCAS	SEM found that the effect of L1 skills on L2 anxiety in high school was indirect through L2 aptitude, L2 achievement, and L1 metacognitive knowledge, indicating the impact of L1 skills is better understood through these L1 and L2 mediators.

Figure 1: Summary of Studies on the Relationships Among L1 Skills, L2 Aptitude (MLAT), L2 Proficiency and Achievement, and L2 Anxiety.

In sum, Sparks et al. speculated that L2 anxiety instruments measure a broad construct that incorporates IDs in students' L1 skills and L2 aptitude *prior to* L2 coursework, IDs in self-perceptions of their language learning ability, or both. Their studies support the premises of Sparks et al.'s LCDH and Cummins' Linguistic Independence and Threshold Hypotheses. In addition, their studies have shown that students' levels of L2 anxiety on the FLCAS and FLRAS reflect their level of L2 aptitude and L2 achievement, i.e., lower anxiety and stronger language ability and vice versa, and suggest that language learning skills are confounding variables for the proposed role of anxiety in L2 learning.

13.4 Purpose of Study

IDs in students' responses on L2 anxiety instruments have been found to be strongly related to their L1 skills, L2 aptitude, and L2 proficiency and achievement. However, no studies have examined whether IDs on the FLRAS would explain the growth in students' L2 reading comprehension beyond the growth explained by skills found to predict reading in an alphabetic orthography. In reading research, the Simple View of Reading (SVR) model has been found to explain the cognitive skills necessary for learning to read and become proficient in an alphabetic orthography (Gough and Tunmer 1986; Hoover and Gough 1990; Hoover and Tunmer 2022). The SVR proposes that word decoding and listening (oral language) comprehension explain most of the variance in reading comprehension. Word decoding requires knowledge of the speech sounds in spoken words and the alphabetic system (letters) by which sounds are represented in print. Listening comprehension represents the linguistic processes used for comprehension of oral language. In some studies, vocabulary has been found to explain additional variance in reading comprehension. The SVR model proposes that decoding and listening comprehension make independent contributions to reading comprehension skills. In L1 reading research, the SVR model has earned voluminous empirical support for its accuracy in predicting students' reading skills (e.g., see Aouad and Savage 2009; Catts 2018; Kim 2015, 2017), and has been supported in many languages with varying orthographic depths including English, Chinese, Spanish, Greek, Korean, and Malay (see reviews by Bonifacci and Tobia 2017; Droop and Verhoeven 2003; Sparks and Luebbers 2018). When employing a latent variable approach, word decoding and listening comprehension have been found to explain the vast majority of variance in reading comprehension (Kim 2015; Foorman et al. 2015). Recent research has supported the tenets of SVR model for learning to read L2 alphabetic orthographies (Jeon and Yamashita 2014; Sparks 2015; Sparks and Patton 2016; Verhoeven and van Leeuwe 2012). Studies in L1/L2 have found that word decoding skill explains more variance in the early stages of learning to read, and the contribution of oral language (listening) comprehension increases in the later grades (e.g., see Francis et al. 2005).

The purpose of the present study is to examine through hierarchical regression analyses whether IDs on the FLRAS would explain unique variance in the growth of L2 reading comprehension skills from the end of 1st to 2nd to 3rd year Spanish beyond that explained by L2 word decoding, L2 listening comprehension, and L2 vocabulary. The outcome of this type of analysis in a longitudinal study could determine whether the FLRAS is measuring an anxiety specific to L2 reading or reflecting IDs in students' language learning skills, in this case, for L2 reading comprehension.

13.5 Method

13.5.1 Participants

The study began with 307 participants randomly chosen from those enrolled in 1st year Spanish courses at one of four high schools in a large suburban school district in the midwest near a metropolitan U.S. city. There were 154 males and 153 females whose mean age was 15 years, 7 months (ranged from 13 years, 7 months to 17 years, 6 months) enrolled in 9th, 10th and 11th grades. Participants included 301 Caucasian, four African-American, and two East Asian students. Two hundred and sixty-six (135 females and 131 males) of the 307 students completed both 1st and 2nd year Spanish, and 51 students (of the 266) completed 1st, 2nd and 3rd year Spanish (22 males and 29 females). Twenty-three of the 307 students did not complete 1st year Spanish, 12 students began but failed to complete 2nd year Spanish, and six students left the school district. All participants were monolingual English speakers with no prior experience in Spanish, were not routinely exposed to Spanish outside school, and spoke only English. Parental permission was obtained for each participant.

13.5.2 Testing Instruments

There were four instruments used to measure participants' L2 reading skills: word decoding, listening comprehension, vocabulary, and reading comprehension. A standardized measure of Spanish achievement, the *Batería III Woodcock-Muñoz Pruebas de aprovechamiento* (Woodcock et al. 2004, 2007) designed for students whose native language is Spanish, was used for measuring participants' Spanish skills in the aforementioned areas.

L2 (Spanish) word decoding. The measure of Spanish word decoding was the *Identificación de letras y palabras* subtest on which the student read aloud a list of increasingly difficult words. For a response to be correct, the student had to decode and pronounce the word correctly. The difficulty level of the words ranged from one-syllable (*vez, pan*) to two- and three-syllable (*joven, ciuidado*) and multisyllabic (*desalmado, municipalidad*) words. Testing continued until a student read six consecutive words incorrectly.

L2 (Spanish) reading comprehension. The measure of Spanish reading comprehension was the *Comprensión de textos* subtest. On the first four items, the student read a phrase (e.g., *casa grande*) and pointed to one (of four) pictures representing the meaning of the phrase. On the remaining items, the student read a short passage and identified a key missing word, i.e., a cloze procedure, which made sense in the context of the passage, e.g., *Luis y Rosa* ____ *amigos*. The items became increasingly difficult by removing picture stimuli and increasing passage length, level of vocabulary, and complexity of syntactic and semantic cues. Most items consist of 1–2 sentences. Testing continued until a student answered six consecutive items incorrectly.

L2 (Spanish) vocabulary. The measure of Spanish vocabulary was the *Vocabulario sobre dibujos* subtest, which measured an individual's speaking vocabulary in Spanish. On two items, the student pointed to one (of four) pictures after the examiner said a vocabulary word, e.g., *la estufa*. On the remaining items, the student identified by name the object shown in the picture. The items began with pictures of objects commonly found, e.g., hand, eye, spoon, to objects that appear less frequently in the environment, e.g., sun, pig, hammer, palm tree. Testing continued until a student was unable to identify six consecutive items.

L2 (Spanish) listening comprehension. The measure of oral (listening) comprehension was the *Comprension Oral* subtest. This subtest measured the ability to comprehend a short, audio-recorded passage and supply a missing word using syntactic and semantic cues. The missing word is located at the end of each item. This oral cloze procedure required the use of listening comprehension, verbal reasoning, and vocabulary skills. The test began with simple sentences, e.g. *Los niños estudian en la* ____, and progressed gradually to more complex passages, e.g., *Los vientos traen aire, los ríos traen* ____. Each item could be repeated twice. Testing continued until a student responded incorrectly to six consecutive items.

Foreign Language (L2) Reading Anxiety

The Foreign Language Reading Anxiety Scale (FLRAS) (Saito, Garza, and Horwitz 1999) was used to determine participants' anxiety for reading in a L2. The FLRAS has 20 items to which students respond on a 5-point Likert Scale ranging from "strongly agree" (5) to "neither agree nor disagree" (3) to "strongly disagree" (1) with a forced-choice, balanced-design format. Students' raw scores were calculated and transformed into z-scores, which were used in all subsequent analyses. The reliability of the FLRAS was checked by calculating Cronbach's alpha, which was .93. A list of FLRAS items is provided in the Appendix.

13.5.3 Procedure

The measures of Spanish reading achievement were administered individually to the participants at the end of 1st, 2nd, and 3rd year Spanish courses by the first author and graduate students trained by him. Participants' raw scores for the four measures were transformed to standard scores ($M = 100$, $SD = 15$) using the *Woodcock-Johnson-III* Normative Update Compuscore and Profiles Program Version 3.1 (Schrank and Woodcock 2008). Because the *Woodcock-Munoz* is a standardized, norm-referenced test calibrated to measure the skills of native Spanish speakers, norms are available for a wide range of grade levels. For this study, participants' scores according to 9th grade native Spanish speaker norms were used.

The FLRAS was administered individually to each participant at the end of 1st year Spanish by the first author and graduate students trained by him.

13.5.4 Results

Table 1 reports the scores of the participants on the Spanish measures. Table 2 presents correlations among the four *Woodcock-Muñoz* subtests and the FLRAS at the end of 1st, 2nd, and 3rd year Spanish courses.

Table 1: Means and Standard Deviations on the L2 Measures for Participants Who Completed 1st, 2nd, and 3rd Year Spanish.

Measure	First-Year		Second-Year		Third-Year	
	M	SD	M	SD	M	SD
L2 Word Decoding[a]	52.8	24.4	70.4	22.4	83.1	14.6
L2 Reading Comprehension[a]	2.4	3.9	6.8	8.8	14.0	12.0
L2 Vocabulary[a]	6.4	6.6	13.1	8.8	17.9	8.6
L2 Listening Comprehension[a]	18.8	9.3	27.2	10.2	34.7	7.2

[a]Standard Scores, $M = 100$, $SD = 15$.
[b]$n = 266$.
[c]$n = 51$.

Hierarchical regression analyses were conducted to examine whether IDs on the FLRAS predicted growth in L2 reading comprehension from 1st–2nd year, 1st–3rd year, and 2nd–3rd year Spanish courses. The regression analyses specified a fixed order of entry for variables to control for the effects of covariates and to test the effects of the FLRAS independent of the influence of other predictor variables. The fixed order of entry for the predictor variables–Spanish word decoding, then Spanish listening comprehension, then Spanish vocabulary–was consistent with L1 and L2 reading research and the SVR model, which have shown that word decoding skill explains more variance in the early stages of learning to read, and that the contribution of oral language

Table 2: Intercorrelations among the FLRAS and the L1 Skill and L2 Achievement Measures.

Measure	1	2	3	4	5	6	7	8	9	10	11	12	13
1. L2 Decoding-1	–	.31	.21	.38	.43	.30	.40	.47	.49	.34	.30	.47	–.32**
2. L2 Reading Comp-1	–	–	.10	.37	.30	.43	.30	.30	.51	.50	.34	.48	–.19**
3. L2 Vocabulary-1	–	–	–	.22	.08	.30	.60	.18	.21	.32	.48	.29	–.31**
4. L2 Listen Comp-1	–	–	–	–	.44	.29	.34	.45	.37	.34	.31	.34	–.26**
5. L2 Decoding-2	–	–	–	–	–	.40	.23	.63	.70	.45	.28	.58	–.38**
6. L2 Read Comp-2	–	–	–	–	–	–	.47	.72	.54	.63	.56	.71	–.37**
7. L2 Vocabulary-2	–	–	–	–	–	–	–	.45	.33	.57	.72	.52	–.37**
8. L2 Listen Comp-2	–	–	–	–	–	–	–	–	.62	.68	.45	.66	–.35**
9. L2 Decoding-3	–	–	–	–	–	–	–	–	–	.54	.46	.66	–.39**
10. L2 Reading Comp-3	–	–	–	–	–	–	–	–	–	–	.64	.74	–.65**
11. L2 Vocabulary-3	–	–	–	–	–	–	–	–	–	–	–	.67	–.52**
12. L2 Listen Comp-3	–	–	–	–	–	–	–	–	–	–	–	–	–.59**
13. FLRAS	–	–	–	–	–	–	–	–	–	–	–	–	–

Note. FLRAS = Foreign Language Reading Anxiety Scale
Note. 1 = 1st Year, 2 = 2nd Year, 3 = 3rd Year
Note. All correlations ≥ .15 are significant at $p < .01$; all correlations from ≥ .12–.15, significant at $p < .05$ level; all correlations below .12 are $p > .05$.

(listening) comprehension and vocabulary increases in the later grades. Three analyses were performed using the participants' scores on the Spanish word decoding, listening comprehension, vocabulary, and reading comprehension measures and the FLRAS to determine whether the FLRAS would predict growth in Spanish reading comprehension after the variance explained by Spanish word decoding, listening comprehension, and vocabulary in previous years had been partialed.

In the first forced entry regression analysis, 1st year Spanish word decoding, listening comprehension, and vocabulary were entered as predictors of Spanish reading comprehension, followed by the FLRAS. The results showed that the FLRAS accounted for additional unique variance (4.1%, $p < .01$) in 2nd year Spanish reading comprehension. Table 3 presents the analysis for 1st to 2nd year Spanish reading comprehension.

In the second forced entry regression analysis, 1st year Spanish word decoding, listening comprehension, and vocabulary were entered as predictors of Spanish reading comprehension, followed by the FLRAS. The results showed that the FLRAS accounted for additional unique variance (30.1%, $p < .01$) in 3rd year Spanish reading comprehension. Table 4 presents the analyses for 1st to 2nd year, 1st to 3rd year, and 2nd to 3rd year Spanish reading comprehension.

In the third forced entry regression analysis, 2nd year Spanish word decoding, listening comprehension, and vocabulary were entered as predictors of Spanish reading comprehension, followed by the FLRAS. The results showed that the FLRAS accounted for additional unique variance (6.8%, $p < .01$) in 3rd year Spanish reading comprehension. Table 5 presents the analyses for 1st to 2nd year, 1st to 3rd year, and 2nd to 3rd year Spanish reading comprehension.

Predictors of L2 Reading Comprehension Over Time from 1st to 2nd to 3rd Year Spanish

Table 3: Criterion Variable Year 2, L2 Reading Comprehension-Year 2.

Step/Variable	R	ΔR^2	ΔF	Final ß	Final F
1. L2 Word Decode-Yr 1	0.3348	.1121	33.20**	0.1173	3.842**
2. L2 Listening Comp-Yr 1	0.4614	.1008	33.35**	0.2702	19.448**
3. L2 Vocabulary-Yr 1	0.4870	.0243	8.32**	0.1235	4.326**
4. FLRAS	0.5278	.0414	14.90**	0.0413	14.900**

Table 4: Criterion Variable Year 3, L2 Reading Comprehension-Year 3.

Step/Variable	R	ΔR^2	ΔF	Final ß	Final F
1. L2 Word Decode-Yr 1	0.3372	.1137	6.03*	.1185	1.061*
2. L2 Listening Comp-Yr 1	0.4099	.0543	3.00	.2192	3.686
3. L2 Vocabulary-Yr 1	0.4650	.0482	2.77	.1754	2.592
4. FLRAS	0.7197	.3018	7.54**	.5606	27.563**

Table 5: Criterion Variable Year 3, L2 Reading Comprehension-Year 3.

Step/Variable	R	ΔR^2	ΔF	Final ß	Final F
1. L2 Word Decode-Yr 2	.4656	.2168	13.56**	.0960	0.723**
2. L2 Listening Comp-Yr 2	.6759	.2401	21.21**	.3255	6.350**
3. L2 Vocabulary-Yr 2	.7533	.1106	12.02**	.2747	6.864**
4. FLRAS	.7973	.0681	8.60**	.3211	8.585**

* $p < .05$ ** $p < .01$

13.6 Discussion

In this longitudinal investigation, participants were administered measures of L2 (Spanish) reading skills at the end of the 1st, 2nd, and 3rd year Spanish courses and a measure of L2 reading anxiety, the FLRAS, at the end of 1st year Spanish. The purpose of the study was to determine whether IDs in reading anxiety on the FLRAS would explain growth in L2 reading comprehension over time after the variance explained by skills directly related to reading–word decoding, listening (oral language) comprehension, vocabulary – and to explain the bulk of the variance for reading comprehension in the SVR model had been partialed.

The answer to the research question was positive. Findings showed that the FLRAS accounted for unique variance in the growth of L2 reading comprehension skills from the end of 1st to 2nd year (4%), 1st to 3rd year (30%) and 2nd to 3rd year (7%) Spanish courses. In a previous study with these L2 learners, the FLRAS explained unique variance in the growth of L2 achievement in Spanish oral and written language skills over time (Sparks, Patton, and Luebbers 2018). However, in that study, a predictor variable, e.g., 1st year L2 reading comprehension, was entered first followed only by the FLRAS in order to explain the growth in 2nd year and 3rd year L2 reading comprehension. But, in the present study, predictor variables that have been found by reading researchers to explain the vast majority of variance in reading comprehension–word decoding, oral language (listening) comprehension, vocabulary–were entered first as predictors of L2 reading comprehension, followed by the FLRAS. Even though the aforementioned three variables have long been found by researchers to explain the bulk of the variance in reading comprehension for several L2s, the FLRAS explained additional unique variance in the growth of L2 reading comprehension from the end of 1st to 2nd to 3rd year Spanish courses. The findings raise the question of whether the additional variance explained by the FLRAS is a measure of students' anxiety, their language skills, or their (accurate) self-perceptions of their language ability.

In two previous studies with this group of participants (Sparks et al. 2018; Sparks, Patton, and Luebbers 2018), findings revealed that IDs in students' anxiety levels on the FLRAS measured *after* exposure to L2 coursework were strongly related to IDs in L1 achievement, L1 cognitive processing (e.g., working memory), and L2 aptitude measured *prior to* L2 coursework. Students' IDs on the FLRAS measured *after* exposure to L2 coursework reflected their IDs in L1 achievement, L1 cognitive processing skills, and L2 aptitude measured *prior to* L2 coursework, i.e., students with the highest level of anxiety had the lowest L1 skills and L2 aptitude, and vice versa. In addition, IDs in anxiety on the FLRAS measured *after* exposure to L2 coursework predicted unique variance in L1 achievement, L1 cognitive processing, and L2 aptitude measured *prior to* L2 coursework. The aforementioned findings show that students' levels of L1 achievement, L1 cognitive processing, and L2 aptitude *preceded* the time at which their L2 anxiety was measured, i.e., *before* they were exposed to the L2. These findings suggest that the growth in L2 reading comprehension attributed to the FLRAS (and FLCAS in previous studies) is likely due to students' language learning ability, their self-perceptions of their language learning ability, or both. Anxiety proponents might claim that these results show that the FLRAS has a significant role in understanding L2 achievement growth. But then, they would have to concede that a survey that purports to measure anxiety also measures language ability, L2 or otherwise, since the growth was in language achievement.

Sparks et al. have conducted a number of studies with the FLRAS and FLCAS. Figure 2 presents a summary of these studies with the results. Over time, the findings have supported a chain of evidence showing that: 1) items on the FLRAS and FLCAS are related to language learning and reading ability, 2) IDs in anxiety are strongly related to IDs in L1 skills, L2 aptitude, and L2 achievement and proficiency, 3) IDs in anxiety measured in high school are related to IDs in students' L1 skills several years *prior to* beginning L2 courses, 4) IDs in anxiety measured in high school explain unique variance in L1 skills in elementary school, 5) IDs in anxiety measured in high school explain the growth in L1 skills from 1st–5th grades, and 6) IDs in anxiety measured in high school explain the growth in L1 reading comprehension from 5th–10th grades. The results of the present study add another link in this chain of evidence. The proposition that the variance explained by the FLRAS for L2 reading comprehension is unrelated to anxiety may seem counterintuitive. However, Sparks et al. have contended that if the FLRAS (and FLCAS) is measuring a unique anxiety for L2 learning, IDs in L2 anxiety measured when enrolled in L2 courses in high school should *not* be found to be related to IDs in L1 skills that were measured *prior to* L2 courses (see Sparks et al., 2018; Sparks, Patton, & Luebbers 2018). In addition, IDs in L2 anxiety measured by the FLRAS (or FLCAS) should *not* explain unique variance in L1 skills or L2 aptitude measured *prior to* L2 study (see Sparks and Ganschow 2007; Sparks and Patton 2013). In several studies, the FLCAS and FLRAS have failed to meet these common sense criteria. Given the aforementioned chain of evidence, the finding that the FLRAS explains unique variance in the growth of L2 reading comprehension is not surprising since this instrument is likely to be a proxy measure for students' L2 reading ability, a measure of their self-perceptions of their L2 reading ability, or both. The accumulated findings from the present study, Sparks et al.'s studies from 1994–2018, and the recent studies by Alamer and Lee (2021) and Sparks and Alamer (2022 in press) provide powerful evidence that FLRAS, and other L2 anxiety instruments, are measuring something other than anxiety.

In an earlier paper, Sparks and Patton (2013) suggested that evidence contradicting the L2 anxiety hypothesis presents a dilemma for its proponents. The dilemma is whether to maintain the position that a "special" anxiety unique to L2 learning is a cause of more or less successful L2 learning and that L2 anxiety

FLCAS	FLRAS
Comprised of 33 items related to language learning ability	Comprised of 20 items related to reading ability
Significant differences among Hi-Ave-Low anxiety groups in L1 skills	Significant differences among Hi-Ave-Low anxiety groups in L1 skills
Significant differences among Hi-Ave-Low anxiety groups in L2 aptitude	Significant differences among Hi-Ave-Low anxiety groups in L2 aptitude
Significant differences among Hi-Ave-Low anxiety groups in L2 proficiency	Significant differences among Hi-Ave-Low anxiety groups in L2 proficiency
Significant differences among Hi-Ave-Low anxiety groups in L1 skills many years prior to L2 courses	Significant differences among Hi-Ave-Low anxiety groups in L1 skills and L2 aptitude one year prior to L2 courses
Significant differences among Hi-Ave-Low anxiety groups in L2 aptitude measured prior to L2 courses	IDs in anxiety in high school explain unique variance in L1 skills and L2 aptitude measured prior to L2 courses
IDs in anxiety in high school explain unique variance in L1 skills measured many years prior to L2 courses	IDs in anxiety in high school explain unique variance in L1 cognitive working memory, metacognitive knowledge prior to L2 courses
IDs in anxiety in high school explain unique variance in growth of L1 skills from 1st–5th grades	IDs in anxiety in high school explain unique variance in L1 reading-related skills (print exposure, reading attitudes)
IDs in anxiety in high school explain unique variance in growth of L1 reading comprehension from 5th–10th grades	IDs in anxiety explain unique variance in growth in oral/written L2 skills over three years of L2 courses
Effect of early L1 skills in elementary school on L2 anxiety in high school was indirect through L2 aptitude and L2 achievement. Effect of L2 achievement on L2 anxiety was direct, and large in magnitude. Results remained stable across different ages and invariant across gender	IDs in anxiety explain unique variance in growth of L2 reading comprehension after growth explained by L2 word decoding, oral language comprehension, and vocabulary had been partialed
	Effect of L1 skills on L2 anxiety in high school was indirect through L2 aptitude, L2 achievement, and L1 metacognitive knowledge, indicating the impact of L1 skills is better understood through these L1 and L2 mediators. Results remained invariant across gender

Figure 2: Summary of Sparks et al.'s Results with FLCAS and FLRAS (1991–2022).

instruments measure anxiety rather than IDs in students' language skills and/or self-perceptions of their language learning ability. The conundrum for the L2 anxiety hypothesis is its confounding variable problem. A confounding variable is one that a researcher fails to control, or eliminate, that damages the internal validity of a study. A study's results may show a false (spurious) correlation between the two variables. Figure 3 depicts the third variable problem in L2 anxiety research and the confounding variables supported by empirical evidence undermining the hypothesis. To date, anxiety researchers have not considered whether a third variable might affect students' responses to L2 anxiety surveys. For example, Horwitz (2010) constructed a timeline of 44 milestones in the development of the L2 anxiety hypothesis, but the studies had not controlled for IDs in participants' language learning ability. Likewise, a review of the L2 anxiety literature by Trang (2012) did not cite empirical studies that measured and controlled for IDs in participants' language learning ability. Moreover, the recent meta-analyses of L2 anxiety studies conducted by Teimouri, Goetze, & Plonsky (2018), Zhang (2019), Botes, Dewaele, and Greiff (2020), and Li (2022) could not analyze the role of IDs in language ability because anxiety studies did not include measures of L1 skills and/or L2 aptitude. While the L2 anxiety hypothesis continues to generate considerable attention, to date, the author is unaware of studies that have avoided the confounding variable problem except for those by Sparks and his colleagues.[3]

Previously, Sparks et al. have proposed several ways in which anxiety researchers could provide evidence to falsify the claim that IDs in L2 achievement are due primarily to IDs in language skills and also provide support for the L2 anxiety hypothesis (Sparks 1995; Sparks and Ganschow 1995; Sparks and Patton 2013). For example, they could conduct studies showing that students with significantly weaker L1 skills and/or L2 aptitude and report high levels of anxiety can have their anxiety reduced and achieve L2 proficiency at the level of students with stronger L1 skills and L2 aptitude. They could also conduct studies showing that there are no differences in L1 skills and L2 aptitude among students reporting differences in their anxiety levels for L2 learning. Or, they could design measures of L2 anxiety that do not explain unique variance or predict growth in students' L1 skills measured several years *prior to* engaging in L2 coursework. Small numbers of students reporting low anxiety and exhibiting poor L2 achievement or reporting high anxiety and exhibiting strong L2 achievement will be present in all academic subjects, including L2

---

[3] L2 anxiety researchers have claimed that educators must "go beyond the [language] aptitude domain to understand the many sources of anxiety. . ." (MacIntyre 2017: 21). But, L2 anxiety proponents have not followed their own advice by conducting studies including measures of L2 anxiety and L2 achievement *and* L1 skills and/or L2 aptitude.

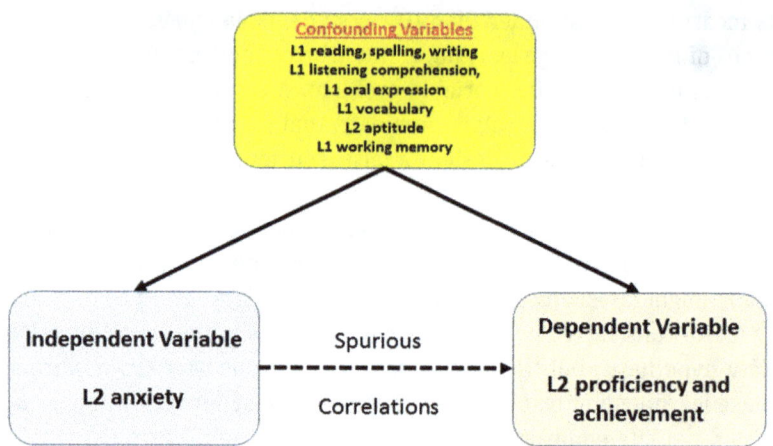

Figure 3: Depiction of the third (confounding) variable in L2 anxiety research.

learning. Anomalies aside, Sparks et al. have demonstrated that IDs on L2 anxiety surveys are related to IDs in L1 skills and L2 aptitude.

13.7 Pedagogical Implications

IDs in students' L2 learning skills–cognitive, social, and affective–have been studied for many years (Dornyei 2009). Research in ID factors such as learning styles, learning strategies, and personality have suffered from conceptual problems and conflicting results (Dornyei and Skehan 2003), and variables such as anxiety are confounded by students' L1 skills and L2 aptitude. Proposed causal connections between anxiety and language learning persist despite contrary evidence suggests, which suggests that L2 educators are interpreting new evidence as confirmation of the hypothesis, ignoring disconfirming evidence, and/or failing to consider alternative explanations. These responses have important pedagogical implications for teaching L2s, three of which are described here.

First, If IDs in language learners' skills are ignored, L2 educators will be unaware that IDs in Learners' anxiety stems from IDs in language skills. L2 educators should be aware that students, even from very early ages, exhibit IDs in their language skills. L2 teachers have often been taught that while ". . . children vary in their rate of [L1] acquisition . . . all, except in the case of severe environmental deprivation, achieve full competence in their mother tongue" (Ellis 2004: 525). However, this view of L1 learning is misguided. Although most children do learn to communicate effectively in their L1, they display normal variation in their rate of acquisition and communication skills, e.g., size of vocabulary, complexity of sentence structures (e.g., Gilkerson et al. 2017; Hoff 2013; Huttenlocher et al. 2010; Kidd, Donnelly, and Christiansen 2018). Moreover, IDs in L1 skills are large and stable across development (Bates, Dale, and Thal 1995; Bornstein and Putnick 2012). Thus, students display important differences in their L1 skills *before* entering the L2 classroom, and IDs in L1 skills have been found to be related to later L2 aptitude and L2 achievement.

Second, if L2 educators are unaware that the IDs in anxiety of more and less successful L2 learners are language-related, they may use pedagogical methods based on falsified theories, e.g., learning styles, cognitive styles, or employ unproven strategies, e.g., raising self-esteem, modifying learner beliefs, that are unrelated to mastery of language skills. Sparks et al. have used the Assumption of Specificity (AOS; Hall and Humphreys 1982) to illustrate the point that the skills necessary for language learning are domain-specific, that is, they are language-related because L2 learning is the learning of language. They have criticized the L2 anxiety hypothesis because anxiety is not specific to language skills or to learning a language. In L1 research, there is no evidence that anxiety plays a role in learning to read or that reducing anxiety improves reading or language skills. Language learning has domain-specific cognitive demands that are not contingent on the presence, or absence, of anxiety.

Third, if L2 teachers assume that differences in students' anxiety are the cause of more and less successful language learning, the probability of teaching the language skills necessary for mastery of an L2 will be diminished. Researchers have shown that the cognitive skills for reading are language-based and that pedagogy for teaching reading should be focused on teaching the domain-specific (language) skills for learning to read (Hoover and Tunmer 2022; Kilpatrick 2015; Stanovich 2000). Like L1 alphabetic orthographies, the skills necessary for learning to read an alphabetic L2 are those related to word decoding and oral language comprehension. Once they learn to decode printed words, students can make use of linguistic processes and knowledge to comprehend the meaning. Debates about how children learn to read print and whether or not reading instruction should emphasize teaching the "skills" necessary for decoding printed words (see Rayner et al. 2002) have often been contentious. However, the empirical evidence has converged around findings showing that children do not learn to read naturally and that the skills for reading (spelling, writing) are best taught directly and explicitly (see Petscher et al. 2020; Seidenberg 2017). Sparks et al. have found that methods that teach the sound-symbol relationships, grammar, and vocabulary of an L2 directly and explicitly, i.e., form-focused instruction, not only improve students' reading skills but also their use and understanding of oral language in the L2 (see Sparks, Artzer et al. 1998). [See also, Sparks (2021) for an explanation of how the SVR model applies to assess students' L2 reading skills in alphabetic orthographies.]

13.8 Conclusions

Horwitz (2010) claims it is "intuitive that anxiety would inhibit the learning and/or production of a second language (L2)" (p. 154). However, empirical evidence has not supported the claim of an anxiety related specifically to language learning. Intuition aside, the claim of a unique anxiety for L2 learning is reminiscent of other special types of anxiety. For example, while "test anxiety" is a familiar explanation for poor scores on classroom and standardized tests, empirical research has not found that test anxiety is a discrete entity (see Lovett & Nelson, 2017), and has shown instead that IDs in anxiety are mediated by IDs in working memory (e.g., see Owens et al. 2012). Likewise, while "math anxiety" is a common explanation for poor performance in math, researchers have found that anxiety about math is negatively correlated with math proficiency (Chang and Beilock 2016) and that cognitive factors, i.e., low math aptitude, low working memory, are associated with anxiety for math (Ashcraft and Krause 2007). Like test anxiety and math anxiety, language anxiety has been shown to be strongly related to cognitive factors. Unfortunately, L2 anxiety is a malleable concept that purportedly includes a surfeit of affective characteristics, e.g., avoidance, safety-seeking, perfectionism, self-esteem, identity, coping (Gkonu, Daubney, & Dawaele 2017: 224).[4] L2 anxiety theory presents problems in explaining L2 learning because it holds the potential to include or exclude anything, or to predict everything. Therefore, it will not explain anything. Platt (1964) suggests that "a theory is not a theory unless it can be disproved; that is, unless it can be falsified by some experimental outcome" (p. 350). To date, researchers have resisted or ignored, experimental outcomes that are not congenial to the L2 anxiety hypothesis.

In sum, the evidence from the present study and others conducted over many years has shown that L2 learning differences are due largely to IDs in

---

[4] The field of second language acquisition (SLA) seems increasingly enamored with socio-emotional explanations for L2 learning, e.g., see *Positive Psychology in SLA* (MacIntyre, Gregersen, and Mercer 2016); Gkonu, Daubney, and Dewaele (2017), with chapters on perfectionism, self-esteem, nonverbal cues, self-image, and social anxiety. The danger of L2 educators' attribution of more/less successful L2 learning to socio-emotional explanations is they pose as uncredentialed mental health pundits, not language learning experts, and present normal, everyday IDs in L2 learning as a quasi-clinical issue, rather than a parallel to IDs in language, mathematics, scientific reasoning, and all other cognitive functions.

students' language learning skills, not anxiety. Instead, anxiety reflects students' L1 ability and L2 aptitude. For the anxiety hypothesis to attain scientific credibility as an explanation for IDs in L2 learning, L2 researchers should accept the challenges presented in this chapter. If they cannot or are unwilling to do so, L2 educators should look elsewhere for explanations for more and less successful L2 learning. The evidence has shown that those explanations are related to IDs in students' language learning ability.

Appendix: FLRAS items

Directions: Statements 1 through 20 refer to how you feel about *reading* Spanish. For each statement, please indicate whether you (1) strongly agree, (2) agree, (3) neither agree nor disagree, (4) disagree, or (5) strongly disagree by writing the appropriate number on the line by each statement. Write an answer for every statement.

___ 1. I get upset when I'm not sure whether I understand what I am reading in Spanish,
___ 2. When reading Spanish, I often understand the words but still can't quite understand what the author is saying.
___ 3. When I'm reading Spanish, I get so confused I can't quite remember what I'm reading.
___ 4. I feel intimidated whenever I see a whole page of Spanish in front of me.
___ 5. I am nervous when I am reading a passage in Spanish when I am not familiar with the topic.
___ 6. I get upset whenever I encounter unknown grammar when reading Spanish.
___ 7. When reading Spanish, I get nervous and confused when I don't understand every word.
___ 8. It bothers me to encounter words I can't pronounce while reading Spanish.
___ 9. I usually end up translating word by word when I'm reading Spanish.
___ 10. By the time you get past the funny letters and symbols in Spanish, it's hard to remember what you're reading.
___ 11. I am worried about all the new symbols you have to learn in order to read Spanish
___ 12. I enjoy reading Spanish.

___ 13. I feel confident when I am reading in Spanish.
___ 14. Once you get used to it, reading Spanish is not so difficult.
___ 15. The hardest part of learning Spanish is learning to read.
___ 16. I would be happy just to learn to speak Spanish rather than having to learn to read as well.
___ 17. I don't mind reading to myself, but I feel very uncomfortable when I have to read Spanish.
___ 18. I am satisfied with the level of reading ability in Spanish that I have achieved so far.
___ 19. Spanish culture and ideas seem very foreign to me.
___ 20. You have to know so much about Spanish history and culture in order to read Spanish.

Recommended Readings

Sparks, Richard & Leonore Ganschow. 1991. Foreign language learning differences: Affective or native language aptitude differences? *Modern Language Journal 75(1)*. 3–16.

In their first paper on this topic, Sparks and Ganschow review the literature on affective factors in L2 learning. In particular, one affective variable, anxiety, is selected for discussion to illustrate their position that L1 achievement may have an impact on an individual's affect when learning an L2. They review Horwitz's FLCAS and show that the items are intimately connected to students' language learning skills. They also review a body of research on L2 aptitude supporting their view that a link exists between L1 learning and L2 aptitude. They present arguments for the examination of L2 learning problems in the context of L1 learning difficulties and propose a new alternative, the Linguistic Coding Deficit Hypothesis.

Sparks, Richard & Leonore Ganschow. 1995. A strong inference approach to causal factors in foreign language learning: A response to MacIntyre. *Modern Language Journal 79(2)*. 235–244.

Authors respond to criticism of their position that language anxiety is a consequence of L1 achievement by using a "strong inference" approach (Platt, 1964). They contend that the ability to use and understand language, rather than affective variables, is the more important causal factor in L2 learning. They explain how a theoretical concept, the Assumption of Specificity, which holds that the locus of L2 learning problems (or success) is reasonably specific to the L2 task, explains more and less success in L2. They summarize the evidence supporting connections between L1 and L2 learning and use the strong inference approach to describe ways researchers could draw more conclusive inferences about the role of language and affective variables for L2 learning.

Sparks, Richard & Leonore Ganschow. 2007. Is the Foreign Language Classroom Anxiety Scale measuring anxiety or language skills? *Foreign Language Annals 40(2)*. 260–287.

The authors report results of a longitudinal study over 10 years in which 54 students were followed and tested with L1 measures in 1st–5th grades and measures of L2 aptitude, L2 anxiety, and L2 achievement in high school. Findings showed that low anxious learners scored significantly higher than high anxious learners on all L1 measures beginning in 2nd grade, and significantly higher than high anxious learners on all L2 aptitude and L2 achievement measures. The FLCAS was negatively correlated with L1 measures of reading, spelling, and vocabulary as early as the beginning of 1st grade, many years before L2 courses. Findings showed that L1 differences among the groups were longstanding and stable and suggested that the FLCAS is likely measuring students' language ability, their perceptions of their language learning skills, or both. Language skills are likely to be a confounding variable for the study of L2 anxiety.

Sparks, Richard & Jon Patton. 2013. Relationship of L1 skills and L2 aptitude to L2 anxiety on the Foreign Language Classroom Anxiety Scale. *Language Learning 63*(4). 870–895.

The FLCAS has been challenged on the grounds that it assesses language learning skills. In this study, 128 students who had been administered measures of L1 skills in elementary school were followed from 1st to 10th grade. Fifty-four students had completed L2 courses in high school where they were administered the MLAT, FLCAS, and additional measures of L1 skills. A Full Information Likelihood Procedure (FIML) was used to conduct a path analysis and hierarchical regressions. Results showed that the FLCAS accounted for significant unique variance in L1 skills in elementary school several years *before* the students' engaged in L2 study, and significant unique variance on the MLAT and L1 skills measured in high school. The FLCAS predicted growth in L1 skills in elementary school, and also from elementary to high school. The authors concluded that there is no *a priori* reason an anxiety instrument should predict growth in L1 skills or explain variance in L2 aptitude. Findings suggested that the FLCAS is measuring individual differences in students' language skills and/or self-perceptions about their language learning skills rather than anxiety unique to L2 learning.

References

Aida, Yukie. 1994. Examination of Horwitz, Horwitz, and Cope's construct of foreign language anxiety: The case of students of Japanese. *Modern Language Journal 78*(2). 155–168.
Alamer, Abdullah & Jihyun Lee. 2021. Language achievement predicts anxiety and not the other way around: A cross-lagged panel analysis approach. Language Teaching Research.https://doi.org/10.1177/1362168821103369
Alamer, Abdullah, Richard Sparks & F. Alrabai. 2022. Increasing language vocabulary decreases language anxiety: A new experimental study using the dual domains latent growth curve modeling method. (Manuscript under review)
Aouad, Julie & Robert Savage. 2009. The component structure of preliteracy skills: Further evidence for the Simple View of Reading. *Canadian Journal of School Psychology 24 (2)*. 183–200.
Argaman, Osnat & Salim Abu-Rabia. 2002. The influence of language anxiety on English reading and writing tasks among native Hebrew speakers. *Language Culture and Curriculum 15*(2). 143–160.
Arnaiz, Patricia & Félix Guillén. 2012. Foreign language anxiety in a Spanish university setting: Interpersonal differences. *Revista de Psicodidáctica 17*(1). 5–26.
Ashcraft, Mark & Jeremy Krause. 2007. Working memory, math performance, and math anxiety. *Psychonomic Bulletin & Review 14*. 243–248.
Bates, Elizabeth, Philip Dale & Donna Thal. 1995. Individual differences and their implications for theories of language development. *Handbook of Child Language* 30. 96–151.

Bonifacci, Paolo & Valentina Tobia. 2017. The simple view of reading in bilingual language-minority children acquiring a highly transparent second language. *Scientific Studies of Reading 21(2)*, 109–119.

Bornstein, Marc & Diane Putnick. 2012. Stability of language in childhood: A multiage, multidomain, multimeasure, and multisource study. *Developmental Psychology 48(2)*. 477–491.

Botes, Eloise, Jean-Marc Dewaele, & Samuel Greiff. 2020. The Foreign Language Classroom Anxiety Scale and academic achievement: An overview of the prevailing literature and a meta-analysis. Journal for the psychology of language learning 2. 26–56.

Brantmeier, Cindy. 2005. Effects of reader's knowledge, text type, and test type on L1 and L2 reading comprehension in Spanish. *Modern Language Journal 89(1)*. 37–53.

Carroll, John & Stanley Sapon. 1959, 2000. *Modern Language Aptitude Test (MLAT): Manual*. San Antonio, TX: Psychological Corp. Republished by Second Language Testing, Inc. https://lltf.net/aptitude-tests/language-aptitude-tests/modern-language-aptitude-test-2/

Catts, Hugh. 2018. The simple view of reading: Advancements and false impressions. *Remedial and Special Education 39 (5)*. 317–323.

Chang, Hyesang & Siam Beilock. 2016. The math anxiety-math performance link and its relation to individual and environmental factors: A review of current behavioral and psychophysiological research. *Current Opinion in Behavioral Sciences, 10*, 33–38

Chen, Tsai-Yu & Goretti B.Y. Chang. 2004. The relationship between foreign language anxiety and learning difficulties. *Foreign Language Annals 37(2)*. 279–289.

Cummins, Jim. 1979. Linguistic interdependence and the educational development of bilingual children. *Review of Educational Research 49(2)*. 222–251.

Dörnyei, Z. 2009. Individual differences: Interplay of learner characteristics and learning environment. *Language Learning, 59*, 230–248.

Dörnyei, Zoltan & Peter Skehan. 2003. Individual differences in second language learning. In Catherine Doughty & Michael Long (eds.), *The handbook of second language acquisition*, 589–630. Malden, MA: Blackwell.

Droop, Mienke & Verhoeven, Ludo. 2003. Language proficiency and reading ability in first- and second-language learners. *Reading Research Quarterly 38(1)*. 78–103.

Elkhafaifi, Hussein. 2005. Listening comprehension and anxiety in the Arabic language classroom. *Modern Language Journal 89(2)*. 206–220.

Ellis, Rod. 2004. Individual differences in second language learning. In Alan Davies & Catherine Elder (eds.), *The handbook of applied linguistics*, 525–551. Malden, MA: Blackwell.

Foorman, Barbara, Sarah Herrera, Yaakov Petscher, Alison Mitchell & Adrea Truckenmiller. 2015. The structure of oral language and reading and their relation to comprehension in Kindergarten through Grade 2. *Reading and Writing 28*. 655–681.

Francis, David, Jack Fletcher, Hugh Catts & Bruce Tomblin. 2005. Dimensions affecting the assessment of reading comprehension. In Scott Paris & Steven Stahl (eds.), *Children's reading comprehension and assessment*, 369–394. Mahwah, NJ: Erlbaum.

Ganschow, Leonore & Richard Sparks. 1996. Foreign language anxiety among high school women. *Modern Language Journal 80(2)*. 199–212.

Ganschow, Leonore, Richard Sparks, Reed Anderson, James Javorsky, Sue Skinner & Jon Patton. 1994. Differences in anxiety and language performance among high, average, and low anxious college foreign language learners. *Modern Language Journal 78 (1)*. 41–55.

Gilkerson, Jill, Jeffrey Richards, Steven Warren, Judith Montgomery, Charles Greenwood, Kimbrough, C., D. Kimbrough, John Hansen & Terrance Paul. 2017. Mapping the early language environment using all-day recordings and automated analysis. *American Journal of Speech-Language Pathology 26(2)*. 248–265.

Gkonou, Christina, Mark Daubney & Jean-Marc Dawaele (eds.). 2017. *New insights into language anxiety: Theory, research, and educational implications*. Blue Ridge Summit, PA: Multilingual Matters.

Gough, Philip & William Tunmer. 1986. Decoding, reading, and reading disability. *Remedial and Special Education, 7(1)*, 6–10.

Hadidi, Effat & Reza Bargezar. 2015. Investigating reading anxiety and performance on reading proficiency: A case of Iranian EFL learners. *International Journal of Language and Applied Linguistics 25*. 50–57.

Hall, James & Michael Humphreys. 1982. Research on specific learning disabilities: Deficits and remediation. *Topics in Language & Learning Disabilities 2(2)*. 68–78.

Hewitt, Elaine & Jean Stephenson. 2012. Foreign language anxiety and oral exam performance: A replication of Phillips's MLJ study. *Modern Language Journal, 96*(2), 170–189.

Hoff, Erika. 2013. Interpreting the early language trajectories of children from low-SES and language minority homes: Implications for closing achievement gaps. *Developmental Psychology, 49 (1)*, 4–14.

Hoover, Wesley & Philip Gough. 1990. The simple view of reading. *Reading and Writing: An Interdisciplinary Journal 2*. 127–160.

Hoover, Wesley & William Tunmer. 2022. The primacy of science in communicating advances in the science of reading. *Reading Research Quarterly 57(2)*. 499–508

Horwitz, Elaine. 1991. Preliminary evidence for the reliability and validity of a foreign language anxiety scale. In Elaine Horwitz & Dolly Young (eds.), *Language anxiety: From theory and research to classroom implications*, 37–39. Englewood Cliffs, NJ: Prentice Hall.

Horwitz, Elaine. 2000. It ain't over 'til it's over: On foreign language anxiety, first language deficits, and the confounding of variables. *Modern Language Journal 84(2)*. 256–59.

Horwitz, Elaine. 2010. Foreign and second language anxiety. *Language Teaching 43(2)*. 154–167.

Horwitz, Elaine, Michael Horwitz & Joanne Cope. 1986. Foreign language classroom anxiety. *Modern Language Journal 70 (2)*. 125–132.

Huttenlocher, Janellen, Heidi Waterfall, Marina Vasilyeva, Jack Vevea & Larry Hedges. 2010. Sources of variability in children's language growth. *Cognitive Psychology 61(4)*. 343–365.

Jeon, Eun Hee & Junko Yamashita. 2014. L2 reading comprehension and its correlates: A meta-analysis. *Language Learning 64 (1)*. 160–212.

Kidd, Evan, Seamus Donnelly & Morten Christiansen. 2018. Individual differences in language acquisition and processing. *Trends in Cognitive Sciences 22(2)*. 154–169.

Kilpatrick, David. 2015. *Essentials of assessing, preventing, and overcoming reading difficulties*. Hoboken, NJ: Wiley.

Kim, Young-Suk Grace. 2015. Language and cognitive predictors of text comprehension: Evidence from multivariate analysis. *Child Development 86 (1)*. 128–144.

Kim, Young-Suk Grace. 2017. Why the Simple View of Reading is not simplistic: Unpacking component skills of reading using a direct and indirect model of reading (DIER). *Scientific Studies of Reading 21(4)*. 310–333.

Li, Rui. 2022. Foreign language reading anxiety and its correlates: A meta-analysis. *Reading and Writing 35*. 995–1018.

Lovett, Ben & Jason Nelson. 2017. Test anxiety and the American with Disabilities Act. *Journal of Disability Policy Studies 28(2)*. 99–108.

MacIntyre, Peter. 2017. An overview of language anxiety research and trends in its development. In Christina Gkonou, Mark Daubney & Jean-Marc Dewaele (eds.), *New insights into language anxiety: Theory, research and educational implications*, 11–30. Blue Ridge Summit, PA: Multilingual Matters.

MacIntyre, Peter & Gardner, Robert. 1994a.The subtle effects of language anxiety on cognitive processing in the second language. *Language Learning 44(2)*. 283–305.

MacIntyre, Peter & Gardner, Robert. 1994b.The effects of induced anxiety on three stages of cognitive processing in computerized vocabulary learning. *Studies in Second Language Acquisition 16(1)*. 1–17.

MacIntyre, Peter, Tammy Gregersen & Sarah Mercer (eds.). 2016. *Positive psychology in SLA*. Bristol, UK: Multilingual Matters.

Marcos-Llinás, Mónica & Maria Garau. 2009. Effects of language anxiety on three proficiency-level courses of Spanish as a foreign language. *Foreign Language Annals 42(1)*. 94–111.

Matsuda, Sae & Peter Gobel. 2004. Anxiety and predictors of performance in the foreign language classroom. *System, 32(1)*, 21–36.

Matsumura, Yuko. 2001. An inquiry into foreign language reading anxiety among Japanese EFL learners. *Eibeibunka: Studies in English Language, Literature and Culture 31*. 23–38.

Onwuegbuzie, Anthony, Phillip Bailey & Christine Daley. 1999. Factors associated with foreign language anxiety. *Applied Psycholinguistics 20(2)*. 217–239.

Otier, Naser Ibrahim & Abdullah Nijr Al-Otaibi. 2019. Foreign language anxiety: A systematic review. Arab World English Journal 10(3). 309–317.

Owens, Matthew, Jim Stevenson, Julie Hadwin & Roger Norgate. 2014. When does anxiety help or hinder cognitive test performance? The role of working memory capacity. *British Journal of Psychology 105(1)*. 92–101.

Petscher, Yaacov, Sonia Cabell, Hugh Catts, Donald Compton, Barbara Foorman, Sara Hart, et al. 2020. How the science of reading informs 21st-century education. *Reading Research Quarterly 55 (1)*.S267–S282.

Phillips, Elaine. 1992. The effects of language anxiety on students' oral test performance and attitudes. *Modern Language Journal 76(1)*. 14–26.

Platt, John. 1964. Strong inference. *Science 146(3642)*. 347–353.

Rayner, Keith, Barbara Foorman, Charles Perfetti, David Pesetsky & Mark Seidenberg. 2001. How psychological science informs the teaching of reading. *Psychological Science in the Public Interest 2(2)*, 31–74.

Rubin, Joan. 1975. What the" good language learner" can teach us. *TESOL Quarterly 1(1)*. 41–51.

Saito, Yoshiko, Thomas Garza & Horwitz, Elaine. 1999. Foreign language reading anxiety. *Modern Language Journal 83(2)*. 202–218.

Schrank, Fredrick & Woodcock, Richard. 2008. Woodcock Interpretation and Instructional Interventions Program (WIIIP, Version 1.0) [Computer software]. *Rolling Meadows, IL: Riverside*.

Scovel, Thomas. 1978. The effect of affect on foreign language learning: A review of the anxiety research. *Language Learning 28(1)*. 129–142.

Seidenberg, Mark. 2017. *Reading at the speed of sight: How we read, why so many cannot, and what can be done about it*. New York: Basic Books.

Sellers, Vanisa. 2000. Anxiety and reading comprehension in Spanish as a foreign language. *Foreign Language Annals 33(5)*. 512–520.

Sparks, Richard. 1995. Examining the linguistic coding differences hypothesis to explain individual differences in foreign language learning. *Annals of Dyslexia 45(1)*. 187–214.

Sparks, Richard. 2015. Language deficits in poor L2 comprehenders: The Simple view. *Foreign Language Annals 48(4)*. 635–658.

Sparks, Richard 2021. Identification and characteristics of strong, average, and weak foreign language readers: The Simple View of Reading model. *Modern Language Journal 105(2)*. 507–525.

Sparks, Richard & Abdullah Alamer. 2022. Long-term impacts of L1 language skills on L2 anxiety: The mediating role of language aptitude and L2 achievement. *Language Teaching Research*. Published online 7/1/22, https://doi.org/10.1177/13621688221104392

Sparks, Richard & Abdullah Alamer. (in press) How does L1 achievement impact L2 reading anxiety? Exploration of mediator variables. (Reading and Writing: An Interdisciplinary Journal.)

Sparks, Richard, Marjorie Artzer, Jon Patton, Leonore Ganschow, Karen Miller, Dottie Hordubay & Geri Walsh. 1998. Benefits of multisensory language instruction in Spanish for at-risk learners: A comparison study of high school Spanish students. *Annals of Dyslexia 48 (1)*. 239–270.

Sparks, Richard & Leonore Ganschow. 1991. Foreign language learning differences: Affective or native language aptitude differences? *Modern Language Journal 75(1)*. 3–16.

Sparks, Richard & Leonore Ganschow. 1993. Searching for the cognitive locus of foreign language learning difficulties: Linking first and second language learning. *Modern Language Journal 77(3)*. 289–302.

Sparks, Richard & Leonore Ganschow. 1995. A strong inference approach to causal factors in foreign language learning: A response to MacIntyre. *Modern Language Journal 79(2)*. 235–244.

Sparks, Richard and Leonore Ganschow. 1996. Teachers' perceptions of students' foreign language skills and affective characteristics. *Journal of Educational Research 89(3)*. 172–185.

Sparks, Richard & Leonore Ganschow. 2007. Is the Foreign Language Classroom Anxiety Scale measuring anxiety or language skills? *Foreign Language Annals 40 (2)*. 260–287.

Sparks, Richard, Leonore Ganschow, Marjorie Artzer, David Siebenhar & Mark Plageman. 1997. Language anxiety and proficiency in a foreign language. *Perceptual and Motor Skills 85(2)*. 559–562.

Sparks, Richard, Leonore Ganschow, Marjorie Artzer, David Siebenhar & Mark Plageman. 2004. Foreign language teachers' perceptions of students' academic skills, affective characteristics, and proficiency: Replication and follow-up studies. *Foreign Language Annals 37 (2)*. 263–278.

Sparks, Richard, Leonore Ganschow & James Javorsky. 2000. Déjà vu all over again: A response to Saito, Horwitz, and Garza. *Modern Language Journal 84(2)*. 251–255.

Sparks, Richard & Julie Luebbers. 2018. How many US high school students have a foreign language reading "disability"? Reading without meaning and the simple view. *Journal of Learning Disabilities 51(2)*. 194–208.

Sparks, Richard, Julie Luebbers, Martha Casteñada & Jon Patton. 2018. U.S. high school students and foreign language reading anxiety: Déjà vu all over again all over again. *Modern Language Journal 102 (3)*. 533–556.

Sparks, Richard & Jon Patton. 2013. Relationship of L1 skills and L2 aptitude to L2 anxiety on the Foreign Language Classroom Anxiety Scale. *Language Learning 63(4)*. 870–895.

Sparks, Richard & Jon Patton. 2016. Examining the Simple View of Reading (SVR) Model for U.S. high school Spanish students. *Hispania 99*. 17–33.

Sparks, Richard, Jon Patton, Leonore Ganschow & Nancy Humbach. 2009. Long-term relationships among early L1 skills, L2 aptitude, L2 affect, and later L2 proficiency. *Applied Psycholinguistics 30 (4)*. 725–755.

Sparks, Richard, Jon Patton & Julie Luebbers. 2018. L2 anxiety and the Foreign Language Reading Anxiety Scale (FLRAS): Listening to the evidence. *Foreign Language Annals 51(4)*. 1–25.

Stanovich, Keith. 2000. *Progress in understanding reading: Scientific foundations and new frontiers*. New York: Guilford.

Teimouri, Yasser, Julia Goetze & Luke Plonsky. 2019. Second language anxiety and achievement: A meta-analysis. *Studies in Second Language Acquisition 41 (2)*. 363–387.

Than, Thi Thu Trang. 2012. A review of Horwitz, Horwitz and Cope's theory of foreign language anxiety and the challenges to the theory. *English Language Teaching 5(1)*. 69.

Verhoeven, Ludo & Jan van Leeuwe. 2012. The simple view of second language reading throughout the primary grades. *Reading and Writing 25(8)*. 1805–1818.

Woodcock, Richard, Ana Muñoz-Sandoval, Kevin McGrew & Nancy Mather. 2004, 2007. *Batería-III Woodcock-Muñoz*. Rolling Meadows, IL: Riverside.

Zhang, Xian. 2019. Foreign language anxiety and foreign language performance. *Modern Language Journal 103(4)*. 763–781.

Zhao, Aiping, Ying Guo & Jaclyn Dynia. 2013. Foreign language reading anxiety: Chinese as a foreign language in the United States. *Modern Language Journal 97 (3)*. 764–778.

Epilogue

14 Individual Differences in SLA–Looking Back and Looking Forward

Richard Sparks & Zhisheng (Edward) Wen

Abstract: In the chapters of this volume, we have discussed key cognitive IDs such as intelligence, language aptitude, metalinguistic ability, learning strategies, self-regulation, working memory and attention/noticing, as well as some selective affective factors (e.g., motivation, anxiety, emotion) that have not been figured prominently in most previous monographs and textbooks of IDs in SLA. In addition, we have discussed topics barely touched directly in previous SLA textbooks, that of learning disability and learning difficulties experienced by L2 learners, which we believe to be relevant and important. Overall, we hope that the chapters in the current volume have succeeded in presenting updated research on these ID factors by authors pursuing diverse perspectives.

Keywords: Individual differences, second language acquisition, intelligence, language aptitude, metalinguistic ability, learning strategies, self-regulation, working memory and attention, noticing, 'deadly sins'

14.1 Recapitulation of chapter summaries and highlights

Overall, we hope that the chapters in the current volume have succeeded in presenting updated research on these ID factors by authors pursuing diverse perspectives. For example, the first section by Adriana Biedroń reported evidence supporting the existence of a critical/sensitive period for L2 learning, and reviewed evidence related to intelligence and L2 aptitude. Notwithstanding, these reviews found a lack of research on the relationship between L2 aptitude components and the cognitive abilities measured by intelligence tests, and concluded that longitudinal studies with large populations are needed to study the relationships between L2 aptitude and cognitive variables.

Section II by Edward Wen reviewed the major theoretical models and assessment procedures for cognitive IDs in working memory and attention generally, and the "noticing hypothesis" in particular. The overall findings showed although a learner needs to consciously notice language input, current empirical evidence falls short of supporting the hypothesis for the simple reason that there are many other internal and external factors influencing the SLA process and outcomes.

In section III, Mark Teng addressed three longstanding issues in L2/SLA research–IDs in metacognition, self-regulation, and use of language learning strategies – and described the roles of these ID variables for effective L2 learning in terms of theory, research, and classroom practice.

Section IV by Richard Sparks expanded current thinking about IDs within SLA by examining three issues related to relationships among L1 skills, L2 aptitude, and L2 achievement and proficiency. The section explored how L2 educators and researchers can assess English reading and writing skills using two well-researched models, the Simple View of Reading and the Simple View of Writing; examined the definition and criteria for the learning disability (LD) concept from an international perspective and the proposed relationship between LDs and L2 learning problems; and questioned whether anxiety for L2 learning is an affective variable or a linguistic variable.

14.2 Problematizing current IDs research

When considering the theme for this epilogue, we recalled Robert DeKeyser's concluding chapter in Wen et al.'s (2019) volume on language aptitude. DeKeyser listed a number of outstanding questions for future research in L2 aptitude that included investigating dependent and independent variables, linking research designs to the proposed dependent/independent variables, proposing practical applications of research, and considering the need for longitudinal perspectives. Another of his proposed questions–the need for theoretical integration–seemed especially salient. For example, DeKeyser noted that although aptitude researchers have conducted studies on a number of issues regarding this question, he stated, ". . . research on aptitude is not just about aptitude" (2019: 324). While maintaining the theoretical relevance of language aptitude, he proposed that studies involving aptitude should be viewed as part of a "very large but structured puzzle."

Like language aptitude, we contend that research involving putative ID variables for L2 learning can also be considered as part of this "puzzle." Some ID variables will be found to constitute a larger piece of the puzzle than other variables. That is, some variables will explain more of the variance in L2 achievement than other variables, and some variables may be found to explain less variance than previously hypothesized. For example, as indicated by the two recent meta-analyses conducted by Li (2015) on language aptitude, and Linck et al. (2014) on working memory, the predictive validity of language aptitude as opposed to working memory is 0.355 versus 0.255. Still, there will be other ID variables that do not fit the L2 acquisition puzzle and should be discarded as viable explanations for IDs in L2 acquisition.

For some, De Keyser's suggestions may be viewed as just another obligatory call for unity and cooperation among L2 researchers from different backgrounds. For those who conduct L2 research with a background in L1 reading and special education (in this case, the first author of this chapter), De Keyser's words brought to mind the process by which the pieces came together to complete the puzzle of how children learn to read. Starting in the 1970s, there has been remarkable progress toward understanding the basic psychological processes that underlie the act of reading. In fact, by the end of the 1990s, so much progress had been made that a leading reading researcher termed this progress the "Grand Synthesis" and described what it meant for the reading field (Stanovich 1998). The synthesis represented how cooperation among different groups of reading researchers in psychology, cognitive science, and neurocognitive fields resulted in a common explanation of the reading process unified by the evidence. Over time, the "science of reading" was informed by an evolving evidence base produced by researchers working on different aspects of the reading process (see Kilpatrick 2015; Petscher et al. 2020; Rayner et al. 2001; Seidenberg 2017). Since then, the unified science of reading has been extended across language and writing systems that explain learning to read and write languages other than English, including both alphabetic and logographic (morpho-syllabic) orthographies (see Joshi and Aaron 2013). The findings from disparate groups of researchers working on different pieces of the reading puzzle have provided converging evidence which has shown that there are universals and operating principles in both word reading/spelling and reading comprehension (Verhoeven and Perfetti 2017).

14.2.1 Siloing vs. cooperation/collaboration

The manner in which the Grand Synthesis for reading developed raises the question of whether there is coordination among those in SLA/L2 fields that could result in a Grand Synthesis that explains how individuals learn an L2. One limitation of the research cited in our volume as well as in previous texts dating to the 1960s (Wong-Fillmore 1979; Skehan 1989, 1991, 1998, 2019; Robinson, 2002, 2005, 2020; Dörnyei 2005, 2009, 2020; Granena 2016; Wen et al. 2017, 2019) is that researcher groups studying IDs in language learning seem to work in "silos," that is, within their own system or subsystem, and do not always engage in reciprocal interaction with others in related areas. In some cases, researchers studying an ID variable may not be familiar with the research on other ID variables for L2 acquisition. One example of "siloing" comes from the study of language anxiety, where researchers claim that a special type of anxiety–foreign language anxiety–is a causal, or at least, important factor in more and less successful L2 achievement. However, most researchers studying this ID variable have taken little note of evidence from the study of other ID variables related to L2 acquisition–L1 attainment and L2 aptitude–which has shown that students' levels of L2 anxiety measured by language anxiety surveys are strongly related to their levels of L1 attainment many years *before* engaging in L2 courses and to their level of L2 aptitude measure *prior to* L2 study. (In his chapter, DeKeyser lamented that L2 audiences comprised of teachers and teacher trainees had never heard of language aptitude tests nor did they know what language aptitude meant.)

Another example is the emphasis on IDs in students' learning styles and the use of language learning strategies. As far back as 1991, Skehan noted the "worrying possibility" that good language learners are those who can use learning strategies, while poor learners may not (288). To date, little evidence has been reported showing that poor language learners can use, or be taught to use, strategies to improve their performance in L2. Likewise, while there has been much interest in learning styles for teaching L2s, there is no evidence from L2 (or L1) research showing that styles are important for L2 learning or that matching learners' styles with teaching methods improves performance (Pashler et al. 2008; Sparks 2006). Why are some researchers and educators unaware of research in IDs related to L2 acquisition and/or reluctant to discard theories or practices that have not generated supportive evidence?

14.2.2 The seven 'deadly sins' of IDs research in SLA

In a recent paper, Dabrowska (2016) identified cognitive linguistics' "seven deadly sins." Although the paper was not written specifically for an L2 audience, several of the sins are related to our earlier points about "siloing" in L2 research. For example, Dabrowska cites an "excessive reliance on introspection," or the use of one's own intuitions as the primary source for theories about language. She notes that this occurs in some cases because many linguists do not have the technical knowledge to use other methods, but in other cases, this practice is an ideological choice because objective methods are incompatible with the "spirit of cognitive linguistics." Another sin that Dabrowska identifies is "not enough serious hypothesis testing," which she describes as the lack of deriving testable predictions from hypotheses, carrying out the tests, and refining hypotheses when appropriate. A third sin is "not treating the cognitive commitment seriously," or not supporting one's analyses by appealing to what is known about human cognitive processing. She explains that while linguists indicate that language relies on general cognitive processes, many seem uninterested in what other cognitive scientists have to say about human cognition. Dabrowska contends that although cognitive linguists have made great strides in studying language, these sins must be addressed if their approach is to produce fruitful results.

The sin listed by Dabrowska that attracted our attention is that of "ignoring individual differences" in language attainment. She indicated that most cognitive linguists "do not look for individual differences and tend to sweep them under the carpet when they find them, with the result that they are usually ignored" (2016: 485). Dabrowska cited several reasons for this practice, but even so, the fact that IDs in language attainment have been ignored is puzzling. SLA/L2 researchers have not refuted or grappled with Cummins' (1979) Linguistic Threshold Hypothesis, i.e., L2 proficiency is moderated by one's level of attainment in L1, even though the first author of this chapter (Sparks) and his research group have published a chain of evidence over 30 years supporting Cummins' hypothesis and showing that there are large differences in students' early L1 attainment and that these differences are strongly related to their L2 aptitude and L2 achievement many years later in high school and college. Likewise, Sparks' research group has provided evidence for Cummins' Linguistic Interdependence Hypothesis by showing that certain first language (L1) knowledge can be positively transferred during the process of L2 (L2) acquisition. In our view, the reluctance to consider the aforementioned evidence on L1-L2 relationships has created a lacuna when attempting to explain IDs in students' ultimate levels of L2 aptitude and L2 acquisition.

14.3 Looking Forward

How could the problem of "siloing" and the commission of the "sins" cited by Dabrowska be addressed by SLA/L2 researchers? Here again, the process by which the "Grand Synthesis" for reading was achieved comes to mind. In the early 90s, reading researchers and reading educators began to diverge on the methods by which they investigated how children learn to read and the problems that some children experience when learning to read. Research scientists were intent on studying the reading process through empirically-based, scientific investigations, while reading educators were using more qualitative methodologies and case studies. At that time, professional organizations in education, special education, and psychology, including the National Reading Conference, were not much interested in the science of reading, particularly in IDs and genetics, so an organization devoted to reading research, the Society for the Scientific Study of Reading, was formed and became the primary professional society devoted exclusively to the study of reading (spelling, writing) science. The organization attracted a large international membership of researchers in diverse fields ranging from educational and cognitive psychology, special education, medicine and genetics, linguistics, speech/language pathology, and neuroscience who studied reading from quantitative and qualitative perspectives. The diversity of the membership made the organization unique and appealed to many researchers, whose collaborations led to the Grand Synthesis.

14.3.1 Richard Snow's legacy and framework for aptitude

In our view, a similar type of project is needed to encourage collaboration among the different strands of L2/SLA researchers and language educators. If such a project could be developed, in which direction should the research proceed? One answer can be found in Richard Snow's (1992) criteria for an "aptitude theory" framework: a) development of language aptitude tests, b) aptitude theory construction, and c) application of language aptitude to practice. This framework would invite input from a wide range of perspectives in the L2/SLA and language education fields. Each of the three criteria is examined here.

Language aptitude tests. This first criterion has been largely successful. Since 1959, researchers from a variety of disciplines have collaborated to construct valid language aptitude measures that have been found to reliably predict L2 outcomes. These batteries include the MLAT, MLAT-E, LLAMA, and Hi-LAB, all of which have been found to explain IDs in L2 achievement (Wen 2021). Although there is room for improvement in the aforementioned batteries and also for the development of new tests, rigorous research in the development of aptitude tests has been a fruitful area for research (Wen, Skehan, and Sparks 2023).

Aptitude theory construction. This second criterion has been less productive because a unified theory that explains L2 acquisition is still being debated. Recently, investigators have advanced new or updated models of language aptitude to explain IDs in language learning. For example, Wen (2015, 2016, 2019) has proposed the phonological/executive (P/E) model of working memory to refine and expand the memory component of John Carroll's aptitude model. At the time Carroll developed his model, the study of memory was limited to the association of form and meaning. The P/E model draws from theories and models of working memory across several disciplines in the cognitive sciences and argues that working memory both constrains and shapes domains, processes and skills of language acquisition (Wen and Skehan 2021). In another aptitude model (i.e., the Staged model; Skehan, 2016, 2019), Skehan has proposed that aptitude works in conjunction with the three major acquisition stages–input-oriented, interlanguage development, output-oriented–that are served by several embedded mechanisms, i.e., input processing, noticing, pattern identification, complexification, handling feedback, error avoidance, automatization. The aforementioned processes work in tandem with existing language aptitude components in Carroll's model and other constraints such as working memory, attention, chunking, and lexicalization. In a slightly different vein, Robinson (2002, 2005, 2020) has conceptualized language aptitude as the combination of more basic cognitive abilities that form aptitude complexes. These aptitude complexes in turn influence L2 task performance, or "task aptitudes," both positively and negatively in real-world situations.

When constructing language aptitude theories, it has always seemed strange that L2/SLA researchers have not considered the primacy of language skills for L2 acquisition. Skehan (2019), too, has noted it seems "a little odd" that there is still a question as to whether language abilities have any special role in language aptitude. Similarly, Sparks and Ganschow (1993, 1995) have maintained for many years that L2 learning is the learning of *language*. They have contended that while other skills will be important for L2 acquisition, variables such as, e.g., motivation, working memory, affective qualities, and personality characteristics, will not be sufficient to compensate for the lack of language ability when learning an L2. For example, an individual with low (to below) average language aptitude but average (to above) average working memory (or strong motivation, low anxiety) will still display problems with L2 learning.

For some time, we have considered that one way to approach the "language is special" notion for language aptitude theory is by considering domain-specific and domain-general variables for L2 aptitude and hypothesizing how the variables in these domains are related to and predictive of L2 acquisition (Sparks, 2022; Wen, Biedroń, and Skehan, 2017). In our view, the IDs that have been considered by SLA/L2 researchers fall into these two broad domains. *Domain-specific* variables are those that are conceptualized as being specific to a particular area, in this case, language learning. Language variables include those language skills measured by Carroll's MLAT, most LLAMA subtests, as well as some of the Hi-LAB subtests. *Domain general* variables are those conceptualized as applying across a variety of cognitive domains and are not specific only to language learning. For example, working memory has also been found to be important for mathematical ability. Motivation will be important for all types of learning. Domain general variables would include certain skills measured by the Hi-LAB, e.g., working memory, sequence learning, processing speed, priming, and other variables proposed by L2 researchers to be important for L2 learning, e.g., motivation and engagement, self-regulation, intelligence (IQ), strategy use, executive functioning (cognitive flexibility, working memory, attention), affective qualities, and personality characteristics. To further elucidate the domain-specific/domain-general approach, we draw on Sparks' and Ganschow's (1995) use of the Assumption of Specificity (AOS), the idea that a brain/cognitive skill is reasonably specific to a particular task.

In the case of L2 acquisition, the AOS would maintain that the brain/cognitive skills necessary for language learning will be those that are language-related. Like Skehan, the AOS contends that language is special for L2 acquisition because L2 learning is the learning of a language. Thus, language abilities are necessary for L2 acquisition, but language acquisition will also draw on domain-general variables. Both domain-specific and domain-general variables will contribute to L2 acquisition and will also be responsible for IDs in language learning capabilities (see also Sparks, 2022).

Since SLA/L2 researchers have not yet developed a comprehensive, unified theory that explains L2 aptitude (and L2 acquisition), we propose a "simple view" of L2 aptitude. The concept (and the name) is borrowed from the Simple View of Reading (SVR) model for L1 and L2 reading in which reading ability has been found to include two domains, word decoding and oral language (listening) comprehension, each of which is comprised of subskills. The SVR proposes that reading comprehension is the product of word decoding and listening comprehension. (See Sparks 2021 and this volume, for a description of the Simple View model for L2 reading and writing and how L1 and L2 reading and writing skills are assessed using the model.) For the "simple view" of L2 aptitude, we propose that language aptitude will be the product of domain-specific and domain-general skills. Domain-specific skills are those that are language-related and will include sound recognition, phonological awareness, phonetic coding (sound-symbol relations), grammar, inductive language ability, and inferencing ability as well as vocabulary and background knowledge in the target language and its culture. Domain general skills are those that are not specifically language-related such as some skills measured by the Hi-LAB, e.g., working memory, sequence learning, processing speed, priming, and other variables proposed by L2 researchers listed earlier. The list of domain-general variables included here is not exhaustive and there are other variables that may be found to be domain-specific skills, e.g., phonological working memory (Wen, 2016).

Application of language aptitude to practice. This third criterion for an aptitude theory proposed by Snow is more complicated. DeKeyer (2019) stated that while aptitude batteries are a fairly reliable tool for selecting learners likely to succeed in language learning, language educators have little use for these batteries because educators do not select their students. He explains that although aptitude treatment interaction (ATI) research should be able to provide guidance for matching learning with treatment, there is little research support for this idea (Dekeyser 2021). But, we ask the following: *why should language aptitude testing apply to practical applications for language teaching?* Aptitude tests were developed for selection and placement in language learning programs and to identify (diagnose) one's level of language aptitude. While there may seem to be a relationship between language aptitude and language teaching, we contend that the path between the two is not straightforward. For example, in the assessment of reading skills, children often are asked to memorize or repeat nonsense syllables, read pseudowords, search the text for a letter, or use colored blocks to demonstrate whether there are differences between phonemes. However, none of these things are normally done in a typical school classroom when teaching reading. Application to the practice of teaching reading or learning to read may follow from a theory, but not from memorizing or repeating nonsense syllables, reading pseudowords, searching the text for a letter, or moving colored blocks.

The point here is that the tools we use to assess and uncover causal explanations for performance in an educational task are not necessarily the same tools that will be used to facilitate the performance of the task in the classroom. One obvious example is the use of another aptitude battery, an intelligence (IQ) test. IQ has been assumed to be a good predictor of overall classroom achievement. However, the results of an IQ test are not directly applicable to the teaching of reading, spelling, writing, math, science, or other school subjects. On the other hand, IQ tests have been used for theory development and for selection and placement purposes, e.g., in gifted and talented programs. Likewise, language aptitude tests can be used for the development of language aptitude theory and to assess language aptitude for selection and placement purposes, but researchers should consider that the results of an aptitude test may not be helpful in assisting a classroom teacher to facilitate students' performance in the language classroom.

14.4 Final Remarks: Towards a Grand Theory of SLA

How could the L2/SLA fields develop their own Grand Synthesis for L2 acquisition? Scholars in many fields have championed the need for, and compatibility of, quantitative and qualitative approaches in research, arguing that the strengths and weaknesses of the approaches establish a complementary relationship, not an incompatible one (Hiver, Al-Hoorie and Larsen-Freeman 2021). We think that the ultimate goal for the study of IDs in SLA/L2 will require joint efforts by scholars from different theoretical backgrounds and those who have expertise from different disciplines such as applied linguistics, education, psychology, neuroscience, and genetics, to name but a few. In *The Republic of Science*, Polanyi (1962) noted, the integrity of science "does not depend on the integrity of individual scientists but on a competitive system that separates the best from the worst independent of any single person's will. By insisting that no one's authority is final . . . far-flung and dispersed communities of scientists are able to do better for science than anyone can do alone" [cited in Wildavsky 1991: 36)].

In addition to the joint efforts of scholars working from multiple perspectives and diverse contexts, Stanovich's remarks for the reading field several years prior to the Grand Synthesis are timely: "Our literature is full of unreplicable findings, single-shot studies, and unexplained anomalies. To pay equal attention to all of this and to try to account for all of it in our reading models when a large chunk of it is noise is a "metatheoretical mistake. Instead, parsimony should be the order of the day" (1989: 366). Like reading or any other field of research, the SLA/L2/language education fields consist of the same issues cited by Stanovich as well as unverified theories, hypotheses based on ideology, the musings of individuals, and other unhelpful information (see Dabrowska 2016). In our view, SLA/L2 researchers should ask important questions (Neisser 1978), even if that means making difficult decisions about some proposed theories and hypotheses for L2 acquisition. As such, we offer some examples of these important, albeit outstanding, questions guiding future research on IDs in SLA.

- Do language aptitude batteries have direct practical applications for language teaching?
- For aptitude theory development, should theories with variables confounded by "third variable" problems be promoted as causal explanations for more and less successful L2 achievement?
- Can motivation for language learning be increased and/or anxiety be decreased with a corresponding measurable increase in L2 achievement?
- For language teaching, should theories without supportive evidence, e.g., learning styles, be presented to language educators as effective teaching methodologies?
- Can language learning strategies be taught, especially to poor language learners, and does the use of strategies lead to measurable improvement in L2 achievement?
- Working memory has been hypothesized to be important for L2 aptitude, but can individuals' working memory be improved?
- How much of the variance will domain-specific variables explain for L2 acquisition?
- Likewise, how much of the variance will domain-general variables explain for L2 acquisition?
- Which domain-specific and domain-general variables can be taught?
- If a domain general skill cannot be taught, what is its practical application for classroom teachers?

These questions and many others should be addressed by SLA/L2 researchers working collaboratively to develop a unified theory of L2 acquisition. That said, we hope that the ideas proposed in this volume will serve as catalysts for boosting future IDs research in SLA in the days to come.

References

Cummins, Jim. 1979. Linguistic interdependence and the educational development of bilingual children. *Review of Educational Research 49*(2). 222–251.
Dąbrowska, Ewa. 2016. Cognitive linguistics' seven deadly sins. *Cognitive Linguistics 27*(4). 479–491.
DeKeyser, Robert. 2019. The future of language aptitude research. In Zhisheng (Edward) Wen, Peter Skehan, Adriana Biedroń, Shaofeng Li & Richard Sparks (eds.), *Language aptitude: Advancing theory, testing, research, and practice*, 330–342. London: Routledge.
DeKeyser, Robert (ed.). 2021. *Aptitude-treatment interaction in second language learning* (Vol. 116). Amsterdam: John Benjamins.
Dörnyei, Zoltan. 2005, 2009. *The psychology of the language learner: Individual differences in second language acquisition*. Mahwah, NJ: Erlbaum.
Dörnyei, Zoltan. 2009. *The psychology of second language acquisition*. Oxford: Oxford University Press.
Dörnyei, Zoltan. 2020. *Innovations and challenges in language learning motivation*. London: Routledge.
Gough, Philip & William Tunmer. 1986. Decoding, reading, and reading disability. *Remedial and Special Education 7 (1)*. 6–10.
Granena, Gisela. 2016. Cognitive aptitudes for implicit and explicit learning and information-processing styles: An individual differences study. *Applied Psycholinguistics 37*(3). 577–600.
Hiver, Phil, Ali H. Al-Hoorie & Diane Larsen-Freeman. 2021. Toward a transdisciplinary integration of research purposes and methods for Complex Dynamic Systems Theory: Beyond the quantitative–qualitative divide. *International Review of Applied Linguistics in Language Teaching*. DOI: 10.1515/iral-2021-0022.
Joshi, R. Malatesha & P.G. Aaron. 2013. *Handbook of orthography and literacy*. Mahwah, NJ: Erlbaum.
Kilpatrick, David. 2015. *Essentials of assessing, preventing, and overcoming reading difficulties*. New York: Wiley & Sons.
Li, Shaofeng. 2015. The associations between language aptitude and second language grammar acquisition: A meta-analytic review of five decades of research. *Applied Linguistics 36*(3). 385–408.
Linck, Jared, Peter Osthus, Joel Koeth & Michael Bunting. 2014. Working memory and second language comprehension and production: A meta-analysis. *Psychonomic Bulletin & Review 21*(4). 861–883.
Neisser, Ulric. 1978. Memory: what are the important questions? In Michael Gruneberg, Peter Morris & Robert Sykes (eds.), *Practical Aspects of Memory*, 3–24. London: Academic Press.
Pashler, Harold, Mark McDaniel, Doug Rohrer & Robert Bjork. 2008. Learning styles: Concepts and evidence. *Psychological Science in the Public Interest 9 (3)*. 105–119.
Petscher, Yaacov, Sonia Cabell, Hugh Catts, Donald Compton, Barbara Foorman, Sara Hart, et al. 2020. How the science of reading informs 21st-century education. *Reading Research Quarterly 55 (1)*.S267–S282.
Polanyi, Michael. 1962. The republic of science: Its political and economic theory. *Minerva I (1)*. 54–73.
Rayner, Keith, Barbara Foorman, Charles Perfetti, David Pesetsky & Mark Seidenberg. 2001. How psychological science informs the teaching of reading. *Psychological Science in the Public Interest 2(2)*, 31–74.
Robinson, Peter (ed.). 2002. *Individual differences and instructed language learning*. Amsterdam: John Benjamins.
Robinson, Peter. 2005. Aptitude and second language acquisition. *Annual Review of Applied Linguistics 25*. 46–73.

Robinson, Peter. 2020. Aptitude and second language acquisition. In Carol Chapelle (ed.), *The Concise Encyclopedia of Applied Linguistics*. Oxford: Blackwell.

Seidenberg, Mark. 2017. *Language at the speed of sight: How we read, why so many can't, and what can be done about it*. New York: Basic Books.

Skehan, Peter. 1989. *Individual differences in second-language learning*. New York: Arnold.

Skehan, Peter. 1991. Individual differences in second language learning. *Studies in Second Language Acquisition 13*(2). 275–298.

Skehan, Peter. 1998. *A cognitive approach to language learning*. London: Oxford University Press.

Skehan, Peter. 2016. Tasks versus conditions: Two perspectives on task research and their implications for pedagogy. *Annual Review of Applied Linguistics 36*. 34–49.

Skehan, Peter. 2019. Language aptitude implicates language and cognitive skills. In Zhisheng (Edward) Wen, Peter Skehan, Adriana Biedroń, Shaofeng Li & Richard Sparks (eds.), *Language aptitude: Advancing theory, testing, research and practice*, 55–78. New York: Routledge.

Snow, Richard. 1992. Aptitude theory: Yesterday, today, and tomorrow. *Educational Psychologist 27*(1). 5–32.

Sparks, Richard. 2006. Learning styles-Making too many "wrong mistakes": A response to Castro and Peck. *Foreign Language Annals 39*(3). 520–528.

Sparks, Richard. 2021. Identification and characteristics of strong, average, and weak foreign language readers: The Simple View of Reading model. *Modern Language Journal 105*(2). 507–525.

Sparks, Richard. 2022. *Exploring L1-L2 relationships: The impact of individual differences*. Bristol, UK: Multilingual Matters.

Sparks, Richard & Leonore Ganschow. 1993. Searching for the cognitive locus of foreign language learning difficulties: Linking first and second language learning. *Modern Language Journal 77*(3). 289–302.

Sparks, Richard & Leonore Ganschow. 1995. A strong inference approach to causal factors in foreign language learning: A response to MacIntyre. *Modern Language Journal 79*(2). 235–244.

Stanovich, Keith. 1989. Various varying views on variation. *Journal of Learning Disabilities 22*(6). 366–369.

Stanovich, Keith. 1998. Twenty-five years of research on the reading process: The Grand Synthesis and what it means for our field. In Timothy Shanahan & F. Rodriguez-Brown (eds.), *Forty-Seventh Yearbook of the National Reading Conference*, 44–58. Chicago: NRC.

Verhoeven, Ludo & Charles Perfetti (eds.). 2017. *Learning to read across languages and writing systems*. Cambridge, UK: Cambridge University Press.

Wen, Zhisheng (Edward). 2015. Working memory in second language acquisition and processing: The Phonological/Executive model. In Zhisheng (Edward) Wen, Malice Borges Mota & Arthur McNeill (eds.), *Working memory in second language acquisition and processing*, 41–62. Bristol: Multilingual Matters.

Wen, Zhisheng (Edward). 2016. *Working memory and second language learning: Towards an integrated approach*. Bristol: Multilingual Matters.

Wen, Zhisheng (Edward). 2019. Working memory as language aptitude: The Phonological/Executive Model. In Zhisheng (Edward) Wen, Peter Skehan, Adriana Biedroń, Shaofeng Li & Richard Sparks (eds.), *Language aptitude: Advancing theory, testing, research and practice*, 187–214. New York: Routledge.

Wen, Zhisheng (Edward). 2021. Language aptitudes. In Tammy Gregersen & Sarah Mercer (eds.), *The Routledge Handbook of Psychology of Language Learning and Teaching*, 389–403. New York: Routledge.

Wen, Zhisheng (Edward) & Peter Skehan. 2021. Stages of acquisition and the P/E Model of working memory: Complementary or contrasting approaches to foreign language aptitude? *Annual Review of Applied Linguistics 4(1)*. 6–24.

Wen, Zhisheng (Edward), Adriana Biedroń & Peter Skehan. 2017. Foreign language aptitude theory: Yesterday, today and tomorrow. *Language Teaching 50 (1)*.1–31.

Wen, Zhisheng (Edward), Peter Skehan, Adriana Biedroń, Shaofeng Li & Richard Sparks (eds.). 2019. *Language aptitude: Advancing theory, testing, research and practice*. New York: Routledge.

Wen, Zhisheng (Edward), Peter Skehan & Richard Sparks (eds.). 2023. *Language aptitude theory and practice*. Cambridge: Cambridge University Press.

Wildavsky, Aaron. 1991. Has modernity killed objectivity? *Society 29(1)*. 33–36.

Wong-Fillmore, Lily. 1979. Individual differences in second language acquisition. In Charles Fillmore, Daniel Kempler & William S-Y Wang (eds.), *Individual differences in language ability and language behavior*, 203–228. New York: Academic Press.

Author Profiles

Zhisheng (Edward) Wen, (Ph.D., Chinese University of Hong Kong) is a Professor of Applied Linguistics in the English Department at the Hong Kong Shue Yan University, Hong Kong SAR, China. Prof. Wen has over 20 years of teaching and research experience in second language acquisition and task-based language teaching (TBLT), cognitive sciences and translation studies, with world recognized expertise in language aptitude and working memory research. Recent books include *"Working memory and second language learning"* (2016, Multilingual Matters), *"Researching L2 task performance and pedagogy"* (Benjamins, 2019), *"Language aptitude"* (Routledge, 2019), *"Cambridge handbook of working memory and language"* (CUP, 2022), *"Language aptitude theory and practice"* (CUP, 2023) and *"Memory in science for society"* (OUP, 2023).

Richard L. Sparks (Ed.D., University of Cincinnati), is a Professor Emeritus of Special Education in the Mount St. Joseph University's Department of Graduate Education, Ohio, USA. His research interests include foreign language learning, reading and language disabilities, and language aptitude. Prof. Sparks has published extensively in both foreign language and learning disability journals. His recent book on *"Exploring L1-L2 Relationships: The Impact of Individual Differences"* was published by Multilingual Matters in 2022.

Adriana Biedroń (Ph.D. University of Adam Mickiewicz, Poznań, Poland) is Professor of English at the Faculty of Philology, Pomeranian University in Słupsk, Poland. Her main areas of research interest and publications are in SLA theory and research, individual differences in SLA, in particular, foreign language aptitude, working memory, intelligence, personality factors and linguistic giftedness.

Mark Feng Teng (Ph.D., Hong Kong Baptist University) is an Associate Professor at the Center for Linguistic Sciences, Beijing Normal University, Zhuhai China. His research portfolio mainly focuses on L2 vocabulary acquisition and metacognition in L2 writing. His extensive list of book and paper publications appeared in leading international publishers and journals. His monographs were published by Routledge, Springer, de Gruyter and Bloomsbury. He also edited and co-edited special issues for several international journals, including *SSLLT, TESOL Journal,* and *Journal of Writing Research*.

Index

Ability Differentiation Hypothesis 56
affect 6, 17, 73, 76, 78, 152, 205
age of onset 7, 19–23, 25–28, 64, 81
agentive behaviors 201
anxiety 62, 73–75, 77–79, 86, 88–90, 92–93, 137, 148, 151–152, 164,171, 178,182, 192,202, 207–208, 223, 241–242, 276, 287–313, 321–324, 327, 330
Aptitude Complex Model 54, 56, 77
aptitude dynamics 53–54, 64, 66
aptitude testing 6, 53, 58, 60–61, 66–67, 328
aptitude-treatment-interaction 3, 53, 63, 77
assessing metacognition 9, 175, 181
assessing self-regulation 201, 206, 210, 217
assessment of strategies 147
Attention 60, 61, 65, 66, 75, 76, 81, 97, 99–101, 104, 106, 109, 125–128, 133, 135–139, 151–152, 155, 161, 175–177, 180, 182, 185, 192, 202, 206, 213, 216, 230, 274, 307, 321, 325, 327, 330
attention control 60, 97, 100–101, 104, 110, 114
Automatization 56, 204, 326

CALF 125, 136–137
CANAL-F 8, 53–54, 56
Cognition Hypothesis (CH) 9, 125, 136
Cognitive Abilities Model 326
cognitive strategies 40, 147–150, 159, 163, 216
complex dynamic systems theory (CDST) 1–2, 5, 66
collaborative research network
compensatory strategies 151, 213
consciousness 9, 97, 125–128, 131, 139, 144, 182
corrective feedback 9, 62, 80, 102–103, 110, 125, 127, 133–134, 137
critical period hypothesis 7, 19, 21

deadly sins 321, 324
Disability 257–269, 277–278
dyslexic 225, 227, 237, 240, 242, 249, 261, 275

embedded-processes model 97
engagement 164, 191, 215
executive functions 43, 97, 102, 104, 111, 113–114, 178

FLCAS 78–79, 287–297, 305–306, 312–313
FLRAS 78–79, 287–288, 290–291, 293–294, 296–298, 300–306
Focus on Form 9, 56, 125, 130, 137, 139
foreign language aptitude 8, 19, 35, 38, 53, 73, 87, 102
Foreign Language Classroom Anxiety Scale 288–289
Fundamental Difference Hypothesis 60

Hi-LAB 3, 8, 53, 59–61, 63, 65, 82, 326–328
Hierarchical Model of Cognitive Abilities
Hyperlexic 225, 227, 237, 239–240, 242, 249

Individual differences 1, 5, 24, 26, 36, 38, 41, 43, 56–57, 62, 65, 73–78, 86, 103, 110, 129, 147, 151, 161–162, 164, 167–168, 183, 192, 194, 214, 218, 261, 266, 280, 288, 292, 313, 321, 325
Intelligence 1, 5–8, 26, 35–49, 53, 57, 59, 62, 66, 74, 79, 83, 85, 87, 101, 112, 259, 268, 270, 278, 321, 327, 329
intelligence and SLA 35
intelligence testing 35

L2 learning 1, 5, 7, 9–11, 25, 27, 29, 57, 63, 98, 101, 109–113, 125–126, 128–129, 131, 134–135, 138–139, 147–148, 175, 193, 202, 257–259, 266–269, 271–280, 287–294, 297, 305, 307–311, 321–322, 324, 327–328
language anxiety 73–74, 86, 287, 289–291, 294, 310, 323–324
language aptitude 4–6, 8, 11, 19–28, 35, 38, 47, 49, 53–54, 58–60, 63, 66–67, 73, 75–76, 82, 86, 102–103, 111, 139, 177, 229, 267–268, 278, 287, 294, 321–322, 324, 326–330
language development 4, 20–21, 38–39, 56, 103, 155, 242, 326
language learning strategies 147–148, 153, 156–164, 168–169
LCDH 8, 53–54, 56, 266, 267, 277, 288, 297
learner agency 201
learning differences 257–258, 260–261
learning difficulties 7, 257–258, 260–261, 279, 321

learning disabilities 257–258, 260–261, 264, 268
Limited Attentional Capacity (LAC)
    Hypothesis 125, 136
linguistic talent 19, 73, 84
LLAMA 8, 46, 53–54, 59–61, 79, 81–82, 326–327
Long-term memory retrieval 61

mental representation 4
Metacognition 6, 9, 150, 155, 175–180, 183–184, 186–193
metacognitive awareness 9, 160, 163, 175, 180–182, 185, 187, 190, 192, 209
metacognitive experiences 175–176, 178–180
metacognitive knowledge 175–182, 184–188, 192–193, 293–294
metacognitive regulation 160, 175, 178, 184
metalinguistic ability 321
metalinguistic awareness 26, 177
MLAT 38, 45–47, 53–54, 58–61, 63–64, 84, 229, 267–276, 291–293, 313
models of intelligence 35–37, 43
motivation 5–6, 38, 44, 49, 59, 62, 73, 76, 80–82, 85–87, 164, 182, 186, 191, 193, 202–203, 205, 207, 215, 242, 276, 292, 327, 330
multicomponent model 99, 109

non-perceivable nonnativeness 26
native-like competence 23, 26
native-like proficiency 20–21, 24, 27, 29–30, 108
Noticing Hypothesis 9, 125, 127–131, 135, 138–139, 321
noticing the gap 57, 125–126, 128, 134
Nurture 41, 125, 127, 137–139

pattern identification 102–103, 326
pedagogical strategies 10, 226, 257
Personality 5, 38, 66, 73–86, 151, 163, 168, 287, 308, 327
Perceptual Reasoning 44
phonological/executive model 8, 97

PLAB 45, 53–54, 59, 82
Polyglots 8, 19, 23, 47, 64, 76, 84–85
Processing Speed 44, 60–61, 327–328
psychological factors 8, 73–74, 77, 83–84, 86

reading comprehension 10–11, 78, 100, 109–111, 149, 162, 187–188, 193, 225–244, 292, 298–306, 323
Recast 56–57, 65, 125, 133–134

second language acquisition 1,19, 24, 53, 76, 100, 102, 147, 175, 184, 201, 206, 217–218, 321
self-reflection 138, 201, 203–204, 211
self-regulation 1, 7, 9, 149, 183, 189–190, 201–207, 210–211, 214–217, 231, 321–322, 327
Simple View of Reading 10, 225–227, 298, 322, 328
Simple View of Writing 225, 230, 322
specific learning disabilities/difficulties 257, 260
strategy choice 9, 147, 161–162
strategy-based instruction 9, 147, 164–169, 189, 215

TBLT 9, 15, 114, 125, 127, 133, 135, 137–140
Theory of Multiple Intelligences 40
Theory of Primary Mental Abilities 39
Triarchic Theory of Human Intelligence 40

ultimate attainment 6, 19–29, 55, 73, 81, 266, 6
Universal Grammar (UG) 1–2
Usage-based accounts 1

verbal comprehension 38–40, 44, 46

WM-SLA nexus 97, 111
word decoding 78, 225–243, 249, 298–309, 328
working memory 1, 4–8, 29, 43–44, 47–49, 56–57, 60–66, 74–75, 80, 85, 87–88, 97, 115, 130, 139, 150, 186, 190, 202, 231, 239, 241–242, 293, 304, 310, 321–322, 326–330

www.ingramcontent.com/pod-product-compliance
Lightning Source LLC
Chambersburg PA
CBHW050513170426
43201CB00013B/1943

9 781501 523663